Dancing Mind, Minding Dance

Dancing Mind, Minding Dance encompasses a collection of pivotal texts published by scholar and researcher Doug Risner, whose work over the past three decades has emphasized the significance of social relevance and personal resonance in dance education. Drawing upon Risner's breakthrough research and visionary scholarship, this book contextualizes critical issues of dance making in the rehearsal process, dance curriculum and pedagogy in 21st-century postsecondary dance education, the role of dance teaching artists in schools and community environments, and dance, gender, and sexual identity, especially the feminization of dance and the marginalization of males who dance.

This book concludes with Risner's prophetic vision for employing reflective practice in order to address social justice and inclusion and humanizing pedagogies in dance and dance education throughout all sectors of dance training and preparation. Beginning with his first book, *Stigma and Perseverance in the Lives of Boys Who Dance* (2009), Risner has distinguished himself as the leading education researcher, scholar, and practitioner to improve young dancers' education and training and in humanistic ways. This book will appeal to dance educators and teachers, dance education scholars and researchers, choreographers, parents and care-givers of dance students, and those who work as teaching artists, arts administrators, private sector dance studio directors and teachers, as well as arts education researchers and scholars broadly. The chapters in this book, except for a few, were originally published in various Taylor & Francis journals.

Doug Risner (PhD, MFA) is a distinguished faculty fellow and professor of Dance and directs the MA in Theatre and Dance: Teaching Artistry program in the Maggie Allesee Department of Theatre and Dance at Wayne State University, Detroit, USA. He conducts research in the sociology of dance training and education, gender in dance, curriculum theory and policy, social foundations of dance pedagogy, online learning, and web-based curriculum design. His books include *Stigma and Perseverance in the Lives of Boys Who Dance* (2009); *Hybrid Lives of Teaching Artists in Dance and Theatre Arts: A Critical Reader* (2014); *Gender, Sexuality and Identity: Critical Issues in Dance Education* (2015); *Dance and Gender: An Evidence-Based Approach* (2017); *Dance, Professional Practice, and the Workplace* (2020); and *Ethical Dilemmas in Dance Education: Case Studies on Humanizing Dance Pedagogy* (2020), which received the 2021 NDEO Ruth Lovell Murray Award for Dance Education and the 2021 Susan W. Stinson Book Award. His most recent edited volumes include *Dancing Across the Lifespan: Negotiating Age, Place and Purpose* (2022) with Pam Musil and Karen Schupp and *Masculinity, Intersectionality and Identity: Why Boys (Don't) Dance* (2022) with Beccy Watson.

Jennifer McNamara (MFA) is an assistant professor of Dance at Mercyhurst University, Erie, USA. Following a twenty-year career as a ballet dancer, she was an adjunct professor at Middle Tennessee State University, Murfreesboro, USA, and taught for New Dialect, Metro (Nashville) Parks and Recreation Dance Division, and the School of Nashville Ballet. A certified Pilates instructor, Jennifer explores the relationships between foundational and aesthetic movement choices; she is also an advocate for justice in dance education. She is a past recipient of the Individual Artist Fellowship (Dance) from the Tennessee Arts Commission, has designed and built costumes, and has been published in *Arts Education Policy Review* and *Masculinity, Intersectionality and Identity: Why Boys (Don't) Dance*, edited by Doug Risner and Beccy Watson. Jennifer earned her MFA in Dance from Hollins University, Roanoke, USA.

Dancing Mind, Minding Dance
Socially Relevant and Personally Resonant
Dance Education

Edited by
Doug Risner and Jennifer McNamara

LONDON AND NEW YORK

First published 2023
by Routledge
4 Park Square, Milton Park, Abingdon, Oxon, OX14 4RN

and by Routledge
605 Third Avenue, New York, NY 10158

Routledge is an imprint of the Taylor & Francis Group, an informa business

Foreword © 2023 Susan W. Stinson
Introduction © 2023 Jennifer McNamara and Doug Risner
Chapter 1 © 1992 SHAPE America
Chapter 2 © 1995 Human Kinetics Publishers, Inc.
Chapter 5 © 2014 National Dance Education Organization
Chapter 7 © 2017 National Dance Education Organization
Chapter 14 © 2018 National Dance Education Organization
Chapter 17 © 2021 National Dance Education Organization
Chapters 3, 4, 6, 8–12 and 15 © 2023 Taylor & Francis
Afterword © 2023 Nyama McCarthy Brown
Chapter 13 © 2014 Doug Risner. Originally published as Open Access.
Chapter 16 © 2010 Doug Risner and Susan W. Stinson. Originally published as Open Access.

With the exception of Chapters 13 and 16, no part of this book may be reprinted or reproduced or utilised in any form or by any electronic, mechanical, or other means, now known or hereafter invented, including photocopying and recording, or in any information storage or retrieval system, without permission in writing from the publishers. For details on the rights for Chapters 13 and 16, please see the chapters' Open Access footnotes.

Trademark notice: Product or corporate names may be trademarks or registered trademarks, and are used only for identification and explanation without intent to infringe.

British Library Cataloguing-in-Publication Data
A catalogue record for this book is available from the British Library

ISBN13: 978-1-032-38208-1 (hbk)
ISBN13: 978-1-032-38209-8 (pbk)
ISBN13: 978-1-003-34395-0 (ebk)

DOI: 10.4324/9781003343950

Typeset in Minion pro
by codeMantra

Publisher's Note
The publisher accepts responsibility for any inconsistencies that may have arisen during the conversion of this book from journal articles to book chapters, namely the inclusion of journal terminology.

The material in this volume has been reproduced using the facsimile method to facilitate easy and correct citation of the original essays. It also explains the variety of typefaces, page layouts and numbering.

Disclaimer
Every effort has been made to contact copyright holders for their permission to reprint material in this book. The publishers would be grateful to hear from any copyright holder who is not here acknowledged and will undertake to rectify any errors or omissions in future editions of this book.

Contents

Citation Information	viii
Notes on Contributors	xi
Foreword	xiv
Susan W. Stinson	
Introduction	1
Jennifer McNamara and Doug Risner	

PART I
Dance Making Pedagogies in the Rehearsal Process — 7

    Prelude — 8

1 Exploring Dance Rehearsal—The Neglected Issues Revealed — 11
   Doug Risner

2 Voices Seldom Heard: The Dancers' Experience of the Choreographic Process — 19
   Doug Risner

3 Making Dance, Making Sense: Epistemology & Choreography — 27
   Doug Risner

PART II
Curriculum and Pedagogy in 21st Century Postsecondary Dance — 45

    Prelude — 46

4 Dance Education Matters: Rebuilding Postsecondary Dance Education for Twenty-first Century Relevance and Resonance — 49
   Doug Risner

CONTENTS

5. Weaving Social Foundations through Dance Pedagogy: A Pedagogy of Uncovering — 65
   Sherrie Barr and Doug Risner

6. Troubling Methods-Centered "Teacher Production": Social Foundations in Dance Education Teacher Preparation — 75
   Doug Risner and Sherrie Barr

7. Leadership Narratives in Postsecondary Dance Leadership: Voices, Values and Gender Variations — 89
   Doug Risner and Pamela S. Musil

PART III
The Role of Dance Teaching Artists in Dance Education — 101

Prelude — 102

8. Hybrid Lives of Teaching Artistry: A Survey of Teaching Artists in Dance — 106
   Doug Risner

9. The Credential Question: Attitudes of Dance and Theatre Teaching Artists — 125
   Doug Risner and Mary Elizabeth Anderson

10. Preparation, Policy and Workplace Challenges of Dance Teaching Artists in P-12 Schools: Perspectives from the Field — 133
    Doug Risner, Sam Horning, and Bryant Henderson Shea

PART IV
Dance, Gender, and Sexual Identity — 147

Prelude — 148

11. Rehearsing Masculinity: Challenging the "Boy Code" in Dance Education — 151
    Doug Risner

12. Bullying Victimization and Social Support of Adolescent Male Dance Students — 166
    Doug Risner

13. Gender Problems in Western Theatrical Dance: Little Girls, Big Sissies and the "Baryshnikov Complex" — 189
    Doug Risner

14. Men in Dance, Bridging the Gap Symposium: Gender Inequities in Dance Education: Asking New Questions — 210
    Doug Risner

PART V
Reflective Practice, Social Justice, and Humanizing Dance Pedagogy 217

    Prelude 218

15 Motion and Marking in Reflective Practice: Artifacts, Autobiographical
Narrative, and Sexuality 224
Doug Risner

16 Moving Social Justice in Dance Pedagogy: Possibilities, Fears and Challenges 232
Doug Risner and Susan W. Stinson

17 Activities for Humanizing Dance Pedagogy: Immersive Learning in Practice 258
Doug Risner

    Afterword 265
    Nyama McCarthy-Brown

    Index 267

Citation Information

The following chapters were originally published in various volumes and issues of the journals *Impulse: The International Journal of Dance Science; Journal of Physical Education, Recreation & Dance Medicine and Education; Research in Dance Education; Journal of Dance Education; Arts Education Policy Review; Teaching Artist Journal;* and *International Journal of Education & the Arts*. When citing this material, please use the original page numbering for each article, as follows:

Chapter 1
Exploring Dance Rehearsal: The Neglected Issues Revealed
Doug Risner
Journal of Physical Education, Recreation & Dance, volume 63, issue 6 (1992) pp. 61–65

Chapter 2
Voices Seldom Heard: The Dancer's Experience of the Choreographic Process
Doug Risner
Impulse: The International Journal of Dance Science, Medicine and Education, volume 3, issue 2 (1995) pp. 76–85

Chapter 3
Making Dance, Making Sense: Epistemology and Choreography
Doug Risner
Research in Dance Education, volume 1, issue 2 (2000) pp. 155–172

Chapter 4
Dance Education Matters: Rebuilding Postsecondary Dance Education for Twenty-first Century Relevance and Resonance
Doug Risner
Journal of Dance Education, volume 10, issue 4 (2010) pp. 95–110

Chapter 5
Weaving Social Foundations through Dance Pedagogy: A Pedagogy of Uncovering
Sherrie Barr and Doug Risner
Journal of Dance Education, volume 14, issue 4 (2014) pp. 136–145

Chapter 6
Troubling Methods-Centered "Teacher Production": Social Foundations in Dance Education Teacher Preparation
Doug Risner and Sherrie Barr
Arts Education Policy Review, volume 116, issue 2 (2015) pp. 78–91

Chapter 7
Leadership Narratives in Postsecondary Dance Leadership: Voices, Values and Gender Variations
Doug Risner and Pamela S. Musil
Journal of Dance Education, volume 17, issue 2 (2017) pp. 53–64

Chapter 8
Hybrid Lives of Teaching and Artistry: A Study of Teaching Artists in Dance in the USA
Doug Risner
Research in Dance Education, volume 13, issue 2 (2012) pp. 175–193

Chapter 9
The Credential Question: Attitudes of Teaching Artists in Dance and Theatre Arts
Doug Risner and Mary Elizabeth Anderson
Teaching Artist Journal, volume 13, issue 1 (2015) pp. 28–35

Chapter 10
Preparation, Policy and Workplace Challenges of Dance Teaching Artists in P-12 Schools: Perspectives from the Field
Doug Risner, Sam Horning, and Bryant Henderson Shea
Arts Education Policy Review, DOI: 10.1080/10632913.2021.2004959

Chapter 11
Rehearsing Masculinity: Challenging the "Boy Code" in Dance Education
Doug Risner
Research in Dance Education, volume 8, issue 2 (2007) pp. 139–153

Chapter 12
Bullying victimisation and social support of adolescent male dance students: an analysis of findings
Doug Risner
Research in Dance Education, volume 15, issue 2 (2014) pp. 179–201

Chapter 13
Gender Problems in Western Theatrical Dance: Little Girls, Big Sissies and the "Baryshnikov Complex"
Doug Risner
International Journal of Education & the Arts, volume 15, issue 10 (2014) pp. 1–22

Chapter 14
Men in Dance, Bridging the Gap Symposium
Doug Risner
Dance Education in Practice, volume 4, issue 1 (2018) pp. 25–31

Chapter 15
Motion and Marking in Reflective Practice: Artifacts, Autobiographical Narrative, and Sexuality
Doug Risner
Journal of Dance Education, volume 17, issue 3 (2017) pp. 91–98

Chapter 16
Moving Social Justice in Dance Pedagogy: Possibilities, Fears and Challenges
Doug Risner and Susan W. Stinson
International Journal of Education & the Arts, volume 11, issue 6 (2010) pp. 1–26

Chapter 17
Activities for Humanizing Dance Pedagogy: Immersive Learning in Practice
Doug Risner
Journal of Dance Education, volume 21, issue 2 (2021) pp. 114–120

For any permission-related enquiries please visit:
http://www.tandfonline.com/page/help/permissions

Notes on Contributors

Mary Elizabeth Anderson (PhD, MFA, MA) is an associate professor and chair of the Maggie Allesee Department of Theatre and Dance at Wayne State University, Detroit, USA, where she teaches courses within the performance and critical/theoretical tracks for students in BA, BFA, and MA programs. Prior to her role as a department chair, Dr. Anderson and Dr. Doug Risner created MA in Theatre and Dance: Teaching Artistry degree program in 2016—the first graduate program of its kind in the US and abroad. Dr. Anderson is also the founding director of the *Performance/Exchange*, one of the department's community engagement and teaching artist training programs.

Sherrie Barr (MFA, CMA) taught dance in higher education for over 40 years, in institutions such as Potsdam State College of NY, University of Oregon, and Michigan State University, and served as a Fulbright lecturer in Lisbon, Portugal. She is now honored to be a courtesy professor of Dance at UO. Her scholarship focuses on dance pedagogy through the juncture of critical pedagogies and somatics, published in *Journal of Dance Education*; *Research in Dance Education*; *Theatre, Dance and Performance Training*; *Journal of Dance and Somatic Practices*; and other journals. Book projects include co-editing/authoring the Community Dance section *Case Studies in Dance Education* and a chapter in the forthcoming text *Future(s) of Performance: The Responsibilities of Performing Arts in Tertiary Education*. Sherrie was privileged to be part of the *Journal of Dance Education*'s Executive Editorial Board from 2012 to 2022.

Bryant Henderson Shea (MFA) is an artist-educator whose physical and theoretical research focuses on the intersectionality of vernacular, urban, and contemporary dance forms; gender studies; and pedagogy. His research has been presented by the National Dance Education Organization, *Journal of Dance Education*, and American College Dance Association. Bryant is an instructor in the MFA Dance Program at The University of Alabama, Tuscaloosa, USA, and a certified physically integrated dance teaching artist with The Dancing Wheels Company. He has been a professor of Dance at Cleveland State University, Willamette University, and Lane Community College and a guest artist at Wayne State University, Alma College, and SUNY Fredonia. Bryant is an accomplished dancer and aerialist whose credits include Celebrity Cruises, The Dancing Wheels Company, SYREN Modern Dance, BEings Dance, Interweave Dance Theatre, and Eugene Ballet. Bryant earned his MFA in Dance and Gender Studies from the University of Oregon, Eugene, USA, and BA in Dance and Public Relations from The University of Alabama, Tuscaloosa, USA.

Sam Horning (BFA) is a dancer, arts administrator, educator, teaching artist, and dance maker interested in detailed improvisation techniques rooted in the information supplied from the body and from nature. As a teaching artist through Dance Exchange, he has led STEAM camps through Jacob's Pillow, dance integration workshops within K-12 schools, guest artist classes and residencies for universities and dance companies, and intergenerational specific programming bringing people together across age and difference. Horning's professional relationship with Dr. Doug Risner began at Wayne State University, Detroit, USA, while he was pursuing his BFA in Dance. Recently, Horning co-authored the article, "Preparation, Policy, and Workplace Challenges of Dance Teaching Artists in P-12 Schools: Perspectives from the Field" (Risner et al., 2021), published in a special issue of *Arts Education Policy Review* devoted to teaching artists in the performing arts.

Nyama McCarthy-Brown (PhD, MFA) is a culturally sustaining pedagogue deeply committed to dance education. She is currently on faculty at The Ohio State University, Columbus, USA, as an associate professor of Community Engagement through Dance Pedagogy. Nyama teaches dance education and contemporary dance with Africanist underpinnings grounded the celebration of all movers. She is also an established scholar, with articles in numerous academic publications. Her book *Dance Pedagogy for a Diverse World: Culturally Relevant Teaching in Research, Theory, and Practice* was published in 2017. Currently she is working on her second book about women of the global majority in ballet. Dr. McCarthy-Brown is an active consultant and workshop facilitator for diversifying dance curriculum for organizations such as San Francisco Ballet School; Cincinnati Ballet; Enrich Chicago; Dance Educators Coalition, Minnesota; Rutgers University Dance Department; University of Buffalo; Ohio Dance; and Dance Education Laboratory.

Jennifer McNamara (MFA) is an assistant professor of Dance at Mercyhurst University, Erie, USA. Following a twenty-year career as a ballet dancer, she was an adjunct professor at Middle Tennessee State University, Murfreesboro, USA, and taught for New Dialect, Metro (Nashville) Parks and Recreation Dance Division, and the School of Nashville Ballet. A certified Pilates instructor, Jennifer explores the relationships between foundational and aesthetic movement choices; she is also an advocate for justice in dance education. She is a past recipient of the Individual Artist Fellowship (Dance) from the Tennessee Arts Commission, has designed and built costumes, and has been published in *Arts Education Policy Review* and *Masculinity, Intersectionality and Identity: Why Boys (Don't) Dance*, edited by Doug Risner and Beccy Watson. Jennifer earned her MFA in Dance from Hollins University, Roanoke, USA.

Pamela S. Musil (MA) is a professor emeritus of Contemporary Dance at Brigham Young University, Provo, USA. Her expertise centers on K-12 dance education, postsecondary dance education, and dance science. Her most recent book publication *Dancing Across the Lifespan: Negotiating Age, Place and Purpose* (2022) was co-edited with Doug Risner and Karen Schupp. Her collaborative research publications with Risner also include "Leadership Narratives in Postsecondary Dance Leadership: Voices, Values and Gender Variations" (*Journal of Dance Education*, 2017) and "Leadership and Gender in Postsecondary Dance: An Exploratory Survey of Dance Administrators in the United States," in *Dance and Gender: An Evidence-Based Approach* (2016) edited by Wendy Oliver and Doug Risner.

Doug Risner (PhD, MFA) is a distinguished faculty fellow and professor of Dance and directs MA in Theatre and Dance: Teaching Artistry program in the Maggie Allesee Department of Theatre and Dance at Wayne State University, Detroit, USA. He conducts research in the sociology of dance training and education, gender in dance, curriculum theory and policy, social foundations of dance pedagogy, online learning, and web-based curriculum design. His books include *Stigma and Perseverance in the Lives of Boys Who Dance* (2009); *Hybrid Lives of Teaching Artists in Dance and Theatre Arts: A Critical Reader* (2014); *Gender, Sexuality and Identity: Critical Issues in Dance Education* (2015); *Dance and Gender: An Evidence-Based Approach* (2017); *Dance, Professional Practice, and the Workplace* (2020); and *Ethical Dilemmas in Dance Education: Case Studies on Humanizing Dance Pedagogy* (2020), which received the 2021 NDEO Ruth Lovell Murray Award for Dance Education and the 2021 Susan W. Stinson Book Award. His most recent edited volumes include *Dancing Across the Lifespan: Negotiating Age, Place and Purpose* (2022) with Pam Musil and Karen Schupp and *Masculinity, Intersectionality and Identity: Why Boys (Don't) Dance* (2022) with Beccy Watson.

Susan W. Stinson (EdD), emeritus professor of Dance, joined the faculty in the Department of Dance at the University of North Carolina Greensboro, USA, in 1979, having been recruited to develop the K-12 licensure program. She served as the department head in Dance 1993–2002 and then as interim dean of the School of Music, Theatre and Dance from July 2012 until her retirement in July 2013. Dr. Stinson's scholarly research in dance education focused on both theoretical issues and how children and adolescents make meaning from their experiences. In addition to multiple journal articles and book chapters, she is the author of two books, including *Embodied Curriculum Theory and Research in Arts Education: A Dance Scholar's Search for Meaning* (2016). National awards include National Dance Association Scholar (1994), National Dance Education Organization Lifetime Achievement Award (2012), and Congress on Research in Dance award for Outstanding Scholarly Research in Dance (2012).

Foreword

Doug Risner is a dance artist and educator, a rigorous scholar (the most published in dance education and one of the most published in dance overall), and a prophetic voice in the field. This book, a selection from among the many publications of his career, attests to his well-deserved reputation. It not only serves as an introduction of his work to new readers but also provides an opportunity for long-time readers to rediscover old favorites from a new vantage point, tracking the development of ideas over time, and in relationship with works they might not have read before. It further offers a chance to discover a remarkable human being as he shares his practice and his thinking while living deliberately in his personal and professional life and the intersections between; to be challenged in one's thinking, about dance education and all of the issues in the larger world with which Doug makes connections; and to collaborate intellectually with the foremost dance education scholar of this generation.

I first met Doug decades ago when he came to UNCG to complete his BFA and begin the MFA program. With Doug's professional dance experience, he taught a number of dance technique courses as a part-time faculty member. I audited his beginning modern dance class while I was still a junior faculty member in Dance at UNCG and immediately respected him. After being my teacher, he then became my student in several graduate courses; I also co-directed his MFA thesis (which became the basis for two publications included in this volume) and served on his doctoral committee.

Doug soon became one of my most trusted colleagues. We frequently exchanged scholarly work in draft form, requesting (and receiving) rigorous critique sent always with a loving heart and a reminder to feel no obligation to accept any of it in making the next revision. In responding to his requests for such critique I often encouraged him to write in a language that his students at the university level could understand and to become visible as a person in his own work, telling his own story as context for what he wrote. Doug's responses to my work challenged me as a thinker and practitioner as well as a writer: Reading his work and his comments on mine pushed me to recognize (with chagrin) on several occasions how I had accommodated to the status quo without realizing it, even in areas where I was recognized as an "expert."

When Doug and I collaborated on a project (always ones he initiated), we each contributed based on our strengths, but I always considered him the lead. I was able to share stories from my own teaching and scholarly life which served to help frame issues, even when the stories became less personal in the final version, to raise questions and to help clarify ideas. Doug, ever the impeccable scholar, contributed extensive literature reviews (introducing me to many sources with which I was unfamiliar), a strength which has undoubtedly raised the stature of his work in the eyes of many scholars. He also brought in data analysis whenever relevant, being far more competent with numbers than I was, and his mixed methods research has offered important examples to others in dance education. The outcomes of this collaboration were always better for our conversations, mostly hidden from the reader. One exception is found in the audio excerpts included in "Moving Social Justice in Dance Pedagogy: Possibilities, Fears and Challenges," Chapter 16 of this volume:

Parts of our ongoing dialogue throughout this process, often incomplete, half-baked, and generally messy, are included in audio excerpts for a number of reasons. First, we seek to draw attention to collaborative thinking, learning, and writing. Second, we hope to illuminate the ways in which the written word, though seemingly effortless from sentence to paragraph, from problem to possible solution, actually makes its frequently awkward and sometimes doubtful path to the printed page. Last, we believe that exposing and confessing our imperfections, inadequacies, and incomplete understandings of the world reveal more of our humanity in our struggle as educators and citizens. (Risner and Stinson, 2010, p. 3)

As the older chapters in this book reveal, Doug's initial work was single authored, which was often required for tenure in those days. However, he makes clear even in the first chapter that he prefers collaboration, and a large number of pieces in this collection are co-authored. Doug has been unique in the field in collaborating not just or even mostly with established scholars but with junior ones as well. He has taken seriously the need to strengthen the future of the field, as much as his own reputation/career. He has selected many co-authors and editors whose scholarly work was not well-known and let their voices be heard, a practice many of us wish we had engaged in more. For example, the section preludes in this volume, written in dialogue with Jennifer McNamara, are an important addition.

I encourage readers of this book to similarly engage with each chapter as a collaboration with the author(s), entering into dialogue with the ideas rather than just receiving them. Doug long ago rejected the "banking method" of education first described by Paolo Freire (1970), which views students as containers into which teachers (and authors) pour knowledge; he would hope for readers to similarly reject it, seeking connections with their own lives and raising critical questions. Doug also uses small group interaction a great deal in his teaching, and he would welcome readers extending the collaboration through engaging in discussions of this work with others.

As noted in his conversation with Jennifer McNamara in the introduction, much of Doug's important work had to be left out of this volume, and I encourage readers to seek out additional sources. Many will offer examples, hard to find among these pages, in which he makes himself more personally visible. However, those who know Doug well will recognize how each piece is indeed connected to his own life, to the issues he faced both professionally and personally. It is especially clear how he listened to the voices of dancers (Part I), professional teaching artists (Part III), and gay males (Part IV). It is also clear to this reader how hard it was for him to question his assumptions about issues he cared so deeply about, as is true for most scholars writing about what is close to home. About professional teaching artists, I was nonetheless pleased to see that he could be transparent in Chapter 10, "Preparation, Policy and Workplace Challenges of Dance Teaching Artists in P-12 Schools: Perspectives from the Field," stating his two primary assumptions and citing Anderson and Risner (2014, p. 280):

[F]irst, dance teaching artists make profound contributions to arts education in P-12 schools, and second, dance teaching artists should receive high quality preparation and support commensurate with their responsibilities and obligations in P-12 schools. (Risner et al., 2021, p. 11)

I also noticed his transparency in reporting that some of the teaching artists in his study expressed reservations about additional training to teach in schools. I was even more pleased to see that he was able to name and reflect briefly on some of the tensions that can arise between teaching artists and specialist teachers in dance who hold certification and often possess extensive significant artistic achievement and credentials, a question that had arisen for me in reading earlier chapters within Part III.

I further applaud his bold courage in questioning some efforts to attract more males to dance, as he did in Chapter 14, the keynote address from the "Men in Dance, Bridging the Gap Symposium: Gender Inequities in Dance Education: Asking New Questions," stating that:

> [e]ven if we believe more male students would benefit our dance programs, we must at some point ask, "How many males is 'enough'?" And "what and who [such as talented female dancers] are we willing to sacrifice to achieve this?" (Risner et al., 2018, p. 26, citing Risner and Musil, 2017, p. 182)

Doug's commitment to populations with life experiences similar to his own was matched by his commitment to those less privileged, which is the focus of Part V in this book. During my own career as dance educator and scholar, I often struggled to merge my long investment in dance education and daily frustrations with increasingly burdensome state requirements for licensure, with my social conscience and desire to make a significant difference in the larger world. For other readers who struggle with this potential conflict in terms of time and energy, Doug's work will be a guidepost and a beacon of hope when there is so much in the world about which to despair.

Most readers of Doug's work, in this volume and others, will feel inspired by not just Doug's hope but his courage, energy, scholarly rigor, and determination to bring overlooked voices into the literature while living his life so fully, no matter the challenges. I am certain he seeks not our gratitude for what he has accomplished so much as the hope that others will be able to continue and expand this legacy.

Susan W. Stinson
Emeritus Professor of Dance
University of North Carolina Greensboro

References

Anderson, M., & Risner, D. (2012). A survey of teaching artists in dance and theatre: Implications for preparation, curriculum and professional degree programs. *Arts Education Policy Review, 113*(1), 1–16. DOI: 10.1080/10632913.2012.626383

Freire, P. (1970/2006). Excerpt from pedagogy of the oppressed. In H.S. Shapiro, K. Latham, & S. Ross (Eds.), *The institution of education* (5th ed., pp. 155–162). Pearson.

Risner, D., Blumenfeld, B., Janetti, A., Kaddar, Y., & Rutt, C. (2018). Men in dance, bridging the gap symposium. *Dance Education in Practice, 4*(1), 25–31. DOI: 10.1080/23734833.2018.1417212

Risner, D., Horning, S., & Henderson Shea, B. (2021). Preparation, policy, and workplace challenges of dance teaching artists in P-12 schools: Perspectives from the field. *Arts Education Policy Review*, AHEAD-OF-PRINT, 1–14. DOI: 10.1080/10632913.2021.2004959

Risner, D., & Musil, P. (2017). Leadership and gender in postsecondary dance: An exploratory survey of dance administrators in the United States. In W. Oliver & D. Risner (Eds.), *Dance and gender: An evidence-based approach* (pp. 158–184). University Press of Florida. DOI:10.5744/florida/9780813062662.003.0009

Risner, D., & Stinson, S. (2010). Moving social justice in dance pedagogy: Possibilities, fears, and challenges. *International Journal of Education & the Arts, 11*(6), 1–26.

Introduction

Jennifer McNamara and Doug Risner

What really matters? And—what are we not paying attention to?

The first is the question that Doug Risner poses to the students in his dance pedagogy course—a version of which I enrolled in online in 2014 through the National Dance Education Organization's (NDEO) Online Professional Development Institute—on almost the first day they click into the virtual classroom. I had recently retired from a two-decade career as a professional ballet dancer, which had taken me quite literally all over the world. The daughter of elementary school educators in the New York State public school system, I was sure that I would never be a teacher, and yet I found myself teaching, at a loss for anything else that seemed necessary in the center of my being. But I also felt wholly unprepared to share what I thought I knew and incapable of communicating the things that I had spent my life learning, practicing, and doing over and over and over. And, to add to my insecurity, I had been rejected by the graduate program I had applied to because my career had not been substantial enough. To be fair, I had danced in mid-sized regional companies during an era when dancers were often hired right out of high school, as I had been, without progressing through a company's preprofessional training program. As such, I did not have an undergraduate degree but was hoping to enter the only MFA program, at the time, that accepted candidates on the strength of their careers. Spoiler alert: I was accepted the second time I applied, several years later. I cannot imagine having gone through the program with a cohort other than the one I joined, nor can I imagine having gone through it without first having begun to unpack all the assumptions that Doug urged those of us in that online class to disentangle from our knowing.

When I enrolled in Doug's pedagogy class, after several years of teaching in a variety of mostly recreational dance programs, I had been working my way through the NDEO's certificate in dance education and had taken courses in movement analysis, research methods, grant writing, and education theory, determined to become a more competent teacher. In my head, competence was associated with competition, as if I could become the "best"—which is, of course, incongruous with the idea of shared learning exchanges: learning happens when we are safe enough and brave enough to not have the answers (physical or theoretical), when we notice difference, and when we celebrate and grieve simultaneously (Risner, 2001), to draw from Doug's doctoral dissertation, which he so kindly allowed me to read as I prepared to write this introduction. Even if I knew everything, had all the answers, and even if the student had the questions that I needed to hear, we might not vibrate on the same or even adjacent wavelengths, and we would miss each other. But at the time, I was expecting a pedagogy course to be brimming with tips and tricks for illuminating the mystery and magic of ballet technique—much like what the students in my pedagogy class expect from me today.

I was *not* expecting to be greeted by those two questions. They were both profound and profoundly bleak, yet simultaneously urgent and hopeful queries posed to a virtual room full of strangers in various stages of their careers, as teachers or otherwise. What really matters? In the end, the stranger, the one who is on the margins of our own margins, is the one who guides us to that knowing.

As unsure of everything as I was at the time, I answered with stubborn faith in the unknown, knowing that it was not enough, and with the anxiety of knowing that it was also not "right," as indentured as I was into the cult of pleasing and perfection. Dancers, in particular during the 1990s and early 2000s, tended to equate and find meaningfulness in pleasing the director, the choreographer, and the audience (but rarely themselves or their value systems) and in seeking perfection—which is, of course, a fallacy. There is only perfect for this moment, in this body, in this place, and in consideration of the accumulated experiences that have led you to this situation. At that early point in my practice, teaching often became simply a regurgitation (and how many other connotations that word has, in the context of perfectionism and the standards of my career) of the things that I had been told and taught.

The course itself and in particular the interactions I had with Doug, through the meticulous, probing feedback he offered, were transformative. I did not, in fact, learn the magic phrases that would transform a student into a "turner" or a "jumper," nor did I learn how to teach dance—instead, I learned how to be in process, in motion, alongside the students who took my classes. I distinguish the difference between these two methodologies by calling into question the ideas about teaching (the person in front of me) *how to do dance steps* and teaching *the person in front of me* (how to do dance steps): one prioritizes the transfer of facts (which are sometimes not so much facts as opinions based on a sliding scale of truth and sometimes are specific to *only* one type of body, aesthetic, or genre), while the other places importance on the people involved in the translation of information and the relationship between them in the shared exploration, unearthing, and navigation of questions and experiences, and embodied and theoretical knowledge.

Within the year after I took his pedagogy course, Doug was diagnosed with terminal cancer; the probing questions that he offered to us as guidance, then, became deeply personal as he wrestled with understanding the very essence of living (the end of) life. He began to organize what his time and attention meant, where they might be best focused, and why. People-pleasing and perfection-seeking, the currency of so much of the dance field at the time (and sadly, still today) seemed like very distant, unimportant ideals. His urgency was palpable.

I know that my answers would be different today, and I know Doug's would be as well. And that is the point: what matters now, what mattered then, what will matter—the accumulated answers are the strands of meaningfulness that make living and dancing an act of profound presence, attuned to matter and the matters of life, of movement, of shift, of expiration and death.

What are we not paying attention to? This is a question I learned to ask because of Doug, too. When we start to identify what matters, what we are attendant to, we start to perceive the spaces in between, inklings of the myriad ideas, thoughts, relationships, moments, people, places, experiences that had not previously brushed against the sphere of our consciousness. This brings me to the idea of centering, like clay on a wheel, that Doug offers in Chapter 1 of this text: when you are centered in the sphere of your consciousness, when you are, in fact, the center, what is so removed from you that you do not notice it? And in that absence, what space is there for shift and growth? In the end, perhaps we are neither the potter nor the clay; perhaps we are the orbiting space between, where possibility lies: what shifting shapes hug the surfaces of clay and hand, and what shifting potential fills the infinite distance between them?

In some ways, our ability to focus attention keenly on a thing is like way the surface tension of a soap bubble shapes its ability to shift and to fill new space as it brushes against the very air, so long as that air is humid. When small ruptures happen, when the water trapped between the layers of soap evaporates, the iridescent orb shimmering in its own tenuous fullness is suddenly, irreparably, and wondrously flung wide open. For the dancer and dance educator, this cycle mimics the precarious balance between knowing—what is inside the sphere of the bubble, and not-knowing—the infinite possibilities that present themselves when the bubble pops. It is the tension of sustaining a dynamic equilibrium in both physical and intellectual practices and of remaining available to both attentiveness and wonder. The invitation to acknowledge and even invite imbalance reminds me, too, of the oft-quoted and paraphrased haiku by the 17th-century Japanese poet and samurai, Mizuta Masahide: *My barn having burned down, I can now see the moon (Mizuta Masahide, n.d.).* It also suggests the way dance—and life—shift in response to both internal and external cadences, the varying rhythms of the center and the margin.

This is the intersection where Doug encourages us to begin questioning—and this crossroad is also where he found himself during his doctoral coursework and research. The sweetness of his dissertation was tempered by urgency, hope, and searing honesty. He noted that the deep and poignant distress of grief, which encompasses a public act of mourning, offers us a point of entry to the creation of a new reality. "I believe it is from this consciousness, when we absolutely refuse to permit what we witness, confess, and grieve to remain unnoticed and without response, that hope and possibility arise" (Risner, 2001, p. 163), he wrote, illuminating the path he traveled and the course he mapped for his future, as well as what he hoped would be the future of dance and dance education itself—knowing, as he wrote it, that the road would be long and arduous.

Knowing, too, as Doug points out in "Making Dance, Making Sense" (Chapter 3 of this text), is always predicated in a particular body, place, time, and context. Knowing is also physical, cognitive, intuitive, and relational. When we begin to know, we also begin to wonder. To become curious. To unknow. And eventually to trouble, disturb, and wrestle with assumptions. When we sit in that place of Keats' negative capability—the idea that a person's potential might be measured by what they do not possess or a willingness to let what is mysterious remains just that—we do not seek to know beyond certainty to irrefutable proof; rather, we are open to possibility, to meaningfulness, to the rhythm of creation and curiosity (Hebron, 2014). We find the deeply resonant moments of our lived experiences, the ones that nurture and sustain our nascent intuitions about movement and stillness, ourselves and others, relationship and process, life and death, and death, and death, and life again: the dance of ongoingness.[1]

Doug's dance with meaningfulness shows up, again and again and again, in the lives he has lived: as student, dancer-performer, creator-collaborator, teacher-educator-mentor, scholar-researcher, and administrator; as husband, father, husband again, and now grandfather; and as a deeply humane, human being who happens to be living into a good death as he navigates terminal cancer. It is our good fortune that he has been reflexively preparing for this next death (for, as Martha Graham is reported to have said, "A dancer dies twice—once when they stop dancing, and this first death is the more painful") since far before his diagnosis. The demi-deaths of each iteration of his humanness have been fertile ground for documenting a life well-lived and well-learned, patiently observed through an autoethnographic lens. From rehearsal to performance, from studio to stage, from back of the room to front of the room to office and back to the studio, to home, the paths have threaded together a practice of philosophical observation, urgent inquiry, and ongoing shift.

Dancing Mind, Minding Dance brings together primary strands of thought interwoven in and through Doug Risner's professional lives as a dancer, choreographer, dance educator, administrator, journal editor, mentor, researcher, and scholar alongside his personal lives as a cis-gender gay male, father, husband (twice), and grandfather. Part I springs from the first iteration of his lived experiences and the first inklings of numerous transitions. Even as a dancer, he was watching himself rehearse and contemplating the significance of the process (over the product) (Risner, 2000). These musings about and inquiry into the dancer's point of view formed the basis of both his MFA and to some extent his doctoral thesis research that followed nearly a decade later, which contributed to valuable insights into the ways rehearsing and co-creating a dance and the ensuing relationships within that space unfold and reverberate for all stakeholders. This was also where Doug's ideas about the aim of education, and dance education in particular, began to crystallize, small seeds of clairvoyance that would, in time, become the foundation of his humanizing dance pedagogy. At this point, however, they served to center him in the greater world, to see the infinite possibilities rippling outward, and to sense, bodily, that centering itself was necessarily a fluid response to the eddies of life—and rehearsal, and process.

When the student is centered in the practice/performance/revelation/journey of education, what does it mean for the teacher to be responsible for someone else's learning? What occurs in the orbiting space between teacher and student, between dancer and choreographer and audience, between now and then? What kind of teacher am I/do I want to be? These guiding curiosities are at the heart of Part II spiral outward in ever-widening waves of inquiry and challenging choices. Doug takes the ideas from the dancer's perspective on significance and meaningfulness in learning and turns that lens to the teachers of the teachers, calling into question ages-old methodologies to focus instead on the social foundations of education, and in particular how they are revealed in the so-called "best practices"—a phrase that should, perhaps, be retired—that privilege one type of student. This is another iteration of the very first question—what (or who) are we not paying attention to—and it is as relevant when speaking about the student-teacher relationship as it is when noting disparities in the way administrators see and are seen at institutions of higher education.

From the perspective of the administrator, Doug was able to guide his inquiry toward the ways dance teaching artists present themselves in the world and the ways they are or are not prepared, supported, and sustained by the institutions charged with doing so. Teaching artists occupy a tenuous sliver in an also tenuous field, and while some of them prefer that chameleon-like ability to slip between the world of dance and the world of teaching, others find the negotiation fraught. Programs to prepare teaching artists vary, appearing and disappearing based on the seeming whim of administrations; they are vaguely regulated, and loosely supported, themselves. But teaching teachers to teach, or perhaps helping them to notice what they are or are not attending to, is deeply meaningful work, for both the mentor and the future students. Doug's sharp insight in this area, his passionate advocacy for and intimate knowledge of what it means to enter that space of sharing as both a teaching artist and a university administrator, reverberates through the research in the third part of this book.

Although Doug is highly respected as a pedagogue and scholar in the field of dance education, I actually first read his work in gender and masculinity studies. He spoke clearly, rationally, and passionately about things I had seen in my career; but he also brought forward, from the intersections of his identity and presentation, nuanced, underlying factors that I had not noticed from the intersections of my identity as a middle class, white, cis-female. The stigma that permeates societal assumptions about males who dance also creates undercurrents in the field: gender and sexual identity politics, the gendering of movement and its effect on dance and dancers, and the marginalization of males by those both inside and outside the field, even as male dancers are also held up as rare, divine beings. And, of course, this loop recreates itself over and over. When I was a newer teacher, the subtle, and not-so-subtle, intertwined narratives in Doug's writing about gender helped me put my own teaching in conversation with the greater dance world, and I am grateful to have had the perspectives Doug brought forward in the articles in the second part of this book to guide my listening, interactions, and questions. Once again, the threads of his thoughts have been interwoven from those musings to these in a fluid, scaffolded manner and have illuminated so many intricate patterns within the field.

Each iteration of Doug's interests and research—his carefully trained gaze helping to gestate and focus his curiosity, his sense of justice, and his advocacy for ethical decision-making—led him to understand, from inside and from a distance, the critical need for a humanizing presence in the dance classroom and studio. The articles in the concluding section of this volume speak from his many years of rehearsing a life (or perhaps living its rehearsal) inside and outside the studio, the classroom, the office, the home. They speak to and of his most personal and fervent work, the bodily and spiritual accumulation of experiences and lessons, the sifting and shifting as layers of space between center and margins blur—and yet maintain the distance necessary to trouble assumptions in the search for a better way. Not a "best practice"—but to know and do better, always better. In motion. A dancing mind.

Note

1 Thanks to author Sarah Manguso for that rich term, the title of one of her autobiographical wonderings (Manguso, 2015).

References

Hebron, S. (2014, May 15). *John Keats and 'negative capability.'* British Library. https://www.bl.uk/romantics-and-victorians/articles/john-keats-and-negative-capability.

Manguso, S. (2015). *Ongoingness*. Graywolf Press.

Mizuta Masahide. (n.d.). In *Wikipedia*. https://en.wikipedia.org/wiki/Mizuta_Masahide.

Risner, D. (2000). Making dance, making sense: Epistemology and choreography. *Research in Dance Education, 1*(2), 155–172. DOI: 10.1080/713694259

Risner, D. (2001). *Blurring the boundaries: Hope and possibility in the presence of the necessary stranger in gay liberation.* (UMI No. 3008895) [Doctoral dissertation, University of North Carolina at Greensboro]. ProQuest.

Part I

Dance Making Pedagogies in the Rehearsal Process

Prelude

"In a metaphor of rehearsal as child's play, one can see that playing does not require a finished product. In much the same way, rehearsal, as distinguished from performance, is a complete activity in and of itself. Engaging dancers more fully in the rehearsal process, choreographers may find performances of the dancers more complete and satisfying." (Risner, 1995, p. 83)

Jennifer McNamara: The voice that is heard so clearly in the pieces that comprise this section suggests, already, the beginning of Doug Risner's search for and construction of a humanizing dance pedagogy. The questions that he revealed, untangled, and wove through his experiences spurred conversations about what it means to know. These dialogues, too, present the idea of centering as not only an intellectual process—the way a teacher talks about centering the mind's eye in order to absorb a lesson—but a physical one as well. Doug uses the analogy of centering clay on a wheel, which he attributes to the potter, poet, and educator Mary Caroline Richards. Centering, or knowing ourselves, is contextual, of course, defined by the boundaries, societal, or other, within which we exist, travel between, and transgress—or transcend, depending on your perspective. When those boundaries are fluid, what more could we know about what it means to exist in another's space, to understand the world in the ways that they do, to see the shimmering edges or the mirage of the center? In dance, how might we really seek to know from someone else's vantage point instead of simply reproducing what we think we know about their context? And, perhaps more poignantly, how does that knowing inform our "right relationships" (Heyward, 1989) in this world? These musings, of course, draw us back to the idea of play and how rehearsal might mirror play as dancers construct or name meaning and knowing through the exploration and assignment of value to the experience in and through the process. What—and whose—story are we telling? And similarly, what are we not paying attention to when we privilege, foreground, or subscribe to one vantage point, often our own?

Doug cites curriculum theorist James McDonald (1974), who noted similarly that the aim of education should be the centering of the person in the world. There is so much richness in that idea, and in some ways, it seems to both predict and mirror a dancer's work—the ways they assimilate others' ideas about themselves as they wriggle to fit into the particular mold of what is currently desirable in the field. And yet fitting into a mold is the antithesis of centering ourselves in the world. A mold is a small, finite, confined space; the world is sprawling, infinite, and shifting. The center changes; it tilts, expands, contracts, and expands again. Centering ourselves in a moving, growing, radiant world invites curiosity. But centering, too, risks perpetuating hegemonic ideals and practices rather than challenging them, especially when the center is seen as a fixed, immutable point. Rehearsal, then, becomes the way to blur the edges of the center even as its nexus, its "right relationships" with the margins, becomes more clearly defined. Rehearsal, rather than performance, of the self and of the dance, is a form of becoming.

Doug Risner: I almost always enjoyed rehearsing more than performing; thirty years ago, though, very little was known about dancers' experiences in the rehearsal process, nor was there much published research, as I pointed out in the sparse references listed for the first two articles included in this section. My affinity for rehearsing, both as a dancer and as a choreographer, was a living, breathing force in my work; I wanted to know, deeply, what it was about rehearsal that I found immensely satisfying, and whether others shared that hunger for blissful, focused, and critically essential immersion in the work at hand. I sought to provide the field a better understanding of dancers in the rehearsal process, how the act of learning choreography unfolded in terms of each person's faith in the process, their faith in the commitment to the work that was being created, often collaboratively, and their faith in fellow co-dancers; more broadly, I was curious how this scaffolded, cooperative work might yield a certain trust in building community, relationships, and artistry.

Thus, Chapter 1, "Exploring Dance Rehearsal: The Neglected Issues Revealed" (1992), and Chapter 2, "Voices Seldom Heard: The Dancer's Experience of the Choreographic Process" (1995), emerged from the questions that guided my MFA thesis, *Dancers in the Rehearsal Process* (1990, UNCG). These pivotal publications were, therefore, foundational to my tenure and promotion at Luther College in 1996. The research study for Chapter 3, "Making Dance, Making Sense" (2000), was published during my second year of coursework for my PhD in Educational Foundations: Pedagogy and Curriculum (1998–2001, UNCG).

JM: The relationship between rehearsal and performance, the relationship between public and private facing lives, the relationship between center and margin—these all formed the basis of Doug's dissertation, a searingly honest reflection of his many journeys between these (at the time fixed) points, seeking to draw them ever closer in hopes of blurring the distinction, to make a whole. And yet—the distance between them is exactly what affords him the power to see the possibility of change that must come, that is critical to his very existence, the continuity, albeit evolving, of the field as a whole, and perhaps even the relationships that stabilize the fabric of society through their gentle fluctuations.

Rehearsal, then, becomes both a metaphor and a way of being; there is trust in the process, faith that one will return again and again and again. There is also a sense that the outcome, perhaps, is less important than the work that is undertaken, the journey of becoming. Rehearsing the "self" in the rehearsal of the dance not only bridges the vast distance between what is and what is not but also offers vantage points for seeing places where these two things might become adjacent or even to merge. Doug's process as a choreographer and the way he sought to understand the dancer's process in the rehearsal brought these ideas to the forefront: as one student noted, "Doing one of these dances is like opening a door into a whole different world…you don't know if it's in the past, the future, or even what planet you're on" (Risner, 2001, p. 66). Rehearsal, like play, is an act of doing and making, always in motion and not necessarily possessing absolute knowledge of the dance or the self, or the intersections of the two, but gathering sensations about what they might be—and what they might not be. Dancers and dance makers learn to leave the door open to possibility, to chance, to change; this porousness means accepting an opportunity to work from both the center and the negative space that surrounds it—to exist in, or even to be the orbiting space between clay and potter, replete and yet somehow still full of unknowing and questions. Doug Risner's writing during this period offers the reader an invitation to enter and experience that space of wonder and otherness.

References

Heyward, C. (1989) *Touching our strength: The erotic as power and the love of God.* Harper & Row.

hooks, b. (1984) *Feminist theory: From margin to center.* South End Press.

MacDonald, J. (1974). A transcendental developmental ideology of education. In J. Gress (Ed.), *Curriculum: An introduction to the field* (pp. 95–126). McCutchan Publishing Corporation.

Risner, D. (1990). *Dancers in the rehearsal process: An interpretive inquiry* [Unpublished master's thesis]. University of North Carolina at Greensboro.

Risner, D. (1992). Exploring dance rehearsal: The neglected issues revealed. *Journal of Physical Education, Recreation & Dance, 63*(6), 61–65. DOI: 10.1080/07303084.1992.10606621

Risner, D. (1995). Voices seldom heard: The dancers' experience of the choreographic process. *Impulse: The International Journal of Dance Science, Medicine, and Education, 3*(2), 76–85.

Risner, D. (2000). Making dance, making sense: Epistemology and choreography. *Research in Dance Education, 1*(2), 155–172. DOI: 10.1080/713694259

Risner, D. (2001). *Blurring the boundaries: Hope and possibility in the presence of the necessary stranger in gay liberation.* (UMI No. 3008895) [Doctoral dissertation, University of North Carolina at Greensboro]. ProQuest.

Exploring Dance Rehearsal—The Neglected Issues Revealed

DOUGLAS S. RISNER

This article offers no specific directions for rehearsing a dance; it is not a rehearsal manual. Rather, it seeks to reveal important issues and questions. The issues revealed continue, rather than answer, the question, "How should choreographers rehearse?"

Choreographers have been making modern dances for nearly a century. While much has been written about the choreographic process (Banes 1980; Cohen, 1965; Foster, 1986;

Stodelle, 1978; Tompkins, 1965), little is known about the meaning dancers make of the rehearsal process. For dancers and choreographers, the process of creating and rehearsing a dance, as distinguished from the final product or performance, is interesting and important. Though often neglected, dancers' experience of rehearsal warrants investigation. What is it about rehearsing that resonates so strongly for dancers? This article seeks to reveal important issues that are hidden and unnoticed during rehearsals.

For dancers and choreographers, the process of making a dance is a centering activity that is based upon humans fully participating in human action. A choreographer begins with a concept and assembles a cast of dancers with whom to work on the creation of a new dance. A rehearsal model will help foster a better understanding of the rehearsal process and the satisfaction that dancers find in rehearsal.

Rehearsal Model

Four distinct stages occur in the development of dance rehearsals. The rehearsal model, presented here in a linear fashion, begins with the *concept and cast* stage. When a choreographer begins a dance, he or she starts with an idea or a concept and a cast of dancers. The concept may not yet be fully developed and the casting of the piece may not be completely articulated at this stage. The choreographer does have dancers, a preliminary set of ideas, and a tentative methodology.

The second stage, *movement investigation*, follows, with the dancers and choreographer exploring movement possibilities. In this stage, the focus is on the search for and the learning of movement. In an open, playful, and spontaneous way, movement and its conception are prominent. Physicality is paramount. Movement phrases may be repeated many times as the dancers become familiar with the movement, its quality, timing, rhythm, dynamic, shape, pattern, and character. The dance product or performance is inevitable, but at this stage the process is primary. The choreographer uses this period to refine the movement phrases; movement choices are explored and edited.

In the movement investigation stage, participants develop a sense of faith and trust in the process itself. The formation of the dance has not yet begun, but there is an understanding that a dance will be created. The movement investigation stage is a paradigm of trust and faith in which the critical process is suspended. It may be faith based on past experience that encourages a mutual belief by the dancers and choreographer that they will return to further the agreed upon goal of making a dance. This stage does not generate the judgment and scrutiny that appear in the pure rehearsal stage and in the actual dance performance.

There are two ways to explore movement in the rehearsal process:

1. The choreographer can develop the movement prior to the rehearsal, then present it to the dancers at a full cast rehearsal. Traditionally, this method is used by choreographers who are interested in seeing their own personal movement performed by a group of dancers. These choreographers usually have a highly developed sense of what movement choices are appropriate for their choreographies. Dancers experience this rehearsal process in a more traditional way; the dancer performs the movement given as articulately as possible.

2. The movement possibilities can develop out of an exchange between the dancers and choreographer during the rehearsal. This method of choreography demands that these

Figure 1 In the *fanning and ordering* stage, dancers experience the sketch of the complete dance—they see for the first time how each individual dancer contributes to the finished work. *Photo*: Chip Peterson.

dancers not only be performers, but also choreographers. For those less experienced in working in this manner, this method can be frustrating and intimidating. Dancers who prefer to copy, with exacting precision, the explicit movement phrases of the choreographer feel uncomfortable when asked to contribute to the choreography. This responsibility can be seen as burdensome and without reward. However, this method, when explained clearly to the dancers, allows them to participate in the making of the dance and to invest themselves more completely in the process.

The *forming and ordering stage* follows or overlaps movement investigation. In the previous stage, movement choices were explored, edited, and refined. A dancer begins to anticipate how the movement phrase will be constructed and ordered by the choreographer. The design of the dance begins to unfold in this forming and ordering stage. Dancers may be asked to manipulate movement; perform movement phrases in unison, solo, or canon; or to perform the movement in other ways. It is in this stage that the vocabulary of the dance is molded into a framework that eventually becomes the dance.

In this stage, dancers experience the sketch of the complete dance. An understanding of the integrated parts of the dance enables the dancers to see for the first time how each individual dancer contributes to the finished work. Having worked rigorously for many rehearsals, the dancers experience satisfaction and relief.

The final stage of the rehearsal process–the *pure rehearsal* stage–begins when the form and content of the dance are complete. This stage focuses on the impending performance. Pure rehearsal brings about "running the dance"–performing the completed dance two or three times over the course of the rehearsal.

In this stage, the choreographer views the dance as a whole unit and comments on the dancers' interpretation and performance. Some changes may be made in what has been achieved in previous stages. Movement may be adjusted to fit the dance's organic wholeness. Time and space may be altered. Motivational directions may be developed.

Pure rehearsal includes "polishing" the dance–continued refinement of execution. Pure rehearsal allows the dancer to develop performance potential, stamina, and dynamic qualities. Emphasis in this stage moves from rote precision of execution to a unified, whole, artistic performance. The dancers' energies are directed toward the approaching performance. As rehearsals continue, dancers work at finding new ways of approaching each run-through while at the same time maintaining the precision and artistic integrity of the dance.

This four-stage model provides a framework for articulating what it is about rehearsing that resonates so strongly for dancers. In addition, the model suggests that dance rehearsal is relevant not only to the making of a dance, but also to dancers' thinking, knowing, and being as people.

Rehearsal as Play

Curriculum theorist James MacDonald (1974) stated: "The aim of education should be the centering of the person in the world." The centering process to which MacDonald refers is based on the work of artist Mary Caroline Richards. Centering as a metaphor arose from her experience of centering clay on a potter's wheel. The physicality of the metaphor makes clear that centering is not just an activity of the mind but of the whole self in time and space. The engagement of the whole self, as an embodied person, is necessary to make meaning of our lives in the world.

Certain processes or activities facilitate centering–the integrating of mind and body. Two that MacDonald acknowledges–play and pattern making, both metaphors for the rehearsal process–are particularly relevant to the dancer and choreographer. The rehearsal period is analogous to a child playing. The child develops an idea or story, tries it out once, and makes necessary changes. The child then evaluates whether the whole scenario is pleasurable and interesting. If so, it is repeated many times and most likely returned to again the next day with some addition or alteration.

The rehearsal process parallels this childlike play structure and gives the choreographer and dancer the same satisfaction. There is a stability in repetition that may be linked to

Figure 2 The rehearsal period is analogous to a child playing. The child develops an idea or story, tries it out once, and makes necessary changes. *Photo*: Chip Peterson.

gaining greater understanding. Through the repetition of hearing, seeing, and doing something, the relationship shared with this "thing" becomes more clearly understood. Within the repetition, the choreographer and dancer are free to explore and "play," as MacDonald suggests in his writings on centering.

MacDonald stated that pattern making "is fundamental for locating oneself in time and space" (1974). Dance rehearsal is the creative and personal ordering of information or pattern making. By establishing patterns in a movement, a dancer transforms reality and creates a specialized order in search of meaning. For a dancer, creative and personal ordering

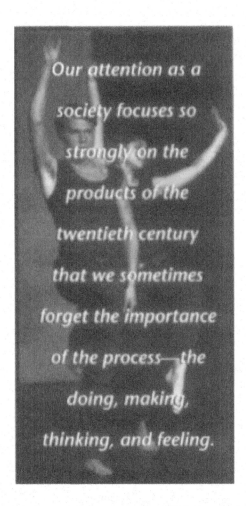

Our attention as a society focuses so strongly on the products of the twentieth century that we sometimes forget the importance of the process—the doing, making, thinking, and feeling.

is essential in the rehearsal of a new dance, regardless of the method of movement invention that the choreographer uses.

When choreographers allow dancers to participate in the creation of movement, the dancers are simultaneously creating movement and meaning. When choreographers give dancers exact movement, the dancers make it their own; they transform it. No two dancers perform the same movement alike. Personal meaning and creativity are essential for dancers to execute precise movement. The choreographer transmits information to the dancers in the form of movement sequences, but to perform these sequences, the dancers enter into a relationship with the movement that allows the creation of a personal order.

The dancers look at and then transform the movement's formal qualities and find shapes, lines, and designs that are interesting. They "play" with the movement, experimenting with quality and dynamic. If this open, playful process within the dancers ceases to exist, the dancers only mimic the choreographer, executing steps without personal engagement with the dance.

This may be more easily understood by returning to the metaphor of a child playing. A child becomes more interested and engaged in a game with predetermined rules and guidelines when he or she is allowed and encouraged to participate in the structure and content of the activity. The child creates a variation of the game or views the game from a different perspective. Children bring themselves creatively to the games they play, actively participating while developing an identity and power of their own.

As suggested by MacDonald's idea of centering for the individual, play is critical. Much of the rehearsal process coincides with the attitude and activity of play. In creating a new dance, choreographers and dancers engage playfully with ideas, music, time, space, and each other. Rehearsing a dance as a playful encounter allows freedom to order and create personal meaning while making a new dance. Creating as play nurtures engagement on a personal level without constant direction and scrutiny. Movement material can be approached in a playful, exploratory manner, without immediate evaluation or judgment.

The rehearsal process as play also encourages "what if...?" movement, which explores movement possibilities by posing creative problem-solving questions. For example, having a dancer do his or her movement phrase entirely on the floor in a playful, nonjudgmental way allows the dancer to explore personal potential for creativity and expression.

Rehearsal as Whole Body Physicality

Many dancers respond strongly to the physical euphoria achieved by repeatedly doing a movement phrase at performance level. Rehearsing a dance as a dancer is a physical experience. Post-modern choreographer Douglas Dunn (1990) has said that "dancers and choreographers come to a physical agreement." Dancers and choreographers agree to explore movement possibilities together, and through this agreement, the dance is created. Meaning is also created in the physical performance of the movement. Returning to the metaphor of dance as play, the physical activity of dance heightens the importance of doing, in this case, the movement.

Knowing something in a physical way differs from knowing in an intellectual way. When dancers are on tour, they immediately take off their shoes upon arrival at the theatre. They want to "know" what the floor is like. Through the physical "doing" of the movement, a dancer moves closer to a greater understanding of the movement, the dance, the other dancers, and him or herself. By simultaneously doing and thinking, a unified, dynamic wholeness is achieved. By being completely present in the physicality of the movement, a dancer encounters an experience of the whole self and relishes the knowledge that, although the movement phrases have been performed many times during a particular rehearsal, he or she will repeat them many times again. Regardless of how dances are constructed, choreographers-if at all interested in dancers actively engaging themselves in the rehearsal process-must acknowledge and nurture each dancer's individuality.

Finding one's own movement in the rehearsal studio is creative as well as personally engaging. Finding and creating engages dancers in the process of dance making and meaning making. This method of choreography requires that dancers have a significant amount of responsibility, especially for their own dancing. Some dancers experience frustration when asked to accept this kind of responsibility. Many see their roles as dancers to be passive receptacles.

Choreographers establish the tone and environment in which their dances are created. By conducting rehearsals that encourage individual dancers to speak, move, and contribute freely, without fear of scrutiny or judgment, choreographers enable the dancers to take a more active role in the process. In an atmosphere where each dancer is viewed as possessing a rich source of ideas, interpretations, and viewpoints, dancers can safely shed the passive receptacle identity and participate as unique, vital components of the dance. Choreographers should consider this a significant issue in their investigation of the relationships they share with dancers.

An individual dancer is not molded and shaped by the choreographer; rather, both choreographer and dancer are transformed during the rehearsal process via an ongoing dialogue with each other and the movement. When both are viewed as contributing to the sum total of the dance, the rehearsal will no longer be oppressive.

Our attention as a society focuses so strongly on the products of the twentieth century that we sometimes forget the importance of the process–the doing, making, thinking, and feeling. Dancers' attention, in many cases, focuses entirely on the dance product and how they look rather than on their experience of making a dance and how they feel when dancing. The dance product, or performance, is inevitable, but the process of making a dance is a potentially rich source of satisfying and meaningful human experience.

Thinking of rehearsal as child's play suggests that playing does not require a finished product. It is a complete activity in and of itself. Of course, as children grow, games begin to have goals with winners and losers. As children encounter the adult world, their attention moves from doing and making to having and possessing.

During the first rehearsals of a new dance, nothing concrete pertaining to the dance may be accomplished, but faithfully, choreographers and dancers will return to the rehearsal studio at the scheduled time to once again share and dance together. There is a faith in the process that something eventually will come about. Faith and trust in the rehearsal situation allow choreographers and dancers to experience deep personal involvement, risk taking, patience, playful encounters, and personal meaning making. New beginnings such as these offer relationships which are based on faith and trust, with people, movement, and ideas.

The rehearsal model described here encourages choreographers to look at each dancer as an individual who possesses a unique style and point of view, and to realize that what resonates most strongly in the rehearsal process for each dancer is distinct. A perspective such as this illuminates the importance of exploring the environment in which one creates a new dance.

References

Banes, S. (1980). *Terpsichore in sneakers*. Middletown, CT: Wesleyan University Press.
Cohen, S. (1965). *Tire modem dance: Seven statements of belief*. Middletown, CT: Wesleyan University Press.
Dunn, D. (1990, April). *Dance, image, and meaning: Twentieth century dance-A refection of its time*. Lecture demonstration with Douglas Dunn & Dancers. The Ewald Scholars' Symposium, Sweet Briar, VA.
Foster, S. (1986). *Reading dancing*. Los Angeles: University of California Press.
MacDonald. (1974). A transcendental developmental ideology of education. In J. Gress (Ed.), *Curriculum: An introduction to the field*, p. 95-126. Berkeley: McCutchan Publishing Corporation.
Stodelle, E. (1978). *TM dance technique of Doris Humphrey*. Princeton: Princeton Book Company.
Tompkins, C. (1965). *The bride and tire bachelors*. New York: The Viking Press.

Voices Seldom Heard: The Dancers' Experience of the Choreographic Process

Douglas S. Risner

This pilot study explores dancers' perspectives of the dance rehearsal process by concentrating on the stories of 3 dancers engaged in the choreographic process. Three significant themes that emerged from the analysis of the interview material include the relationship of dancer and choreographer, the relationships shared between dancers, and the experience of new beginning. The study concludes that the rehearsal process is a social situation that is based on a shared faith and trust in the process itself; the rehearsal process allows for individual affirmation in diverse ways. The emergence of these themes illustrates the importance of continued questioning and evaluation of the rehearsal process.

I'm tremendously affected by relationships among dancers-it completely affects how I dance.
(Suzanne, age 27)
It's awkward finding out whether the choreographer is going to favor someone and use them over and over again. **(Kim,** age 23)
If there's something the choreographer doesn't like, I want him to tell me.
(Michelle, age 20)

Dancers, as bodies, minds, and spirits, are integral to the choreographic process. Without the dancers, the choreographer has no means, no materials with which to create his or her work. Although seemingly primary to the act of choreography, the dancers' experiences of the choreographic process have not been explored fully. Much has been written about choreographic pioneers (Cohen, 1965; Foster, 1986; Stodelle, 1978) and innovators (Banes, 1980; Kreemer, 1987; Tompkins, 1965); little is documented about the dancers' experiences of the choreographic process. Though often neglected, dancers' experiences of rehearsal warrant investigation (Risner, 1992). Within this investigation of dance rehearsal, one important question that emerges is, How do choreographers wish to rehearse?

To explore the dancers' perspectives of the rehearsal process more fully, this pilot study concentrates on the stories of 3 dancers with whom I recently created a dance. I sought a research methodology that would retain the richness of each experience contained in the stories. Those interviewed are not objects of research, but subjects of research. While the researcher can never be truly objective, the purpose of this qualitative research, in Robert Donmoyer's (1985) words, "is not to subsume particular events under general categories but to alter the general categories and constructs to better accommodate the novelty of the particulars" (pp. 64-65). Within this methodology, larger themes of human experience present themselves, other realities can be embraced, and relationships to others' experiences can be seen.

Crucial to this research was that I be able to observe and talk with the participants in the rehearsal process. The demands of the dance made it necessary to select dancers with at least 4 to 5 years of experience in dance rehearsal and performance.

One of the dancers who participated in this study recently completed a BFA degree in dance at a large university in the South and was 20 years old. Recalling her mother telling her that she always knew her daughter was going to be a dancer, this participant has been dancing since the age of 4. Michelle (a pseudonym) described herself as a very logical person who likes what is "real." She saw dance as a way of expressing herself.

Another participant was born in Texas and moved to North Carolina to pursue dance in high school at a state school for the performing arts. While she performs and takes dance classes at a university, her academic major is history. Justifying her studies in history, she stated, "People don't take dancers seriously, so I'll have something to fall back on." In her early 20s, Kim (a pseudonym) has danced since she was very young. Trained extensively in modern dance and ballet, she has performed frequently during the last 5 years. Describing herself as a meticulous person, she stated, "I like rehearsals to run smoothly and organized."

The third participant began dancing at an early age, continuing with ballet in high school and modern dance in college. For many years she traveled through out the United States and Europe, performing with small regional dance compa nies. A free-lance newspaper writer, she sees dance as the one thing in her life that remains constant. This participant was in her late 20s and will be referred to as Suzanne.

Procedures for conducting this study included interviewing the dancers, writing a personal reflection on the rehearsal process, making notes following each rehearsal, and reading journals I asked the dancers to keep. I read and reread the material generated, seeking to identify major themes that would reveal the meanings the participants made of the rehearsal process.

Each participant was interviewed twice during the 4-week rehearsal period. The first interview occurred during the 1st week of rehearsal and lasted between 30 and 45 minutes. The second interview occurred during the 3rd week of rehearsal. Each interview focused on questions that would allow the dancers to speak freely about dancing and rehearsing.

The interview questions were used as a springboard to allow the participants to talk candidly about themselves. The dancers were asked question such as, "Can you talk about what rehearsal is like for you?" Questions that would result in specific yes or no answers were avoided. The objective was to encourage the dialogue to travel in any direction, guided more by what the participants felt was significant, rather than being guided toward a specific answer by the researcher. The first interview was transcribed; the second interview was summarized follow ing the session from the researcher's notes. After reading the transcriptions a number of times and consulting the summarized notes, I edited the interview material before proceeding further with the analysis.

An overall observation of these women revealed they were highly skilled dancers with an incredible appetite for movement, dialogue, and direction. Their similarities included strong faith in themselves, in dance, and in the choreogra phers with whom they worked. They all shared a firm conviction that dancers should respect and accommodate the choreographer's vision. In addition they believed that dancers, in the rehearsal process, have a mutually agreed upon goal of making a dance.

Although they shared many similar views, each was also a unique and interesting individual. Michelle spoke openly about her preference for being told exactly what to do in the rehearsal situation, "I like them [choreographers] to say this is the step you do, and do it on this count, and this is exactly how it's done." Suzanne explained the stable force of dance in her life, admitting, "I'm always after a new horizon, and dance is the one thing that has been consistent." Kim shared her concern about working with a new choreographer: " After a few days you find out whether a choreographer is going to waste your time." Each participant spoke and wrote openly and honestly; all fully engaged themselves in the inquiry.

The Dancers' Stories

As I explored the stories of the 3 dancers in relationship to one another and brought the stories together conversationally, three significant themes emerged: the relationship of dancer and choreographer, the relationships shared between dancers, and the experience of new beginnings. Each of these themes is important to the shaping of the larger picture constructed by these stories.

Dancer-Choreographer Relationship

For the most part, these dancers viewed the relationship between choreographer and dancer to be somewhat one-sided, with the dancers' responsibilities including following directions, satisfying the choreographer, and working for the general benefit of the group and the dance. Michelle and Kim articulated the importance of working with a choreographer who is firm, clear and exact in instructions. Michelle, spoke about a previous experience, "He [the choreographer] didn't know what he wanted. I didn't like that way Qf working." She felt choreographers should be prepared and organized: "We did nothing, nothing in those rehearsals." Kim echoed Michelle's viewpoint:

> I don't want to waste my time because it's precious, and I don't think other people should have to waste their time either. There are some choreographers that just "slough" around, and they make you make up everything, and then they take credit for it.

Kim and Michelle described themselves as organized, logical, and exacting people; they expect the same from choreographers with whom they work. Kim concluded, "I'm an organized person, and I like rehearsals to run smoothly and organized."

Michelle pointed out that the relationship between the dancer and the choreographer should be respectful: " A good relationship would be that even if you hated every single move, you'd give him [the choreographer] the benefit of the doubt." Michelle also asked for honesty in this respectful relationship: "If there's something the choreographer doesn't like, I want him to tell me."

Kim felt there was a hierarchical relationship between the choreographer and the dancers, believing that a choreographer "directs and puts people in places while they're doing certain movement." She continued, "I don't know if the choreographer's job is just to make a dance, because I think the dancers make the dance, too." Kim believed the relationship should be based on honesty, too, but concluded, "I think the dancer is second in the hierarchy after the choreographer.'

Both Kim and Michelle believed that the relationship dancers share with the choreographer affects how they will perform and look on stage. Their views tended toward the pragmatic. Michelle was interested in satisfying the choreographer: "There's still that sense of not knowing if you're doing what he wants. After you show it to him, you feel like he might hate it. ... I just don't want to look stupid." Kim spoke openly about the relationship this way: "It's awkward finding out whether the choreographer is going to favor someone and use them over and over again. ... That's sort of a frightening thing, you know? ... Are we going to look good?"

Suzanne made no distinctions between her relationship with the choreographer and the other dancers, believing most, if not all, of the responsibility is carried by the group as a whole working unit, people dancing together of their own free will. Suzanne said, "The whole thing, we're all in this together, because we want to be.'

Relationships Dancers Share

Each of these participants held strong and unique beliefs about the relationships dancers share in the rehearsal studio. For Suzanne, the relationships in rehearsal are ways of being and knowing, a paradigm for connected living. Kim viewed the relationships with other dancers as competitive, often awkward, a problem-solving venture to be worked out efficiently. For Michelle, these relationships allowed her to emulate the more advanced dancers; these relationships were also a way of gathering more information about the movement. Suzanne talked about the connectedness she felt in the rehearsal situation:

> I'm tremendously affected by relationships among dancers-it completely affects how I dance. In the circles I've worked in there's always been a conscious effort to make people feel like people. I would call it a communal feeling-we're all in this together, and we all enjoy it together. I see it as a common labor.

Suzanne's interest in the social aspect and the camaraderie were not echoed in the words of Michelle, whose interest in other dancers seemed to be linked to the notion of challenge and gaining greater movement skills. Michelle stated, "I watch Kim to see if there's something she likes and the way she does the movement." Revealing her interest in other dancers Michelle said, "I've never worked with such professionals. It's so challenging to me." Michelle was inspired by others in the studio: "I look at them for the nice qualities they have, then I try."

Kim's view of her relationships with other dancers differed from both Suzanne and Michelle in that she felt a competitiveness and awkwardness at the root of the situation. Kim spoke about working with the other dancers:

> I haven't ever worked with Michelle or Suzanne and so that makes it real awkward and uncomfortable. There's competitiveness, too, in the sense of who is the choreographer going to use. It is awkward because you don't know how you're gonna look with the person or how you're gonna work with the person and share responsibility.

Speaking of the struggle for control that Kim often felt from other dancers in rehearsal, Kim's beliefs about her relationships with other dancers seemed to be based on the effect those dancers will have on her own performance. Realizing that other dancers are highly skilled was often scary for her: "Is another person going to make one person look really bad because they're better than the others?" Ultimately, Kim asked whether people liked her. Each participant's view may be linked to such a universal question, and their relationships in rehearsal may be correlative to searching for such affirmation.

New Beginnings

Being in a strange and unknown environment, like early rehearsals for a new work, can be frightening. Through Kim's voice, one hears how awkward new situations can be. Curiosity about new relationships with other dancers, she has revealed, provokes a response that is often tense and uncomfortable. In this same situation, Suzanne finds joy and excitement in a new environment that can facilitate possibilities for connecting with the new world around her. Suzanne explained, "I 'm fond of throwing myself into a strange and new environment." Her interest in meeting people and listening, as well as talking, was evident when she said, "I can totally forget about myself. I am real interested in other people." For Suzanne the rehearsal process is as much about social interaction as it is about dance; "I do the best I can [referring to dance] and then I'm interested in what other people are doing." Her convictions about connectedness, meaning, and the larger meditative questions in life are summarized when she spoke about other dancers with whom she has worked:

> I just feel like a lot of the attitude is it's a job-to goin, go through the ropes-I heard this in the last concert I was in. I couldn't believe people were complaining, "Oh, God! It's taking so long "Well, why do you do it? I'm in control here. The day I want to stop doing this, I will, but I will never sit around and complain about it.

What is interesting about Kim and Suzanne's differing viewpoints is that each woman was greatly affected by her response to new situations. Suzanne's interest in new situations enabled her to remain in control and think meditatively. Kim resolved her apprehensions by working diligently and attempting to figure out those with whom she shares a relationship in rehearsal. By holding her own, competitively, in the rehearsal situation, Kim more clearly defines herself to others and can then feel less tense and more comfortable.

Listening to these stories, one sees how each participant views the rehearsal process uniquely and how each perceives herself in relation to the dance and the other dancers. Michelle finds solace in organization, logic, and order. **Kim** re ceives great affirmation from presenting herself to others. Suzanne feels most complete and whole when connecting with others in the creative process.

Significant Issues

From the dialogue exchanged between the three dancers, the significance of relationships in the rehearsal studio emerges. Both Michelle and **Kim** have a firm belief that there is a pronounced hierarchy within the rehearsal situation, with dancers as secondary. They view the choreographer as one who gives exact, precise directions; the choreographer always knows exactly what he or she wants. As a choreographer, I feel this description might be somewhat limiting, depicting a situation that would not be conducive to creating out of an atmosphere of connectedness or group interaction.

Kim indicated that she was confused about the relationship when she said, "I don't know if the choreographer's job is just to make a dance, because I think the dancers make the dance, too." Yet in the hierarchical relationship she describes, it would be difficult to credit dancers with any empowerment other than working well, that is, doing what they are told.

Kim and Michelle also feel that the choreographer can greatly affect how they look and perform. The choreographer is seen as possessing the key to their dancing, either keeping their dancing locked away, or unlocking their abilities for all to see. This view advocates a dancer whose primary functions are to follow directions, question minimally, and appease the choreographer.

Finding one's own movement in the rehearsal situation is both creative and personal. This finding and creating engages the dancer in the process of dance making and meaning making. This method of choreography requires that dancers bear a significant amount of responsibility-foremost, a responsibility for their own dancing (Risner, 1992). Michelle and Kim often find this manner of rehearsing unpleasant. Some dancers become frustrated when asked to accept this kind of responsibility. Kim said, "They [choreographers] make you make up everything." Michelle stated, "I like to be shown exactly what to do." The view of responsibility as possibility is not shared by these dancers. They see the roles of dancers as passive and receptive. This is a significant issue that choreographers should consider in their questioning of the nature of relationships between choreographer and dancer. Suzanne's vision is much more active and participatory in that she sees the rehearsal situation as communal. Her relationship with the choreographer is not dissimilar to that of herself and other dancers.

The dialogue regarding relationships between the dancers allows many social aspects to emerge. All of the dancers, in some way, commented how these relationships determine how each dancer functions in the rehearsal. Michelle sees these relationships as possibilities for more information to better her own performance. She sees the potential to gain greater insight about the movement and its execution. Kim finds the social aspect of these relationships to be frightening, because it might affect her performance in a negative fashion. The social part of rehearsal is also awkward for her due to the struggle for control she often feels. Suzanne relishes the social aspect of these relationships to the point that a connectedness to the group is necessary for her to maintain interest in dancing.

Relationships between dancers in the rehearsal process may be a means of self-definition. Michelle may only feel whole and complete if she can emulate the most advanced dancer in the rehearsal. Suzanne may feel most complete when she is in touch with the entire cast. Kim displaces feelings of awkwardness when she has the opportunity to prove herself to the group. This research boldly illustrates the social context of the rehearsal process. Choreographers should be aware that dancers are, at all times, individuals with feelings, agendas, and visions.

In discussing these relationships, it is necessary to return to a question I asked earlier: How may choreographers wish to rehearse? One can see from the dialogue that although the dance product, the performance, is inevitable, the process of making a dance is a potentially rich source of engaged, satisfying, human experience. Dancers, in many instances, focus primarily on the dance product and how they look, rather than on their experience of making a dance and how they feel. Choreographers may wish to encourage dancers not only to think about their impending performance, but also to reflect upon the experience of creating the dance. In a metaphor of rehearsal as child's play, one can see that playing does not require a finished product. In much the same way, rehearsal, as distinguished from performance, is a complete activity in and of itself. Engaging dancers more fully in the rehearsal process, choreographers may find performances of their dancers more complete and satisfying.

From the dialogue, one can see that the participants have differing responses to new situations. These responses directly affect the activity in rehearsal and help to more clearly articulate a definition of self.

Finding new rehearsal situations awkward and frightening, Kim often feels apprehensive about other dancers and the relationships she will enter into during the rehearsal period.

Kim resolves the conflict by clearly articulating through the rehearsal process who she is as a dancer. After presenting herself thoroughly as a dancer who is technically precise, extremely quick, and a diligent worker, her identity is more clearly distinct. She then feels more comfortable and less tense. During this time, Kim learns all she can about the other dancers and their dance capabilities, which leads to some of her apprehensions. When Kim is satisfied that she is as worthy as all of the other dancers, she can more fully enjoy the rehe;:,rsal process.

For Suzanne, new beginnings and situations are viewed as possibilities for sharing and connecting with other individuals. Her view is quite different from Kim's and is based solely on her faith in relationships with others and on herself as a social being,' 'I'm interested in what other people are doing." Her convictions about social interaction with other dancers are strong. Suzanne defines herself by connecting with others.

The first few rehearsals of a new dance may produce very little actual choreography, but faithfully, choreographers and dancers return to the dance studio at the agreed upon time to once again create together. There is a faith in the rehearsal process that a dance will be completed and performed. This group faith in the rehearsal process is often accompanied by a sense of timelessness, as if rehearsals will continue as long as necessary. This sense of timelessness, facilitated by a faith in the rehearsal situation, allows dancers to experience deep personal involvement, risk taking, playful encounters, and profound personal understanding. Dance rehearsals offer relationships with people, movement, and ideas that are based on faith and trust.

Conclusions

This research renders no specific instructions for rehearsing a dance. Quali tative research such as this reveals important issues about dance making and the dancers with whom choreography is created. Through the dialogue exchanged between the participants, this study reveals a way of looking at the nature of the individual dancer and choreographer and his or her desire to relate to the other in the rehearsal process.

In the final analysis, it is clear that the social context of the rehearsal process is a significant theme. The emergence of this issue is surprising and illustrates the importance of continued questioning by choreographers. The danc ers' stories reveal a great desire to relate to one another in the rehearsal situation. It has been shown that the relationships the dancers share help to define each as an individual. Therefore, it would seem appropriate for choreographers to acknowledge and nurture the social context within the rehearsal and, at the same time, recognize the complexity of the issue.

A sensitivity to the social aspects of the dance rehearsal may allow choreog raphers to understand that rehearsing is not only dancing, but also a means for dancers, as people, to satisfy needs, exchange ideas, and share feelings. The dancers' stories illustrate the diverse ways dancers respond to and participate in the rehearsal studio.

Choreographers may find it helpful to ask themselves what kind of relation ships they share with dancers. Do these relationships allow and encourage an open exchange? This knowledge continues rather than answers the question, How might one rehearse? The answer is multilayered. Heightened awareness is central to understanding the social complexity of the dance rehearsal studio. Contempla tion of these important issues will continue to be addressed in my rehearsal situation.

This study has also revealed that some dancers focus entirely on the dance product, or performance. Their energies are directed toward how they look and what can be done to look better. Their experience of making a dance and reflecting on the process has not been cultivated in their careers. For many choreographers, myself included, within an open, playful, expansive environment, rehearsal can be a complete activity in and of itself. Choreographers may guide dancers to a more complete understanding of the rehearsal process by engaging the dancers in the doing, feeling, thinking, and making of a dance. In so doing, choreographers might well expect to see their completed works performed in a more physically powerful, emotionally rich, and intellectually informed way.

It has also been seen that each of the participants feels a sense of faith or trust in the rehearsal process. Choreographers and dancers faithfully return to the studio, week after week, trusting that at some point in the future they will all possess a dance. There is faith that something eventually will come to fruition. The involvement with the process without orientation toward the product seems to abstract time. This timelessness of the rehearsal period may come about because of trust. Faith and trust in the rehearsal studio allow strong personal commitment, risk taking, affirmation, and personal meaning making.

My hope is that each participant in this study has been clearly and fairly heard. Having grown through this experience of investigating the rehearsal studio, I will continue this research and ask questions about relationships shared in the dance rehearsal process. By exploring the dancers' experience of the choreo graphic process, choreographers validate, acknowledge, and nurture dancers' primary function in the act of choreography.

References

Banes, A. (1980). *Terpsichore in sneakers.* Middletown, CT: Wesleyan University Press. Cohen, S. (1965). *The modern dance: Seven statements of belief.* Middletown, CT: Wesleyan University Press.

Donmoyer, R. (1985, April). *Distinguishing between scientific and humanities-based approaches to qualitative research: A matter of purpose.* Paper presented an annual meeting of the American Education Research Association, Chicago, IL.

Foster, S. (1986). *Reading dancing.* Los Angeles: University of California Press.

Kreemer, C. (1987). *Further steps.* New York: Harper & Row.

Risner, D. (1992). Exploring dance rehearsal-the neglected issues revealed. *Journal of Physical Education, Recreation and Dance,* **63(6),** 61-65.

Stodelle, E. (1978). *The dance technique of Doris Humphrey.* Princeton, NJ: Princeton.

Tompkins, C. (1965). *The bride and the bachelors.* New York: The Viking Press.

Making Dance, Making Sense: Epistemology & Choreography

DOUG RISNER

ABSTRACT *This interpretive inquiry explores the construction of knowledge by dancers in the rehearsal process. Although seemingly primary to the act of choreography, the dancers' experiences of the choreographic process have not been explored fully. Though often neglected, the dancers' experience of rehearsal warrants further investigation for dance educators. Through the dancers' narratives, an account of the nature of knowing emerges from which an epistemology, or theory of knowledge, is theorized.*

Following a review of the relevant literature in dance education and epistemology, an interpretive methodology is used as a framework for collecting and interpreting the narrative accounts of ten university dancers with whom the researcher recently created a new piece of choreography. Four significant epistemological clusters are discussed, most notably knowing as interpersonal construction, knowing as re-membering the body, and the contextual situatedness of knowing from a particular body, place, and time. The study reveals important epistemological issues for further dance research agendas.

Introduction

Dancers, choreographers, dance educationists, and researchers today find themselves frequently crossing important interdisciplinary boundaries, educational borders, and critical social frontiers. Projects of critical pedagogy, feminist theory, cultural studies, and interpretive/narrative research are appearing in university dance departments throughout the world. Making dances, in all their various forms, methods, and structures, is a central part of what dancers and choreographers do on a daily basis; however, how dancers make sense, create meaning, learn, and know these dances often goes without interrogation. This work seeks to elaborate upon current expansive and crossover dance education research, and to question how this research can enliven our students, our choreographies, and our lives in general. It should be clear that the ways in which we rehearse, choreograph, teach, and write signify the ways in which we encounter the world, and more importantly, shape the totality of the world in which we live. More specifically this research asks, 'what is it we can learn about the values, or what we think is important in our choreography, teaching, or research?' Or put more simply, as choreographer John Gamble asserts, 'Our dances clearly show for us what we have been paying attention to.' This project, then, seeks to ask among other things, 'what haven't we paid attention to?'

The choreographic processes of many twentieth-century dance pioneers (Cohen, 1965; Foster, 1986, Stodelle, 1978) and innovators (Banes, 1980; Jones, 1989; Kreemer, 1987; Tompkins, 1965; Van Dyke, 1996) have been documented. Although seemingly primary to the act of choreography, the dancers' experiences of the choreographic process have not been explored fully. Though often neglected, the dancers' experience of rehearsal and performance warrants investigation (Risner, 1992). The social nature of the rehearsal process in dance allows choreographers to understand that rehearsing is not merely dancing, but also an important means for dancers, as people, to make meaning, to satisfy needs, exchange ideas, and to share frustrations (Risner, 1995). In other words, to make sense out of the world these dancers encounter. For professional choreographers these issues may be secondary, or relatively insignificant in comparison to the high value placed on the dance product. Exploring the world in which our dance students reside is critical for the dance educator; investigating how these students make meaning or construct knowledge of that world is precisely the aim and the work at hand for this paper.

This interpretive inquiry explores the construction of knowledge by dancers in the rehearsal process and performance of a dance I recently choreographed. Through their words and particular stories heard here, an account of the nature of knowing emerges from which an epistemology may be theorized. Epistemology, from the Greek *episteme*, 'knowledge,' and *logos*, 'explanation,' is the study of the nature of knowledge. Within this study, philosophers analyse, often controversially, the defining features, conditions, and limitations of knowledge. Since Plato's *Meno* and *Theaetetus* (c.400 B.C.), epistemologists have attempted to articulate the essential, defining components of what it is to know.

For the purposes of this research, a brief outline of the kinds of knowledge discussed in the field of epistemology will be helpful. Philosophers have identified various ways of knowing: for example, propositional knowledge (knowing *that* something is so) is rooted in theory or a set of organising ideas. Non-propositional knowledge of something (e.g. knowledge by acquaintance or direct relationship) is grounded in the propinquity of sensation, feeling and intuition. Knowing generated by knowledge of *how* to do something hinges upon practical application or skill (Audi, p. 234). There are numerous other species of knowledge of interest to dance educationists, as well as particular models of knowing. Louis Arnaud Reid (1969) developed an extensive body of work conceptualized around a rubric of knowledge in the arts, and borrowing from Bertrand Russell, Reid developed the notion of 'acquaintance knowledge' as enriched sensate experience. Howard Gardner's (1983) theory of multiple intelligences also translates well to this epistemological project. Feminist standpoint epistemology informs this work, for instance, Belenky, et. al. (1986) note important differences between separate and connected ways of knowing. Connected knowledge arises from intimacy, equality, and relationship. Separate knowledge, on the other hand, commences from separation, objectivity, and distance. This narrative project also owes much to epistemologist Lather's (1986) work, which asserts that 'we use our research to help participants understand and change their situations', and at the same time contemplate the potential for praxis (understanding and change) for ourselves and research participants. It is not within the scope or means of this paper to discuss the whole of epistemological study, which might very well include knowledge generated in live performance. Nor is it possible to give an exhaustive interrogation of knowledge from a range of aesthetic points of view (e.g. knowing a dance by means of appreciation). Volumes could be, and have been written on aesthetics (see Best, 1974; McFee, 1994) and epistemology (See Alcoff & Potter, 1993; Harding, 1993).

The work at hand explores the nature of knowing for dancers as this knowledge emerges in the rehearsal process. From the unique story of each dancer, brought together conversationally with the others, common themes of experience can be heard. These ways of knowing, or epistemologies, as evidenced by the dancers' stories, are often rooted in the experience of the whole body and frequently conjoin *knowing that* and *knowing how*. Put more simply, their stories of knowing commence from an epistemic stance, or place of knowing that often combines theory and practice and frequently transcends traditional epistemology altogether.

In addition, the uniqueness of each account illustrates the significance of knowing from a particular body, place, time, and context. This paper offers a view of knowing which attempts to more fully justify an epistemology from the margin, the dancer's place of knowing. One that does not necessarily move from this historically-distanced place of integrated body to one more centralized and wholly cerebral. To do so would only replicate the traditional epistemic stance, one predicated on a universal, general account of the nature of knowledge, denying the knower and the situatedness of the knower in a social context.

Methodology

Qualitative interpretive research takes as one of its central tenets that research should render a larger understanding of what it is to be human in the world.[1] Dance educationists Stinson & Anijar (1993) assert the aim of interpretive research is to elicit meaning and understanding rather than proving or disproving facts. My concern in this project is 'personal meaning making' and the ways in which dancers come to know in the rehearsal situation. Knowledge, in qualitative research, is socially constructed and contains multiple truths and realities, as Reid (1986) questions:

> Are there not other kinds of knowledges, perhaps many other kinds, in which knowledge is not so cut-off, so sterilized, from other aspects of personal life, the life in which feeling plays an important part, and where knowing is the functioning of a person responding as a whole human being? (p. 2)

Subjectivity and 'personal meaning making' are worthwhile and valuable when researching human experience, and more specifically dancers engaged in the choreographic process.

Given these assumptions, I sought a methodology that would retain the richness of each experience contained in the dancers' stories. Those interviewed are not objects of research, but rather, subjects of research. The dancers' stories form the bulk of the data in this narrative project whereby each person is a knower who authors stories of his or her own experience; narrative authority takes a very different epistemological stance (Olson, 1995). Acknowledging that the researcher can never be truly objective, the purpose of qualitative research in Donmoyer's (1985) words, 'is not to subsume particular events under general categories but to alter the general categories and constructs to better accommodate the novelty of the particulars' (p. 64). Within this methodology larger themes of human experience present themselves and other realities can be embraced.

Personal meaning reveals itself in a diversified manner and therefore dictates that the researcher choose a methodology that allows for an emergence of dialogue, dialogue that is open to shifts and turns along the winding path of the subject's story. Stinson, Blumenfeld-Jones and Van Dyke (1988) assert that, 'personal meaning is not always immediately available to consciousness, ready to be expressed briefly and quickly' (p. 4). When open to a multitude of possibilities, the unexpected or surprise narrative account reinforces the significance of interpretive research for scholars interested in fleshing out more of the whole story.

Of course, what we want to know informs how we conduct our research. The questions we ask shape the words and stories we record, analyse, and interpret. Inextricably linked to the interpretive methodology employed, the questions pursued by the narrative researcher are therefore broad and heuristic in order to allow and facilitate individual authorship. It is important to note that in formulating a particular research question, researchers in many ways also 'decide' the answer; given the nature of humanities-based research rooted in questions of meaning, the liabilities appear minimal. Interpretive inquiry, then, often illuminates a slice of the proverbial pie previously unseen or unexpected. Narrative research reveals the plurality of our human experience as evidenced by the singularity of our individual existence.

Additionally, how one intends to use research findings also determines one's research methodology and thereby exposes its inherent value system. Interpretive inquiry makes no claim to a value-free, unbiased system, but rather acknowledges the multiple social constraints and inequalities operating in our culture and how those value-charged traditions can be exposed. Statistical predictability and law-like regularity while central to scientific empirical research, for the aims of this work, undermine the epistemological situatedness and contextuality of the knower's voice. Eisner (1981) reminds researchers that artistic qualitative research focuses on individual experiences, their meanings, and what others make of them. More than just unraveling particular values through story in order to 'explain away' through language and symbol, interpretive research seeks explanation and understanding in order to emancipate and maximize human potential to freely create a more just world. Dancers' voices, all too often silenced (Stinson et al., 1990; Risner, 1995; Shapiro and Shapiro, 1995), should be more clearly heard. To perform this research in a manner that was in agreement with my assumptions and research philosophy, I chose a methodology drawn from phenomenological and hermeneutic inquiry. (See Braxton, 1984; Stinson, et al., 1988; Risner, 1995.)

Rehearsal Process and Research Procedures

As time limitations warranted, I limited my research to include a semester-long rehearsal period. The rehearsal process for this dance included approximately 40 hours of rehearsal, which spanned an eleven-week period in which 75-minute rehearsals were held twice per week. All dancers regularly attended rehearsals and participated in the reflective writing and interview process. The rehearsal period culminated in a fully produced work entitled, *Download*, which was included in a series of dance concert performances at the end of the semester, as well as generating this piece of research.

The subjects of this research were ten undergraduate and graduate students at a large state university, eight women and two men; their ages ranged from 18 to 25. Geographically, the group was representative of seven states in the US and one additional country. Some were highly experienced dancers with strong technical training and extensive performance credits. Others had more limited training and stage experience. Of the group of ten student dancers, seven were pursuing degrees in dance, four at the graduate level. Three of the subjects were enrolled in other disciplines: journalism, music composition (graduate level), and interactive arts respectively. My overall impression of this group of dancers could be described as energetic, attentive, creative, diverse, and willing.

As the choreographer/researcher, I am currently a doctoral fellow in the Department of Educational Leadership and Cultural Foundations, as well as an adjunct faculty member in the Department of Dance at this university. While in residence my teaching responsibilities have included modern and jazz dance technique at all levels, dance appreciation, and social foundations of education. As a frequent guest artist and master teacher, my choreographies have been performed throughout the US.

This seven-minute repertory piece, *Download*, with a musical score by Rhys Fulber and Bill Leeb, was the culmination of a cycle of dances that were designed to be genderless[2] in character and focused on problematizing movement sequences for dancers in sets of couplings and sometimes trios. I created five movement phrases; together with the dancers, two additional phrases were created. One choreographic device I employed evolved over a series of dances I made in the mid-1990s. Choreographed movement phrases were given to dancers first, then restrictions and constraints were placed upon each partner. For example, dancers were asked to attach themselves to their partners in various ways—hand in hand, arm over shoulder, back to back, etc. Given these contradictions (or possibilities), the dancers' problem-solving skills (rightfully including their own imaginations) formed the choreographic solutions that would ultimately become sections of the dance. The movement style for this dance was sharp, angular, and percussive. I emphasized fully-committed performance with athletic abandon, all the while demanding technical precision. Another choreographic tool I used for collaborative movement invention with the dancers was rooted in the dancers' responses to a series of verbal cues. Their movements, which when completed, were organized by superimposing rhythms borrowed from other phrases in the dance. The layered effect of this device produced movement sequences that were highly individualized, gesturally communicative, and often interestingly neurotic.

Procedures for conducting this study included interviewing the dancers, reading journals I asked the dancers to keep, writing my own personal reflection on the rehearsal process, and viewing rehearsal videotapes. Each participant dancer was interviewed twice during the eleven-week rehearsal period. The first interview occurred during the third week of rehearsal and lasted between 30 and 45 minutes. The second series of interviews occurred during the tenth week of rehearsal. Each interview focused on questions that would allow the participants to speak freely about dancing, rehearsing, learning and knowing.

Posed in a semi-structured, yet open-ended fashion, broad interview questions were used as a springboard to allow the dancers to speak candidly about themselves, the rehearsal process, and how each came to know the dance. Questions that would result in specific 'yes' or 'no' answers were kept to a minimum and highly specific questions, other than biographical information, were avoided. This allowed for a discussion prompted more by the dancers' epistemological interests rather than by a large sampling-type survey instrument which might be used for generalization over a large population. For my purposes, I posed broad questions to allow the dancers' voices to navigate their own personal histories and meaningful experiences of dance rehearsal. The dancers were asked questions such as:

- Could you talk about your experience of doing this dance?
- Can you speak about learning this choreography?
- How do you know the dance?
- How do you know that you know the dance? and
- What specifically does it mean to know a dance?

The second series of interviews were used to revisit significant issues heard earlier, either in their journals or in the first interview. Interviewing procedures were always predicated on nourishing honest dialogue that could travel in any direction, elicited more by what the dancers felt was important epistemologically, rather than directed toward a specific answer by the researcher. As choreographers, teachers, and researchers, and more to the point, as people we all find significant meaning in unique and sometimes different ways; therefore, the interviews often include diverse issues and concerns within the rubric of knowing and claims to knowledge.

The first tape-recorded interview was summarized following the session from the researcher's notes; the second was transcribed, resulting in nearly a hundred pages of data. The dancers' reflective writings and interview transcriptions were returned to them for their own self-editing, deletion, and addition. The dancers' journal entries and my observations of the rehearsal process generated another fifty pages of summarized data. After reading the transcriptions a number of times and consulting my summarized notes, I edited the interview material before proceeding further with the analysis. The analysis of the data generated was based generally on procedures of interpretive inquiry (Stinson, et al., 1990). Extraneous material was eliminated and emerging themes in each account were identified.

From these reductions, the subject's stories were brought together in a dialogue fashion for further discussion. An independent researcher then checked the reductions. Commonalities were woven together thematically, while every effort to retain the richness of individual particularities and dissonances was sought. The emergent discussion revealed a wider perspective of what it is to know as a dancer in a piece of choreography. These epistemological notions are clusters of ideas which spiral around the following themes: knowing as an interpersonal construction, knowing by doing, knowing as memory, and knowing as certainty. Each of these thematic clusters overlaps one another, much like choreography with few or seamless transitions. The interrelatedness of different ways of knowing, much like 'theme and variation' movement motifs in choreographic passages, should also be emphasized. I encourage readers to view these knowledge clusters as fluid and continuous, rather than discrete, unrelated categories. Having said that, for the purposes of this paper I will discuss these clusters of ideas separately, all the while intimating the complex weave the dancers' stories tell and the sophisticated ways of knowing that emerges.

Knowing as an Interpersonal Construction

In the words of many of the dancers' stories, the significance of knowing in relationship with others is heard. Although each dancer interprets the group relationship uniquely, the profound nature of interacting with others in the rehearsal process and during the performance of the dance is instructive for interrogating the nature of knowing in the rehearsal studio. Redfern (1973) alludes to this species of knowing as 'interpersonal understanding' in the following:

> By getting outside oneself, as it were, one sees (even idiosyncrasies) by contrast and comparison—for example, when trying to reproduce someone else's movement sequences, or conversely when one observes others making similar attempts in respect to one's own. Self-knowledge and knowledge of others seem to go hand in hand, and in education are of particular importance when young people are often concerned with problems of their own identity, and interested in how others—people they actually know, and not characters in fiction or history—'tick'.(p. 112)

Jordan, a nineteen-year-old journalism major, speaks of the foundational aspect of the group as a social unit, locating herself within the group early on in the rehearsal process. She states, 'What came first before mastering any movement phrases was a realization of my place in the relationship with the fellow dancers—that was to one day become the dance.' Mark, a twenty-one year old dance major, states, 'It was like I was a piece in a jigsaw puzzle, made of nearly identically shaped pieces.' Isabelle relates her experience of working with others and constructing meaning from her relationship with the group in the following:

> At the beginning of the process I was not working off of the dancers around me. I was trying to dance the piece by myself, and I learned that if I use them, depend on them, and give the same back to them it makes everything better. During my experience of the dance I learned how to dance as a group.

Each of the dancers sees an important connection between knowing the dance and engaging in meaningful relationships with others in the group. What each account has in common is the broad picture each subject paints, a puzzle, a geography, a community constituted by metaphors that allow dancers to conceive of themselves and the knowledge they create in relation to others.

> The dance requires complete trust and dependency on others–especially knowing where people are in space .... so you don't run into them, and also, knowing that people are there, there to catch you!

These words are Derek's, a graduate student in music composition, who has performed in four dance concerts this year at the university. Ally, aged twenty-four, is a Master of Fine Arts (MFA) student in dance. She has had extensive training in jazz, tap dance, ballet, pointe work, and modern technique. Ally states, 'I feel very empowered doing the piece, experiencing everyone giving me energy and my giving energy away.' Her words speak similarly to Derek's in that each sees a mutually beneficial relationship in trusting and depending upon others in the process, a social give and take. Ally's and Derek's stories describe a way of knowing predicated on *knowing that*, a theory or set of social assumptions in this instance which undergird their experience of the choreographic process. In addition their stories speak again to Redfern's (1973) criticism of Langer's (1953) belief that in dance all actualities disappear. Redfern firmly believes, as do Ally and Derek, that in fact dancers do relate and construct knowledge 'in a very real way as they touch, hold, lift, swing one another around, synchronize their movements, vary their distance and so on' (p. 112).

Christina, a graduate student pursuing an MFA in performance and choreography, reveals that for her the interpersonal nature of knowledge made possible in working with others comes about after she as an individual learns the movement. Her words indicate an escalation of her social awareness in rehearsal leading toward performance:

> As I move along, the process becomes more and more of a social event. I start considering the others' opinions, movement choices, solutions ... there is more dialogue and communication. I find these skills good to be developed in dance. This dance made me be more social and aware of others.

For Christina, social relationships in rehearsal are linked to the formal relationships between dancers in the choreography. She states, 'I liked watching the process from learning the phrase to putting it into context and the way it created relationships between the dancers.' Her words indicate a separation; first she, as an individual learns the movement, then as the dance is structured, she becomes more aware of the social element, in order to completely know the dance. Lauren, a 23 year-old graduate of an Integrative Studies in the Arts programme, shares her views on the interpersonal development of knowledge in learning movement and sequence in the following passage:

> Isabelle and I worked with Christina—just the three of us. That was the first time I felt I actually learned all the phrases and their sequence. Then I could practice them on my own. It's working that way—one on one. That's how I learn ... that's how I know.

Lauren's words indicate the significance of a personal connection with Isabelle and Christina beyond the regularly scheduled rehearsals in allowing her to know the dance. Her words, like those of Christina and Derek, speak to the epistemological role of the engaged, observing dancer whereby knowledge is gained by watching and appreciating others within a community.

My previous research on the dancers' experience of the rehearsal process has shown that the social context, although often ignored, is an important source for further investigation; the relationships dancers share help to define each as an individual (Risner, 1995). The dancers' stories recounted here highlight the deeply profound nature of constructing knowledge in relationship with others. Interacting with other dancers in the rehearsal process and during the performance of the dance is instructive for illuminating a theory of knowledge in the choreographic process, although it should be noted that each dancer interprets the relationship to the group uniquely. It can be heard in these accounts that to know the dance is to know others in the same project of locating themselves within a community. It is a view of knowing or an epistemic stance that is situated in and dependent upon a social context. Harding's (1993) work on feminist standpoint epistemologies is particularly useful at this juncture. Her argument reaffirms the emergent knowledge claims heard in the dancers' narratives, and at the same time, deconstructs feminist empiricism she feels only replicates the objective, distanced positivist stance of which she is critical. Harding asserts, 'communities, not primarily individuals, produce knowledge'(p. 65).

Knowing by Doing

Nearly half of the ten dancers speak at length regarding the significance of physically doing the dance as a way of knowing, or in epistemological terms, *knowing how*. This notion linking knowing and doing interestingly provokes further questions about how dancers view knowledge and the frequent mind-body duality that accompanies most traditional epistemological thought which historically privileges propositional knowledges, or *knowing that*. Is it possible to know the dance without doing it? Must a dancer do the dance to know it? Or does doing the dance justify the knowledge claim, rather than constitute it? The following accounts would suggest the actual doing of the dance is primary to the construction of knowing and subsequently challenge the focus of epistemology on propositional over practical forms of knowing.

> I learned this dance very quickly and easily. I pick up phrases mentally very quickly. Once I have the phrase sequence of movement in my head, I then have a need to *do it*. Doing it, not talking about it and analysing it verbally.

Mark's words introduce the important idea of doing as a form of knowing. Isabelle speaks similarly of doing as a means of knowing. She says, 'I know the dance by throwing myself completely into it, like it is a different world. It's a different world because I have never been there before, but it is comfortable and confident.' This connection between doing and knowing is also important for Ally. She clarifies seeing and then doing the movement when she says, 'see it first, just watch, then do it, and do it in sequence over and over ... that's how I know'.

For dance educationists and choreographers this description of *knowing how* and its practical connection to technical skill may seem obvious, however the ramifications for epistemology are important. Traditional epistemic views hold that knowledge generated by skills does not adequately produce the truth necessary to validate this practical knowledge as significant. For an insightfully thorough discussion of incorporating *knowing how*, or practical knowledge, in traditional modes of knowing see Dalmiya and Alcoff (1993). What may not be so obvious for dance educators, is the significance dancers place on the physical epistemology of doing the dance, repeatedly. I return to Mark's narrative as an example. His words indicate that he understands the movement and sequence quickly, but in order *to know* the dance he has the need *to do it*. With this awareness, dance educators and choreographers might re-think and remember their own dance histories, physicalities, and values as actively performing dancers. It may well be the case that what we attend to when creating our dances is in conflict, if not neglectful, of what dancers need epistemologically to know and to perform (our) the dances.[3]

Maria and Derek both speak to the notion of doing as knowing, when each speaks about being on *automatic pilot* when performing the dance in entirety. Maria, a first year undergraduate dance major states, 'what I feel when I really know a dance is when I can do it with my eyes closed, on automatic pilot. For my body it becomes automatic — this is when I know the dance'. Derek says:

> In parts of the dance, my body takes over and almost enters a sort of hypnotic, or automatic pilot, especially when the dance gets aerobic and I feel like I can't go on anymore. That's when I stop thinking with my mind and just do it with my body.

Both of these dancers might well be speaking in similar tones with which Reid (1969) spoke when discussing 'acquaintance knowledge' as enriched, sensate experience. *Automatic pilot* status for these dancers is achieved, it would seem, only after successfully mastering knowing *that* and knowing *how*. Mark, Ally, Derek, and Maria all approach knowing and doing from an integrated mind and body connection, although each at certain times emphasizes the necessity for the body as constituted physically to 'take over.' The epistemology described, predominantly *knowing how* or practice, is one predicated on a physicalization of the knowledge, for both learner and knower. Performing a dance for the 112th performance is tremendously different from the evening it was first premiered. The dancers' narratives heard here clearly indicate the epistemological primacy of the body. We will return to this point later in this paper as the dancers' stories spiral around the primacy of the body and body memory.

Knowing as Memory

Nearly all of the dancers' narratives address issues regarding memory and remembering. Some equate memory with remembering the dance within the context of the music; others speak of remembering the structure of the dance's programme, or the equations, which give the dance its formal programme. Others describe a body memory in which the body itself is re-ordered, re-assembled given the particularity of the dance at hand. These epistemological clusters around memory reaffirm postpositivist views of multiple, situated, and contextual knowledges and at the same time reassert the body, previously denied, as the mediator of all knowledge. Memory, or the putting of things back together, speaks to what these dancers know. For Jordan and Rebecca, the musical score for the dance serves as a way of knowing, one that comes about through the atmosphere and relationship the music provides. It is from this place between reason and sensing that these dancers locate themselves, and come to know their place in the choreography. Cheryl and Ally remember the programme of the dance as a mode of knowing in which smaller equations and specific counts comprize their epistemology. A large number of the dancers reveal a memorization embedded in the body; Maria, Derek, Isabelle, Christina, and Cheryl all speak at great length about the body's ability to know and to re-member, to put back together or to re-assemble the body. For these dancers, to remember is to re-organize the body specifically for the dance at hand. It is an epistemology that combines *knowing that* and *knowing how*, a way of constructing knowledge from theory and practice, propositional and practical knowledge that re-integrates the mind and the body.

Musical Memory

Rebecca has danced since she was three years old; her training is primarily based in ballet, jazz, and tap dance. In addition she has studied clogging, Graham technique, belly dancing, and ballroom dance. At twenty-five, she is completing her first-year of an MFA programme. Her words indicate the importance of the rhythm and music together in learning and knowing the dance. Rebecca states, 'The first thing I do is understand and remember the rhythm of the movement as it is married to the music. I have to feel them together.' For Rebecca, knowing the dance is knowing the movement with the music. She continues, 'The music triggers ... when I hear it, what I'm trying to remember.' Jordan's words reveal her strong connection to the musical score as almost an ontology (or way of being) of her experience of dancing, or as she describes, 'an atmosphere my body remembers.' Her account speaks to the centrality of music in relationship to knowing in dance:

> I knew *Download* (title of the dance) the day we started running the dance with the music. A whole mood and atmosphere was created and in turn dictated how my body, my face, my expression, my everything was performed. I've always been very music sensitive. Dance to me has always been the most natural, primal, organic response to music. My body remembers because it zeros in to the atmosphere when I hear the music. When there's no atmosphere, there's no memory.

Again, it is necessary to reiterate that what these dancers sense, intuit, and feel may be what Reid clarified as 'acquaintance knowledge' or enriched experience. By virtue of the music, the propositional knowledge (knowing that), and knowing how (technical, practical knowledge), these dancers articulate knowing from a place, or epistemic stance that is constituted by feeling and intuition which transcends traditional epistemology. Or put more simply as Reid (1969) questions, 'we have a deeper, richer acquaintance in the experience ... why are we not allowed to call this 'knowledge'? (p. 214).

Programme Memory

Ally and Cheryl describe knowing as a means of understanding the dance's structure and the equations that manipulate the content of the dance. Understanding the inherent structure and process is foundational for revealing these dancers' epistemic stance. Cheryl, a twenty-two-year-old MFA student writes:

> Learning this dance was a very structured experience for me. I felt as if I was learning something that was very clear, clean and direct. I resonated most with the choreographic process. I look at the whole dance as a mathematical formula, and it was a matter of finding the solution for myself.

Ally's words illuminate the significance of knowing the programme, sequence, and order as central to her way of knowing. She states, 'I know the dance because my mind has stored the programme for my muscle's movements and I can remember the programme and sequence of steps.' Knowing the dance for Cheryl and Ally is both knowing the programme intellectually and knowing the physical solution—*knowing that* and *knowing how*, each necessitated by the other. Ally continues, 'I can recall this order at any time. I can even visualize myself doing each step with the other dancers. I am constantly thinking: order.' Interestingly, her visualization of the intellectual programme includes a situatedness in the social community of the dance, rather than in her individual intellect, which once again points to the intricate and interrelated epistemological weave.

Body Memory

A number of the dancers reveal a memorization embedded in the body. As indicated earlier, these epistemological notions are clusters of ideas that spiral around and among one another. This point is instructive in order to excavate the overarching epistemology that arises as one that is interwoven and multiple. For example Cheryl, although as revealed earlier indicates the mathematical equation as the radical point for constructing knowledge in the dance, also believes that the body and its respective parts solve, or re-member the formula that is the dance. Cheryl's words reiterate the emerging epistemological combination of theory and practice in knowledge construction. She states later in an interview, 'I know this dance through my limbs–legs, arms, head. I know the movement from my individual body parts. I've never thought about that before.' Derek's account of body memory is based on his experience of membering the parts of the body in distinct ways in respect to the particular dance he is rehearsing or performing. His candid reflection intimates the profound nature of knowing the dance by re-membering the body. Derek writes:

> In this dance, my body is membered in such a fashion that it can twist and contort spontaneously and quickly. My body feels almost 'short' or rather 'compact.' I would also warm-up differently for each piece. I feel that my body becomes a sort of shape-shifter … .I have the same body, it's just assembled differently. It's a sort of 'costume change'… in each dance I stepped into a different arrangement of body parts.

Maria intimates knowing from a body memory and dancing in a state of *automatic pilot* recounted earlier when she says, 'In every dance I do, I feel certain body memory which I felt in this dance. This automatic pilot—when I can do a dance with my eyes closed and without thinking.' For Maria, these notions of knowing as doing, and knowing as body memory are intertwined, spiralling around one another. Her reflections reveal a deeply profound connection to the body and to the pure physicality of dancing a dance repeatedly. Maria continues, 'I feel when I really know a dance ... my body becomes automatic ... .doing a dance over and over again until my muscles actually seem to be thinking 'squeeze on count 3,' 'lengthen on count 8.' Isabelle, having shared her views on knowing as a social construction, and also knowing by doing, or in her words, 'completely throwing yourself into the dance,' states later in her reflective writing, 'In this dance, I know the dance by sending energy out from all the parts of my body.' Her epistemic stance also spirals between these central notions of how one knows a dance. Christina's words speak to her keen awareness of her body, as its parts constitute it. She says, 'I am constantly aware of what each part of my body is doing. It's like having body-members in complete control.'

Clustered notions of memory and remembering for these dancers are significant to the respective ways of knowing that emerge from their narratives. It is instructive for choreographers and dance educators to understand the multiple ways and the situated contextuality in which re-membering can be perceived, and its utility in the rehearsal process seems noteworthy. Shapiro's (1999) argument for the reassertion of the body in critical pedagogy echoes the dancers' claims to knowledge: 'My attempt is to illuminate the body as that which mediates and holds in memory the experiences of our lives, and in so doing, create critical discourse for the body.' (p. 31) It can be heard in these narrative accounts that to interrogate an epistemology of the choreographic process is to also understand the composite design of knowledge construction, a spiralling process of the social, the self, body memory, and the relationships formed.

Knowing as Certainty

In the words of some of the dancers we hear that knowing to some degree is associated with a confidence derived from being sure of themselves in rehearsal. To be unsure, it seems from their stories, is to not know. Certainty becomes inextricably linked with knowing for these dancers. Our educational landscape and dominant cultural codes have historically valued certainty over ambiguity, reason over intuition, and mind over body. The complexity of the nature of knowledge in the rehearsal process reveals more of its sophisticated texture, valuing mind-body integration on the one hand, and absolute certainty on the other. It may in fact be that dancers, given the ambiguity and multiple possibilities of any given dance performance, necessarily need to possess an absolute certainty of the choreography in the rehearsal context. It should be noted that only three of the ten dancers spoke about this issue; it seemed, however, to be of great significance to them. I have included it in this discussion, not only because of the passionate and persuasive ways in which their narratives spoke, but also because of the implications for deconstructing traditional epistemology, which privileges certainty, reason, and intellect.

Cheryl states, ' I was never unsure of the movement or the movement quality. I always knew where and how I was supposed to be.' Maria relates her understanding of knowing as certainty and confidence in the following:' I admired the piece and felt very, very confident while performing—it was one of those pieces that I was so sure of, you know. I actually wasn't very nervous before performing.' Christina's words indicate, in much the same way as the others, the significance of being sure as a measure of what it is to know. She states, 'Ready and sure about my knowledge of the dance I could perform with security, energy and no sense of hesitation.' Each of these dancers implies the importance of feeling secure, ready, and certain as crucial to knowing the dance and central to its performance.

As mentioned earlier in the *knowing as doing* section of this paper, the sophisticated nature of an epistemology of the choreographic process often provokes further questions for theorising in dance education. Is certainty the goal of knowledge construction in dance rehearsal? Does confidence merely justify the knowledge claim? Or is it perhaps, that to know is to be certain? Clearly for some of these subjects, to be uncertain is to not know; certainty becomes profoundly enmeshed with knowledge. Similarly in the first section, the social context of the rehearsal studio is a means to locate one's self and make meaning. The dancers' desire for certainty may also be a way to confront paradigmatic opposites of mind and body, self and society, in this case certainty and ambiguity.

Conclusions: making sense

This modest, yet worthwhile project owes much to the pioneering efforts and noteworthy contribution of many dance scholars, most notably to Susan Stinson, Louis Arnaud Reid, Jill Green, David Best, and H. Betty Redfern, whose work has both inspired and transformed dance research methodologies and contemporary dance educational thought. It is from their legacy that the unique stories of each dancer emerge and common themes of experience can be heard. As dance educators and choreographers continue their creative and scholarly work into the twenty-first century, dancers' experience of the choreographic rehearsal process remains an area for further important research and theorising. The conspicuous absence of literature on the dancers' experience may well be a barometer of the hegemonic and dominant cultural codes that continue to silence dancers. These treat them more like mindless workers or robotic machines, incapable of making any significant contribution, rather than recognising their worth as whole human beings who create meaning, knowledge and understanding in (our) the dances and in the future, their own dances. This project seeks not only to give voice and authority to these individuals that are primary to our choreographies, but also to move to an understanding that at all times, dancers are singular authors and subjects of their own life histories and experiences that construct a plurality of meanings. Dancers don't just do dances; they live lives.

Through the subjects' words and particular narratives heard here, an account of the nature of knowing emerges from which an epistemology is revealed. It is an epistemology that conjoins *knowing that* and *knowing how* in the contextual situatedness of knowing from a particular body, place, and time. By bringing the dancers' stories into conversation with one another, a wider perspective of what it is to know as a dancer in a piece of choreography is revealed as a series of clusters which spiral in and around four significant themes. This intricate epistemology laces together important themes for further discussion and exploration about our rehearsals and choreographies.

Knowing in relation to others through social practice and interpersonal construction of knowledge illuminates the multiple and complex ways in which dancers come to know a piece of choreography, most notably by knowing *others* in community. The social aspect of rehearsal intimated here allows for a deeply meaningful interrogation of self and group. The significance of physically doing the dance as a way of knowing, speaks to dancers' incredible appetite for movement and *moving* as a valid epistemic stance, and serves as a reminder that dancers want to dance, sometimes even more profoundly than they want to be a part of the choreographer's creative process. For many dancers, not doing the dance, and more to the point, not repeatedly doing the dance, is not knowing. This reassertion of the body as a rich source of knowledge construction is a strong critique of the traditional epistemic stance which de-values practical knowing. In addition, the narratives heard here clearly reassemble the western duality of mind and body as a unified site for knowledge construction, and echo critical pedagogues who contend that all knowledge is body-mediated.

It has also been seen that dancers often view confidence and certainty as linked to knowing a particular dance. The question of certainty regarding epistemology as discussed earlier is much too vast a subject to argue in this brief interpretive inquiry; however, it would be highly instructive to hear clearly the dancers' assertions that to be confident and sure in rehearsal is to truly know the dance. The dancers' need for certainty in rehearsal may be connected to the ambiguity of performance, or better put, this ambiguity may be balanced by certainty, just as the narratives indicate a balance of mind and body, and of self and society. The epistemological clusters around memory reaffirm postpositivist notions of contextually-situated knowledges. For many of the dancers, knowing embedded in various and diverse forms of memory and re-membering, whether that memory be musical, programmatic, or bodily, informs the rehearsal, choreographic, and performance process in a fuller way. From these emergent themes, dance educationists and choreographers are encouraged to understand the complex weave of knowledge construction for dancers in the rehearsal studio as a spiralling process of self, society, body, memory, and the profoundly meaningful relationships intertwined. It is clear that any assumption that takes as its primary tenet that dancers learn and know a piece of choreography in the same, uniform way is clearly mistaken. Given these diverse ways of meaning-making and knowing, choreographers might reconsider the ways in which they create and rehearse their dances, and more to the point, dance educationists might benefit from interrogating how dancers learn and how dancers come to know. As with all interpretive research, more questions frequently arise. Here are a few for consideration:

- What assumptions guide the choreographer's rehearsal process?
- What values are embedded within these processes?
- Where do these assumptions and values come from?

- Might it be that choreographers rehearse in ways similar to their own training and learning styles?
- If so, what benefits and limitations are continually being reproduced in their rehearsals and choreographies?

Finally, given the findings of this research, dance educators might pursue questions regarding their own perceptions about the dancers that breathe life into their dances:

- Do I rehearse in ways which acknowledge, affirm, and celebrate different ways of knowing?
- What personal meaning making is nurtured in my rehearsals?
- And lastly, in returning to John Gamble's assertion in the introduction to this paper: What haven't I paid attention to?

It has been my great desire in this project to have the subject's voices clearly heard in order for dance educationists, researchers, choreographers, and dancers to understand more completely, and to reflect upon, the epistemological implications of the choreographic process. Narrative research through particular stories, often reveals issues previously hidden and in doing so, frequently more important questions, rather than generalizable answers, arise. This work is offered in such a spirit that through the unique epistemological voices heard in the choreographic process, we move beyond singular, universal explanation toward research that allows a more plural understanding of ourselves, and our student dancers as unique individuals with emerging commonalities.

NOTES

[1] Dance researchers whose work is embedded in methods and procedures of qualitative interpretive inquiry, such as in this study, owe much to the significant contribution of important figures in the field. In addition to those scholars referred to in the text of this paper, it is also important to note that this postpositivist research is rooted in much of the pioneering work of Glaser and Strauss (1967) 'The discovery of grounded theory'; Green and Stinson (1999) 'Postpositivist research in dance'; Kvale (1983) 'The qualitative research interview'; Moustakas (1990) 'Heuristic research design'; Reason (1994) 'Human inquiry in action'.

[2] I use the term 'genderless' to communicate my concern in this cycle of dances for movement assignment that would be potentially gender indiscriminate. Which is merely to say, that all movement would be performed to its fullest extent by all members of the company regardless of an individual's predisposition to one particular sex or another. My colleagues and reviewers have reminded me, of course, that this would inevitably be impossible—given the intricate nature in which gender is socially constructed and culturally carved. While it is certainly appropriate to acknowledge the complexity of gender enculturation, I am equally convinced that trivialising such attempts is unwarranted.

[3] I have spent a great deal of time agonizing over the ownership of the dances I now create: Who do these dances belong to anyway? If, as this research supposes, dancers' voices and contributions are significant and worthwhile, then how does one refer to these collaborations? For the sake of ethics, certainly not space, then it seems appropriate to refer to them as '(our) the dances' for the duration of the article.

REFERENCES

ALCOFF, L., & POTTER, E. (1993) When feminisms intersect epistemology, in: L. ALCOFF & E. POTTER (Eds) *Feminist Epistemologies* (New York, Routledge).
AUDI, R. (Ed.) (1995) *The Cambridge Dictionary of Philosophy* (Cambridge, Cambridge University Press).
BANES, S. (1980) *Terpischore in Sneakers* (Middletown, CT, Wesleyan University Press).
BELENKY, M., CLINCH, B., GOLDBERG, N. & TARULE, J. (1986) *Women's Ways of Knowing: the development of self, voice, and mind* (New York, Basic Books).
BEST, D. (1974) *Expression in Movement and the Arts* (London, Lepus Books).
BRAXTON, J. (1984) *Movement experience in modern dance: a phenomenological inquiry*. Unpublished doctoral dissertation, University of North Carolina at Greensboro.
COHEN, S. (1965) *The Modern Dance: seven statements of belief* (Middletown, CT, Wesleyan University Press).
DALMIYA, V. & ALCOFF, L. (1993) Are 'old wives tales' justified? in: L. ALCOFF & E. POTTER (Eds) *Feminist Epistemologies* (New York, Routledge).
DONMOYER, R. (1985) 'Distinguishing between scientific and humanities-based approaches to qualitative research,' Paper presentation at American Education Research Association annual meeting, Chicago, IL.
EISNER, E. (1981). On the differences between scientific and artistic approaches to qualitative research, *Educational Researcher*, 10, pp. 5–9.
FOSTER, S. (1986) *Reading Dancing* (Los Angeles, University of California Press).
GARDNER, H. (1983) *Frames of Mind: the theory of multiple intelligences* (New York, Basic Books).
GLASER, B., & STRAUSS, A. (1967) *The Discovery of Grounded Theory: strategies for qualitative research* (Chicago, Aldine).
GREEN, J., & STINSON, S. (1999) Postpositivist research in dance, in: S. FRALEIGH & P. HANSTEIN (Eds) *The Art of Research: systematic inquiry* (Pittsburgh, University of Pittsburgh Press).
HARDING, S. (1993) Rethinking standpoint epistemology: what is strong objectivity? in: L. ALCOFF & E. POTTER (Eds) *Feminist Epistemologies* (New York, Routledge).
JONES, B. (1989) *Body Against Body* (Barrytown, NY, Stanton Hill Press).
KREEMER, C. (1987) *Further Steps* (NewYork, Harper & Row).
KVALE, S. (1983) The qualitative research interview: a phenomenological and hermeneutical mode of understanding, *Journal of Phenomenological Psychology* 14, pp. 171–196.
LANGER, S. (1953) Feeling and Form (London, Routledge & Kegan Paul).
LATHER, P. (1986) Research as praxis, *Harvard Educational Review*, 56, pp. 257–275.
McFEE, G. (1994) *The Concept of Dance Education* (London, Routledge).
MOUSTAKAS, C. (1990) *Heuristic Research: design, methodology, and applications* Newbury Park, Sage Publications).
OLSON, M. (1995) Conceptualizing narrative authority: implications for teacher education, *Teaching & Teacher Education: An International Journal of Research and Studies*, 11(2), pp. 119–135.
REASON, P. (Ed.) (1994) *Participation in Human Inquiry* (London, Sage).
REDFERN, H. (1973) *Concepts in Modern Educational Dance* (London, Henry Kimpton Publishers).
REID, L. (1969) Meaning in the Arts (London, Allen & Unwin).
REID, L. (1986) *Ways of Understanding and Education* (London, Heinemann).
RISNER, D. (1992) Exploring dance rehearsal—the neglected issues revealed, *Journal of Physical Education, Recreation and Dance*, 63(6), pp. 61–65.
RISNER, D. (1995) Voices seldom heard: the dancers' experience of the choreographic process, *Impulse: The International Journal of Dance Science, Medicine, and Education*, 3, pp. 76–85.
SHAPIRO, H. & SHAPIRO, S. (1995) Silent voices, bodies of knowledge: towards a critical pedagogy of the body, *Journal of Curriculum Theorizing*, 11(1), pp. 49–72.
SHAPIRO, S. (1999) *Pedagogy and the Politics of the Body: a critical praxis* (New York, Garland Publishing).
STINSON, S.W., BLUMENFELD-JONES, D. & VAN DYKE, J. (1990) Voices of young women's students: an interpretive study of meaning in dance, *Dance Research Journal*, 22, pp. 13–22.

STINSON, S.W. & ANIJAR, K. (1993) Interpretive inquiry in dance education, *Impulse: The International Journal of Dance Science, Medicine, and Education*, 1, pp. 53–64.
STODELLE, E. (1978) *The Dance Technique of Doris Humphrey* (Princeton, NJ, Princeton).
TOMPKINS, C. (1965) *The Bride and the Bachelors* (New York, The Viking Press).
VAN DYKE, J. (1996) Choreography as a mode of inquiry: a case study, *Impulse: The International Journal of Dance Science, Medicine, and Education*, 4, pp. 318–25.

Part II

Curriculum and Pedagogy in 21st Century Postsecondary Dance

Prelude

"Each teacher's pedagogy is personal, and if not carefully examined and reflected upon regularly, teachers will teach the way they were themselves taught." (Risner and Barr, 2015, p. 89)

Jennifer McNamara: The collected articles in this section reflect the point where I met Doug Risner for the first time, although they span time both before and after I was a student in the National Dance Education Organization's Online Professional Development Institute courses that he taught. Rereading them as I prepared to write the introduction and preludes for this edited volume reminded me of those elemental questions: What matters? What am I not attending to? The articles speak to the work of wondering, seeking, and hoping, things that I had forgotten how to do, somewhere between now and that first transformational experience I had in Doug's pedagogy class. Perhaps the bleakness I was feeling, in and of itself, is a comment on the field of dance, dance education, dance teacher preparedness and wholeness, and the journey of learning often pushed aside in the midst of the compounding expectations and never-ending race to stay one step ahead, which are intertwined into a teacher's ongoing work. As I encountered the articles again, I realized I was reading them as a student, both satiating and sparking my own curiosity—and that is exactly what they should call forth in the reader: a hunger for and a joy in recognizing why we must commit to the work of teaching in the ways that we must learn to do.

Doug Risner: After 25 years in postsecondary dance, I published the sole-authored Chapter 4, "Dance Education Matters: Rebuilding Postsecondary Dance Education for Twenty-first Century Relevance and Resonance" (2010a). It emerged from my doctoral study in curriculum and pedagogy in the College of Education at the University of North Carolina-Greensboro (UNCG 1998–2001) as well as my experiences as chair of the Department of Dance at Wayne State University (2003–2009) and my administrative role and responsibilities for redesigning the Bachelor of Fine Arts in Dance and Bachelor of Science in Dance degree programs.

The other chapters in this section were researched, written collaboratively, and co-authored with colleagues who are also practitioners and scholars who share with me many similar research interests and concerns about the direction of curriculum and pedagogy in post-secondary dance education in the 21st century. Each chapter calls into question traditional approaches to undergraduate dance degree program curricula, which still today often privileges Bachelors of Fine Arts degrees while marginalizing Bachelors of Science and Bachelors of Arts degree programs in dance and BS and BA dance major students. In addition, this section emphasizes the importance of understanding the social foundations of education and dance education pedagogy. From this perspective, teaching methods defined as "best practices" are questioned. Best practices for whom? What students are left out or ignored in best practices models? Moreover, what are the outcomes of methods-centric teacher production? Who is left behind in a "best practices" pedagogy and curriculum that is designed for, defined by, and then universalized as a white, upper middle-class student/learner?

JM: These questions as well as the opening quote that provides context for this prelude should be at the heart of the ongoing evolution of dance, dance pedagogy, and dance education practices. Taken collectively, however, the articles point out that this critical work of forward shift is often pushed aside in favor of production: of aesthetic, of bodies, of continuity and therefore continued lineage and legacy.

Postsecondary education is the logical site for radical change, revolution, and evolution, but the systems it is designed to interrogate center its power in a still, small space. Creating shift, as Doug advocates for in his searing and sweet doctoral thesis, which he so generously allowed me to read, must be done with bold tenderness (Risner, 2001). Incremental shift, like "best practices," a phrase which should, perhaps, be retired, leaves out those who are not privileged nor part of the center, those who don't belong, and those who already exist in the always-shifting margins. This is not where dance, dance education, or dance pedagogy should strive to locate themselves, and so it is up to us to reframe the ways in which we engage with the critical work of teaching and learning. These chapters serve as both cautionary tales and guidebooks carrying hope for a future in dance that transcends outdated ideas of "best practices" and methods-centric teacher production by uplifting new ideas about social frameworks for pedagogy, leadership in postsecondary education, and a commitment to educating teachers.

Simply teaching as we were taught when we were children (or adults), regurgitating ideas we haven't even tasted for ourselves, not stopping to question our assumptions—this is where the dance field fails its students, practitioners, makers, and ultimately itself, stagnating in unexamined ideas about the body, movement, advocacy, art, communication, and all the things we seek to know in both embodied and theoretical ways and to share with students, audiences, and strangers (Risner, 2010a). Doug's foregrounding of social foundations as essential components in dance education draws from the earliest models of public education in the US. They provide the means for us to transcend our current limitations and frustrations, and they bring us back to the idea of a shared, communal humanity.

Doug's theory of education as a practice of co-learning not only draws from the deep ideas in bell hooks' writing and philosophies on education, community, hope, love, and self but also honors the legacy of community schools in the US and nudges the idea of student-centered learning a bit more toward a model of co-labor between two individuals who bring a literal body of experience to their endeavors. The arc of his work, which gathers threads from across the span of his experiences, so clearly suggests a humanizing dance pedagogy, even as he grappled with a multitude of other ideas along the way—and each piece was integral to the story of the whole. By de-emphasizing the production of teachers and instead bringing into focus the relationships—right relationships—that are the point of exchange, the blurred boundaries, and the widened orbits, Doug Risner illuminated what it means, in the end, to teach and to learn, connected to both strangers and partners in the act of growing into the fullness of human experience. He sets the tone for this work both humbly and astutely in his pedagogy classes, reminding students that "[w]e will learn what we learn from, and with, one another. There is no other real learning that will take place in this course" (Risner, 2010b, p. 204).

References

Risner, D. (2001). *Blurring the boundaries: Hope and possibility in the presence of the necessary stranger in gay liberation.* (UMI No. 3008895) [Doctoral dissertation, University of North Carolina at Greensboro]. ProQuest.

Risner, D. (2010a). Dance education matters: Rebuilding postsecondary dance education for twenty-first century relevance and resonance. *Arts Education Policy Review, 111*(40), 123–135. DOI: 10.1080/10632913.2010.490761

Risner, D. (2010b). *Challenges and opportunities for dance pedagogy: Critical social issues and "unlearning" how to teach.* In T. Randall (Ed.) Global Perspectives on Dance: Research and Pedagogy, Conference Proceedings of the Congress on Research in Dance, pp. 204–209. Leicester, U.K. June 2009. DOI: 10.1017/S2049125500001114

Risner, D. & Barr, S. (2015). Troubling methods-centric "teacher production": Social foundation in dance education teacher preparation. *Arts Education Policy Review, 116*(2), 78–91. DOI: 10.1080/10632913.2014.944965

Dance Education Matters: Rebuilding Postsecondary Dance Education for Twenty-first Century Relevance and Resonance[1]

Doug Risner

Abstract

Postsecondary dance education is at a crucial juncture in its history in academe. Emerging from women's physical education programs in the 1930s, the profession's realignment with the arts broadly and arts-based education specifically has been characterized by ambitious goals and steady growth through the 1990s. However, a number of critical developments over the past decade have displaced many previous gains and undermined the overall stability and integrity of the field. Four primary challenges are investigated in this article: curricular equity, expansive dance education programs, graduate study opportunities, and national leadership. I urge dance educators and administrators to re-envision and expand P–12 dance education in the liberal arts tradition to include private studio, commercial-sector, dance in community and related teaching professions. This article provides recommendations and strategies for developing relevant and resonant twenty-first-century dance education programs beyond current confines.

[1]This article was originally published in *Arts Education Policy Review* 111(4), pp. 123–135. Reprinted with permission.

Thirty years ago, Buryn's suggestion that "not knowing where you're going, you pay more attention to where you are, wherever that is" (Buryn 1980), woke American culture up to its need for re-envisioning a more nuanced balance of life, career, meaning, and, by extension, aesthetic experience, in ways that seem even more relevant today. Throughout the 1980s, we not only found ourselves, but we also adopted the notion that it is not the destination that is important, but, instead, it is the quality of the journey that matters. Like most dancers I know, I found the "journey model" exceptionally appealing, primarily because I, like many in the dance profession, did not know exactly where I was going.

I propose that while the journey model for dance in higher education has experienced significant growth over the past twenty-five years, it has not been sure of where it is going either. Still, college and university dance programs offering a major or minor have increased threefold since the mid-80s (Bonbright 2002). Coincidentally, my academic and administrative career spans exactly the same period—first as a young faculty member, then as a tenured associate professor, followed by a move to research administration and then chair of a department, and now back to the dance faculty. My academic journey is not dissimilar from the trajectory that dance education has tracked, with its initial ambitions, steady growth, diversification, and then (somewhat) a return to where it started—being much more informed, but still facing many of the same challenges from nearly three decades ago.

Like other arts faculty who swap careers from professor to administrator and back to faculty member, I spent considerable energy upon my return to the faculty in rebuilding, repairing, and rehabilitating my teaching. I had to look seriously at where I was, what had happened to the profession pedagogically, and then what I needed to do to effectively slip back into the ranks of the faculty. Here, I will advocate that the same is true for the challenges confronted by dance education today. For many of the same reasons, this kind of work is necessary because we have been paying attention to other things—meeting others' needs, pursuing others' goals and often documenting external, frequently ill-informed objectives (Hope 2008). Although I enjoyed most of my administrative positions, especially those in which my work had positive outcomes for students' lives, they did take me away from many of my basic needs as an effective educator and engaged teacher. Similarly, postsecondary dance education must look seriously at its own status, its basic needs, and the urgent necessity of its own repair and rebuilding.

Paying more attention to where we are is critical for dance education's future in higher education. The immediate challenges before us require us to direct our energies toward four primary areas: curricular equity, expansive dance education, graduate study, and national leadership. In terms of curricular equity, we must look carefully at the professionalization of the bachelor of fine arts (BFA) that continues to fuel most of the growth in dance departments across the nation. Given already limited resources and some of the harshest economic realities in memory, what level of equity does dance education—its curricula, programs, and faculty—hold? Similarly, we must expand and elaborate the definition and value of P–12 dance education curriculum in broad and inclusive ways. When we look closely at the aims of teaching, learning, pedagogy, community engagement, and cultural understanding, our P–12 dance education programs, if carefully reframed, can serve numerous dance professions and career paths for many more students than we currently serve in the hyperprofessionalized, exclusive BFA environment. Third, we must confront the obstacles of limited graduate study opportunities in dance education and the ways in which these limitations repeatedly confound the field's viability, growth, research, and leadership, both presently and in the future. Finally, we must grapple with the need for national leadership in postsecondary dance education.

Although the National Association of Schools of Dance (NASD) provides critically important direction and meaningful counsel for meeting standards in departmentally reflective and engaged ways, it does not survey the field for dance education equity, nor is it intended to do so or advocate for such a goal. Although the National Dance Education Organization (NDEO) has continued to play a significant role in arts-based dance education in P–12, private sector, higher education, and related dance education contexts, neither its mission nor its aims extend to postsecondary dance curricula or degree programs. Therefore, national leadership in dance education must come from within the field, by and for those who have a direct stake in its viability and future.

Unless indicated otherwise in this essay, I employ the term "dance education" to refer to the P–12 school and private studio age group, as well as postsecondary teacher preparation programs for these populations. This distinction is important to make at the outset to understand the expansion and relevance of dance education curricula for professional degree programs at the undergraduate and graduate levels I advocate later in this work.

Dance Education and Curricular Equity

Dance education teacher preparation programs in higher education, unlike like music education and visual arts education, remain on the periphery of postsecondary arts across the United States. Admittedly, dance is significantly dwarfed by other arts disciplines in higher education, both in terms of student enrollment and faculty and staff. However, even among the largest dance units (i.e., ten or more full-time faculty) that offer dance education degree programs, few have more than one dance education position on their faculty. In most dance programs, the dance educator—if there is one—also holds substantial teaching responsibilities beyond and outside their area of teacher preparation. These additional duties create substantial challenges for dance education faculty who are responsible for time-intensive, preservice teaching supervision and student teaching observation and evaluation.

Much of the fringe status and perception of dance education is a byproduct of long-standing "artist versus educator" binaries that privilege dance performance and choreography while marginalizing commitments to teaching, pedagogy, and dance in the community (Risner 2007;

Kerr-Berry 2007), regardless of the fact that the vast majority of undergraduate dance majors will not seriously pursue or attain professional dance careers in performance or choreography (Montgomery and Robinson 2003; Bennett 2009). The impact of pejorative discourses about dance education pervades important administrative decisions about staffing, resources, space usage, and fiscal priorities. Dance educators' marginal status also figures prominently in questions of tenure, promotion, and research credibility and funding (Clark 1994; Risner 2006). These inequities deserve further investigation, both internally for dance units and at upper administrative levels. To conduct such an investigation, we must begin by looking carefully at where we are now and how dance education continues to endure its marginalized, undervalued place in the overall schema of postsecondary dance.

The Ramifications of BFA Professionalization in Dance

In order to unpack dance education's curricular inequity, we must clearly see the emphasis on and impact of BFA professionalization in our programs over the recent past. Three decades of successful realignment of dance in academe within colleges and schools of fine and performing arts (as opposed to its placement in physical education) have contributed considerably to the ever-increasing development of new BFA programs in higher education in the United States (Risner 2008). When coupled with dominant discourses that undervalue dance education and teaching, well-intentioned efforts directed toward professional degree parity with other arts disciplines have unfortunately overemphasized dance as a performing art form at the expense of liberal arts and dance education programs.

According to data from Higher Education Arts Data Services (HEADS), BFA degree programs in dance increased by 33 percent over the last five years (Higher Education Arts Data Services [HEADS] 2004; HEADS 2009). Taken alone, this professionalization articulates the field's fervent commitment to establish dance as a separate arts discipline that is equal and valid alongside music, theater, and visual arts in postsecondary education. However, when this increase is seen in conjunction with the health and vitality of dance education degree programs, competing narratives quickly emerge. Although BFA programs continue to experience unprecedented growth, dance education programs have in fact decreased by 13 percent over the same five-year period (HEADS 2004; HEADS 2009). Although the BFA professionalization of dance in the university is certainly critical to long-term success, the persuasive political narratives that undergird and facilitate these kinds of dramatic priority shifts require the field's immediate attention and action. More to the point, sacrificing important dance education and liberal arts degree programs for BFA professional preparation programs forfeits numerous opportunities for expanding dance and dance education into American life and culture. I want to convey the urgency of the need to address these recent shifts in postsecondary dance for a number of reasons, which I elaborate in the following sections.

Competitive Resources in Difficult Economic Times

From the data reported earlier, we see the highly competitive environment that dance education faces as departments' priorities move increasingly toward BFA programs and needs. This competition for human and financial resources, which we are already losing, is exacerbated by the scrutinizing corporate value systems of postsecondary education. Demands for increased productivity that emphasize credit hours generated and numbers of majors push departments for ever increasing, quantifiable, and measurable outcomes. For people in the performing arts with heavy production seasons and needs, this one-size-fits-all corporate mentality ignores the extensive resources and personnel that are needed to nurture and maintain quality programs. The intensive specialization of BFA requirements; an increased number of courses in technique, choreography, and dance studies; and increased performance requirements make these programs expensive. The cost of faculty hires with prestigious professional credentials, high quality dance production, and noted guest artist residencies also requires substantial financial investment.

A primary focus on developing and sustaining the demands of rigorous BFA programs, however, has sharply redirected departments' resources at the expense of dance education programming, teacher preparation programs, and faculty hires in dance education. Under these corporate-based conditions and harsh current economic realities, administrative decisions between dance degree programs often lack parity. Over the past decade, postsecondary dance administration has been forced to negotiate dance's competitive survival, often at the price of dance education programs.

Moreover, current fiscal realities position dance education in academe in an even more precarious situation. As state legislatures across the nation balance immense budget deficits, frequently on the back of postsecondary institutions, dance education programs and faculty lines are particularly at risk for cuts and nonreplacement of vacant faculty lines (Green 2008). Because postsecondary dance educators often hold part-time or fractional positions, budget tightening in difficult economic times affects these faculty disproportionately. What is most confounding in this unfortunate scenario is the narrow but intense focus of dance programs on BFA curricula, when, in actuality, the vast majority of these students will not likely dance professionally or pursue professional careers (Montgomery and Robinson 2003; Bennett 2009). Rather, most dance students will cultivate relevant and meaningful careers in dance education and related professions in studio, community, presenting organizations, dance technology, production, advocacy, and administrative realms. When we look at where we are as a field, it should be obvious that re-envisioning dance education in more expansive ways holds the most promise and potential for influencing dance education policy and the viability of broad dance education curricula and degree programs in postsecondary dance.

Expansive Dance Education

For dance education, part of the process of looking candidly at where we are as a field is to see clearly the constrained configuration of current dance education programs and the limited appeal that our programs garner, in terms of undergraduate student interest and upper administration support. A portion of these constraints obviously comes from state certification requirements and education unit mandates. Others, however, come from us, because we have allowed the breadth of dance education to be concealed, reduced, or ignored entirely. Regardless, dominant perceptions equate the whole of dance education solely with P–12 dance teacher preparation.

Every instance in which we fail to articulate the significance of teaching, pedagogy, community awareness and engagement, technology, and research that is made possible through dance education contributes to the marginalization of the field. The work of expanding dance education in undergraduate curricula and thereby establishing its viability and relevance is a threefold process: (1) articulation of the breadth of dance education and pedagogy for current programs, (2) expansion of dance education to include private studio and community settings, and (3) developing new programs in dance education and related professions degree programs.

Articulating the Breadth of Dance Education and Pedagogy

Limited views and misperceptions of liberal arts degree programs in dance and dance education abound. From deans to students, prospective students, and their parents, the viability and practicality of these programs remain ambiguous for important stakeholders. As a prospective student's parent told me at a recent audition, "My daughter doesn't want to teach little kids, so she's only auditioning for the BFA program." Or, as a college dean responded recently to the unit's first formal request for a full-time dance education and technology faculty line (the first appeal of its kind for a department that has certified dance teachers for over thirty years), "Until you can demonstrate the need for P–12 dance teachers, I won't consider the request." And, finally, during an advising appointment, a BFA third-year student who teachers regularly in a local dance studio asked, "Why do I have to take a course in dance teaching? I've been teaching at my hometown studio since I was fourteen." Each of these examples illustrates the need for better articulation of the range and scope of dance education and pedagogy in postsecondary dance, while keeping in mind the multiple and complex forces that influence administrative priorities and decision making.

Effective articulation, especially in the current postrecession environment, begins by first addressing the intimate educational connections between the dance artist and the dance teacher/educator. For far too long, the significance of informed teaching skills and expertise has been underrated in the training of dancers, especially in professional degree tracks. "Artist versus educator" discourses that privilege technique and performance continue to hold sway in the public mind. However, the majority of professionally trained dancers earn a considerable portion of their dance income outside of performance, from wages generated from their own teaching or teaching-related positions.[2] Therefore, as the BFA student's previous question indicates, we must

---

[2]Montgomery and Robinson (2003) reported that 61 percent of undergraduates in dance held jobs other than performance.

articulate the importance of teaching and pedagogy preparation for all dance students through our curriculum offerings, degree requirements, and advising.

For guidance, we can turn to guidelines and standards from the NASD. Baccalaureate degrees with P–12 teacher preparation programs receive extensive and productive accreditation attention from this organization (National Association of Schools of Dance [NASD] 2009, 89–92); however, this guidance may have limited application in expanding the utility of dance education curricula beyond the confines of P–12 preparation. In terms of general liberal arts degree programs in dance (BA, BS),[3] dance pedagogy is discussed only minimally in operational guidelines for dance studies and electives, along with living dance, dance notation, anatomy and kinesiology, choreography, philosophy of dance, dance ethnology, and music for dance (NASD 2009, 84–85). Guidelines for teaching in professional degree programs (BFA) are equally brief but more specific:

> VIII.B.4. Teaching. Students must develop basic knowledge and skills in dance pedagogy. The program should include the equivalent of at least one course in pedagogy and teaching experience. (NASD 2009, 88)

Because NASD provides considerable flexibility in the unit's adaptation of guidelines and standards, it is difficult to know the ways in which this standard is satisfied by the sixty-five NASD-accredited institutions with BFA programs, or to know how the other 652 nonaccredited dance major and minor programs across the United States (Bonbright 2002, 65) address teaching and pedagogy preparation.[4] However, NASD guidelines provide an important framework for more intense attention to dance education curricular expansion in professional degree programs.

It will be beneficial to elaborate a reciprocal dialogue that acknowledges not only the positive impact of high-quality technique, performance, and choreography curriculum on teacher preparation programs, but also the influence of dance education coursework for professional BFA programs and their graduates, whose careers will inevitably include some kind of teaching and community education.[5]

Expanding Dance Education in Studio Settings

Historically, the nature of the relationship between postsecondary dance and private dance studios[6] has been rightly described as "an often hostile condition of disconnection" (Cohen 2002). These long-standing disconnections have emanated from multiple asymmetrical value systems related to dance, children, artistry, commercialism, economics, competition, production, and education, among others (Risner, Godfrey, and Simmons 2004). Although dance in academe has, from its earliest beginnings, been predisposed to creative and educational values for children and adolescents (Hagood 2000), private dance studio programs have been influenced by commerce and the demands of the market. As Posey explains:

> In the private sector, the public's perception of dance education determines what they will buy and marketing strategies are developed accordingly. This has an impact on the curricula offered at private schools of dance. In order to meet operating expenses, the private dance school must offer classes that someone will buy, and thus economic reality intrudes and influences both its artistic and educational values. (Posey 2002, 44)

Until recently, postsecondary dance has been reluctant to acknowledge or address the commerce-based framework from which successful private sector dance education operates. Without conveying oversimplification, in many instances, dance in academe has adopted a dismissive approach to private studio dance education altogether. However, the trivialization of the economic pressures of running a private dance school is often based on little to no experience of people in higher education who rarely bear responsibility for the fiscal health and economic well-being of their postsecondary dance departments.

---

[3] I refer here to NASD guidelines and standards for baccalaureate degrees that do not include specific P–12 teacher preparation programs.
[4] See Note 1.
[5] For professional dancers, teaching-related positions include rehearsal direction; reconstruction; teaching artist; artist-in-residence work in schools, higher education, and community settings; and teaching of movement-related systems such as Pilates, Feldenkrais, Alexander technique, and yoga.
[6] I use the term *private dance studio* to refer to dance instruction delivered in for-profit studios, schools, academies, and centers, whose students are primarily three to eighteen years of age.

Expanding dance education to address private studio teaching preparation will require a clear appraisal of where we are currently—that is, to see that our energies are primarily directed toward P–12 dance education and state certification for teachers. Although these efforts are vitally important, the asymmetry of focusing only on teacher certification is revealed in the numbers themselves. According to the NDEO, nearly six thousand K–12 schools in the United States offer dance as part of their curriculum; however, private dance studios and schools in the United States number 32000. By failing to expand dance education in this sector, we not only ignore a significant population, but also dismiss its potential growth and, for postsecondary settings, greater cultural engagement in our communities.

Based on previous research, expansion would begin by developing current dance education programs with new options that address private sector concerns in conjunction with higher education expertise and curricular resources (Risner, Godfrey, and Simmons 2004). The private studio option might include such topics as the commerce of private sector dance education, parental expectations, the absence of multiple commercial choices in costume and music selection, childhood studies and child development, and age-appropriate movement and choreographic themes.

Without dance education expansion and curricular development, as Posey suggests, opening and operating a dance school in today's economy frequently forces owners to learn from their own experiences while operating a highly competitive business (Posey 2002). Often, this situation means that private sector dance educators are self-taught and must build business strategies and teaching values without the benefit of sound comprehensive degree preparation. At the same time, their economic reality repeatedly translates to a need to please their clientele (i.e., parents and students) in order to retain them in a competitive market. Within such a buyer's-market framework, they must also work to develop their own artistic choices and educational integrity, all too often without the benefit of serious study or informed learning. Expanding dance education programs to address these needs will mean developing a more cohesive understanding of shared goals and mutual concerns in dance education broadly.

Community Dance in Postsecondary Dance Education

Historically, dance and dance education have shared important social bonds with their communities, both by definition and out of necessity. Many dance companies depend heavily upon community support and volunteerism. During the early 1980s, national and corporate funding agencies began to place stringent directives on arts funding to include a strong social service component. As Green notes:

> Most often, the term "community dance" has been associated with particular programmes that arose in places such as the United Kingdom and Australia during the 1970s. Although there were community dance initiatives prior to this period, I am particularly referring to what has become known as the "community dance movement." Some of these initial efforts were associated with youth projects and other community advocacy services, often in an attempt to elicit government funding. (2000, 54)

While particular projects often focus on unique needs, the community dance movement is generally characterized as actively developing and delivering dance-based programs aimed at reaching disenfranchised populations, communities, and individuals (Eddy 2009; Green 2000; Houston 2005; Unrau 2000). At their root, many community dance projects seek social inclusion by empowering participants who are perceived as excluded from the mainstream (e.g., at-risk children, core city populations, differently-abled persons, seniors, incarcerated populations, persons who are physically or mentally challenged).

Professional dance artists working with communities form another important group in the area of community dance (Sweeney 2003) and include modern dance choreographers such as Deborah Barnard, Emily Burns, David Dorfman, Pat Graney, Bill T. Jones, Liz Lerman, Stuart Pimsler, and Jawole Willa Jo Zollar. Large professional dance companies, especially those working in ballet, have also developed community programs—although these programs' aims are often directed more toward revenue generation and young talent recruitment, rather than toward social inclusion and reaching disenfranchised populations. Although research in professional dance company outreach and community dance is highly limited, in a study of twenty-five dance companies, Mead (2004) reported the ways in which the aims, mission, and delivery of educational outreach may be only tenuously linked to effective dance education or dance education expertise. Mead's findings come as no surprise when we see more clearly where we stand as a discipline in the United States. Unlike postsecondary dance in the United Kingdom, here, we have all but ignored dance education outside the onerous and rigid licensure requirements of the K–12 model.

Institutional data from Community Arts Network[7] and Community Dance,[8] two nonprofit organizations providing support, resources, and research for community arts education, identify three institutions that currently provide undergraduate programs with community dance curricula in the United States: a minor, a certificate program, and a concentration. In comparison, data for the United Kingdom report twenty-four undergraduate programs with specialization in dance in the community (seven degree majors, seven minors, and ten concentrations). Community dance education in higher education in the United Kingdom balances core skills, knowledge, and understanding in dance with a course of study connected directly to dance teaching. This pedagogical imperative emphasizes working with different groups of people, dance in education and community settings, project planning, dance facilitation, work-based learning, dance management, and historical and contextual studies relating to community dance—its purpose, place, and identity (Community Dance 2009). I strongly advocate considering a similar approach for expanding postsecondary dance education in the United States.

A vital and relevant U.S. dance education in the twenty-first century must include private studios and schools and community dance in its curricula, practice, and research. By specifically focusing on mutual concerns and inherent, yet untapped, connections among studio training in the private sector, community dance education, and degree programs in higher education, we can begin to envision productive relationships that squarely place the physical, emotional, and communal health of all student dancers and our communities at the core of dance education.

Graduate Study in Dance Education in the United States

Up to now, this article has focused primarily on the status of undergraduate dance education—its current strengths and limitations, as well as potential models for rehabilitation and expansion.

---

[7] See Community Arts Network at http://www.communityarts.net.
[8] See Community Dance at http://www.communitydance.org.uk.

To fully assess where we are, however, we must also look at graduate study opportunities in dance education. A number of sources provide an overall picture of scarcity, deficiency, and decline.

Master's-Level Dance Education

Based on data from the sixty-five NASD-accredited institutions, initial master's degree programs (MA, MEd, MS) have decreased 22 percent over the last five years, while MFA programs have increased 15 percent (HEADS 2004; HEADS 2009). Of initial master's degree programs in dance education, a 50 percent decrease is reported for the same period. In terms of degrees awarded from 2003 to 2009, the number of MFA graduates has increased 39 percent, while the number of initial master's degree graduates has decreased 26 percent, and master's level dance education has seen a 100 percent decline. These date recapitulate in a more pronounced way what I have noted happening at the undergraduate level. The attention, resources, and priorities of dance units in the United States are squarely focused on development and maintenance of performance-oriented BFA and MFA degree programs.

Current data from the NDEO[9] report sixty-two master's degree programs in dance in the United States, with MFAs representing 53 percent of all programs, initial master's level degrees representing 37 percent, and dance education master's degrees representing only 10 percent (six programs[10]). In terms of context, 2007 data from HEADS reported the following arts education master's level programs: 343 music education programs, 67 art education programs, and 3 dance education programs (HEADS 2007). When faced straightforwardly, these limited opportunities for graduate study speak powerfully to the urgency of rehabilitating postsecondary dance education at both the bachelor's and master's level.

---

[9] Educational statistics are difficult to track for dance education as a result of the exclusion of dance and dance education from important national assessments and reports. The NDEO synthesizes data from a number of sources to provide baseline statistical information for the field. See http://www.ndeo.org/content.aspx?page_id=22&club_id=893257&module_id=55774.

[10] Master's programs in dance education are currently offered by the following six institutions: New York University, Steinhardt School of Culture, Education, and Human Development; SUNY-Brockport; Temple University; University of Hawaii; University of Idaho; and University of North Carolina- Greensboro.

Doctoral Study in Dance

The dearth of master's programs in dance education is exacerbated by the lack of opportunities for advanced study at the doctoral level. Of the four doctoral programs currently offered in dance in the United States,[11] there are no doctoral programs in dance education.[12] Looking at the history of the dance doctorate and its recent direction over the past decade will be helpful for understanding the larger argument advanced here for repairing graduate study and rehabilitating advanced degree opportunities in dance education.

Tracing the history of the dance doctorate is difficult, because early dissertations on dance emerged from other, nondance disciplines—a dominant trend that continues today. The earliest recorded doctoral thesis is William Fenton's "The Seneca Dance: A Study of Personality Expression in Ritual," completed at Yale University in 1937 (Hagood 2000). Lulu Sweigard's 1939 Ed.D. dissertation, "Bilateral Asymmetry in the Alignment of the Skeletal Framework of the Human Body," from New York University is credited as the first doctoral thesis in dance education (Dance Education and Research Descriptive Index 2009). Thirty dissertations on dance had been completed by 1960.

Graduate study in dance benefited from the overall postsecondary "dance boom" from 1965 to 1980, although most growth was experienced and sustained in BFA and MFA tracks. For the period 1971 to 1981, Brennan cites 256 completed doctoral degrees, of which the leading doctoral institutions in dance (ranked in order by number of dissertations) were: New York University, Texas Woman's University, University of Wisconsin–Madison, and Columbia University (Hagood 2000).

From the early 1980s through the mid-1990s, postsecondary dance struggled to maintain its bountiful enrollments from the previous decade and suffered significantly under the emergent "corporate university" model, especially in terms of human and physical resources such as inadequate facilities and reduced or eliminated faculty lines as the result of tightening budgets and their requisite cuts. This time frame also saw the elimination of the prestigious University of Wisconsin–Madison's doctoral degree program. In 1993, however, a new Ph.D. program in dance at the University of California–Riverside was established in Dance History and Theory, the nation's first doctorate to emerge from dance, rather than from health, physical education, or recreation (Hagood 2000).[13] Completed doctoral dance dissertations from 1982 to 1994 numbered 243, on par with the previous period but failing to match the growth trajectory of the previous four decades.

During the late 1990s, decreases in enrollment, administrative pressures, and leadership changes brought about the decline of two previously productive doctoral programs in dance.[14] With so few institutions offering advanced study, the loss of the Wisconsin doctoral program and two additional doctoral programs significantly impacted the field. Doctoral institutions during this period also eliminated practice-based Ed.D. programs, focusing their energies instead on the research-based Ph.D. The impact of these events has been especially detrimental to doctoral work opportunities in dance education in the last decade, as revealed by the following data.

Doctoral Degrees and Dissertations

Most doctorates in dance in the United States are awarded outside the academic dance unit, as illustrated in Table 1. Of the 219 doctoral degrees conferred from 1999 to 2008, 72 percent were awarded in other disciplines. The predominant Ph.D. comprised 85 percent of all doctoral degrees. Because the doctor of education degree is no longer available in dance, as noted earlier, it is no surprise that the Ed.D. accounted for only 4 percent of doctorates awarded from dance programs during this period. Therefore, post-master's dance

---

[11] The doctorate in dance is currently offered by the following four institutions: Temple University; Texas Woman's University (fully low-residence program); Ohio State University; and University of California–Riverside. Outside of dance per se, performance studies doctoral programs that include dance studies are New York University, Tisch School of the Arts; and Northwestern University's performance studies doctoral program.

[12] The longstanding Ed.D. and Ph.D. programs in dance education at New York University's Steinhardt School of Culture, Education, and Human Development have been suspended indefinitely. The unit maintains its master's programs in dance education. The master's program in dance education at Columbia University Teacher's College, which produced thirty-three doctorates with dance education content from 1948 to 1998, has been discontinued.

[13] The interdisciplinary-based doctoral program in Dance History and Theory at the University of California–Riverside graduated its first Ph.D. in 1998. The doctorate has recently been retitled Ph.D. in Critical Dance Studies.

[14] See Note 12.

Table 1 Doctoral Degrees in Dance/Dance content, 1999–2008

Degree	Conferred in dance (N = 61) n	%	Conferred in other (N = 158) n	%	Total doctorates n	%
Ph.D.	52	24	135	62	187	85
Ed.D.	9	4	21	10	30	14
Psy.D.	0	0	2	>1	2	1
Total	61	28	158	72	219	100

Source: ProQuest 2009.

education students interested in a practice-based Ed.D. curriculum and applied research must pursue doctoral study outside the dance unit.

A comparison of doctorates in dance and dance education over the same period shows an overall flat-line for all doctoral study, with approximately 10 percent growth (see Table 2). Upon closer inspection, however, degrees in dance education or with dance education content (Ph.D. and Ed.D.) have decreased 45 percent during the past decade. Although dance education degrees made up nearly half of all completed dance doctorates from 1999 to 2003, the last five years have seen that number drop to only 22 percent.

Longitudinal data from 1939 to 2008 indicate a strong growth trajectory for dance education dissertations from the 1940s through 2000, but a sharp decline emerged during the past decade (see Table 3). The average annual number of completed dissertations in dance education today is approximately the same as it was in 1989, numbering about four dissertations per year. For context and comparison, Jones (2009) reported 213 completed dissertations in music education for the year 2005 alone.

From 1999 to 2008, the majority of dance education doctorates (62%) were conferred by academic units other than dance, with the Ph.D. constituting three-quarters of all degrees, as shown in Table 4. The Ed.D. in dance accounted for 25 percent of all doctorates in dance, while 23 percent of all doctorates conferred by other disciplines were Ed.D. degrees. Without the Ed.D. in dance, postsecondary dance stands to lose

Table 2 Dance and Dance Education Doctorates Awarded, 1999–2008

Degree	1999	2000	2001	2002	2003	2004	2005	2006	2007	2008
Dance	17	14	19	14	12	12	18	10	22	25
Dance education	11	10	6	5	5	3	5	2	3	6
Difference	6	4	13	9	7	9	13	8	19	19
Total awarded	28	24	25	19	17	15	23	12	25	31

Source: ProQuest 2009.
Note. Data from Higher Education Arts Data Services is highly limited for this comparison.

Table 3 Dance Education Dissertations, 1939–2008 (N = 202)

	1939–50	1951–64	1965–79	1980–2002	2003–08
Dissertations	9	13	48	108	24
Yearly average	0.75	0.92	3.20	5.00	4.00

Sources: Bonbright and Faber 2004, 14; ProQuest 2009.

Table 4 Doctoral Degrees with Dance Education Content, 1999–2008

	Conferred in dance ($n = 21$)		Conferred in other ($n = 35$)		Total doctorates	
Degree	n	%	n	%	n	%
Ph.D.	15	27	27	48	42	75
Ed.D.	6	11	8	14	14	25
Total	21	38	35	62	56	100

Source: ProQuest 2009.
Note: There are currently no doctoral programs in dance education.

nearly a third of its doctoral students, as Table 2 shows.

Conversely, prospective dance education doctorates may elect the Ph.D. in dance, which brings into question doctoral faculty preparedness for guiding dissertations in fields of study for which they may have little or no expertise, credentials, or interest. At the extreme, we may be losing prospective dance education doctoral candidates altogether. The 20 percent decline in dance education dissertations from 2003 to 2008 illustrated in Table 3 provides evidence that this attrition could be the case.

Of the 62 percent of dance education doctorates conferred outside of the dance discipline, the majority of degrees were awarded in education (54%), followed by art education (11 percent) and psychology (11%), as listed in Table 5. Music/music education and physical education accounted for 6 percent of degrees respectively. The presence of these conferring disciplines outside of dance are not surprising. When students confront the absence of doctoral programs in dance education, many select an education doctorate in curriculum, teaching, foundations, or leadership.

As postsecondary dance has moved out of the auspices of health and physical education to realign itself with the fine and performing arts, a doctorate in arts education offers an interdisciplinary program with collaborative and bridging opportunities for dance in arts education. The emergence of dance and movement therapy and psychology of the arts and artists makes psychology another logical option for doctoral study in dance education.

Although these areas and the remainder of small-percentage disciplines outside of dance have cogent ties to dance education, a core body of knowledge in dance education theory and practice remains subjugated to the instrumental means

Table 5 Doctoral degrees with dance education content conferred from other disciplines, 1999–2008 ($N=35$)

Degree	n	%
Education	19	54
Art education	4	11
Psychology	4	11
Music/music education	2	6
Physical education	2	6
Theater/drama	1	3
Applied linguistics	1	3
Counseling	1	3
Humanities	1	3

Source: ProQuest 2009.

and ends of other, larger disciplines. More simply, doctoral dance education is only as important as its ability to translate other disciplines' aims, serving as an alternative lens for education, art education, psychology, music education, and physical education. In these multiple interdisciplinary scenarios, all of which are worthy and valid, the intrinsic value of dance education is minimized and undervalued. Additionally, the knowledge base created from these dissertations likely prioritizes and enlarges other disciplines, rather than centralizing dance education practice and research needs.

Nearly a third (30%) of all dissertation topics in dance education over the past decade have focused on curriculum and pedagogy (see Table 6). Given the fact that 54 percent of dance education doctorates are completed in education, the prevalence of these topics is predictable, at least in instrumental terms. One of those 17 doctorates in curriculum and teaching was my own Ph.D.

Table 6 Dissertation topics conducted in dance education, 1999–2008 ($N = 56$)

Degree	n	%
Curriculum and pedagogy	17	30
Community dance	5	9
Administration/higher education	3	5
Creative/collaborative process	3	5
Creative dance	3	5
Dance science/somatic study	3	5
History and criticism	3	5
Multicultural education	3	5
Elementary education	2	4
Developmental psychology	2	4
Health/wellness	2	4
Interdisciplinary arts/integrated arts	2	4
Special education/differently-abled	2	4
Technique and choreography	2	4
Contact improvisation	1	2
Kinesthetic learning	1	2
Notation	1	2
Technology	1	2

Source: ProQuest 2009.

(Risner 2001); therefore, I am aware of both the strengths and limitations of taking one's doctorate outside dance. Although my doctoral preparation and expertise in curriculum theory and teaching in higher education has served me well, what I did not learn in my program is very similar to what the field has not learned over the past ten years. Because our collective doctoral efforts have focused primarily on teaching and curriculum in higher education, we have learned very little about dance in elementary, middle, and high schools. Even less has been learned in critically important areas such as integrated arts education, kinesthetic learning, and technology.

In summary, the lack of graduate programs in dance education has had numerous deleterious effects on the field and requires the profession's immediate attention. First, the scarcity of opportunities for students to engage and develop postgraduate expertise in dance education must be addressed. The absence of a terminal degree in dance education presents critical challenges for maintaining and growing the field. Second, the profession suffers further from the lack of leadership created by the shortage of graduate programs and doctoral graduates. Third, with new knowledge nearly at a standstill, how can dance education move forward in research and best practices? Although many other deficiencies exist, the lack of graduate study opportunities contributes heavily to the dearth of quality research and scholarship. Seeing where we are in our graduate programs means both facing the limitations elaborated here and acknowledging that if we ignore them, as I believe we have, our inaction will repeatedly confound the field's viability, growth, research, and leadership.

Re-Envision, Rebuild, and Resonate

Knowing where we are as a field allows us to think much more clearly about where we are going—or better, where we need to go. As I have suggested here, postsecondary dance education must look candidly at its status, its basic needs, and its potential to repair, rebuild, and resonate with multiple stakeholders and constituencies outside and beyond performance degree programs in dance. Having outlined this need, I recognize that the challenges before us are formidable ones.

In no way do I forecast quick and easy solutions to the obstacles that are already in place or lie ahead. The recommendations and strategies I describe here, however, do find their roots in energies and resources that are currently available or may be available based on what we know. In this spirit, readers are encouraged to digest and then put into action the following plan in terms loosely arranged around the notion of "how this might happen."

I revisit four primary areas discussed earlier and then present strategies for re-envisioning each set of challenges, including remediation of curricular equity, expansive and resonant dance education, rebuilding of graduate study, and national leadership commitment.

Remedies for Dance Education Curricular Equity

In addition to the approaches discussed earlier, a large part of achieving curricular equity and parity of dance education programs means developing strategies that will have a strong appeal for our colleagues and administrators who focus on performance-based curricula and professional degree programs. The most compelling arguments for this population will likely be those that articulate how dance education, conceived in its broadest sense, will benefit BFA and MFA students. Although this approach recapitulates, to some degree, the instrumental values I criticized earlier, the underlying notion here is to recast dance education curricula as something that professional degree programs need to be successful.

A recent survey of graduate program directors in postsecondary dance (Risner 2009) found that MFA programs rated the following areas as most important to their programs: artistic practice (82%), improvisation/choreography (69%), and performance (62%). Although the category of teaching and pedagogy was rated low (33%) in terms of importance to program, the significance of teaching preparation for postsecondary settings was emphasized repeatedly in qualitative responses regarding MFA graduate research coursework and career preparation. More to the point, because the MFA, as the terminal degree for studio faculty pursuing positions in higher education, seeks to prepare highly proficient teachers, the door is open for clarifying and advocating an expanded role for informed teaching and pedagogy coursework at the master's level.

MFA graduates pursuing careers in professional performance and choreography will likely teach, either to supplement their income or to fulfill an outreach activities requirement of the dance company for which they perform. The rise in prominence of the "teaching artist" over the past decade is a visionary example of rethinking the limitations of artist versus educator binaries. As Booth asserts, "A teaching artist is an artist, with the complementary skills and sensibilities of an educator, who engages people in learning experiences in, through, or about the arts" (2003, 11). The Association of Teaching Artists (ATA) identifies three basic capacities necessary for all teaching artists: understanding your art form; understanding classroom environment, pedagogy, and human development; and understanding the collaborative process of working in a school environment (Association of Teaching Artists 2009). I can think of no MFA programs in the United States that address these competencies beyond specific art form understanding.

The argument for BFA students is somewhat similar and equally as pragmatic. Many are already teaching in studios and in the community without the benefit of dance education coursework such as pedagogy, methods, creative dance for children, or teaching practica. Nor do they understand the importance of this kind of career preparation. Undergraduates in professional tracks have much to learn about teaching, pedagogy, cultural awareness, and community engagement. Here again there is a considerable necessity to articulate why BFA and MFA programs need and will benefit from healthy and vibrant dance education curricula. I encourage readers to articulate these connections for themselves in their own institutional contexts and then advocate the mutually beneficial relationship between professional programs and dance education coursework.

Expansive and Resonant Dance Education Programs

As should be clear, I strongly advocate a new and expansive definition of postsecondary dance education for the twenty-first century that still continues to include P–12 teacher preparation and certification as vital components. But for this area to be viable and relevant, further expansion of the concept of "dance education" is necessary. A resonant and relevant dance education program will likely find its first success within a liberal arts degree framework (BA, BS, BSEd) that includes core coursework in teaching in multiple sectors (studio, community, outreach, alternative settings) and related dance professions (e.g., advocacy, administration, production, dance science, and technology). Re-tooling liberal arts bachelor's degrees in this direction allows a new postsecondary responsiveness to students who might otherwise fall short of BFA audition requirements, or who might choose nondance degree programs with greater career preparation and job opportunities. At the same time, an expansive dance education degree could also serve the field and our communities in new and profoundly important ways. Expanding dance education to address these needs fosters enhanced cultural relevance and community resonance.

Although expansive programs could take a number of different approaches and perspectives, some central aims and components might include:

- To provide relevant and comprehensive liberal arts study of dance beyond traditional technique and performance training paradigms
- To offer an integrative program in the study of dance, community, and culture with multiple opportunities for students to enhance technical skill, investigate shifting social and global concerns, and cultivate diverse career preparation in broad dance teaching contexts and professions

- To present accessible courses of dance study blending inquiry and practice that prepare students to be imaginative and innovative leaders for improving people's lives and social circumstances through dance education and related professions
- To offer degree options and opportunities in dance teaching; commercial and private sector dance; administration, policy, and advocacy; production and technology; dance science and body therapies; and dance in community and alternative settings

Rebuilding Graduate Study in Dance Education

From the data presented previously, one of the most significant challenges for rebuilding graduate programs in dance education is likely tethered to communication of the dire situation of postsecondary dance education at the graduate level to the field itself. This article and its data attempt first to alert, and then to galvanize readers in multiple sectors of dance education. Without strong and accessible graduate study opportunities, the profession cannot sustain itself. In addition to the strategies outlined earlier, I will make a few cursory recommendations for both people in postsecondary graduate programs and those units currently considering or developing graduate programs in dance.

- Identify local, institutional, and regional needs for graduate study in dance education in its broadest definition. What populations might be served by initial master's level study outside narrowly defined programs that position the MA/MEd/MS as a generic, intermediary credential leading to the doctorate? In what ways could initial master's programs focus broadly on pedagogy, teaching, community, and dance in alternative settings in addition to and beyond teacher certification? See, for example, NASD guidelines for specific standards for dance education degrees at the initial master's level (NASD 2009, 104–07).
- For MFA-granting institutions, review the level and quality of expertise that graduates currently develop and attain in the area of postsecondary teaching preparation. For guidance, see NASD standards for graduate degrees combining research and practice orientations, as well as teaching for all graduate programs (NASD 2009, 100–03). Contemplate the significance of balancing the dominant programmatic thrust of artistic practice, choreography, and performance with important career preparation in teaching, pedagogy, and cultural and community engagement. Because the MFA is the terminal studio degree for postsecondary teaching positions, consider implementing a teaching artist core curriculum with multiple course options or electives.
- For all graduate programs, explore the curricular possibilities made available through technology, distance learning, and consortium partnerships with other graduate programs. Important curricular innovations in dance frequently happen in small pockets, developed by talented yet isolated faculty members. Consult graduate faculty colleagues in other master's and doctoral programs for innovative practices and new curricular designs. Explore partnering opportunities and reciprocal enrollment possibilities for students between institutions.

The Need for National Leadership in Postsecondary Dance Education

As I began to conduct this research and compile increasing amounts of data, I became more and more miffed that so little attention is paid to the status and well being of postsecondary dance education in the United States. My frustration peaked when I finally realized that no one is minding the dance education store. The virtual storekeepers have been our respective state departments of education, which mandate teacher preparation certification requirements, as they are legally bound to do. Dance educators and administrators have dutifully done what we were told to do and considered that to be more than enough. However, without national leadership, our collective attention has focused so narrowly on meeting these directives that I believe we have forfeited the larger aims of dance education and the wider mission and role of dance education in the higher education dance field.

Although national leadership must come from within the field, by and for those who have a direct stake in dance education's viability, relevance, and future, there are a number of resources and strategies that can provide energy and support for these efforts:

- Development of national leadership may come from partnerships with organizations that advocate on behalf of postsecondary dance and, in some instances, dance education.
  - NASD and the Council of Dance Administrators (CODA) could play important roles in assembling administrators and dance educators to discuss the status of dance education and its future. The establishment of ad hoc committees and working groups, as well as workshops and plenary sessions, could identify key challenges and future directions for healthy and vibrant postsecondary dance education.
  - NDEO, dedicated to fostering dance education in multiple sectors, may serve an even larger role in advocacy, policy, and curriculum development assistance.
- Outside postsecondary dance per se, leadership partnerships might also be forged with national and international organizations with constituent populations that comprise dance educators and teaching artists, including Community Arts Network; Community Dance; and the Association of Teaching Artists.
- Doctoral study opportunities will require national leadership and institutional commitment. In addition to the potential support listed previously:
  - The profession will benefit from consulting current master's level dance education programs first, as these institutions may be well-positioned to introduce new or reinstate previous doctoral programs in dance education.
  - For units that currently grant master's degrees in dance education and belong to an institution that also offers a robust doctoral program in education, possibilities for partnering in a dance education doctoral option within the education unit's Ph.D. or Ed.D. program should be explored.
  - Additional support for the development of doctoral programs in dance education can be sought from the Carnegie Foundation's Initiative on the Doctorate (http://www.carnegiefoundation.org/CID) and the Council of Graduate Schools' Preparing Future Faculty Project (http://www.preparing-faculty.org).

Final Thoughts: "Both/and" Decision Making

As a former department chair and a BFA, MFA graduate, I am well acquainted with the political negotiations and complex interplay of developing professional degree programs while simultaneously attempting to nurture and sustain liberal arts and dance education programs. Within this curricular negotiation, an "either/or" approach to decision making often surfaces in which dance unit priorities are determined in fragmented ways. From this either/or view, departments frequently address particular parts of their programs rather than the interconnected whole of the unit. Unified thinking necessitates a move away from fragmentation to "both/and" thinking about the breadth and depth of our programs.

Although likely unintentional, the proliferation of BFA and MFA programs has likely exacerbated the divisive "artist versus educator" dichotomy. From such, a highly limited or specialized view of excellence has emerged as the gold standard for all dance degree programming in higher education. From this dominant narrative, dance programs have systematically begun to define and understand excellence solely as excellence in technique (e.g., for ballet and modern dance), performance, and choreography. Unfortunately, this powerful mindset ignores much of what dance educators are teaching and, more important, the creative potential of all young dance students, most of whom will not perform professionally with major national dance companies. However, these dominant values do corroborate the rampant specialization of undergraduate dance programs: over-valorizing artistic production of the dancer while grossly underestimating the meaningful learning processes in dance education and related professions. The most fallacious argument operating here is that we must choose either one or the other. From the current corporate lens in higher education, we—and I implicate myself here as well—have likely acquiesced to pick one track and pursue it almost exclusively. This narrowed focus has been the trajectory for much of postsecondary dance for the past decade and a half; dance education has not been prioritized on this trajectory. At the same time, the complex pressures that our upper administrations confront wield substantial influence on our programs. Many factors influence decision making by university administrators: economic pressures, resource parity between programs, enrollment, credit hour production, facility needs, health and safety, and status of the arts in academe, among others. However, the outcome of these factors frequently results in either/or scenarios that force dance units into similar kinds of either/or decisions, whether implicitly or explicitly. As I have argued here, when the value of dance education is tied exclusively to P–12 teacher preparation and state certification, postsecondary administration often misperceives the larger aims of dance education generally, as well as the importance of teaching, pedagogy, community outreach and engagement, technology, and research made possible through dance education programs, curricula, and faculty positions.

Knowing that administrative leadership rarely encourages thinking in "both/and" ways, our charge will also include forging understandings that evidence long-term, meaningful connections between postsecondary dance education curricula and professional degree preparation and community engagement. To make advances in these tenuous times, our progress must be aligned with strategies that ensure solid gains in which stability and growth are well planned and possible to execute. As we chart the future terrain of postsecondary dance education, I hope we will begin by seeing both where we are and where we are going.

References

Association of Teaching Artists. 2009. Getting started as a teaching artist. www.teachingartists.com/gettingstartedTA.htm (accessed September 5, 2009).

Bennett, D. 2009. Careers in dance: Beyond performance to the real world of work. *Journal of Dance Education* 9 (1): 27–24.

Bonbright, J. 2001. *Database of higher education institutions offering dance minor and major programs*. Bethesda, MD: National Dance Education Organization.

———. 2002. The status of dance teacher certification in the United States. *Journal of Dance Education* 2 (2): 63–67.

Bonbright, J., and R. Faber. 2004. *Research priorities for dance education: A report to the nation*. Bethesda, MD: National Dance Education Organization.

Booth, E. 2003. Seeking definition: What is a teaching artist? *Teaching Artist Journal* 1 (1): 5–12.

Buryn, E. 1980. *Vagabonding in the USA*. Berkeley, CA: And/Or Press.

Clark, D. 1994. Voices of women dance educators: Considering issues of hegemony and the education/performer identity. *Impulse* 2 (2):122–30.

Cohen, P. 2002. Partnership potential between private dance schools and dance programs in higher education: Connections and disconnections. *Journal of Dance Education 2* (2): 50–51.

Community Dance. 2009. http://www.communitydance.org.uk (accessed September 5, 2009).

Dance Education and Research Descriptive Index. 2009. Silver Spring, MD: National Dance Education Organization. http://www.ndeo.org/content.aspx?page_id=1106&club_id=893257 (accessed September 1, 2009).

Eddy, M. 2009. The role of dance in violence-prevention programs for youth. In *Dance: Current selected research*, Vol. 7, ed. L. Overby and B. Lepczyk. Brooklyn, NY: AMS Press. 93–143.

Green, J. 2000. Power, service and reflexivity in a community dance project. *Research in Dance Education 1* (1): 53–67.

Green, L. 2008. Battle of the budget. *Dance Teacher 30*(9): 74–78.

Hagood, T. 2000. *A history of dance in American higher education: Dance and the American university*. Lewiston, NY: Edwin Mellen Press.

Higher Education Arts Data Services. 2004. *Dance data summaries 2003–2004*. Reston, VA: Higher Education Arts Data Services.

———. 2007. *Art and design data summaries 2006–2007*. Reston, VA: Higher Education Arts Data Services.

———. 2007. *Dance data summaries 2006–2007*. Reston, VA: Higher Education Arts Data Services.

———. 2007. *Music data summaries 2006–2007*. Reston, VA: Higher Education Arts Data Services.

———. 2007. *Theatre data summaries 2006–2007*. Reston, VA: Higher Education Arts Data Services.

———. 2009. *Dance data summaries 2008–2009*. Reston, VA: Higher Education Arts Data Services.

Hope, S. 2008. Requirements, cultural development and arts education. *Arts Education Policy Review 110* (1): 3–5.

Houston, S. 2005. Participation in community dance: A road to empowerment and transformation? *New Theatre Quarterly 21* (2): 166–77.

Jones, P. 2009. The doctor of musical arts in music education: A distinctive credential needed at this time. *Arts Education Policy Review 110* (3): 3–8.

Kerr-Berry, J. 2007. Dance educator as dancer and artist. *Journal of Dance Education 7* (1): 5–6.

Mead, D. 2004. Dance company education and outreach: A time to review what we do. In *Merging worlds: Dance, education, society and politics*, ed. D. Risner and J. Anderson, 285–90. Silver Spring, MD: National Dance Education Organization.

Montgomery, S., and M. Robinson. 2003. What becomes of undergraduate dance majors? *Journal of Cultural Economics 27*:57–71.

National Association of Schools of Dance (NASD). 2009. *National Association of Schools of Dance Handbook 2009–2010*. Reston, VA: National Association of Schools of Dance.

Posey, E. 2002. Dance education in dance schools in the private sector: Meeting the demands of the marketplace. *Journal of Dance Education 2* (2): 43–49.

ProQuest. 2009. Dissertations and theses. http://proquest.umi.com (accessed July 30, 2009).

Risner, D. 2001. Blurring the boundaries: Hope and possibility in the presence of the necessary stranger. Ph.D. diss., University of North Carolina at Greensboro.

———. 2006. Equity in dance education: Where are we now? *Journal of Dance Education 6* (4): 105–08.

———. 2007. Current challenges for K–12 dance education and development: Perspectives from higher education. *Arts Education Policy Review 108* (4): 17–23.

———. 2008. Equity in dance education: Momentum for change. *Journal of Dance Education 8* (3): 75–78.

———. 2009. *Survey of dance graduate programs in the US: Research priorities*. Detroit, MI: Wayne State University. http://www.dougrisner.com/html/cordcepa_research.html (accessed May 1, 2010).

Risner, D., H. Godfrey, and L. Simmons. 2004. The impact of sexuality in contemporary culture: An interpretive study of perceptions and choices in private sector dance education. *Journal of Dance Education 4* (1): 23–32.

Sweeney, S., ed. 2003. Living in a political world? A symposium hosted by the Dance UK in collaboration with Dance Umbrella, South Bank Centre, London. http://www.criticaldance.com/magazine/200401/articles/LivinginaPoliticalWorld20031000.html (accessed June 5, 2009).

Unrau, S. 2000. Motif writing in gang activity: How to get the bad boys to dance. In *Dancing in the millennium*, ed. J. Crone-Willis and J. LaPointe-Crump, 172–79. Washington, DC: Congress on Research in Dance.

Weaving Social Foundations through Dance Pedagogy: A Pedagogy of Uncovering

Sherrie Barr and
Doug Risner

ABSTRACT Today's dance educators enter classrooms populated by increasingly diverse students in which teachers' pedagogical knowledge necessitates heightened understandings of race, ethnicity, social class, gender, and sexuality. Uncovering taken-for-granted assumptions, dominant stereotypes, and educational structures that reproduce social inequalities in schools requires teacher preparation in social foundations of education. This qualitative study examined an undergraduate dance pedagogy course weaving social foundations content taught through a critical feminist pedagogical perspective over a three-year period. Narrative data were drawn from student ($n = 59$) writing assignments and discussion posts. Inclusion approaches for social foundations are presented. The range and diversity of student narratives amplify the challenge of, and the need for, the inclusion of social foundations in dance teacher preparation.

Conversations about what defines dance and what constitutes dance education in the twenty-first century invigorate the field of dance pedagogy. Today, characteristics of postmodern disciplines such as cultural pluralism, gender, sexuality, queer studies, somatics, ableism, and ability are as apparent in onstage dance performances as in offstage dance education conversations (Antilla 2008; Shapiro 2008; Burnidge 2012). Dance educators and researchers are reimagining pedagogies that go beyond contradictions between a teaching methods-based approach and the changing dance education landscape (Stinson 2010). All these richly diverse conversations concerning effective and meaningful pedagogy serve to facilitate teacher candidates "to learn to think critically rather than reverentially about their art and their chosen profession" (Stinson 1991, 29). Through embracing personal experience in learning, teacher candidates can also explore the possibilities of an "engaged pedagogy" (hooks 1998/2006, 138), one that offers inroads to "find personal relevance and meaning when entering and engaging content" (Ottey 1996, 31).

Yet, discipline-specific pedagogy courses focusing on *what* is to be taught and *how* it can be most efficiently accomplished still remain the emphasis within many teacher preparation programs in the United States (Risner 2010a). Methods-based instruction ignores the individual student's personal meaning in relationship to learning. To remedy such oversight, questions focusing on *why* in relation to the broader culture need to be addressed. These are the types of theoretical queries underlying social foundations of education theory in which scholars and theorists explore issues of class, race and ethnicity, sexuality, and gender, and ways these issues, historically and in society today, impact educational institutions. Within this field of study, "Social foundation courses emphasize the why of democratic public education, for what purposes, in whose benefit, to what ends; thus they centralize the aims of freedom, equality, human dignity, and social justice" (Risner 2010a, 206). Integrating social foundations issues into dance pedagogy recognizes the evolving nature of dance education and dance pedagogy.

In this article, we examine an undergraduate dance pedagogy course taught from a critical feminist perspective. The course weaves issues of social foundations throughout assigned readings, writings, discussions, and teacher feedback. Central to our inquiry is an exploration of student attitudes and beliefs pertaining to issues of social foundations. Primary resources for the research were student reflective writings from course assignments. Using students' writings in this way values their voices as being as relevant as that of the teacher, a tenet embedded within the course's pedagogical framework. It also underscores two of the course's stated student learning outcomes:

- Greater self-reflection on one's own teaching theory and practice; the ability to question and improve one's own teaching practice systematically.
- Heightened awareness and sensitivity to social and cultural issues in teaching.

Finally, in honoring student voices in this inquiry, we bring into focus the alignment between learning outcomes and the two fundamental questions students focused on throughout the course: What kind of teacher do I want to become? What does it mean to be responsible for someone else's learning?

CONTEXT AND METHODS

While Risner was on sabbatical, Barr, recently retired from another institution in the state, taught several of his courses, including Dance Pedagogy. Our discussions about the course initially focused on its scope and general aims, ways in which the course fit into the program's overall dance education curriculum as well as within the university's identity as a large urban research institution, and, because Dance Pedagogy is a web-based course, the ins and outs of online teaching. Our discussions soon morphed into dialogues about individual teaching struggles and endeavors that highlighted our beliefs about the pedagogy of dance pedagogy. We discovered a common commitment to facilitate students in an engaged reflective praxis. We also found a shared belief in critical feminist pedagogies and social foundations to be a meaningful vehicle for student growth and learning.

To further situate this research, a brief overview of the dance program and its students is given. The program offers a BFA professional degree and a liberal arts BS degree in dance professions. Dance Pedagogy is an upper level, three-credit course, open only to dance majors. It is required of BS students; some BFA students take the class to satisfy their one-course requirement in teaching. Noteworthy is that many students teach at various local studios while enrolled in the class, and all BS and BFA students had some sort of studio dance teaching in their background. The course's appeal to the program's diverse student population can be best understood by its purpose, as stated on the syllabus:

> To develop students' theoretical and applied understandings of critical pedagogical concerns in dance education including teaching and learning theory, social and cultural issues in education, cultural diversity, and reflective practice.

This statement holds additional significance, as it addresses the BS program's commitment to educating socially engaged dance practitioners and "preparing students to be imaginative and innovative leaders for improving people's lives and social circumstances through dance and related professions" (Risner 2013, 58).

The Dance Pedagogy course catalog description reads: "an overview of theory and practice of dance teaching in arts education with particular foundational emphasis on social and cultural aspects of pedagogical theory in multiple settings (K12, private studio, higher education, and dance in community)." Course content is structured as nine sequential units within a 15-week semester. Assignments include summary and position papers, reflective writings, peer feedback, field observations and reports, social immersion projects, and final semester reflections. Students are encouraged to use the Pedagogical Reflection board for dialogue pertaining to readings and assignments, for peer feedback, or simply to share "aha" moments. In addition, small discussion groups (three or four students) meet after posting assignments to discuss questions and reactions about the completed unit. Formative assessment feedback by the teacher is given to students for units longer than one week. The scope of instructor feedback, peer comments, and varied course assignments supports the authors' commitment to teaching from a critical feminist pedagogical perspective: that is, a frame to help students question and challenge their assumptions and practices about teaching dance (Risner 2014).

The course structure became the gateway to designing our inquiry. To explore how students perceived issues of social foundations, we turned to students' discussion board posts and reflective writings. These writings became our data.[1] Data were obtained from a three-year period (2011–2013) in which the course was taught and, in addition to discussion posts, included reflective papers, immersion projects, and field observation reports. The demographics of the fifty-seven enrolled students were 84 percent female and 16 percent male; 75 percent white and 25 percent African American. Data were mined to discover emergent exemplar and divergent themes pertaining to attitudes in relation to social foundations. Analyzing the data in this manner became our springboard to examine multiple and sometimes contradictory dimensions within students' beliefs and attitudes.

Writing assignments, especially reflective papers, provided students with opportunities to make sense of their experiences, establish what was important to them, and explore connections to their beliefs about pedagogy. Having such an investigative platform available to students made their writings an abundant and rich resource. In this article, we offer our findings "to give readers an opportunity to reflect, to pay attention to what they might otherwise miss in their own teaching settings" (Green and Stinson 1999, 104) rather than to prescribe any particular assignment.

BACKGROUND

The following overview provides a summary of integral areas of study employed in the course. Although separately presented, the interplay of theoretical areas throughout the course must be emphasized. The background contextualizes the focus and scope of intellectual thought in relationship to students' ongoing query of: What kind of teacher do I want to become? What does it mean to be responsible for someone else's learning?

Social Foundations

The field of social foundations examines the complex relationship between education and culture and unrecognized ways dominant society impacts education. Scholars and theorists explore the structures within educational institutions to better understand the philosophies, politics, and practices and their impact on teaching and learning (Lewis 2013). With a praxis orientation of theory and practice, teachers are provided with investigative spaces to both identify culture–education relationships and attempt to understand why, especially why things are the way they are. By engaging in such a humanistic inquiry, uncovered realizations can reveal tensions and problems that might seem insurmountable. Yet, as Sharon Welch (1999) asserts, "We need a sense of self and community fluid enough to learn from and with difference and mistakes" (cited in Risner and Stinson 2010, 9) to imagine the world in new ways.

To realize such transformative learning, instruction and content must extend beyond the classroom. This perspective recognizes the impact of the broader culture and sociocultural realities on learning. Integrating social foundations in teacher preparation courses through critical feminist pedagogies supports and informs the construction of this perspective. By bringing the "hidden curriculum" (Stinson 2005) to light, teacher candidates "are exposed to and to grapple with counterintuitive and counternormative ways of thinking about and engaging with our educational system" (Butin 2005, 215). A classroom filled with young students energetically rapping and interacting with each other is not necessarily a sign of chaos or disrespect. Yet, it is precisely because reactions to such behavior can be counterintuitive to learning that studying social foundations becomes fundamental to teacher preparation (Butin 2005; Risner and Stinson 2010; Lewis 2013).

As commonly accepted traditions and taken-for-granted assumptions come into question, students discover incongruities within their own educational histories. Examining inconsistencies can give rise to meaningful teaching and learning moments, leading to pertinent questions about why. For instance, probing dominant assumptions of often-held beliefs about a good dancer's specific body type conflicts with the premise that all children can dance and engage in the art form's intrinsic merits. As a course of study, social foundations provides a frame to better understand why such an assumption is part of embedded inequities, values, and complexities of educational institutions. When expanding awareness of social issues, the frame also offers students necessary spaces to probe their own attitudes in relation to socioeconomic structures in education, including values as teachers and citizens of society.

Critical and Feminist Pedagogies

Critical pedagogy finds its roots within the thinking of Brazilian philosopher and educator Paulo Freire. His ideas challenge "the banking concept of education in which the scope of action allowed to the students extends only as far as receiving, filling, and storing the deposits" (Freire 1970/2006, 155). The critique underscores a basic premise within critical pedagogy that knowledge is not discovered facts, but rather a process, socially constructed (Ottey 1996; McLaren 2009). To pedagogically enter into this premise, responsibilities for students and teachers must come into play, each party becoming "an active participant, not a passive consumer," offering "a way of thinking about pedagogy which emphasize[s] wholeness, a union of mind, body and spirit" (hooks 1998/2006, 137).

As a field of studies, critical pedagogy is a transformative and democratic pedagogy, committed to teaching in ways that seek to provide all people equal access to educational opportunities. Underlying principles serve to unmask the ways in which race, class, gender, ethnicity, and sexual orientation create inequalities in educational structures, and taken-for-granted assumptions are examined to demystify inequities within educational structures. Sadly, the imbalance of equal access, ranging from curriculum and classroom environment to instructional methods and assessment, is quite real with significant consequences (Stinson 1991, 2005, 2010; Risner 2010b). With this backdrop, critical pedagogy can be understood as a perspective about education, an approach to theories and practices of education serving as a "tool that connects the student, teacher, and content in a way that transforms the learning process into one that develops active participation in democracy" (Shor 1992, cited in Ottey 1996, 32). Darder, Baltodano, and Torres (2009) confirm this perspective in discussing critical pedagogy as "a culture of schooling that supports the empowerment of culturally marginalized and economically disenfranchised students" (9).

The tenet of hegemony holds particular relevance in critical feminist pedagogues' commitment to transforming undemocratic educational settings. When teachers interrogate their hegemonic beliefs, they are also acknowledging "responsibility to critique and transform . . . classroom relationships" (Darder, Baltodano, and Torres 2009, 12). The principle becomes increasingly germane to dance teacher preparation when examining pedagogical practices stemming from "traditions, practices, or beliefs . . . no longer serving us within the discipline," which, in turn, leads to questioning if "previous models are either flawed or not keeping pace with the changing needs of education and the world at large" (Musil 2010, 111). The critique underscores why dance educators can no longer afford to "ignore the important question: 'Why is this knowledge being taught in the first place?'" (McLaren 2009, 62).

Addressing questions of why invites a careful look at the relationship between the learner and content. Central to critical feminist pedagogies, especially in its concepts of empowerment, leadership, and community, is the primacy of the individual learner (Shrewsbury 1997; Stinson 1998). Locating the focal point of learning within the student, a teaching–learning paradigm emerges that invites each student to engage in learning as a "whole person with a complex social/cultural/dancerly identity . . . to experience the ways in which values, meaning, and personal histories closely relate to physicality" (Dyer 2009, 227). A democratic feminist pedagogy further supports this approach to learning through an environment that actively honors diversity of experience, culture, and personal identity (Stinson 1991, 1998; Shapiro 1998; Dyer 2009; Musil 2010; Burnidge 2012). This is a pronounced shift from traditional pedagogy "with the teacher as narrator" (Freire 1970/2006, 155) to a feminist pedagogy in which the teacher

> [i]s above all a role model of a leader. S/he has helped members of the class develop a community, a sense of shared purpose, a set of skills for accomplishing that purpose, and the leadership skills so that teacher and students may jointly proceed on those tasks. (Shrewsbury 1997, 172)

Shifting toward a feminist pedagogy encourages teaching to be a shared responsibility between instructor and student, remediating previously taken-for-granted relationships based on authority. When teaching becomes a mutual responsibility of power, the potential for students to find empowerment is heightened (Shrewsbury 1997). For dancers studying pedagogy, feelings of empowerment can initially be disconcerting. Age-old adages like "Teach as I was taught" and "Leave your emotions at the studio door" surface and become a competing narrative with new perspectives about teaching. Critiquing the first adage leads students to constructively examine idolized teachers on whom they have chosen to model, or model unwittingly due to the hegemonic nature of authoritarian dance pedagogy. Employing a critical feminist social foundations lens to see one's teachers or to question the role of emotions in one's learning intensifies the critique. The examination also invites students to question their own place of privilege in relation to educational inequities. Pedagogy becomes personal, the journey of getting to know oneself sometimes feeling like an emotional roller coaster ride. Students find themselves critically examining, perhaps for the first time, the relationship between one's dancer self, teacher self, and teacher-of-others self.

Sherry Shapiro (2008) recalls ways in which the art form of dance has historically tended to embrace difference as a way to celebrate the human condition. She challenges dance educators to build on this history while educating the next generation:

> Any act of education is an act of transcendence that reminds us that education, any education, must engage our students in all of their different narratives—narratives that are shaped by ethnicity, harnessed by social class, and textured by culture. (266)

Shapiro's challenge can also remind students and their teachers that to ask "Why am I doing this?" can be a stepping stone to further interrogate: What kind of teacher do I want to become? What does it mean to be responsible for someone else's learning?

WEAVING SOCIAL FOUNDATIONS THROUGH DANCE PEDAGOGY

The following section provides examples from two units integrating social foundations content. The units served as theoretical underpinnings while establishing the backdrop for weaving issues of social foundations throughout the course. Each unit is described in terms of its scope, purpose, and assignments. Student writings, the primary data of this research, are discussed in relation to each unit's content as a means to highlight students' attitudes and illustrate ways of integrating social foundations into teacher preparation.

Although units are discussed as distinct entities, the course is structured in a helical spiral, allowing course content to unfold while illuminating potential connections students can forge in thought and action between units. In addition, with each recurrence of core theoretical ideas, students grapple with learned concepts in a more informed way. We share the insights gained from examining the challenges, reflections, and experiences of the students. These insights are as much about the values as they are the complexities of integrating social foundations and critical feminist pedagogies into teacher preparation courses.

Social Foundations of Education[2]

Social foundations of education are introduced in a three-week unit presented in two parts: The first part investigates societal frameworks of politics, economics, class, race, ethnicity, and culture that influence education; part two examines these issues as a reflection of American culture-at-large. Assignments for both parts adhere to a key tenet within social foundations: Schools and the kind of schooling a student receives can often reproduce privilege and inequity of the larger culture. For one assignment, students choose one of the required readings and articulate that author's perspective of education and problems and solutions presented in the essay. They are also asked: If you could talk with this author, what questions would you have for her or him? These prompts encourage students to engage with the author's ideas and to use their personal experiences to further examine the potential value of those ideas.

The example we present here focused on race and privilege, which served as an entrée into social foundations theory. Student reflections were in response to instructor prompts connected to the assigned reading, Peggy McIntosh's (1990/2006) essay, "White Privilege: Unpacking the Invisible Knapsack." These included the following:

1. Choose an example of white privilege described in the reading to which you can relate. Discuss why you selected this example and describe your insights.
2. What did you find difficult to understand from your own experience? Describe why.
3. Can you identify "invisible racism and prejudice" in your world today? If yes, describe; if no, does that mean it doesn't exist? Explain.

An analysis of the assignment's posts revealed that the notion of privilege was as often about students reflecting on privilege as an abstract concept as it was how the realities of privilege impacted their daily lives. The largest number of responses (43%) highlighted this group of students' newly found awareness about "white privilege" as described by McIntosh. Over a third of the student responses (35%) recognized its existence, whereas nearly a quarter (22%) took issue with McIntosh's essay.

Responses expressing a newfound awareness also revealed an element of surprise about the very real possibility of people receiving privilege due to racial and gender identification:

> *Robert:*[3] I had to put myself in the shoes of another in order to realize the level of difference there still is in racial advantages.
> *Abbey:* I never realized how much my ethnicity is not held against me. I never have to worry if people will think ill of my entire race for the way that I act.
> *Deborah:* I grew up in these white schools, in white suburbs hearing all about white people problems. And then I would come home and flip on the TV and the majority of people on television were attractive white people. This really shaped my world into this tight closed little community without a lot of deviation.

The voices of African American students dominated responses, although not exclusive of white students, that recognized the existence of white privilege. Reflections from both races included some sense of personal involvement:

> *Talia:* I believe the issue is more understood by those who do not reap from the benefits of privilege. Those who receive privileges are sometimes blind to the benefits and they view the benefits as being deserved and earned, instead of unearned.
> *Serena:* Some whites have become so accustomed to [privilege] that they think it is neutral. It takes a very sophisticated person with strong metacognition to acknowledge that their ethnic group has been a beneficiary of unearned privilege.
> *Annika:* How is it that someone that was not born and raised in this county can come here and have better advantage in life then me, [an African American woman], and my children?
> *Karen:* [A]ll these barriers need to be broken down. There should be no differences in privileges. It's our fault that there are barriers.
> *Jasmine:* Why has there not been a consistent daily effort to find a solution to this problem? Why can't we focus on daily research of legislation that can improve disadvantages for those in need [minorities]?
> *Louis:* I already know when I audition with the white male dancers who [are] going to make it in the piece. I feel the white male dancers don't have to work as hard to get noticed by a teacher.

Students who took issue with McIntosh's essay were exclusively white. The sense of personal identity was equally pronounced in their responses:

> *Rhys:* This close-minded and harsh speaking of 'white privilege' is horrendous. This article is simply outdated and the mentality of McIntosh is sickening.
> *Kelly:* To say that I am privileged specifically because I am white is equal to saying that I would be less privileged if I was not white. Either way, an assumption has been made with a disregard to any other information about a person. There are plenty of unprivileged white people, as well as privileged whites.
> *Rose:* Assuming that I have more money than a black man or woman is no better than saying I'm the racist or I have the advantage, because I don't.
> *Marlena:* The idea that, 'we are taught not to see white or gender privileges' is a line of crap! . . . Current law makes it illegal to discriminate against a person because of the color of their skin. I don't believe that I get more advantages in life over a person of color. In fact, in some places, it is quite the opposite.

When looking at the three response categories (newly found awareness, recognition of white privilege, denial of white privilege) as a whole, we can view the emotional range of responses through Milton Bennett's (1993) model of intercultural sensitivity that establishes a continuum defined by two polarities. The model also highlights responses overlapping categories along the continuum. Within this assignment, the emotionally charged statements of taking issue and recognizing the existence of white privilege illustrate the continuum's endpoints. Responses falling within two categories were typically found when students included their families and upbringings in their reflections about their awareness of privilege:

> *Erin:* I have not necessarily thought too much about white privilege ... people even in my own family have participated in this negative racial stereotyping.
> *Tinley:* These topics ... were readily discussed in my household, but I was also conditioned never to expect anyone to really understand, let alone actually address in a class.
> *Shauna:* I went to school with majority of blacks and I was popular. I always had to work hard because I strive[d] to be the best. I have experienced [what] I call favor/privileges given to another person, but I cannot call any personally.
> *Thomas:* I was entirely oblivious to my own ignorance as was nearly everyone else in the community. It was an eye-opening experience coming to [college] and learning about all of these different cultures that I had never seen or even heard about before .... Maybe I am simply part of the problem.

The attitudes that students had once accepted were now being interrogated as incongruities were being uncovered. Student narratives were as much about perceptions of themselves as their perceptions of how the world works. For those reflecting on privilege in relation to their own histories, connections between social foundations and education became more pronounced. Yet, this was the students' entry-level experience with social foundations. Issues that McIntosh and others raised would be revisited, not to force a change in anyone's attitude, but to encourage students to remediate their attitudes and to connect those beliefs to their developing personal pedagogy.

Critical and Feminist Pedagogies[4]

In this two-week unit, students examined critical and feminist pedagogy, focusing on feminist theory's emphasis on gender. Here, assignments shifted from summary writing to position statements in which students make informed and articulate responses to readings, including asking critical questions about an author's argument and rationale, offering examples from personal experiences, and providing reasoned positions of their own. The course's overarching questions (What kind of teacher do I want to become? What does it mean to be responsible for someone else's learning?) gained relevance in this unit as past dance experiences became more central to their investigations. Guidelines for the final assignment were to consider what they learned throughout the unit, using Sue Stinson's (2005) "The Hidden Curriculum of Gender in Dance Education" to reflect on stereotypes and unspoken messages about gender, race, and other issues that are too often implicitly taught in the dance class. In addition, the assignment openly invited students to include their histories, as dancers and teachers, in their narratives.

Within the submitted assignments, 42.5 percent demonstrated a matter-of-fact attitude in recognizing the significance of critical feminist pedagogy to their development as teachers. Over a third of the responses (37.5%) expressed an active curiosity to continue exploring possibilities within this pedagogical frame, and 20 percent primarily focused on competing narratives that unfolded for them during this unit's studies.

The following exemplifies those narratives expressing recognition and value of critical feminist pedagogies through this unit's learning:

> *Shauna:* I learned the limits in education of banking method transmission theory education. This method of teaching limits the freedom in learning.
> *Heidi:* Realizing gender stereotypes and doing [our] part to change them is not only important to our own teaching but to the lives of our students and their futures.
> *Deborah:* The hidden curriculum concept really blew my mind. We are teaching about gender whether or not we intend to. I just realized that I talk to my little girls in class in a much different way than I do my [older] girls.
> *Christian:* Giroux had me questioning ... how my [high school] teachers went about their own lessons and rules. Stinson ... had me evaluating my own self as a teacher, though teacher of dance, and questioning how rigid or flexible [I am].
> *Steven:* [T]he classroom is more a 'machine' than I thought, controlling what we learn and how we learn it ... I had just assumed that [critical feminist pedagogy] was pedagogy that reflected the ideas of women, but I am starting to understand how critical these theories are.

Students who wanted to probe teaching possibilities within critical feminist pedagogies reflected:

> *Clare:* I always knew that many, if not most of these issues ... existed, but never really asked so deeply into 'why' they existed. I am now much more aware of asking my own questions.
> *Marlena:* I need to be more open when I teach, to question my experiences and think about how I apply my values in the classroom as a teacher.
> *Erin:* I want to change these [negative pop culture] images to be able to help other girls and boys become aware of these issues ... I am interested [in] asking questions that will help me continue to mold my own pedagogy.

The self-reflexivity in the preceding statements can be readily aligned with tenets of critical feminist pedagogies. Their statements are also antithetical to authoritarian and methods-based instruction that most of these students experienced at some point in their childhood education and dance training. Such competing narratives are exemplified in the following statements:

> Christian: I have been coined the 'fun teacher,' because I do allow students to talk to me, and keep my classroom a bit more casual. I'm not sure if that is a pedagogic method, or more or less my keeping business in the studio, therefore generating myself a job.
>
> Catherine: We are always taught to be quiet and take direction, but I wonder how can we promote discipline without being authoritarians as teachers?
>
> Jasmine: I have, however, always tried to prepare my students for the American social culture by teaching dance etiquette in the classroom but I am now questioning those methods due to the fear of preparing them for the methods of the banking system . . . Yikes!

The presence of competing sensibilities within each statement is not surprising. Many students had reached their current level of dance expertise through methods-based training in private studios and were continuing that tradition as they taught in some of those same studios. In wrestling with different pedagogic perspectives, students looked for prescriptive methods of teaching within a critical feminist frame. This search for answers was especially evident in two groups: one wanting to explore feminist pedagogies further and the other focusing on competing narratives. Quandaries were voiced in students' reflective narratives as well as in comments to peers:

> Clare: (Reflection) I have found that many of the writers within this unit have approached sharing their perspectives through various angles and suggestions rather than a mere problem-solution.
>
> Jasmine: (Comment to Clare) [T]he authors shared their perspective but didn't give more suggestions on how to apply the techniques discussed to the classroom.
>
> Heidi: (Reflection) [Gender oppression] makes it difficult for women later in life to develop a voice and sense of personal identity as they spent so many years striving to fit the mold created by their dance teachers, studios, and peers.
>
> Sophie: (Comment to Heidi) I was in very strict dance classes when I was younger and there [were] only girls. I have never thought about how this may have affected me, or how I conduct myself today.

All responses, as with the Social Foundations unit, overlapped thematically. But now, the presence of all three categories within individual reflections was also in play. This vacillation of categories highlights a "disequilibrium of . . . assumptions of the world and each other . . . reveal[ing] certain political, social, and cultural contradictions" (Smith 2013, 127). For example, students' questioning of taken-for-granted assumptions underscored contradictions between their genuine feelings about favorite teachers from their early dance training–"caring, dedicated nurturing, generous"–and the trappings of the traditional technique class–"discipline, getting it right, being perfect."[5]

To some extent and to varying degrees, students' posts reflected their growing sensitivity to the complexities of teaching from a social foundations and critical feminist pedagogical perspective. Narratives also revealed ways dance had positively impacted their lives. Students wanted to share their joy and empowerment through dancing as much as the discipline and skills they had learned from their teachers. Each in their own way recognized that there were no, as Abbey states, "blatant solutions." She further comments:

> Sometimes it is easy to look at these problems and think there is no hope but if we intellectually and physically investigate the root causes, we can take a stand and move the world toward a better, more harmonious future.

DISCUSSION

Studying issues of social foundations is to confront one's assumptions and values. It also provokes being uncomfortable because accepted norms are called into question. Deborah hints at her discomfort when acknowledging how the "hidden curriculum concept really blew my mind" and asking if "there is a fine balance between stamping out gender roles and losing all identity with some sort of gender?" The importance of such self-reflexivity is confirmed by Ann Dils (2007) through her query regarding social foundations and dance education:

> [M]otion is a means of reshaping who we are, how we are represented, and the meanings those representations hold for others is central. . . . Might these ideas be useful to deliberations about the educational worth of dancing as it is enacted in schools? (110–11)

The tensions between each student's awareness of sociocultural issues and previously unquestioned traditions were poignant. For these students, ownership of their attitudes became a frame to interrogate identities and unfolding personal pedagogies. Michelle Knight-Diop and Heather Oesterreich (2009) confirm the importance of feelings and emotions "as sites of knowledge to create cultural rules of interactions that promote and/or hinder [their] preparation as teachers" (2679). This was surely the case for Louis when coming to grips with believing that he was always seen through a racial lens, or Rose feeling annoyed about others' expectations that she relate to perspectives beyond her own.

Numerous incongruities surfaced as students tried to make sense of their educational histories and evolving professional identities. Christian spoke to this tension in thinking about feminist pedagogy in connection to his private studio teaching situation: "I almost hate myself for saying this, but no studio and no parent would allow for an uncontrolled, potentially dangerous, environment." Although aware of this potential tension, Abbey focused on being empowered when teaching from a social foundations feminist teaching perspective, as it is "more about what kinds of people you are teaching students to become, rather than the actual subject matter."

Students continually grappled with differences between identities of dancer selves and teacher selves. However, their excitement about a critically reflexive praxis did not erase the genuine concerns about tossing away the authoritative discipline that was so essential to their dance training. These concerns raised other questions, often about the very purpose of dance education. Elise wondered, if "very young dancers . . . accustomed to creative dance . . . may not be able to grow as an adult dancer if their basis of dance . . . is . . . creative dance." Dawn Clark (1994) recognizes such potential conflicts for emerging teachers when addressing persistent tensions between the educator and performer aspects within an educator's professional life. Her questions of: "'Who am I?' as an educator," and "'Where do I fit?'" (122) could have as easily been posed by the pedagogy students. Studying social foundations and critical feminist pedagogies provided students a platform to develop a personal pedagogy, to create a balance between personal and professional values. It was a beginning.

CONCLUSION

We began this article by acknowledging that today's dance teachers enter a profession filled with multiple challenges and diverse student populations. Social issues of class, race, ethnicity, gender, and sexuality are shifting the educational landscape, as well as attitudes about effective and meaningful pedagogy. Informed primarily by *what* to teach and *how* most efficiently to teach and test it, traditional teacher preparation fails to meet the needs of future dance teachers and students of dance. Traditional methods-based teacher preparation too easily duplicates an understanding of the world that is no longer accurate or relevant. Erica McWilliam (2005) cautioned a decade ago, "By re-enacting such pedagogical habits, we make a culture of teaching and learning that parallels a predictable and regular social world" (1). That today's world is neither predictable nor homogenous reinforces the need for teachers to develop pedagogies that consider and then challenge *why* things are the way they are.

Students in this inquiry explored pedagogical possibilities in an undergraduate course employing critical feminist approaches integrated within an introduction to social foundations of education. Student writings and reflections frequently focused on heightened awareness of self, highlighting their teacher selves but without acknowledgment of the learner in the educational environment. Some students recognized their privilege; however, they also stayed within their own comfortable world of experience, unable to discern the marginalization of others that unearned privilege produces and maintains. Yet, other students strongly advocated for change. Several students expressed surprise about the existence of inequities within educational settings, whereas others voiced concern about their own educational histories. In sum, the range of student responses only amplifies the challenges of, and the need for, the inclusion of social foundations in teacher preparation.

We conclude by returning to the two fundamental questions the students contemplated throughout the semester: What kind of teacher do I want to become? What does it mean to be responsible for someone else's learning? There was no expectation that students would reach conclusive answers by the end of the semester. Like one's evolving pedagogy, answering these questions is a life-long endeavor. To bring this inquiry to a close, we share a few end-of-semester student reflections.

Annika suggested, "I believe as teachers we sometimes get lost in how important we are and who is looking to us for inspiration." Sophie reflected on teacher responsibility and creating community: "We can never walk in someone else's shoes. But, we can share our experiences, feel others, and create a sense of community among one another." She concluded, "This course has made me realize how much responsibility a teacher has." Louis noted the recurring *why* factor, and that all teachers should possess the ability "to understand their environment, the conditions in which their students live, and how to challenge students, engage their learning styles in a way that is not demeaning but empowering."

Karen reflected on her learning and role as a dance educator: "Each reading taught me a little bit more about myself. I did not necessarily agree with everything I read but like we learned in [this course]," she contended, "sometimes it is okay to get angry, at least you know you are thinking. I am not simply a dance instructor." Cecily spoke about empowerment: "I want to guide young girls on a positive path that will help them find confidence and security in themselves. I don't want to let my students down." Advocating cooperation rather than competition, Erin stated, "We need to teach children how to learn to assist others and cooperate with one another, because it is an important life skill, more important, in my opinion, than competing to be on top." Thomas suggested, "It is crucial to teach children to be more accepting and compassionate." Later he implored, "The effects we [teachers] have on children today can have immense repercussions tomorrow–to understand the power behind shaping young minds–we need to pay special attention."

The knowledge gained through social foundations alone will not eliminate the challenges that teachers encounter when entering today's classroom doors. Yet, exploring social foundations can provide students with a critical lens to begin considering their personal pedagogy in relation to the broader culture. We hope this discussion continues to invigorate conversations about pedagogy to best prepare future generations of dance teachers.

NOTES

1. Institutional review board approval was obtained for use of student writing in this research.
2. For Unit Two readings see Asher (2006); Belenky et al. (2006); Gray (2006); Loewen (2006); McIntosh (1990/2006); Spring (2006); Risner (2005); and Wood (2006). For videos, see *Killing Us Softly 4:*

Advertising's Image of Women (2010); *People Like Us: Social Class in America* (2001); and *What a Girl Wants: How the Media Diminishes the Value of Young Women* (2001).
3. All student names are pseudonyms to protect privacy.
4. For Unit Three readings, see Freire (1970/2006); hooks (1998/2006); Risner (2007); Shapiro (1998); and Stinson (1998, 2005). For videos, see *Generation M—Misogyny in Media & Culture* (2008), and *Tough Guise: Violence, Media, and the Crisis in Masculinity* (1999).
5. In Unit One, students were asked to identify their favorite teachers. These descriptors come from those discussions.

REFERENCES

Antilla, E. 2008. Dialogical pedagogy, embodied knowledge, and meaningful learning. In *Dance in a world of change*, ed. S. Shapiro, 159–79. Champaign, IL: Human Kinetics.

Asher, T. 2006. Girls, sexuality and popular culture. In *The institution of education*, ed. H. S. Shapiro, K. Latham, and S. Ross. Fifth edition, 305–08. Boston: Pearson.

Belenky, M., B. Clinchy, N. Goldberger, and J. Tarule. 2006. Connected teaching. In *The institution of education*, ed. H. S. Shapiro, K. Latham and S. Ross. Fifth edition, 125–35. Boston: Pearson.

Bennett, M. J. 1993. Towards ethnorelativism: A developmental model of intercultural sensitivity. In *Education for the intercultural experience*, ed. M. Paige, 21–71. Yarmouth, ME: Intercultural Press.

Burnidge, A. 2012. Somatics in the dance studio: Embodying feminist/democratic pedagogy. *Journal of Dance Education* 12(2):37–53.

Butin, D. 2005. Guest editor introduction: How social foundations of education matters to teacher preparation: A policy brief. *Educational Studies: A Journal of the American Educational Studies Association* 38(3):214–29.

Clark, D. 1994. Voices of women dance educators: Considering issues of hegemony and the educator/performer identity. *Impulse* 2(2):122–30.

Darder, A., M. Baltodano, and R. Torres. 2009. Critical pedagogy: An introduction. In *The critical pedagogy reader*, ed. A. Darder, M. Baltodano, and R. Torres. Second edition, 1–20. New York: Routledge.

Dils, A. 2007. Social history and dance as education. In *International handbook of research in arts education*, ed. L. Bresler, 103–12. New York: Springer.

Dyer, B. 2009. Finding self, honoring learners: Sociopolitical reflections on the teaching of American contemporary dance technique and theory. In *Dance: Current selected research*, vol. 7, ed. L. Y. Overby and B. Lepczyk, 223–67. New York: AMS Press.

Freire, P. 1970/2006. Excerpt from *Pedagogy of the oppressed*. In *The institution of education*, ed. H. Shapiro, K. Latham, and S. Ross. Fifth edition, 155–62. Boston: Pearson.

Generation M—Misogyny in Media & Culture. 2008. Produced and directed by Thomas Keith, DVD. Northampton, MA: Media Education Foundation.

Gray, E. 2006. The culture of separated desks. In *The institution of education*, ed. H. S. Shapiro, K. Latham, and S. Ross. Fifth edition, 273–79. Boston: Pearson.

Green, J., and S. W. Stinson. 1999. Postpositivist research in dance. In *Researching dance*, ed. S. H. Fraleigh and P. Hanstein, 91–123. Pittsburgh, PA: University of Pittsburgh Press.

hooks, b. 1998/2006. Engaged pedagogy. In *The institution of education*, ed. H. S. Shapiro, K. Latham, and S. Ross. Fifth edition, 137–41. Boston: Pearson.

Killing Us Softly 4: Advertising's Image of Women. 2010. Produced and directed by Sut Jhally, DVD. Northampton, MA: Media Education Foundation.

Knight-Diop, M., and H. Oesterreich. 2009. Pedagogical possibilities: Engaging cultural rules of emotion. *Teachers College Record* 111(11):2678–704.

Lewis, J. 2013. New challenges, new vision: Why social foundations and teacher education partnerships matter. *Educational Studies: A Journal of the American Educational Studies Association* 49(2):169–82.

Loewen, J. 2006. The land of opportunity. In *The institution of education*, ed. H. S. Shapiro, K. Latham, and S. Ross. Fifth edition, 193–201. Boston: Pearson.

McIntosh, P. 1990/2006. White privilege: Unpacking the invisible knapsack. In *The institution of education*, ed. H. Shapiro, K. Latham, and S. Ross. Fifth edition, 239–42. Boston: Pearson.

McLaren, P. 2009. Critical pedagogy: A look at the major concepts. In *The critical pedagogy reader*, ed. A. Darder, M. Baltodano, and R. Torres. Second edition, 61–83. New York: Routledge.

McWilliam, E. 2005. Unlearning pedagogy. *Journal of Learning Design* 1(1):1–11.

Musil, P. 2010. Perspectives on an expansive postsecondary dance. *Journal of Dance Education* 10(4):111–21.

Ottey, S. 1996. Critical pedagogical theory and the dance educator. *Arts Education Policy Review* 98(2):31–9.

People Like Us: Social Class in America. 2001. Produced and directed by Andrew Kolker and Louis Alvarez, DVD. Washington, DC: The Center for New American Media.

Risner, D. 2005. What Matthew Shepard would tell us: Gay and lesbian issues in education. In *Critical social issues in education: Democracy and meaning in a globalizing world*, ed. H. S. Shapiro, 237–249. Boston: Lawrence Erlbaum.

———. 2007. Rehearsing masculinity: Challenging the "boy code" in dance education. *Research in Dance Education* 8(2):139–53.

———. 2010a. Challenges and opportunities for dance pedagogy: Critical social issues and "unlearning" how to teach. In *Global perspectives on dance: Research and pedagogy, Conference proceedings of the Congress on Research in Dance*, ed. T. Randall, 204–09. Cambridge, MA: Congress on Research in Dance.

———. 2010b. Dance education matters: Rebuilding postsecondary dance education for twenty-first century relevance and resonance. *Journal of Dance Education* 10(4):95–110.

———. 2013. Curriculum revision in practice: Designing a liberal arts degree in dance professions. *Journal of Dance Education* 13(2):56–60.

———. 2014. Hold on to this! Strategies for teacher feedback in online dance courses. *Journal of Dance Education* 14(2):52–58.

Risner, D., and S. W. Stinson. 2010. Moving social justice: Challenges, fears and possibilities in dance education. *International Journal of Education & the Arts* 11(6):1–26. http://www.ijea.org/v11n6/ (accessed February 24, 2014).

Shapiro, S. B. 1998. Toward transformative teachers: Critical and feminist perspectives in dance education. In *Dance, power, and difference*, ed. S. Shapiro, 7–21. Champaign, IL: Human Kinetics.

———. 2008. Dance in a world of change: A vision for global aesthetics and universal ethics. In *Dance in a world of change*, ed. S. Shapiro, 253–72. Champaign, IL: Human Kinetics.

Shor, I. 1992. *Empowering education: Critical teaching for social change*. Chicago: University of Chicago Press.

Shrewsbury, C. 1997. What is feminist pedagogy? *Women's Studies Quarterly* 25(1/2):166–73.

Smith, K. 2013. Covert critique: Critical pedagogy "under the radar" in a suburban middle school. *International Journal of Critical Pedagogy* 4(2):127–46.

Spring, J. 2006. Thinking critically about history: Ideological management, culture wars, and consumerism. In *The institution of education*, ed. H. S. Shapiro, K. Latham, and S. Ross. Fifth edition, 73–78. Boston: Pearson.

Stinson, S. W. 1991. Reflections on teacher education in dance. *Design for Arts in Education* 92(3):23–30.

———. 1998. Seeking a feminist pedagogy for children's dance. In *Dance, power, and difference*, ed. S. Shapiro, 23–47. Champaign, IL: Human Kinetics.

———. 2005. The hidden curriculum of gender in dance education. *Journal of Dance Education* 5(2):51–7.

———. 2010. Questioning our past and building a future. *Journal of Dance Education* 10(4):136–44.

Tough Guise: Violence, Media, and the Crisis in Masculinity. 1999. Produced and directed by Sut Jhally, DVD. Northampton, MA: Media Education Foundation.

Welch, S. 1999. *Sweet dreams in America: Making ethics and spirituality work*. New York: Routledge.

What a Girl Wants: How the Media Diminishes the Value of Young Women. 2001. Produced by Elizabeth Massie, directed by Matthew Buzzell, DVD. Northampton, MA: Media Education Foundation.

Wood, G. 2006. Can we have schools that work? In *The institution of education*, ed. H. S. Shapiro, K. Latham, and S. Ross. Fifth edition, 21–7. Boston: Pearson.

intent of this article. However, a study of this kind in the future could provide important quantitative data on teacher preparation curricula in dance education. Although the ability to widely generalize findings from the present study to the larger population is limited, we believe these findings may be helpful to others incorporating, or contemplating the integration of, social foundations into arts pedagogy and curriculum.

BACKGROUND

Beginning with social foundations, moving to critical pedagogies, and then concluding with their translations to dance education and teacher preparation, we provide an overview of each field as it has developed in the United States. These summaries are not exhaustive; rather, for the purposes of this article, we focus on historical and contemporary context, current research, and current applications to dance teacher preparation. Readers from the fields of music, theater, and visual arts education are encouraged to contemplate these developments in terms of their own contexts, values, and commitments for teacher education and preparation.

Social Foundations of Education

The National Center for Education Statistics (2010) defines the field of social and philosophical foundations of education as:

> A program that focuses on the systematic study of education as a social and cultural institution, and the educational process as an object of humanistic inquiry. Includes instruction in such subjects as the philosophy of education, history of education, educational literature, educational anthropology, sociology of education, economics and politics of education, educational policy studies, and studies of education in relation to specific populations, issues, social phenomena, and types of work. (Classification of Instructional Programs [CIP] Code 13.091)

The field of social foundations first emerged at Teachers College Columbia University in the 1930s. There, educators "stressed the role of the school, allied with other progressive forces, in planning for an intelligent reconstruction of US society where there would be a more just and equitable distribution of the nation's wealth and the 'common good' would take precedence over individual gain" (Liston and Zeichner 1991, qtd. in Swain 2013, 124). The expectation was that student teachers "were to consider, engage, and contribute to the reformation of social injustices. In short, teachers were to be actively responsible for shaping a collective future" (Swain 2013, 124). Within this approach, social foundations courses at Teachers College, as well as teacher preparation courses throughout the country today, frequently ask students to consider challenging questions about access, equity, fairness, privilege, oppression, and participation in a democratic society's education system. This approach of framing teacher preparation by asking education students critical questions about the sociocultural aspects of schooling has had its critics, who claim it to be "un-American both in methodology and consequences" (McCarthy 2006, 144). Then and now, social foundations educators argue that the central aim of equality in U.S. education remains grossly unmet (Johanningmeier 1991) and that "the [originators of the social foundations program at Teachers College] intended to draw upon the unique resources of each discipline to examine fundamental and urgent social problems and issues, thus promoting authentic interdisciplinary reliance and collegiality" (Warren 1998, 120).

Following World War II and through the 1970s, the critical and cross-disciplinary emphasis of social foundations programs led to the rapid development of such programs in institutions across the United States (Provenzo and Provenzo 2009), the establishment of the American Educational Studies Association in 1968, and the first published standards for social foundations programs in 1978 (Tozer and Miretsky 2000). The emergence of critical pedagogy in the late 1970s was particularly timely for social foundations theorists and educators, especially those interested in questions about power, authority, and privilege. The combination of an interdisciplinary social foundations paradigm and innovative critical pedagogical approaches resonated deeply with dance education theorists and teachers, which we discuss later in this section.

In 1983, President Reagan's National Commission on Excellence in Education published the report *A Nation at Risk: The Imperative for Educational Reform*, which "provided an indictment of U.S. education, citing high rates of adult illiteracy, declining SAT scores, and low scores on international comparisons of knowledge by American students as examples of the decline of literacy and standards" (Provenzo and Provenzo 2009). The report issued a severe critique of teachers and teacher preparation programs, leading to the widespread perception "that teacher education programs lack rigor and teachers lack adequate knowledge of the content areas they teach" (Lewis 2013, 180), impairing students' ability to "compete in the global work force" (Swain 2013, 125). Social foundations educators contended that the underlying problems of illiteracy, declining test scores, and "failing" schools were linked directly to the vast inequalities inherent in the educational system itself and the deadening effects of "teach to the test" mandates, not to teachers or teacher preparation programs (Shapiro 1984; Purpel 1985).

Twenty years later, social foundations theorists concluded that NCLB represented the culmination of the corporate-based accountability efforts initiated by *A Nation at Risk* (Novinger and O'Brien 2003; Purpel and McLaurin

2004). However, they also importantly highlighted that NCLB stressed equity, as its primary goal was eliminating the achievement gap between groups by 2014. Most recently, Lewis (2013) notes, "There has been little emphasis on the development of the cultural competency of teachers or a focus on appropriate pedagogical strategies that impact student learning"—foci that are inherent in social foundations curricula for teacher candidates (173). At the same time, required coursework in social foundations in teacher preparation programs has been marginalized (Neumann 2009), though steady articulation of its relevance continues today:

> Foundations courses are important to the preparation of culturally competent teachers because they provide prospective teachers with an understanding of educational philosophies, the politics of education and educational practices and how these impact schools, the teaching profession, and K–12 student learning. (Lewis 2013, 173)

Critical Pedagogies

Education theorist and critical pedagogue Ira Shor describes critical pedagogy as:

> Habits of thought, reading, writing, and speaking which go beneath surface meaning, first impressions, dominant myths, official pronouncements, traditional clichés, received wisdom, and mere opinions, to understand the deep meaning, root causes, social context, ideology, and personal consequences of any action, event, object, process, organization, experience, text, subject matter, policy, mass media, or discourse. (1992, 129)

Critical pedagogies as they are employed today find their roots in the liberatory philosophy and praxis-orientation of Paulo Freire ([1970] 2006) and his critique of the "banking" concept of education, "in which the scope of action allowed to the students extends only as far as receiving, filling, and storing the deposits" (155). In the banking model, "narrating teachers deposit information in the minds of passive receiving students" (Ottey 1996, 32); knowledge is assumed to be "a gift bestowed by those who consider themselves knowledgeable upon those whom they consider to know nothing" (Freire 2006, 155). As students increasingly hone their capacity to receive, store, and regurgitate information, their capacity to develop critical consciousness about the world is equally diminished (McLaren and Leonard 1993). Critical pedagogues argue that developing one's consciousness (what Freire described as "conscientization") is essential for informed praxis—engaging and repeating a helical spiral of theory, applied practice, evaluation and reflection, and informed action—in liberating education (Risner 2005). The outcome of collective praxis is social transformation (McLaren 2000).

Since the early 1980s, extensions and adaptations of critical pedagogy have proliferated in interdisciplinary forms and educational realms (Breault 2011). As hybrid critical pedagogies materialized, connections to the aims and goals of social foundations also grew (Provenzo and Provenzo 2009). While preserving a Freirean stance of critique, authority, power and social change, hybrid forms frequently shifted away from Freire's social-class emphasis to focus on race and ethnicity, gender, sexual orientation, age, ability, nationality, religion, moral and ethical issues, and political activism, among other emphases (Thiessen et al. 2013). In order "to help students develop consciousness of freedom, recognize authoritarian tendencies, and connect knowledge to power and the ability to take constructive action" (Giroux 2010), critical feminist pedagogy—informed by feminist, postcolonial, critical race, and queer theories—uniquely focuses on gender and gendered teaching.

Teaching in ways that transform students from passive recipients of information to engaged learners actively participating in constructing knowledge has been a long-held goal of critical feminist pedagogy (Currie 1992). Over three decades ago, Adrienne Rich (1979) articulated the difference between receiving an education and claiming an education: "Although receiving an education is to come into possession of; to act as receptacle or container for; to accept as authoritative or true—claiming an education is to take as rightful owner; to assert in the face of possible contradiction" (231).

Chow et al. (2003) emphasize that "the distinguishing factor" between the two forms of education "is feminist thinking's emphasis on using a gendered lens to examine social constructions of masculinity and femininity as forming a central stratifying cleavage within society" (260) that is reproduced in education and schooling (Gray 2006). While critical feminist pedagogies are diverse and vary in relation to teaching contexts and age and level of students, their underpinning concepts address the following core principles: (1) an understanding of female epistemologies and women's ways of knowing (Gilligan 1982; Belenky et al. 1986; Belenky et al. 2006); (2) a commitment to relationships of equality and shared power among learners and teachers (Lather 1991; hooks 1994; hooks 2006); (3) a recognition of the value of creating collaborative community within the classroom where all voices are heard (Gore 1993; Ladson-Billings 1994); (4) an emphasis on consciousness raising, diversity, justice, and possibility while respecting diverse personal experience and agency (Greene 1986; Ellsworth 1997; McIntosh [1990] 2006); (5) a concern for caring and student empowerment, learning, and independence as learners (Noddings 1984; Ellsworth 1992); and (6) the responsibility to challenge traditional pedagogy and its social, cultural, political, and economic inequities (Anyon 1980; Gray 2006).

Obviously, these core principles cannot be claimed exclusively by critical feminist pedagogues; as Stinson (1998b) notes, "what educator would admit to disagreement with the goal of helping students become independent learners who can work with others?" (31). However, the overall systematic commitment to incorporating these values into education—from curricula to course design to pedagogy and instruction to assessment and evaluation—is singular in its scope and ability to critically engage teacher candidates in reflective dialogue about the what, how, and why of their teaching in order "to change society by [recognizing] their power to become agents of change" (Stinson 1998b, 31). Toward these ends, critical feminist educators endeavor to nurture the abilities of students to envision a world that is "not yet" (Giroux 1988, 175), a vision that many dance educators have found increasingly resonant over the past three decades, as discussed in the following section.

Critical Feminist Pedagogies in Dance

Dance education theorist and feminist pedagogue Sherry Shapiro (1998) asserts:

> A feminist pedagogy insists that education must start from the lived experiences of our students' lives... Our bodies provide an emotional mapping of who we are and how we have been shaped by the dominant society. (9, 12)

The emergence of critical and feminist pedagogies in dance education can be traced directly to the work of dance curriculum theorist and educator Susan Stinson in the mid-1980s. Stinson, like a number of critical dance education theorists who would follow,[1] completed her doctorate in social and cultural foundations of education at the University of North Carolina at Greensboro, a program founded by David Purpel and James MacDonald in 1972. In her 1984 dissertation, "Reflections and Visions: A Hermeneutic Study of Dangers and Possibilities in Dance Education," Stinson:

> [s]earches for meaning in three areas: her personal life, her professional life as a dancer/dance educator, and herself as citizen of the world. She examines herself and her work in the same way she approaches a work of art, in order to find meaning in her experience as a dance educator [and] moves from large questions relating to the world and human existence to specific scenarios common in dance education. (Moffett 2010, 18)

From this vantage point, Stinson was the first to illuminate the emphasis of traditional dance pedagogy schools on obedience and silent conformity in which dancers reproduce what they receive, rather than critique, question, or create it. Over time this kind of environment produces passive followers rather than active leaders and may also contribute to further gender bias in dance education (Stinson, Blumenfeld-Jones, and Van Dyke 1990). Since the early 1990s, critical feminist pedagogues in dance have begun to challenge prevailing aesthetic, social, economic, and political ideologies and their subsequent social and cultural implications for dance education, especially those that relate to power and the ensuing asymmetrical relationships (Adair 1992; Van Dyke 1992; Green 1999; Green 2000).

With notions of equality as a prominent common thread, critical feminist pedagogy in dance education examines how socially embedded assumptions about gender and dominant structural power relations produce unjust educational and sociocultural outcomes (Arkin 1994; Clark 1994; Shapiro 1998; Stinson 1998a; Stinson 1998b). At the same time, multiculturalism and cultural diversity in dance have continued to receive considerable attention in critical feminist pedagogy, especially in terms of curricular inclusion and innovation (Asante 1993; Mills 1994; Mills 1997; West 2005; McCarthy-Brown 2009). Additionally, the inclusion of issues of sexual diversity, homophobia, and bullying in schools has become commonplace in critical and feminist dance pedagogy (Gard 2001; Gard 2003; Mozingo 2005; Risner 2002; Risner 2009; Risner 2014a).

Background Summary

Teacher preparation programs in dance that integrate social foundations through critical and feminist pedagogies seek to balance the importance of developing a teacher candidate's pedagogy with the methods and instructional strategies that ultimately align as closely as possible with that pedagogy. Questions rooted in larger human experience and societal situations, including those related to gendered learning and teaching, diverse learning styles, multicultural curricula, hidden curricula, socioeconomic factors, gender equity, and disparities in the educational achievement gap among ethnic and racial groups, prepare teacher candidates for the level of consciousness and intentionality that is necessary for effective and meaningful teaching in today's complex world. As Breault (2011) notes:

> The artist engaged in art as well as the teacher engaged in pedagogy becomes acutely aware of the nuances, flows, and tensions within their work so they can move closer to their images of the ideal. Thus consciousness, intentionality, refinement, and belief are critical elements in any pedagogy. Although pedagogy requires some larger ideal or set of beliefs to give it life and form, instruction does not. (634)

REVIEW OF NATIONAL STANDARDS

With the current policy landscape sketched and the background of social foundations and critical pedagogical approaches in dance teacher preparation described, we now turn our attention to relevant national standards. We recognize that teacher certification requirements vary, sometimes significantly, by state and institution. Therefore, the most effective and meaningful direction will likely come from the national level, which we present here. Three sets of standards for teacher preparation are examined, with specific emphasis on common threads of social foundations preparation for teacher candidates; two of these standards are specifically for dance education, and the third is for social foundations of education. The dance education standards include the National Association of Schools of Dance's *Standards Handbook*; the National Dance Education Organization's *Professional Teaching Standards in Dance Arts;* and the American Educational Studies Association Committee on Academic Standards and Accreditation's *Standards for Academic and Professional Instruction in Foundations of Education, Educational Studies, and Educational Policy Studies* (also known as the "Social Foundation Standards") (see Table 1).

As the sole accrediting agency for U.S. college and university dance programs, the National Association of Schools of Dance (NASD) and its standards represent the only binding national requirements for teacher preparation in dance education, addressing such matters as curricular structure, content, and time requirements. In addition to required content in dance and general academic studies, National Association of Schools of Dance accredited programs for teacher preparation should include professional education requirements equal to at least 15 to 20 percent of the entire program (eighteen to twenty-four semester credit hours), described as "those courses normally offered by the education unit that deal with philosophical and social foundations of education, educational psychology, special education, history of education, etc. Student teaching is also counted as professional education" (National Association of Schools of Dance 2013, 101).

The twofold challenge in meeting this standard for many dance education programs lies first in its reliance on the "education unit" (e.g., college of education) to require and effectively deliver this kind of coursework, which Neumann (2009) and Lewis (2013) have confirmed receives little to no emphasis in general teacher education programs today. And second, many dance education programs may not have qualified faculty to teach social foundations content, with the exception of student teacher supervision.

The praxis-incorporative approach for social foundations presented in this article finds its grounding in the goals of the NASD standards and the commonalities of the collective standards for teacher preparation. As Table 1 indicates, numerous overlapping and complementary areas of consensus emerge:

- To perceive the art form within sociocultural contexts
- To understand the significance of diversity in teaching and learning settings
- To experience learning as open dialogue for change and problem-solving
- To foster interdisciplinary awareness for meaningful critique and evaluation
- To facilitate experiential, collaborative learning through immersive experiences
- To engage in analysis through challenging inquiry and reflective praxis

When taken together, these values raise important questions about the appropriateness and effectiveness of "how-to" methods instruction for preparing teacher candidates who can critically develop and reflectively refine their pedagogy and purpose, as well as articulate the meaning of their work in an increasingly diverse, complex, and challenging world. Equating the development of teacher values to the practice of technical skills eliminates the crucial human element in teaching and learning.

INTEGRATING SOCIAL FOUNDATIONS INTO DANCE EDUCATION

In the following section, we describe one approach for integrating social foundations into dance teacher preparation, based on an undergraduate dance pedagogy course designed by Risner and taught by Barr (in 2013) and Risner (from 2009 to present) at a large, urban research university in the U.S. Midwest. As a preface, we begin with an overview of the pedagogical approaches employed and a description of the course, including its context. We then provide examples of social foundations integration in the areas of historical foundations and culture and education, including competition, individualism, and personal gain; race, ethnicity, class, and gender; and sexuality and sexual orientation. Recommendations for readers are offered throughout, as well as insights on student perspectives and responses.

Pedagogical Approaches

A critical pedagogical approach to teaching seeks to help teacher candidates expose, question, and challenge taken-for-granted assumptions and practices that limit, marginalize, and disenfranchise human agency and freedom. Education is never neutral, but instead a series of complex asymmetrical power relationships that are frequently hidden and unexamined. Feminist pedagogy expands this perspective by looking more closely at commonly held assumptions about gender in teaching and learning. Because traditional dance pedagogy schools students for obedience and emphasizes conformity, critical feminist pedagogy in dance positions gender as a conscious variable in all aspects of dance education and validates and affirms individual differences in gender, ethnicity, and culture.

TABLE 1
Undergraduate Teacher Preparation in Dance and Social Foundations, Relevant Standards Summary

	National Association of Schools of Dance[a]	Professional Teaching Standards in Dance Arts[b]	Social Foundations Standards[c]
Content requirement/description	Professional education shall comprise 15–20% of program: 18–24 credit hours in philosophical and social foundations of education, educational psychology, special education, and history of education. Student teaching is also counted as professional education. (101)	By promoting student growth through the study of dance, accomplished teachers not only introduce students to movement/performance skills, diverse subjects, and cultural issues, but also introduce them to ways of seeing dance within and across social, historical, and political contexts. (8)	Professional preparation shall include at least one course, preferably two or more, in the social foundations: philosophy, history, and sociology of education; education theory; social and cultural foundations; and policy studies. (110)
General characteristics	• Ability to teach effectively in a variety of settings • In-depth focus on educational philosophies and theories • Ability to communicate with learners of diverse backgrounds and cultures • Ability to adjust teaching styles to the needs of learners (102)	• Capitalize on individual student backgrounds by analyzing how people and cultures provide stimuli or inspiration to create dance (10) • Establish environments that encourage and support creative thought and expression, critical analysis, questions, reflective decision-making, and experimentation (15)	• Understand the full significance of diversity in a democratic society and how that bears on education • Understand and apply critical perspectives on education and schooling • Critically analyze current educational policies and practices (111)
Theoretical and historical perspectives	• Ability to form, articulate, and defend individual critiques, critical analyses, and evaluations about dance • Knowledge of dance as a communication medium and developmentally as an agent of civilization (103)	• Integrate theories and principles from allied disciplines, such as anatomy, kinesiology, aesthetics, anthropology, history, cultural studies, and others as may be appropriate • Embed dance history in instruction providing contexts and origins of dance movement, styles, and theories (11–12)	• Prepare preservice educators for interpretive uses of knowledge germane to education • Establish lifelong learning through critical reflection on education within its historical, philosophical, cultural, and social contexts (112)
Teaching competency	• Ability to assess experiential backgrounds and orientations of individuals and groups of students and to plan educational programs to meet assessed needs • Ability to accept, amend, or reject methods and materials based on personal assessment of specific teaching situations • Ability to relate dance to other art forms and fields of study and to engage in discussions concerning the value and place of dance within individual communities (103)	• Honor individual student abilities and interests (8) • Create a safe atmosphere where students are encouraged to express their own ideas and values (15) • Incorporate critical reflective practice to improve personal pedagogy and student learning (23) • Foster student exploration of the different purposes dance can serve in diverse cultures (12) • Enhance learning through collaboration on diverse topics and activities (18)	• Ability to facilitate students' holistic development, supporting their pursuit of intellectual freedom, and to foster students' civic engagement and individual autonomy • Ability to develop students' reflective, deliberative, and participatory citizenship skills in a democratic society • Ability to advance students' innovative and collaborative problem-solving and to engage students' critical and analytical capacities (114–15)
Practical/field experiences	Pre-service teachers should engage in observation and discussion of field-based teaching/learning experiences in diverse settings. Opportunities for various types of teaching and directed observation throughout the degree program should be provided. (104)	Teachers are observed by an administrator or fellow teacher as part of their professional development, allowing for reflection with observation debriefings that focus on a teacher's strengths and offer assistance in areas that need improvement. (21)	Preservice teachers should investigate and consider their own values, beliefs, and teaching practices by examining race/ethnicity, gender, and social class and how they affect teaching and learning in classrooms as well as in formal and informal educational settings. (116)

Note: Page numbers in parentheses are from the sources: [a]National Association of Schools of Dance (2013); [b]National Dance Education Organization (2011); [c]American Educational Studies Association Committee on Academic Standards and Accreditation (2013).

From a critical feminist perspective, we attempt to model examples of connected teaching, shared authority, informed "failure," the value of uncertainty, and committed self-reflection that can be translated into action (Risner 2008).

Course Description and Context

Foundations of Dance Pedagogy, an upper-level course for dance majors, is required of Bachelor of Science (B.S.) students, including those seeking teacher certification in dance.[2] The majority of students enrolled teach at various local dance studios. The dance program's diverse student population is addressed in the course purpose defined in the syllabus: "To develop students' theoretical and applied understandings of critical pedagogical concerns in dance education including teaching and learning theory, social and cultural issues in education, cultural diversity, and reflective practice." This aim aligns with the BS program mission of "preparing students to be imaginative and innovative leaders for improving people's lives and social circumstances through dance and related professions" (Risner 2013, 58).

The Web-based course contains nine sequential modules delivered over a fifteen-week semester through Blackboard Learn+, version 9.1. As a three-credit online course, students are expected to devote a minimum of nine hours per week to the class. Modules vary in length from one to three weeks. Small discussion groups (three to four students) meet regularly. Course materials include readings, films/videos, and task-based materials. Assignments and experiential projects include summary and position papers, reflective writings, peer feedback, field observations, social immersion projects, and semester reflections. Formative assessment feedback is provided to students for modules longer than one week in duration.[3] Students post all assignments online for each module; separate boards are also used for ongoing dialogue and conversation (Class Lounge, Course Questions, and Pedagogical Reflections). Successful completion of the course satisfies the university's writing-intensive general education requirement.

Recommendations

Consider where an emphasis on social foundations and critical feminist pedagogy might best fit within a current dance course required for teacher preparation. Alternatively, consider incorporating this content incrementally throughout a number of required classes in cooperation with other dance faculty. Teacher candidates appreciate and benefit from seeing critical pedagogical theory in action. For example, see approaches offered by Burnidge (2012), Alterowitz (2014), and Leonard (2014).

Historical Foundations

Although many teacher candidates have been students of dance for as long as they can remember, most have not had an opportunity to critically look at their own education in historical, philosophical, or reflective ways. In order to develop students' informed understanding of education philosophy and historical foundations, the course commences with an overview of dance education—its historical background, context, and current national agenda in the United States. Three readings constitute the course's primary content: Ann Dils (2007), "Social History and Dance as Education"; John Dewey ([1897] 2006), "My Pedagogic Creed"; and Jane Bonbright ([2000] 2007), "National Agenda for Dance Arts Education." Larger philosophical questions about the aims and purposes of education and teaching are explored, such as: What is the role of education in a democratic society? How does arts education play a role in overall education? What historical developments and philosophical approaches led to the inclusion of dance education in public schools?

Alongside this historical learning, students examine and reflect upon their own education, schooling, and dance education and training, beginning with a reflection on their "favorite teacher" while growing up (What was it about this teacher that you remember the most? Describe an important lesson or learning experience with this teacher that you still carry with you today). When assembled, their collective reflections depict a "passionate, caring, energetic, and dedicated" teacher who "encouraged, inspired, pushed, and supported" students. These descriptors serve as an important discussion starter for investigating pedagogy—the art and science of teaching. Upon completion of this module, students are able to:

- Articulate an understanding of the role of education in a democratic society
- Demonstrate knowledge of the history and philosophy of dance education in the United States
- Formulate an informed rationale for the importance of arts education and dance education
- Reflect upon their understanding of pedagogy and what it means to be a teacher

With this grounding, students over the duration of the semester focus on two central questions: What kind of teacher do I want to become? What does it mean to be responsible for someone else's learning?

Recommendations

Depending on background and experience, some students may initially need guidance in making meaningful connections between their own dance training (often in a studio setting) and the educational and pedagogical concepts presented. When possible, develop writing cues and discussion prompts that are inclusive, drawing attention to the importance of identifying relationships and influences. For example, teaching dance in the early twentieth century liberated women from the confines of domesticity and allowed them to create more independent lives outside the restraints of the home while still remaining "respectable."

If space in the teacher preparation curriculum is limited, consider developing a unit on the historical foundations of dance education for incorporation into a required dance history course; collaborate with another dance faculty member if appropriate. Teacher candidates and other undergraduate dance majors will benefit from seeing the evolution of dance teaching within the history of dance.

Culture and Education: Competition, Individualism, and Personal Gain

Teacher candidates enter postsecondary programs with a good deal of personal knowledge about the U.S. educational system, in which most have excelled. By virtue of acceptance to the university and admittance to the teacher education program, many have achieved high grade-point averages, attended "good" schools, received high school honors, and won university scholarships within the cumulative process. In short, many have done everything not only "right" but well; therefore, their view of schooling is often highly positive. While we welcome them to our programs, their preparation as effective teachers in an increasingly diverse world requires helping them critically unpack much of the economic, political, social, and cultural influences that brought them to us. To these ends, we examine dominant societal notions that valorize competition, individualism, personal gain, and individual achievement, and how these ideas play out in education and schools. Teacher candidates' understanding of the complex relationships between culture and education is central to this learning.

Three concise readings provide social foundations content: Joel Spring (2006), "Thinking Critically About History"; Elizabeth Gray (2006), "The Culture of Separated Desks"; and George Wood (2006), "Can We Have Schools That Work?" Using students' personal educational experiences as a backdrop for examining culture and education requires preparing them to think in critical ways by asking "why" questions that seek to get beneath their taken-for-granted assumptions about people and society. For example, why is winning important in our culture? Who benefits from this value system? Why are winners important in education? To whose advantage is the "few winners/many losers" paradigm? How do these values exemplify democratic public education? Students are asked to engage directly with each author's educational perspectives, problems addressed, and recommendations or solutions offered, as well as with the prompt, "If you could talk with this author, what questions would you have for her/him?"

Having interrogated values of competition and individualism, we then turn to dominant notions about personal gain and individual achievement by returning to and capitalizing on teacher candidates' personal experiences and lives. The Personal Capital Inventory, designed by Risner, is a comprehensive checklist comprised of possessions (and access to others' possessions), resources, benefits, financial support, honors and awards, achievements, and opportunities. Completing the inventory helps students understand how personal gain, individual achievement, and privilege infuse most of their experiences—and for many, how much this "capital" is entwined in their identity and taken-for-granted assumptions, and how much meaning it has provided in their lives. We cycle back to the students' inventories later in the semester to allow them to locate themselves and their experiences in a global context. Upon completion of this module, students are able to:

- Articulate an understanding of the economic, political, and social nature of culture and education in the United States
- Analyze dominant forms of education, including their strengths and limitations
- Formulate an informed understanding of pedagogical approaches that support the collective good in a democratic society

Recommendations

Based on the demographics and previous dance training of teacher candidates in the program, contemplate possibilities for translating the values of commercial dance competitions into larger societal values of competition and individual achievement. It may be the case that some counternarratives (see Giroux et al. 1996) of cooperation and collective accomplishment go unacknowledged as important oppositional values. Illuminating these contradictions can be powerful for developing teacher candidates' critical analysis, not only in this instance, but also for other conflicted areas of teacher preparation with which students will grapple.

It should be increasingly apparent that this praxis-incorporative approach attempts to drape social foundations content and learning around each teacher candidate's window of experiences, beliefs, and values. As students acclimate to this approach and become comfortable asking critical "why" questions, many will begin to understand that "the personal is political" (Hanisch 1969), and that their evolving pedagogy is intimately tied to who they are and who they want to be as a teacher in a changing and politicized world (Risner 2009). Given the personal engagement required in this work, some students will need additional support, while others will need only a push or a nudge. Beyond the instructor's interventions, consider peer-learning approaches such as small discussion or study groups, and feed-forward strategies like individual learning plans or targets for students' future assignments (Duncan 2007).

Culture and Education: Race, Class, and Gender

In order to teach effectively in an increasingly diverse U.S. society, teacher candidates must understand and be prepared to address educational issues of race, ethnicity, social class, gender, and sexual orientation in teaching and learning. Dominant cultural assumptions about "difference" and school inequities based on race and social class ("good schools" vs. "bad schools") significantly impact the kind of education P–12 students receive. Today's undergraduate students in postsecondary dance programs are more racially diverse than the dance faculty who teach them: white non-Hispanic females (77%) comprise the vast majority of all dance faculty (Higher Education Arts Data Services [HEADS] 2013). All teacher candidates need to see people, discuss issues, and confront problems that relate to their lives and experiences.

Three readings present content on race, ethnicity, and social class in relation to education and schooling: Peggy McIntosh ([1990] 2006), "White Privilege: Unpacking the Invisible Knapsack"; James Loewen (2006), "The Land of Opportunity"; and Carol Burris and Kevin Welner (2005), "Closing the Achievement Gap." Three films provide additional content: *The Pathology of Privilege* (Jhally 2006); *Class Dismissed* (Alper 2005); and *People Like Us: Social Class in America* (Kolker and Alvarez 2001). Based on these learning experiences, students return to their Personal Capital Inventory completed earlier and reflect upon any changes in their perspectives on the relationship between schooling, race, and social class. We then ask students to locate themselves (using their inventory) in relation to the Global Village: Earth as a Village of 100 People project[4] (One World—Nations Online Project 2014) by identifying both their majority and minority status. This exercise further enhances teacher candidates' awareness of privilege, access, excess, and responsibility, and how this awareness impacts their developing pedagogical perspective.

Recommendations

Teacher candidates respond to race, ethnicity, and social class content in numerous ways and to varying depths—many experience guilt about their privileged status and frustration that children receive unequal educations; others respond primarily by expressing gratitude to parents for the student's comfortable lifestyle and success. A few students feel genuine sadness about other people's circumstances but credit their own hard work for earning what they have. Consider pedagogical approaches that validate student responses while also challenging students to think more deeply about the context from which their responses emerge. Teacher candidates need to understand that feelings and emotions are real and tangible; many were likely raised to believe that we live in a just and fair world for all—to learn otherwise frequently shatters the world as they've known it. Help students turn their new knowledge toward pedagogies of empathy and understanding of others' experiences and contexts. Teacher candidates also need to understand that while their own personal experience is important and valid, it is also highly limited—representing only one perspective, emerging from a set of particular circumstances and environments, often ones they did not determine or choose. Applying this perspective to understanding their own students' experience and context will be critical for effective and meaningful teaching.

Gender, Sexuality, and Sexual Orientation

Social foundations issues in education rooted in gender look closely at dominant cultural assumptions about femininity, masculinity, sexuality, and sexual orientation.

Gender issues are significantly framed by current media depictions of what girls/women and boys/men should be and do—how they should act, behave, and look appropriate to their gender. Popular media and advertising send messages to girls and women that emphasize feminine perfection, self-doubt in females, and how and what girls should be—most of which emerge from a masculinist perspective. Much of popular culture is focused on sexualized images and content, which are being projected more and more onto children and adolescents. These media images speak forcefully and repeatedly, and schools are not immune to them. As we have noted earlier, schools often reproduce a society's dominant attitudes. Traditional styles of teaching and pedagogy are rooted in similar masculine perspectives. Critical gender pedagogues have developed alternative pedagogical approaches in which connection and dialogue replace separation and lecture. Social issues of sexual orientation and gender identity play out in many ways in the education system, as schools and their curricula struggle to find effective ways to address teasing, harassment, and homophobic bullying and violence (Risner 2014a). Schools and teachers are often unprepared to provide support and meaningful protection to vulnerable students.

Gender and education content is presented in three readings: Tizzy Asher (2006), "Girls, Sexuality, and Popular Culture"; Belenky and colleagues (2006), "Connected Teaching"; and Doug Risner (2005), "What Matthew Shepard Would Tell Us." Two readings on gender in dance education are included as well: Sue Stinson (2005), "The Hidden Curriculum of Gender in Dance Education"; and Doug Risner (2007), "Rehearsing Masculinity: Challenging the 'Boy Code' in Dance Education." Three films expand upon the content of the readings: *What a Girl Wants* (Buzzell and Massie 2001); *Killing Us Softly* (Jhally 2010); and *Tough Guise: The Crisis in Masculinity* (Jhally

1999). Writing prompts and discussion group cues ask students to identify dominant messages, decipher message content and gender perspective (who's sending the message), and describe how they have personally experienced these messages. We conclude with the question, What gender messages do you believe are most harmful to young boys and girls?

Recommendations

Based on responses from students ($n = 59$) who have completed this course, most teacher candidates engage enthusiastically with gender content and discussion, especially the central aims of connected teaching of drawing out knowledge from students and not telling them what to think, but instead asking students to "think more." Teacher candidates also relate to the critique of traditional pedagogy's "doubting method," in which students' ideas are viewed as inferior, put down, or dismissed altogether. However, some struggle with acknowledging the important premise that connected teachers don't know the answer to everything (Belenky et al. 2006). Students' inability to make this connection may be due in part to their identities as dancers and the previous dance training they have "received." Consider ways to illustrate that imperfection is not a flaw, but rather that strong teachers aren't afraid to learn or fail. In tandem, tether conversations about "imperfection" to dominant popular discourses and media representations of femininity; the female body; gay, lesbian, bisexual, transgender, and queer persons; homophobia; and bullying. Teacher candidates will benefit from understanding these issues as part of larger educational concerns for human dignity and respect for all people, as well as part of the kind of teaching environments they will create and model.

INTEGRATING SOCIAL FOUNDATIONS PROJECTS

The course design uses a spiral progression, rather than a linear approach to social foundations and their intersections with educational theory and practice. The helical structure of the spiral places critical issues of race, ethnicity, class, and gender at the center of a learning cylinder around which students' experiences, questions, and reflections gradually wind, simultaneously receding from and drawing near, each time becoming hopefully more informed. Two experiential projects illustrate the aims of social foundations inclusion and the particular ways that weaving this content within a spiral course progression can enhance teacher candidate learning. Risner (2005) summarizes:

> Advancing and retreating in a methodological coil enables students to see not only the interrelatedness and complexity of social constructions of privilege and marginality, but also to reflect upon their own place within these hierarchical structures. (238)

Social Immersion Project

The purpose of the Social Immersion Project is to facilitate teacher candidates' better understanding of the social issues raised in class readings, films, and discussions through students' actual involvement with and experience of life situations different from their own. By design, the project seeks to create stimulating, socially immersed learning opportunities that momentarily reduce the abstractions of poverty, homelessness, hunger, mental illness, racism, gender bias, and social inequities, among others. Students select one of the following immersion projects:

- 74-cent meals: For one week, live on $0.74 per meal. You may multiply the allowable amount to create a budget for the week.[5]
- Same clothes: Wear exactly the same clothes for one week. You may wash them once.
- Volunteerism: Volunteer for a week at a food bank, soup kitchen, homeless shelter, helpline, hospice, or other social service agency.
- Public transportation: Use *only* public transportation for one week.

As they select their project, students are encouraged to think about the privilege that allows them options and to remind themselves that many people don't have these kinds of choices in their lives. The central aims of this project are that teacher candidates: (1) experience the range of other people's experiences, albeit briefly and in a limited way; and (2) expand their development as reflective teachers who will be able to teach comfortably and effectively in diverse settings, environments, and locations.

Critical Field Observations

Conducting critical field observations of other teachers' dance classes in varied settings provides teacher candidates with important experiential learning that can contribute to their understanding of pedagogical theory and practice through a social foundations lens. Traditional field observation in dance focuses primarily on the teacher, teaching methods, and classroom management. Critical field observations examine teacher and student action equally, focusing on the description of relationships between teacher and student, student and student, and the whole group, as well as communication patterns and equity, engagement, and pedagogical values and priorities. Observations are conducted in K–12 schools, community settings, private schools and academies, and postsecondary institutions. Teacher candidates observe in at least three different settings, with a fourth observation scheduled at their discretion and based on teaching interests. Each observation is documented separately using a fieldwork notes template designed by Risner, which when completed provides extensive data for a critical analysis written by the student in the form of a comprehensive field observation report. Most teacher candidates find this project stimulating and worthwhile, especially the chance to see teachers' pedagogies in action—whether they find the teacher effective or not—and to use the pedagogical theory and social foundations they have learned to constructively critique each pedagogy observed. Beyond these realizations, critical field observations allow teacher candidates to understand on a deeper level that each teacher's pedagogy is personal, and that if not carefully examined and reflected upon regularly, teachers will teach the way they were themselves taught.

CONCLUSION

This article began with the recognition that preparing dance specialist teachers means preparing them to enter schools in an increasingly diverse and politicized world, an educational policy landscape entrenched in technical production, teacher-proof curriculum, high-stakes testing, and methods-centric teacher preparation. Some ramifications of this landscape elaborated earlier include significantly narrowed teacher preparation programs and curricula stripped of social foundations of education. We asserted that larger questions about the purpose, meaning, and function of democratic education in the United States remain important for preparing effective teachers, and presented a praxis-incorporative approach to social foundations inclusion in dance teacher preparation programs, a goal supported by a review of national standards. Although fully committed to this approach, we recognize that knowledge of social foundations alone will not solve today's vast educational policy challenges or the troubled schools they create and that dance teacher candidates will encounter. No single curriculum revision or alternative approach can resolve the inherent educational disparities and inequities of current policy and mandates; however, that doesn't mean these should be ignored, go unexamined, or be tacitly affirmed by indifference and silence. The least we can do is to prepare teacher candidates with strong personal pedagogies and value systems, individuals who know the challenges and are ready to confront inequities faced by their students, programs, and schools. Inclusion of social foundations in teacher preparation is a first step.

We return to two central questions dance pedagogy students seek to answer over the duration of the course described in this article: What does it mean to be responsible for someone else's learning? What kind of teacher do I want to become? Answering these questions requires that preservice teachers give equal consideration to their identity as teacher-self and their identity as teacher of others. This dual consideration is one of the most prominent missing links in methods-centric teacher preparation, in which standardized "how-to" technical solutions to nearly any situation may have little to nothing to do with the particular teacher's values, beliefs, pedagogy, or relationships with students.

In conclusion, when we take seriously the enormous responsibility for someone else's learning, which we believe committed teachers do, and if we accept the charge of preparing teachers who are culturally, socially, and politically informed, which we believe we should, then teacher candidates deserve to be exposed to a far wider range of social and cultural foundations in education. It is our hope that this article contributes to larger conversations about arts and dance teacher preparation; however, given current challenges and debates, we wonder if collective energies and a commitment to viewing arts teacher preparation through a larger social and cultural lens are sufficient. We hope so.

NOTES

1. In addition to Susan Stinson (class of 1984), other dance education graduates of the doctoral program in social and cultural foundations of education at the University of North Carolina at Greensboro include Jan Van Dyke (1989), Donald Blumenfeld-Jones (1990), Peggy Hunt Richter (1991), Sherry Shapiro (1991), Katherine Lee (1993), Doug Risner (2001), Adrienne Sansom (2005), and Yolanda Medina (2006).
2. In addition to BS core coursework (12 credits), required dance courses in technique and performance (18 credits), dance studies (17 credits), cognates (6 credits), and a capstone (3 credits), teacher certification students also complete required dance coursework in secondary teaching methods; creative dance for children; and student teaching, fieldwork, and assisting. The college of education requires an additional 19 credits, which do not include any social foundations courses or content.
3. See Risner (2014b) for formative and summative assessments for Web-based learners in this dance pedagogy course.
4. An amended version of the Global Village was developed for this course using a variety of additional resources.
5. This figure is based on Michigan Temporary Assistance to Needy Families (TANF) food assistance for a family of three at or below the poverty line.

REFERENCES

Adair, C. 1992. *Women and dance: Sylphs and sirens.* New York: New York University Press.

Allison, A. 2013. No art teacher left behind: Professional development that really matters in an age of accountability. *Arts Education Policy Review* 114 (4): 178–90.

Alper, L., dir. 2005. *Class dismissed: How TV frames the working class* [DVD]. Northampton, MA: Media Education Foundation.

Alterowitz, G. 2014. Toward a feminist ballet pedagogy: Teaching strategies for ballet technique classes in the twenty-first century. *Journal of Dance Education* 14 (1): 8–17.

American Educational Studies Association Committee on Academic Standards and Accreditation: Tutwiler, S., K. deMarrais, D. Gabbard, A. Hyde. P. Konkol, H. Li, Y. Medina, J. Rayle, and A. Swain. 2013. Standards for Academic and Professional Instruction in Foundations of Education, Educational Studies, and Educational Policy Studies, 3rd. ed. *Educational Studies* 49(2): 107–18.

Anyon, J. 1980. Social class and the hidden curriculum of work. *Journal of Education* 162 (1): 1–17.

Arkin, L. 1994. Dancing the body: Women and dance performance. *Journal of Physical Education, Recreation and Dance* 65 (2): 36–38, 43.

Asante, K. 1993. African-American dance in curricula: Modes of inclusion. *Journal of Physical Education, Recreation & Dance* 64 (2): 48–51.

Asher, T. 2006. Girls, sexuality and popular culture. In *The institution of education*, 5th ed., ed. H. S. Shapiro, K. Latham, and S. Ross, 305–08. Boston: Pearson.

Bartolome, L. 2004. Critical pedagogy and teacher education: Radicalizing prospective teachers. *Teacher Education Quarterly* 31 (1): 97–122.

Belenky, M., B. Clinchy, H. Goldberger, and J. Tarule. 1986. *Women's ways of knowing: The development of self, voice, and mind*. New York: Basic Books.

———. 2006. Connected teaching. In *The institution of education*, 5th ed., ed. H. S. Shapiro, K. Latham, and S. Ross, 125–35. Boston: Pearson.

Beveridge, T. 2010. No Child Left Behind and fine arts classes. *Arts Education Policy Review* 111 (1): 4–7.

Bonbright, J. 2007. National agenda for dance arts education. Paper presented at the Dancing in the Millennium Conference, Washington, DC, July 19–23.

Breault, D. 2011. Pedagogy. In *SAGE encyclopedia of curriculum studies*, ed. C. Kridel, 634–35. Thousand Oaks, CA: Sage.

Burris, C., and K. Welner. 2005. Closing the achievement gap by detracking. *Phi Delta Kappan* 86 (8): 594–98.

Burnidge, A. 2012. Somatics in the dance studio: Embodying feminist/democratic pedagogy. *Journal of Dance Education* 12 (2): 37–53.

Buzzell, M., dir., and E. Massie, prod. 2001. *What a girl wants: How the media diminishes the value of young women* [DVD]. Northampton, MA: Media Education Foundation.

Chow, E., C. Fleck, G. Fan, J. Joseph, and D. Lyter. 2003. Exploring critical feminist pedagogy: Infusing dialogue, participation, and experience in teaching and learning. *Teaching Sociology* 31 (3): 259–75.

Clark, D. 1994. Voices of women dance educators: Considering issues of hegemony and the education/performer identity. *Impulse* 2 (2): 122–30.

Currie, D. 1992. Subject-ivity in the classroom: Feminism meets academe. *Canadian Journal of Education* 17 (3): 341–64.

Dewey, J. (1897) 2006. My pedagogic creed. In *The institution of education*, 5th ed., ed. H. S. Shapiro, K. Latham, and S. Ross, 101–07. Boston: Pearson.

Dils, A. 2007. Social history and dance as education. In *International handbook of research in arts education*, ed. L. Bresler, 103–12. Dordrecht, The Netherlands: Springer.

Duncan, N. 2007. "Feed–forward": Improving students' use of tutors' comments. *Assessment & Evaluation in Higher Education* 32 (3): 271–83.

Ellsworth, E. 1992. Why doesn't this feel empowering? Working through the repressive myths of critical pedagogy. In *Feminisms and critical pedagogy*, ed. C. Luke and J. Gore, 90–119. New York: Routledge.

———. 1997. *Teaching positions: Difference, pedagogy, and the power of address*. New York: Teachers College Press.

Freire, P. (1970) 2006. Excerpt from *Pedagogy of the oppressed*. In *The institution of education*, 5th ed., ed. H. S. Shapiro, K. Latham, and S. Ross, 155–62. Boston: Pearson.

Gard, M. 2001. Dancing around the "problem" of boys and dance. *Discourse: Studies in the Cultural Politics of Education* 22 (2): 213–25.

———. 2003. Being someone else: Using dance in anti-oppressive teaching. *Educational Review* 55 (2): 211–23.

Gilligan, C. 1982. *In a different voice: Psychological theory and women's development*. Cambridge, MA: Harvard University Press.

Giroux, H. 1988. Border pedagogy in the age of postmodernism. *Journal of Education* 170 (3): 162–81.

———. 2010. Lessons to be learned from Paulo Freire as education is being taken over by the mega rich. Accessed February 2, 2014, at http://firgoa.usc.es/drupal/node/47936.

Giroux, H., C. Lankshear, P. McLaren, and M. Peters. 1996. *Counternarratives: Cultural studies and critical pedagogies in postmodern spaces*. New York: Routledge.

Gore, J. 1993. *The struggle for pedagogies: Critical and feminist discourses as regimes of truth*. New York: Routledge.

Gray, E. 2006. The culture of separated desks. In *The institution of education*, 5th ed., ed. H. S. Shapiro, K. Latham, and S. Ross, 273–79. Boston: Pearson.

Green, J. 1999. Somatic authority and the myth of the ideal body in dance education. *Dance Research Journal* 31 (2): 80–100.

———. 2000. Emancipatory pedagogy? Women's bodies and the creative process in dance. *Frontiers* 21 (3): 124–40.

Greene, M. 1986. In search of a critical pedagogy. *Harvard Educational Review* 56 (4): 427–42.

Hanisch, C. 1969. The personal is political. In *Feminist revolution*, ed. K. Sarachild, C. Hanisch, F. Levine, B. Leon, and C. Price, 204–05. New York: Random House.

Higher Education Arts Data Services (HEADS). 2013. *Dance Data Summaries 2012–2013*. Reston, VA: HEADS.

hooks, b. 1994. *Teaching to transgress*. New York: Routledge.

———. 2006. Engaged pedagogy. In *The institution of education*, 5th ed., ed. H. S. Shapiro, K. Latham, and S. Ross, 137–41. Boston: Pearson.

Jhally, S., dir. 1999. *Tough guise: Violence, media, and the crisis in masculinity* [DVD]. Northampton, MA: Media Education Foundation.

———. 2008. *The pathology of privilege: Racism, white denial and the costs of inequality* [DVD]. Northampton, MA: Media Education Foundation.

———. 2010. *Killing us softly 4: Advertising's image of women* [DVD]. Northampton, MA: Media Education Foundation.

Johanningmeier, E. 1991. Through the disarray of social foundations: Some notes toward a new social foundation. *Educational Foundations* 5 (4): 5–39.

Kolker, A., and L. Alvarez, dir. 2001. *People like us: Social class in America* [DVD]. Washington, DC: Center for New American Media.

Ladson-Billings, G. 1994. *The dreamkeepers: Successful teachers of African American children*. San Francisco: Jossey-Bass.

Lather, P. 1991. *Getting smart: Feminist research and pedagogy within the postmodern*. New York: Routledge.

Leonard, A. 2014. Democratic bodies: Exemplary practice and democratic education in a K–5 dance residency. *Journal of Dance Education* 14 (1): 1–7.

Lewis, J. 2013. New challenges, new vision: Why social foundations and teacher education partnerships matter. *Educational Studies* 49 (2): 169–82.

Liston, D., and K. Zeichner. 1991. *Teacher education and the social conditions of schooling*. New York: Routledge.

Loewen, J. 2006. The land of opportunity. In *The institution of education*, 5th ed., ed. H. S. Shapiro, K. Latham, and S. Ross, 193–201. Boston: Pearson.

McCarthy, M. 2006. The rise and fall of ED200F. *Educational Studies* 39 (2): 134–45.

McCarthy-Brown, N. 2009. The need for culturally relevant dance education. *Journal of Dance Education* 9 (4): 120–25.

McIntosh, P. (1990) 2006. White privilege: Unpacking the invisible knapsack. In *The institution of education*, 5th ed., ed. H. S. Shapiro, K. Latham, and S. Ross, 239–42. Boston: Pearson.

McLaren, P. 2000. Paulo Freire's pedagogy of possibility. In *Freirean pedagogy, praxis and possibilities: Projects for the new millennium*, ed. S. Steiner, H. Krank, P. McLaren, and R. Bahruth, 1–22. New York: Falmer Press.

McLaren, P., and P. Leonard. 1993. *Paulo Freire: A critical encounter*. New York: Routledge.

Mills, G. 1994. Umfundalai: One technique, three applications. *Journal of Physical Education, Recreation & Dance* 65 (5): 36–38.

———. 1997. Is it is or is it ain't: The impact of selective perception on the image making of traditional African dance. *Journal of Black Studies* 28 (2): 139–56.

Moffett, A. 2010. Dance as inquiry: Critical thinking in dance education. M.A. thesis, University of Oregon. Accessed February 2, 2014, at http://hdl.handle.net/1794/10691.

Mozingo, K. 2005. Lesbian lacunae: Invisible spaces in dance education. *Journal of Dance Education* 5 (2): 58–63.

National Association of Schools of Dance. 2013. *National Association of Schools of Dance handbook 2013–14.* Reston, VA: National Association of Schools of Dance.

National Center for Education Statistics. 2010. Integrated postsecondary education data system: Classification of instructional programs (CIP). Accessed February 2, 2014, at http://nces.ed.gov/ipeds/cipcode/cipdetail.aspx?y=55&cipid=88072.

National Commission on Excellence in Education. 1983. *A nation at risk: The imperative for educational reform.* Accessed February 10, 2014, at http://www2.ed.gov/pubs/NatAtRisk/index.html.

National Dance Education Organization. 2011. *Professional teaching standards in dance arts.* Silver Spring, MD: National Dance Education Organization.

Neumann, R. 2009. Highly qualified teachers and the social foundations of education. *Phi Delta Kappan* 91 (3): 81–85.

———. 2010. Social foundations and multicultural education course requirements in teacher preparation programs in the United States. *Journal of Educational Foundations* 24 (3–4): 3–17.

Noddings, N. 1984. *Caring: A feminine approach to ethics and moral development.* Berkeley: University of California Press.

Novinger, S., and L. O'Brien. 2003. Beyond "boring, meaningless shit" in the academy: Early childhood teacher educators under the regulatory gaze. *Contemporary Issues in Early Childhood* 4 (1): 3–31.

One World—Nations Online Project. 2014. The Global Village: Earth as a village of 100 people. Accessed September 30, 2013, at http://www.nationsonline.org/oneworld/global-village.htm.

Ottey, S. 1996. Critical pedagogical theory and the dance educator. *Arts Education Policy Review* 98 (2): 31–39.

Picower, B. 2011. Resisting compliance: Learning to teach for social justice in a neoliberal context. *Teachers College Record* 113 (5): 1105–34.

Provenzo, E., and A. Provenzo. 2009. *Encyclopedia of the social and cultural foundations of education.* Thousand Oaks, CA: Sage.

Purpel, D. 1985. *Schools and meaning: Essays on the moral nature of schooling.* Lanham, MD: University Press of America.

Purpel, D., and W. McLaurin. 2004. *Reflections on the moral and spiritual crisis in education.* New York: Peter Lang.

Rich, A. 1979. *On lies, secrets and silence: Selected prose (1966–1978).* New York: Norton.

Risner, D. 2002. Sexual orientation and male participation in dance education: Revisiting the open secret. *Journal of Dance Education* 2 (3): 84–92.

———. 2005. What Matthew Shepard would tell us: Gay and lesbian issues in education. In *Critical social issues in education: Democracy and meaning in a globalizing world*, ed. H. S. Shapiro, 237–49. Boston: Lawrence Erlbaum.

———. 2007. Rehearsing masculinity: Challenging the "boy code" in dance education. *Research in Dance Education* 8 (2): 139–53.

———. 2008. The politics of gender in dance pedagogy. *Journal of Dance Education* 8 (3): 94–97.

———. 2009. *Stigma and perseverance in the lives of boys who dance: An empirical study of male identities in Western theatrical dance training.* Lewiston, NY: Mellen.

———. 2010a. Challenges and opportunities for dance pedagogy: Critical social issues and "unlearning" how to teach. In *Global perspectives on dance: Research and pedagogy, conference proceedings of the Congress on Research in Dance*, ed. T. Randall, 204–09. Cambridge, MA: Congress on Research in Dance.

———. 2010b. Dance education matters: Rebuilding postsecondary dance education for twenty-first century relevance and resonance. *Journal of Dance Education* 10 (4): 95–110.

———. 2013. Curriculum revision in practice: Designing a liberal arts degree in dance professions. *Journal of Dance Education* 13 (2): 56–60.

———. 2014a. Bullying victimisation and social support of adolescent male dance students: An analysis of findings. *Research in Dance Education* 15 (2): 179–201.

———. 2014b. Hold on to this!: Strategies for teacher feedback in online dance courses. *Journal of Dance Education* 14 (2): 52–58.

Risner, D., and S. Stinson. 2010. Moving social justice: Challenges, fears and possibilities in dance education. *International Journal of Education & the Arts* 11 (6). Accessed January 3, 2011, at http://www.ijea.org/v11n6/.

Sabol, F. R. 2010. *No Child Left Behind: A study of its impact on art education.* National Art Education Association and National Art Education Foundation project report. Accessed December 31, 2012, at http://www.arteducators.org/research/NCLBProjReport2-10.pdf.

———. 2013. Seismic shifts in the education landscape: What do they mean for arts education and arts education policy? *Arts Education Policy Review* 114 (1): 33–45.

Shapiro, H. S. 1984. Crisis of legitimation: Schools, society, and declining faith in education. *Interchange* 15 (4): 26–39.

Shapiro, S. B. 1998. Toward transformative teachers: Critical and feminist perspectives in dance education. In *Dance, power, and difference: Critical and feminist perspectives on dance education*, ed. S. B. Shapiro, 7–21. Champaign, IL: Human Kinetics.

Shor, I. 1992. *Empowering education: Critical teaching for social change.* Chicago: University of Chicago Press.

Spring, J. 2006. Thinking critically about history: Ideological management, culture wars, and consumerism. In *The institution of education*, 5th ed., ed. H. S. Shapiro, K. Latham, and S. Ross, 73–78. Boston: Pearson.

Stinson, S. W. 1984. Reflections and visions: A hermeneutic study of dangers and possibilities in dance education. Ph.D. diss., University of North Carolina at Greensboro.

———. 1998a. Places where I've been: Reflections on issues of gender in dance education, research, and administration. *Choreography and Dance* 5 (1): 117–27.

———. 1998b. Seeking a feminist pedagogy for children's dance. In *Dance, power, and difference: Critical and feminist perspectives on dance education*, ed. S. B. Shapiro, 23–47. Champaign, IL: Human Kinetics.

———. 2005. The hidden curriculum of gender in dance education. *Journal of Dance Education* 5 (2): 51–57.

Stinson, S., D. Blumenfeld-Jones, and J. Van Dyke. 1990. Voices of young women dance students: An interpretive study of meaning in dance. *Dance Research Journal* 22 (2): 13–22.

Swain, A. 2013. The problem with "nuts and bolts": How the emphasis on "highly qualified professionals" is undermining education. *Educational Studies* 49 (2): 119–33.

Thiessen, D., E. Campbell, R. Gaztambide-Fernandez, S. Niyozov, S. Anwaruddin, C. Cooke, and L. Gladstone. 2013. Perspectives on pedagogy. *Curriculum Inquiry* 43 (1): 1–13.

Tozer, S., and D. Miretzky. 2000. Professional teaching standards and social foundations of education. *Educational Studies* 31 (2): 106–20.

Van Dyke, J. 1992. *Modern dance in a postmodern world: An analysis of federal arts funding and its impact on the field of modern dance.* Reston, VA: American Alliance for Health, Physical Education, Recreation, and Dance.

Warren, D. 1998. From there to where: The social foundations of education in transit again. *Educational Studies* 29 (2): 117–30.

West, C. S. 2005. Black bodies in dance education: Charting a new pedagogical paradigm to eliminate gendered and hypersexualized assumptions. *Journal of Dance Education* 5 (2): 64–69.

Westheimer, J., and J. Kahne. 2007. Introduction. *Equity and Excellence in Education* 40 (2): 97–100.

Wood, G. 2006. Can we have schools that work? In *The institution of education*, 5th ed., ed. H. S. Shapiro, K. Latham and S. Ross, 21–27. Boston: Pearson.

Leadership Narratives in Postsecondary Dance Leadership: Voices, Values and Gender Variations

Doug Risner, PhD

Pamela S. Musil, MA

ABSTRACT Dance in the U.S. university finds its beginnings in the visionary leadership of women. Since the mid-1910s, dance faculty and students in higher education have been predominantly female. Gender in postsecondary dance today remains much the same, with the exception of dance leadership, which is increasingly male. This narrative inquiry is drawn from a mixed-method study ($n = 75$) that examined the lives of administrative leaders—defined as chairs, directors, heads, or coordinators—who lead departments or programs of dance in colleges and universities in the U.S. The purpose of the exploratory investigation was to develop a status report drawn from quantitative survey data and qualitative interview narratives of administrators in postsecondary dance with particular attention to gender. This inquiry focuses on representative data of nine participants from the larger study. Findings are presented on participants' leadership approach; support for work; work–life balance; and research, creative activity and teaching. Gender implications are discussed.

Dance in the U.S. university finds its earliest beginnings in the visionary leadership of women since the mid-1910s: Blanche Trilling and Margaret H'Doubler at the University of Wisconsin; Gertrude Colby at Teachers College; Bird Larson at Barnard College; Martha Hill and Mary Jo Shelly at Bennington College and New York University; and Ruth Lovell Murray at Wayne State University, among others. Their pioneering and tireless efforts led to the establishment of dance as an independent discipline in academe. The 1950s expansion of dance programs and departments resulted in increasing numbers of dance faculty, mostly women (Ross 2002), and later the founding of the Council of Dance Administrators (CODA) and the second generation of strong female leadership during the 1970s "dance boom": Alma Hawkins at the University of California, Los Angeles; Elizabeth Hayes at the University of Utah; Helen Alkire at The Ohio State University; and Nancy Smith (Fichter) at Florida State University (Hagood 2000). Dance faculty and students in higher education were predominantly female.

The growth of professional degree offerings (BFA, MFA) in the 1990s fortified the academic presence, professionalization, and relevance of postsecondary dance, which in turn began to attract males to university dance faculties (Risner 2010). "Once clearly the domain of women," as Jan Van Dyke (1996) noted at the time, "now many college dance faculties are striving for gender equity regardless of the numerical dominance of women as dance students" (537). By 1994, males comprised 37 percent of postsecondary dance faculty (Higher Education Arts Data Services [HEADS] 1994). Still, females continued to serve as leaders of the wide majority (80 percent) of dance departments and programs as chairpersons, heads, or directors (Stern 1994, cited in Van Dyke 1996). However, gender equity concerns and questions about male privilege of the time persisted: Will increasingly gender-diverse dance faculties satisfy the large population of female students' needs? Or, will young females "come to regard academic dance programs as just one more place where men are given special consideration. Will male dance student enrollment rise with the increase in male faculty?" (Van Dyke 1996, 538).

According to HEADS (2015), 20 years later female students constitute the vast majority of postsecondary dance major students (86 percent), and males comprise 34 percent of dance faculties (down three percent from 1994). However, the National Association of Schools of Dance reports that men now lead over 42 percent of dance departments and programs in the United States (HEADS 2015), an increase of five percent in just the last four years (HEADS 2011, 2015). This narrative inquiry is drawn from a larger mixed-method study ($n = 75$) that examined the professional lives of administrative leaders—defined as chairs, directors, heads, or coordinators—who lead schools, departments, or programs of dance in postsecondary colleges and universities in the United States. The purpose of the investigation was to develop a comprehensive status report, comprised of quantitative (survey) data and qualitative (interview) narratives, of administrative leadership in postsecondary dance with particular attention to gender. This study focuses on representative, qualitative narratives of nine participants (six women, three men) from the larger study pool. Throughout this article, selected findings from the survey will provide a larger context for the participants' interview data.

RESEARCH STUDY DESIGN

Readers are urged to see the authors' chapter, "Leadership and Gender in Postsecondary Dance: An Exploratory Survey of Dance Administrators in the United States," (Risner and Musil 2017) for the full survey findings from which the participants' survey data were drawn and interview questions for this article were eventually formed. Together, that chapter and this article document the findings of the larger, three-year mixed-method study.

Interpretive research frameworks give researchers the tools to render a better understanding of what it is to be human in the world and to generate meaning and understanding rather than proving or disproving facts (Denzin and Lincoln 2011). Meaning is revealed in diverse ways and requires that researchers engage conceptual frameworks and methodologies that account for multiple perspectives, contextualization, and complexity. The realities of participants or subjects are considered multiple, socially constructed, and contextual (Creswell 2014). As interpretive researchers for nearly three decades, we, the authors, continually strive to model the values and methods of qualitative research. At the outset, we note our roles as current and former dance department head, area head, and senior associate chair in large university settings (private and public) and the bias that could emerge from many years in leadership positions. Therefore, we employed co-researcher and external colleague checks for removing confirmation bias, culture bias, leading questions, and wording bias. We briefly outline the purpose and need for using a mixed-method design from a dual perspective: that of a pragmatic researcher's approach (what works best now) and that of a critical researcher's approach (what empowers positive social change and action). John Creswell (2003) explained the pragmatic researcher's turn:

> Truth is what works at the time; it is not based in a strict dualism between the mind and a reality completely independent of the mind. Thus, in mixed methods research, investigators use both quantitative and qualitative data because they work to provide the best understanding of a research problem. (12)

The void in published, quantitative research on dance administration and those who lead postsecondary programs and departments required quantifiable baseline data from which tentative generalizations could be cautiously formulated. For that reason, gathering and analyzing quantitative survey data on a relatively large scale about dance administrators' professional lives, meaning and purpose, workload and responsibilities, salary, work satisfaction, and influential experiences and people were necessary. Simultaneously, but from an interpretive research perspective, the processes and methods of qualitative research design and generated data permit researchers to build concepts, develop grounded theories, and seek emergent patterns through interpretation and contextual analyses (Denzin and Lincoln 2011). We believe, when combined with a critical perspective, as R. Burke Johnson, Anthony Onwuegbuzie, and Lisa Turner (2007) do, that:

> Qualitative dominant mixed methods research is the type of mixed research in which one relies on a qualitative, constructivist-poststructuralist-critical view of the research process, while concurrently recognizing that the addition of quantitative data and approaches are likely to benefit most research projects. (124)

Frederick Erickson (2005) expanded this perspective further by articulating interpretive design from a critical approach:

> The interpretive qualitative researcher would say that the question "what is happening?" is always accompanied by another question: "and what do those happenings mean to those who are engaged in them?" And a critical qualitative researcher would add a third question, "and are these happenings just and in the best interests of people generally?" (7)

Thus, this study and analysis employed a mixed-method, qualitative-dominant design from a critical interpretive perspective.

Methodology

A four-part methodology was employed for the larger research study: (1) review of literatures in postsecondary dance leadership and administration; (2) analyses of data assembled annually by HEADS in conjunction with institutionally accredited members of the National Association of Schools of Dance (NASD) from 1994 to 2015; (3) the authors' extensive online survey of dance administrators ($n = 75$) who lead postsecondary dance departments and programs in the United States; and (4) interviews with selected participants ($n = 9$) of geographic diversity, described later in this section. Each of the nine participants selected was interviewed once; interviews were 45 to 75 minutes in duration. Human subject investigation approval was obtained from Risner's university.

At the conclusion of the survey, participants were invited to indicate their interest in completing a follow-up interview. Of those who responded affirmatively, nine participants (six females, three males) were selected for semistructured interviews. Selections were made in an effort to represent the demographics of the larger study pool: to represent both genders equitably and ensure diversity of race, cultural background, institutional and program size and type, and length of time in leadership positions. Interviews took the shape of guided conversations based on each participant's earlier survey responses, allowing participants to speak candidly about themselves and their experiences and allowing the researcher to revisit topics and themes in greater depth and detail (Kvale and Brinkmann 2008). Therefore, each interview protocol was unique to each participant's previously completed survey responses. Interview questions were organized in three main areas taken from the survey: leadership approach, support for participants' work, and work–life balance. Participants were encouraged to share stories and give examples when possible. All were asked whether they believed leadership characteristics, challenges, or other information indicated in their survey responses had anything to do with gender. Each participant was also asked to discuss the open-ended comments he or she had made at the survey's conclusion about the recent gender shift occurring in postsecondary dance leadership (i.e., increasing male leadership according to NASD and HEADS data).

Interviews were recorded digitally, transcribed, and then destroyed. Analysis of data generated was based on procedures of interpretive inquiry (Lincoln and Guba 2004). Extraneous material was eliminated and emerging themes and patterns in each narrative account were identified and coded (Bernard and Ryan 2009). Musil conducted the interviews, which were transcribed by a student research assistant. Both authors verified edited transcript reductions prior to coding and analyses.

The authors acknowledge that the research topic is complex and carries the risk of researcher bias in presentation and analysis. To limit the potential for bias, Musil coded the transcripts using the three interview categories as a starting point. Narratives that further clarified or subdivided the three interview categories were counted as a subthemes. Fourteen subthemes emerged (see Table 1). Transcripts were analyzed for subtheme frequency, relevance to the larger study, and female–male divergences, particularly as they either aligned or contrasted with survey results. Those occurring with most frequency were viewed to have greater relevance for discussion. A low frequency was also addressed if it had particular application to leadership, or it represented a gender contrast. Because this study seeks to explore current realities and attitudes related to gender in dance higher education leadership, we chose to negotiate the gender binary while seeking simultaneously to recognize that gender functions between binaries and that factors beyond gender might also be at play within any given narrative.

Participants

Of the nine participants interviewed, six were female and three were male (see Table 2). Nearly all were tenured senior faculty (full professors and associate professors); Beth's institution does not grant continuing tenure. Time in current administrative position varied from 1 to 28 years. Although most participants had served four years or fewer in their current positions, many had previously chaired programs at other institutions. The number of full-time faculty in the participants' particular dance unit (school, department, or program) ranged from one to ten, with gender composition of full-time faculty on average 62 percent female and 38 percent male, when calculated across all nine interview participants' institutions. Representative survey data from the larger study ($n = 75$) provide context for rank and tenure status by gender (see Table 3) and workload (administration, teaching, research and creative activity, service, and fundraising and development) by gender (see Table 4).

TABLE 1 Recurring Themes by Participant

Participant	a	b	c	d	e	f	g	h	i	j	k	l	m
Mindy	X	X	X	X	X	X				X	X	X	
Susan	X	X		X	X	X				X	X	X	
Beth	X	X	X	X	X	X				X		X	X
Julia	X		X	X	X	X				X	X	X	
Candace	X		X	X	X	X				X	X		X
Rachel	X			X	X	X				X	X		X
Mike	X	X	X		X		X		X	X		X	
Paul	X		X		X	X		X	X	X		X	X
Ben	X		X	X	X	X	X	X					

Note: a = value and growth of dance programs; b = differences between dance and the academy; c = influences of culture and upbringing; d = student-centered values; e = democratic and collaborative leadership styles; f = power, privilege, status, and institutional hierarchy; g = roles of leader and follower; h = professional boundaries; i = creative work as outlet; j = workload size and pressures; k = challenges of family life, children in academe; l = lack of staff support; m = little or no desire for higher echelon leadership.

TABLE 2 Description of Participants

Participant	Gender/Ethnicity	Title	Administrative Structure	Rank/Tenure Status	Institution Type	Highest Degree, Years In Position
Mindy	Female Hispanic	Dance Program Director	Department of Performing Arts	Associate professor tenured	Public community college	Master's (initial), 12 years
Susan	Female White	Dance Program Head	School of Theatre, Dance & Performance Studies	Associate professor tenured	Public university	Master's (initial), 2 years
Beth	Female White	Department Chair	College of the Arts	Professor untenured	Private college	Master's (initial) 28 years
Julia	Female White	Department Chair	Department of Dance	Professor tenured	Public university	PhD, 1 year
Candace	Female White	Department Chair	Department of Dance	Professor tenured	Public university	PhD, 2 years
Rachel	Female White	Department Chair	Department of Theatre & Dance	Professor tenured	Private college	MFA, 4 years
Mike	Male White	Director of Dance	School of Theatre & Dance	Assistant professor tenure track	Public university	PhD, 4 years
Paul	Male Black	Director of Dance	Department of Theatre & Dance	Associate professor tenured	Public university	MFA, 9 years
Ben	Male Asian	Dance Program Area Head	Department of Theatre & Dance	Associate professor tenured	Public university	MFA, 2 years

TABLE 3 Full Mixed-Method Study: Rank and Tenure Status by Gender

	Female ($n = 54$)		Male ($n = 21$)		Total	
	n	%	n	%	n	%
Professor	23	42	10	48	33	44
Associate professor	16	30	8	38	24	32
Assistant professor	9	17	2	9	11	15
Lecturer/instructor	6	11	1	5	7	9
Tenured	36	68	14	67	50	68
Tenure track	5	9	1	5	6	8
Nontenure track	12	23	6	28	18	24

Note: $n = 75$. From Risner and Musil (2017, 164).

TABLE 4 Full Mixed-Method Study: Workload as Percent Time by Gender

	% Female	% Male	% All
Administration	41	45	42
Teaching	36	27	33
Research/creative activity	11	13	12
Service	9	11	10
Fundraising/development	3	4	3

Note: From Risner and Musil (2017, 165).

BACKGROUND IN LEADERSHIP STYLES

It is not within the scope of this analysis to provide an exhaustive review of literature in leadership styles, particularly within the corporate model, where the literature is vast and descriptions of leadership styles abound. Literature on gender and leadership practice in higher education is also growing and although a comprehensive review is impractical, select works offer insights that have relevance to this study. Margaret E. Madden's (2005) review of gender and leadership in higher education addresses confluences that characterized leadership styles and goals among female administrators during specific historical periods. Madden problematized institutionally masculinized hierarchies and challenged gender stereotypes within hierarchical contexts such as higher education. Such stereotypes include overt or subconscious beliefs that career women are not nice, not feminine enough, and less likely to display important leadership qualities. Men are perceived as more likely to delegate, provide intellectual stimulation, and solve problems (5).

Jill Blackmore (2013) offered a critical feminist examination of historical leadership trends that have affected education. She asserted that more attention should be given to the intersection of gender, culture, religion, and class within leadership models. Perhaps of greatest applicability to this study are the works of Sandra Acker (2012) and Dana Christman and Rhonda McClellan (2012), which tackle the complexities and potential pitfalls of labeling and categorizing gendered behaviors within higher education leadership contexts, particularly when gender is viewed primarily as a binary of sexed bodies. Acker (2012) suggested that stereotypically gendered leadership behaviors should no longer be viewed as ascribed gender, but rather, as performed gender; and that viewing governance decisions through a series of different lenses will help us better understand women in academic leadership roles (424). Cristman and McClellan's (2012) study of men and women administrators' resiliency in leadership sought to identify how leaders gender themselves, concluding that most male and female leaders move between so-called gendered behaviors as a function of good leadership practice.

Literature in Dance Leadership

Beyond the work of Van Dyke (1993, 1996) and Hagood (2000) referenced earlier, literature regarding dance leadership and administration is sparse (Solomon 1983; Lee 1984; Whiteman 1992); little empirical research has been conducted about postsecondary dance leadership and administration (Risner 2007, 2010), although what has emerged raises important issues for further inquiry. Feminist discourse identifies specific leadership practice in the arts such as sharing of power, collegiality, collaboration (Garber et al. 2007), "exchange of energy" (Irwin 1995, 18), and feminist role models in administrative leadership (Thurber and Zimmerman 1996). Nearly two decades ago, former department head and dean Sue Stinson warned of the level of sacrifice women take on as administrators "who try to climb the tenure track while simultaneously taking care of everyone but themselves" (Stinson 1998, 123). At the same time, in the quest to keep dance and the art form at the center of focus while meeting the accelerating demands of the increasingly corporate-driven world of academia, effective leadership becomes progressively more important (Fichter 2002). However, dance historian and critic Janice Ross (2002) suggested that:

> Practitioners of the arts are often not the best educational advocates and theorists for the arts. The situation of not being an artist can give one more credibility with administrators and policymakers. The more neutral vantage point of an engaged outsider can be a powerful perspective from which to affect educational and institutional policy. In this manner one tends to frame arguments for academic acceptance from the outside in. (121)

The dance chairperson's role in insuring that both faculty concerns and student needs are met "frequently calls for a triangulation of sorts, not so much a balancing act—like a teeter totter, but more like a three-legged table made more stable by virtue of a third grounding, or in this instance a third perspective from the dance chair" (Risner and Prioleau 2004, 344). For dance administrators, quality of student instruction is frequently the chief mitigating factor in this triangulation, as the administrator seeks to advocate for students and at the same time serve as a representative of the dance faculty to the upper administration (Risner 2007). The lack of opportunity for advanced study at the doctoral level significantly limits the field's growth in leadership and administration; of the four doctoral programs currently offered in dance in the United States, there are no doctoral programs with an emphasis in dance administration, education, or leadership (Risner 2010).

The need for strategic and visionary planning for the next generation of dance leadership in academe has been voiced (Hagood 2000; Risner and Prioleau 2004; Risner 2007, 2010; Musil 2010). Postsecondary leadership has received considerable attention at the recent meetings of the think tank, Dance 2050: What Is the Future of Dance in Higher Education?, sponsored by the National Dance Education Organization and formed in 2011. The working group seeks "to function proactively, articulating and substantiating potentially radical innovation in dance in higher education, while fostering the leadership required to forge structural change" (Kolcio 2013). In the group's vision statement, "The Future of Dance in Higher Education" (Kahlich 2012), leadership abilities are to be cultivated "at the undergraduate level in dance programs and continues with proactive support for those moving through the tenure and promotion process; many dance educators/artists continue to become academic administrators at all levels" (11).

VOICES AND VALUES

With this background charted, we turn to the narratives of nine dance administrators who participated in semistructured interviews based on each participant's responses to an extensive online survey (Risner and Musil 2017). In addition to that quantitative data, the survey also gathered qualitative responses to open-ended questions about gender and postsecondary leadership in dance. Participants were given a copy of their survey responses for reference during the interview. We present the interview narratives organized by three areas of the participants' work and lives, taken directly from survey subheadings: leadership approach, support for participants' work, and work–life balance. Narratives are edited for succinctness. Gender implications within each area are discussed. Themes of race, cultural background, and sexual orientation also emerged in several interviews, as these topics intersected with gender and leadership. Although space does not permit a thorough examination of those issues here, some have naturally found their way into the narrative.

Leadership Approach

Primary interview questions in this area included the following:

- Can you talk about your approach to leadership?
- What's most important to you in your role?
- What guides your decision making?
- Why is this approach important to you?
- Where do you believe your values come from?

Participants were encouraged to share stories and examples throughout the interview.

Approaches and educational values among interviewees had significant ideological similarities in self-described leadership style and philosophy. All participants, to some degree, indicated using democratic, consensus-building, nonhierarchical, community decision making, or similar leadership styles.

Beth, a full professor and chair of a conservatory program for 28 years, stated, "I've been trying to create a student-centered environment in which each person feels valued and respected as an individual—a nonhierarchical relationship between the students and faculty where there really is a sense of a shared dedication to learning and growth and breadth." Paul, an associate professor and director of dance for nine years, stressed the importance of consensus building in what he termed the "hippie approach" where all voices are communally brought to the table. Ben, who is relatively new to dance administration, shared, "I would say my approach would be more democratic. I'm from Hawaii and we have such a genuine engagement with each other, even if they're not blood relatives; it's a sense of having everyone's opinions matter." Currently on tenure track as an assistant professor and director of dance, Mike noted, "Overall I like the idea of a leader creating opportunities for others to shine and nurturing an environment for others to grow in ... a leader has to be open ... a very good listener."

Although ideological values were similar, other indicators suggest differences in leadership practice. For example, two male participants referenced and differentiated notions of leading versus following. Ben stated, "I like to lead. I like to lead with willing, capable followers. I find as a good leader, you're also a good follower. I'm not saying this in terms of bragging, I just honestly, generally, and modestly, say that I enjoy leading." Mike specified what it means for him to lead and be followed: "It's not so much about the leader but it's about the followers, and if you don't have any followers you're really not a leader. I try to lead by example—I think it rubs off." Later, Mike also referenced leadership in terms of having one's "hand on the pulse and to see who they're leading and who's behind them." The narratives of Ben and Mike could help us better understand the potential link between the willingness to lead and gender. Paul described himself in autonomous and independent terms when discussing his decision-making practice. Although he indicated that he governs via community input, he also discussed subsequent decisions as his own unilateral acts.

Women discussed leadership in terms of community decision making rather than leader–follower models. As Julia, a full professor and chair, described, "Trying to create a cohesive unit so that we can move forward and have all voices be heard is really important to me." Rachel, a full professor and chair, spoke of leadership in nonhierarchical terms and related it to her consensus-building process. "I am not a very hierarchal or top-down leader and I bristle at most of that. One of my signature strengths is relationship. I draw on different people's strengths, ask clarifying questions, and help a group come to an understanding of the direction they want to go." Although subtle, this differentiation might indicate differences in how men and women perceive themselves within the dance leadership role.

Variations: Gender and Leadership Approach

In fact, the survey data gathered ($n = 75$) in the larger study indicate significant gender differences in how male and female administrators perceive themselves in the leadership role. Male administrators perceived their strengths in providing, guiding, forward thinking, and managing, whereas female administrators' perceived strengths were tied to leading through collaboration and support of students and faculty. When interviewees were asked about the role gender might play in some of the survey data, their responses were cautious; many were hesitant to make generalizations regarding gender and dance administration. However, all of the women were aware of perceived gender biases within academic leadership models, whereas Mike and Ben seemed less inclined to recognize these biases.

Attitudes about the role of gender and its impact within leadership were mixed, and covered a range of topics including gendered leadership qualities, personnel, pay scales, and general gender bias. Beth, who recently retired, indicated that:

> [Leadership] is not dependent on gender. It's dependent on other qualities and values, but my leadership style is completely female. Yes, why I do what I do is a very female perspective—we are raised to serve and believe me, as a Jewish female, I was really raised to serve. It's natural for me to go to that place of supporting, and the one thing that I love about my job is watching people grow.

Julia's comments had a similar tone:

> Of course, you have to be cautious. I would say among middle-aged, cisgendered women that, yes, they see themselves as helpful and supportive and that's a version of femininity that they have learned growing up and embraced—much more the servant-leader position than the visionary leader or the leader who makes decisions only on merit or the number of grants you bring in, those kinds of monetary making decisions. Yes, but it's not just that I'm a woman. It's that I'm a white middle-aged woman that sees myself as a traditional woman.

Of the female participants, Beth and Susan felt women are more conditioned than men to nurture, serve, and support—traits that had served both of them well as leaders. Candace, a professor and chair, was reluctant to overgeneralize:

> I'm loathe to make too many generalizations, but I have found that women tend to be more organized as administrators. Where

I think there is a gender thing is I often see men progressing really well in research and women not, and it's because women do tend to end up taking these administrative roles. So I'm not surprised women have strengths in administration... that women see that they have more strengths than challenges [as administrators], or that the men find more challenges because I think they're not socialized to be administrators within the academy.

When survey participants ($n = 75$) were asked why they became dance administrators, males were three times more likely than females to report, "I wanted to increase my income," and "My previous experiences in leadership were positive." The most divergent gender response between participants was "I had a strong mentor/role model," which men selected at five times the rate of women. When asked whether or not gender plays a part in the decision to take a leadership position, Candace suggested:

I've found that men generally avoid administrative roles ... by either actively or just unwittingly being really bad at them. I think sometimes it's strategic. Whereas women, I think, are constructed to be effective communicators, are able to multitask in quite extraordinary ways, are able to be superorganized and methodical both around operations and in terms of vision. But I have met some good male administrators, so I don't want to completely universalize men as being bad administrators. My strongest role models have been women, and I've also had some really bad female administrators as well. But generally the ones who've resonated with me have been women.

When asked to describe their motivations for entering the field of dance administration, 72 percent of female survey participants selected the statement, "I became a dance administrator because I enjoy supporting students and faculty" (50 percent of males selected this response). A number of interviewees linked supporting students to effective leadership. When Susan, an associate professor and dance program head, was asked if she felt her impulse to support students was linked to gender, she stated, "Absolutely, I'm sure it's gender. Of course it is. I mean, the whole assessment process has been nurtured by women. And I use the word nurture deliberately. It's really hard to know if that's because in dance we are a matriarchy. My mentors, for the most part, are all women." Ben echoed similar sentiments: "Not to sound sexist, but I think [the impulse to support] comes more naturally [to women] than men. I think the maternal instinct is probably what that is about." Julia, like 48 percent of female survey participants, reported personnel and staffing issues as one of the most challenging aspects of her work (see Table 4). In her interview she revisited her notions of women and caring about others:

Yes, absolutely. Again, understanding that gender is anomalous. I think some heads don't really lose much sleep about whether person X is unhappy, or whether they're treating people equally in the department. I think some people enjoy manipulating faculty against each other. Again, I think it's the middle-aged, traditional women thing, that making sure others are happy and feel good about themselves and their work is really important.

With the exception of Beth and Candace, the other seven interviewees believed that women face more challenges than men in leadership positions in terms of being heard within the academy itself. Mindy, a program director for 12 years, suggested, "I think that immediately when people see you as a woman they think that you're maybe not as effective as a male department head." Paul echoed her sentiment in his observation that his female colleague in the department (the only female in a department of all white men except Paul, who is African American) is not often heard until Paul or someone else voices what the female colleague has already said. Later, Paul reinforced this sentiment: "For the most part, if I say something, it gets heard and I feel that my gender probably has some impact."
In reference to increasing numbers of male administrators in dance, Beth indicated:

To a certain extent, I feel that in a field where we're 70 percent women and 30 percent men, the leadership should reflect that. I would hate to see higher education become yet another area in which all of the people in the lower positions, that is students and faculty, are women and all of the people at the top are men. That would be sad to me.

Julia echoed this thought noting, "I think that having a male head would be a very bad idea—create a kind of paternalistic hierarchy that would be very unwelcome ... having a woman and having a dance person (as a chair) is tremendously validating for dance faculty." She concluded by emphasizing that with a female chair, "We have somebody that can represent our own issues and values."

Most interviewees acknowledged the dominance of white male culture that persists in the academy's leadership structure and approaches, as well as the perceptions about women that emerge and are maintained from such masculinist constructions. Paul expounded on challenges faced by women in explicit and thoughtful ways, confirming that "the good old boys' institution is alive and well," but he also noted that shifts have occurred in a positive direction. The majority of females signaled prevailing sociopolitical attitudes and challenges, as Candace suggested:

I think the academy has carried institutional sexism throughout its entire history. I think that is still very much in place. It's incredibly subtle, but I think that men typically get more opportunities to do research and to not have to take on administrative roles, and I think women typically get the burden of service in administration. I think some of that comes out of the way in which we are socialized in the work place. And some of it comes from just the history of the academy and women's place within it.

Susan shared her perspectives about gender bias in the institution as it relates to unequal pay for similar work:

I know great male leaders in dance and they all make more money than I do. I don't think that people mean to be sexist or gendered ... I think it's just the default. If somebody came into [my] position now, and it was a white male, he would automatically be offered more than my salary. If I were replaced by a woman, she would be offered less than my salary... and it will have nothing to do with their experience or their competence. I think it's just automatic and unconscious. The men dance leaders I know are fabulous at what they do and totally deserve the money they make... but we deserve it, too.

It is important to note that four of the nine interviewees differentiated men in the dance discipline—either explicitly or implicitly—as different from men generally in terms of stereotypical male behavior. In her interview, it was important to Susan to say, "We do have gender issues but not in the dance area. We have a little dance tribe over here and we like each other." Ben reported, "We will have our disagreements like any groupings of people, dance or otherwise, but I think for the most part we're always—I would say 99 percent—always on the same page." These individual narratives begin to shape a larger narrative that diverges from traditional male stereotypes within the higher education dance workplace. Shared governance and collaborative leadership, often generalized to females and espoused by the female interviewees in this inquiry, were also seen as important elements of dance administration for the male participants. Christman and McClellan (2012) asserted that effective leadership behaviors are difficult to ascribe within neat binary roles and suggest a new paradigm—a "middle space" that replaces static dichotomies with a more fluid continuum that functions without regard to gendered stereotypes (663). This type of continuum seems to be present within dance postsecondary leadership.

Support for Participants' Work

Interview questions about the support their work as dance administrators receives were based on each participant's responses to a Likert support scale included in the online survey, which asked them to rate specific persons, groups of people, and organizations that support their work (Risner 2009). Follow-up interview questions included the following:

- As you look at your ratings again, does anything in particular stand out to you?
- Is there one specific source of support that is most helpful to you?
- Can you talk more about your satisfaction/dissatisfaction?
- What do you attribute to your level of satisfaction?

This portion of the interview concluded with the question, "Do you see any links or connections between gender and support for your work?"

Each of the nine interviewees addressed heavy workloads. As Mike put it, "We undertake a lot, especially at the beginning until we build the program where you can delegate and have more people and faculty who can take things on." Substantial workloads, lack of effective staff support, and funding were the most pervasive indicators of support dissatisfaction for participants' work. "All those hats that we wear," Mindy said, "so the kind of support that we need is help [with] administrative work." Beth summed up some of dance administrators' self-inflicted challenges in maintaining heavy workloads without sufficient support:

> Virtually all of the administrative work of our department is done either by me or by my department coordinator... anything that she doesn't have time for, I do. I lay some of the blame for overwork on myself, but I think that the equation at most universities is: "insufficient resources, plus incredible overwork on the part of the administrator, equals excellent department." We're really doing it with smoke and mirrors and there's no reason on earth for our department to be as good as it is when you look at the actual resources available. My dissatisfaction is trying to do too much with too little.

Survey data indicated that males perceived significantly higher levels of support satisfaction than females. Overall support satisfaction showed similar gender differences (see Table 5): the majority of males (51 percent) reported they were *highly satisfied* and *satisfied*, whereas only 36 percent of females reported the same combination. Statistically, that females expressed considerably lower levels of support satisfaction brings up important questions about the environments in which women administrators work and lead dance programs, as well as others' perceptions and attitudes about female leadership in the academic workplace.

Lower levels of support satisfaction for women could be tied to workplace experiences such as Beth's heard earlier in which she performs all of the administrative duties required of her position and then does the remainder of the department coordinator's workload, too. This "someone's got to do it" rationale might give female administrators professional cover for what in fact is likely a good deal of personal sacrifice (Stinson 1998), which males in this inquiry do not appear to experience or acknowledge. For example, in the same situation of work overload, Mike's strategy is to delegate the work to others as soon as possible once he has established standard operating procedures:

> In a leadership position you have to know to delegate; you have to stand back, in a way, and let things happen. You initiate and you create an environment for things to happen, but you can't be everywhere; you can't wear all the hats. So it's slowly getting

TABLE 5 Full Mixed-Method Study: Support Satisfaction by Gender

	% Female	% Male	% All
Highly satisfied	6	6	6
Satisfied	30	41	33
Somewhat satisfied	43	23	38
Dissatisfied	17	18	17
Highly dissatisfied	4	12	6

Note: From Risner and Musil (2017, 167).

Research and creative activity is perceived as an important part of work–life balance among administrators. In the larger study's survey (Risner and Musil 2017), when asked to respond to the statement, "As a dance administrator, I have been able to maintain an active research/creative activity profile," participants reported *strongly agree* (10 percent), *agree* (48 percent), *disagree* (36 percent), and *strongly disagree* (6 percent). There were no significant gender differences. In this study, all three male interviewees acknowledged the importance of their creative work as an enlivening factor in their work as a dance administrator; and five of the six female administrators discussed their research and creative work as part of the workload balancing act, addressing complexities in finding time for research. "As long as I also get to do my creative work, amongst all this crazy administrating," Ben stated, "that's important for me." "I get so much administration," Candace said, "that I then have to find other time in my life to do [my research] beyond the working day." Rachel lamented, "It was like trying to get water out of a rock –I could not squeeze anything else out of my life. You need to attend to the most basic needs of your child; you try to meet day-to-day demands as a teacher; [and] for me, the one that got short-changed was always the work of an artist." What could be emerging here might have less to do with gender and more to do with the occupation itself. Heavy workloads for dance administrators impinge on personal lives regardless of gender or the language participants use to discuss their labor.

Variations: Gender and Work–Life Balance

Although both male and female participants in the larger study reported significant challenges relating to work–life balance, the challenges emerged more strongly in female administrators' interviews, especially when discussing and maintaining critical relationships, such as one's health, and parenting. Rachel lamented the difficulty of compartmentalizing one's life as a caregiver:

> Women faculty I know are trying to juggle various care giving roles, whether it's caring for elderly parents, which tends to fall to the daughters, or if as a parent. In a faculty meeting, at ten minutes to five, you see every woman in the room who has kids in day care get up and walk out. You don't see the dads get up and walk out. Someone else is picking up the kids from day care.

Susan stated:

> There is no way that I could live how I'm living now, when my kids were home. My husband can be understanding in a way that my kids could not be. So I think that I'm able to do more research and creative work now than I was able to do when the kids were home. That's why my career is taking off now … and I think that higher education needs to understand this.

Mindy believes that many women in postsecondary education endanger their own health with years and years of 60-hour work weeks, as she cautioned:

> I don't have health concerns, but I'm in my 40s; I can see how 20 years from now if I'm still doing the same amount of hours and load and all of that, how it could actually lead to health concerns; and not necessarily anything I'm doing differently, but just in the amount of stress on the actual body. I don't have children, but I have a lot of friends that leave these kinds of jobs to do other things that require less time because they do want to start families or want to have kids.

It is important to note that the larger study's survey did not delve into elements that would potentially influence work–life balance, like marital status, children and parenting, spousal or elder care, summer employment, and personal health, among other influences. Given the tentative but persuasive findings in this inquiry, future studies are needed to better understand the ways in which dance administrators, especially women, effectively balance personal and professional lives, as well as the role models they present, intentionally or not, for students and faculty pursuing tenure and promotion.

FURTHER THOUGHTS

The purpose of this narrative inquiry was to develop a better understanding of the experiences of dance administrators (chairs, heads, directors, and coordinators) as part of the authors' comprehensive status report of administrative leadership in postsecondary dance with particular focus on gender and its role within leadership structures and practices. This study, focused on representative, qualitative narratives of nine participants (six women, three men) from the larger study pool, confirmed many of the quantitative findings from the survey, revealed some anticipated qualitative findings from the survey, and some unexpected outcomes regarding leadership approaches, work support satisfaction, and work–life balance issues.

As the first empirical inquiry of its kind conducted within the United States, this exploratory inquiry uncovered and acknowledged the existence of some long-standing issues within postsecondary dance leadership and raised some new questions. However, to make sweeping generalizations or conclusions at this time would be imprudent. Qualitative research often produces more questions than answers, seeking to better understand people, processes, and relationships. Throughout this article we have highlighted what we believe are primary themes in the interview data, and we have posed a number of questions for readers' contemplation, ones that we hope will stimulate leadership and gender discourses and inspire future empirical research in this area. Multiple opportunities for prospective research studies include lack of support structures among female administrators; how male and female administrators' strengths reflect what they value in leadership traits; and issues surrounding male privilege, including disparities relating to academic credentials, salaries, and career advancement. Matters affecting both genders include the role of childrearing and family structures in tenure, advancement and work–life balance, and the impact of increasing male leadership on both male and female students' postsecondary dance experience and education.

Further inquiry on these and similar topics will guide the discipline toward a more informed professional community, one leading postsecondary dance into the third decade of the twenty-first century.

Throughout the voices heard in this study, we are reminded of the limitations that any lens presents for understanding human experience. The act of research observation, and its attendant analysis, immediately frames experience in a certain light and perspective. Of particular importance to us is the notion that gender is socially constructed, fluid, and likely overrated for understanding how any one individual works or studies in dance. In this inquiry we have witnessed and discussed a number of stereotypes that have some basis in reality, but for the occupation of administrator itself, not so much for the gender. For example, Sue Stinson (1998) compared much of the chair's work in dance to departmental housekeeping that no one else wants to do. In this study, we have heard the notion of "wearing many hats" and its related translation of "multitasking," which seems to be associated more with the job rather than gender. Margaret Madden (2005) cautioned us to remember:

> Indeed, individuals' behavior probably varies greatly from situation to situation, but there is not sufficient evidence from sound empirical observation of women and men in real academic leadership settings to begin to quantify the extent of variability between or within genders. A feminist analysis is useful only if it helps women and men understand and respond to constraints on their behavior from gendered expectations and contexts, not if it perpetuates false stereotypes about women's leadership style. (6)

Gender stereotypes about women in dance leadership and administration falsely generalize them even when a fair number have some link to reality; however, stereotyping also draws a conclusion that often produces social difference and in some cases, social distance that cuts off real learning about other people and their practices. The aim of this research has been precisely the opposite, especially in terms of the ever-increasing political dimension of postsecondary administration in U.S. universities and colleges. Therefore, we have sought to present these nine administrators as individuals, each in her or his own complexity. Because we know full well that even seemingly positive stereotypes could be oppressive or used oppressively by the dominant group whose authority wields its unquestioned power to reduce and define groups and individuals to a narrow derogatory "type," this narrative inquiry explicitly seeks to support women and men serving as dance administrators to redefine themselves in free and liberating ways.

REFERENCES

Acker, S. 2012. Chairing and caring: Gendered dimensions of leadership in academe. *Gender and Education* 24(4):411–28.

Bernard, R., and G. Ryan. 2009. *Analyzing qualitative data: Systematic approaches*. London: Sage.

Blackmore, J. 2013. A feminist critical perspective on educational leadership. *International Journal of Leadership in Education* 16(2):139–54.

Christman, D., and R. McClellan. 2012. Discovering middle space: Distinctions of sex and gender in resilient leadership. *The Journal of Higher Education* 83(5):648–70.

Creswell, J. 2003. *Research design: Qualitative, quantitative, mixed methods approaches*. Thousand Oaks, CA: Sage.

———. 2014. *Research design: Qualitative, quantitative, and mixed methods approaches*. Fourth edition. Thousand Oaks, CA: Sage.

Denzin, N., and Y. Lincoln. 2011. Discipline and practice of qualitative research. In *The Sage handbook of qualitative research*, ed. N. Denzin and Y. Lincoln, 1–19. Thousand Oaks, CA: Sage.

Erickson, F. 2005. Arts, humanities, and sciences in educational research and social engineering in federal education policy. *Teachers College Record* 107(1):4–9.

Fichter, S. N. 2002. The quest for center: Creating a culture for learning in a corporate world. *Arts Education Policy Review* 103(5):3–7.

Garber, E., R. Sandell, M. Stankiewicz, and D. Risner. 2007. Gender equity in the visual arts and dance education. In *Handbook for achieving gender equity through education*, ed. S. Klein, 359–80. Mahwah, NJ: Erlbaum.

Hagood, T. 2000. *History of dance in American higher education*. Lewiston, NY: Edwin Mellen.

Higher Education Arts Data Services (HEADS). 1994. *Dance data summaries 1993–1994*. Reston, VA: Higher Education Arts Data Services.

———. 2011. *Dance data summaries 2010–2011*. Reston, VA: Higher Education Arts Data Services.

———. 2015. *Dance data summaries 2014–2015*. Reston, VA: Higher Education Arts Data Services.

Irwin, R. 1995. *A circle of empowerment: Women, education, and leadership*. Albany, NY: State University of New York.

Johnson, R., A. Onwuegbuzie, and L. Turner. 2007. Toward a definition of mixed methods research. *Journal of Mixed Methods Research* 1 (2):112–33.

Kahlich, L., ed. 2012. *Proceedings: DANCE 2050—The future of dance in higher education*. Bethesda, MD: National Dance Education Organization. http://www.ndeo.org/content.aspx?page_id=22&club_id=893257&module_id=123461 (accessed October 21, 2015).

Kolcio, K. 2013. Event information for DANCE 2050 in 2013. http://www.ndeo.org/content.aspx?page_id=87&club_id=893257&item_id=318561 (accessed October 21, 2015).

Kvale, S., and S. Brinkmann. 2008. *Interviews: Learning the craft of qualitative research interviewing*. Thousand Oaks, CA: Sage.

Lee, S. 1984. Dance administrative opportunities. *Journal of Physical Education, Recreation and Dance* 55(5):74–75.

Lincoln, S., and E. Guba. 2004. But is it rigorous? Trustworthiness and authenticity in naturalistic evaluation. *New Directions for Evaluation* 1986(30):73–84.

Madden, M. E. 2005. 2004 Division 35 Presidential address: Gender and leadership in higher education. *Psychology of Women Quarterly* 29 (1):3–14.

Musil, P. 2010. Perspectives on an expansive postsecondary dance. *Journal of Dance Education* 10(4):111–21.

Risner, D. 2007. Current challenges for K–12 dance education and development: Perspectives from higher education. *Arts Education Policy Review* 108(4):17–23.

———. 2009. *Stigma and perseverance in the lives of boys who dance: An empirical study of male identities in Western theatrical dance training*. Lewiston, NY: Edwin Mellen.

———. 2010. Dance education matters: Rebuilding postsecondary dance education for twenty-first century relevance and resonance. *Arts Education Policy Review* 111(4):123–35.

Risner, D., and P. Musil. 2017. Leadership and gender in postsecondary dance: An exploratory survey of dance administrators in the United States. In *Dance and gender: An evidence-based approach*, ed. W. Oliver and D. Risner, 158–83. Gainesville, FL: University Press of Florida.

Risner, D., and D. Prioleau. 2004. Leadership and administration in dance in higher education: Challenges and responsibilities of the department chair. In *Conference proceedings of the National Dance Education Organization: Merging worlds: Dance, education, society and politics*, ed. D. Risner and J. Anderson, 343–51. East Lansing, MI: National Dance Education Organization.

Ross, J. 2002. Institutional forces and the shaping of dance in the American university. *Dance Chronicle* 25(1):115–24.

Solomon, R. 1983. Dance into administrator: Chairing the department or life at the top. *Journal of Physical Education, Recreation and Dance* 57(2):66–67.

Stern, R. D. 1994. *1994-95 Dance Magazine college guide*. New York: Mcfadden Communications.

Stinson, S. 1998. Places where I've been: Reflections on issues of gender in dance education, research, and administration. *Choreography and Dance* 5(1):117–27.

Thurber, F., and E. Zimmerman. 1996. Empower not in power: Gender and leadership roles in art teacher education. In *Gender issues in art education: Content, contexts, and strategies*, ed. G. Collins and R. Sandell, 144–53. Reston, VA: National Art Education Association.

Van Dyke, J. 1993. *Modern dance in a postmodern world: An analysis of federal arts funding and its impact on the field of modern dance.* Reston, VA: AAHPERD.

———. 1996. Gender and success in the American dance world. *Women's Studies International Forum* 19(5):535–43.

Whiteman, E. F. 1992. Management competencies for dance administrators in higher education. In *Dance in higher education*, ed. W. Oliver, 114–17. Reston, VA: American Alliance for Health, Physical Education, Recreation and Dance.

Part III
The Role of Dance Teaching Artists in Dance Education

Prelude

"As teaching artists negotiate the complexity of 'guest-hood' upon entry into P-12 educational environments, they do so alongside reconciliation of their creative interests and artistic praxis within regulations, rules, and policies of respective school locales." (Risner et al., 2021, p. 11)

Jennifer McNamara: The rich and complicated story of Doug Risner's earlier years was one I did not know when I first met him, but it has illuminated much about his passion for teaching, the mercurial qualities and flexible thinking he models, and the practicality with which he draws these elements together in his pedagogical approach. His multifaceted approach to teaching, detailed in the articles of this section, includes outcomes for all parties as equitable components and partners and is clearly indicative of Doug's early training, which, in some ways, both contradicts and simultaneously mirrors my own. He knew that he wanted to be teacher before he knew that he wanted to be a dancer; I had no interest in teaching or dancing (I wanted to be a firefighter). His first-grade teacher, Mrs. Shaffer, approached each student as an individual, each with different needs, and made sure to focus on their strengths rather than on their shortcomings. At six years old, he frequently invited neighborhood friends to his house to play school—and of course, he was always the teacher. I, on the other hand, emphatically turned my back on teaching, from the age of six until I was in my mid-twenties, because it seemed impossibly daunting to be responsible for someone else's learning—although my parents, both public-school teachers, were brilliant models of how to do it well.

Doug and I both started dancing in the second grade, though: his teacher, Miss Phyllis, and my teacher, Miss Gloria, were the types who saw the future rather than only the present. They instilled in us the belief in hard work, doing our best, and never giving up, skills that are often lumped in with the currently fashionable idea, in the uneasy late pandemic years, of practicing resilience. But resilience has also earned a reputation as yet another idea that is perpetuated by racist policies: resilience, in spite of its supposed reliance on the self, actually rests on access to support systems that are often withdrawn from the communities that need them the most, including access to arts and education. This is where Doug's early years as an educator clearly drew on his reverence for and learning from Miss Phyllis, incorporating methodologies that were never negative or demeaning, and instead focused on the porous places where new ideas seep into the consciousness and reveal new possibilities in the spaces between body and mind, between teacher and student, between dancer and maker.

Doug Risner: Much of my early dancing career, 1980–1984, comprised performances with a small contemporary dance company in Pittsburgh, Janet Gillespie & Present Company, of which I was a member, and also taught jazz, modern, and ballet technique for its associated school, the Dance Gallery. During that time, my work also extended to encompass teaching artist gigs for dance companies and social service programs, including Pittsburgh Ballet Theatre School, Abraxas Foundation for Troubled Youth, and Western Pennsylvania School for Blind Children. From 1985 to 1997, working in various college and university dance programs across the US, I choreographed original programs for university dance touring programs and community outreach events; this type of work was common for both educational institutions and professional dance companies in the era of accessible grant funding for arts outreach [now often rebranded as "community engagement" in an effort to address and distance itself from ideas about "white saviorism" embedded in the previous term, Jennifer notes] by the National Endowment for the Arts (NEA), among other governmental entities. Often times these works were based on classic children's books (*The Bremen Town Musicians; The Giving Tree; Where the Wild Things Are*) and were frequently paired with original musical scores. Because I had read (and danced) these books so many times with my young daughter Hannah Risner (b. 1984), whom I cherished, I felt particularly drawn to make them into works I could share with others, especially for young children and adolescents across the US.

Like many dance teaching artists during this period, I frequently presented week-long residencies in postsecondary dance departments and programs and often brought one of my undergraduate students with me as an assistant. As a team we would present masterclasses during the day and then teach and rehearse a dance work from my choreographic repertoire selected by the host institution from a number of potential pieces that their students could perform on campus and on tour. I found this type of teaching artistry quite meaningful for everyone involved, for several reasons: (a) dance faculty at other institutions benefitted from not having to create yet another work for students; (b) students were exposed to a different approach to creating/learning choreography collaboratively; (c) young children in schools were introduced to dance; and (d) my student assistants also benefitted significantly—learning how to adapt, compromise, and make quick decisions and choices to benefit the overall residency experience for the host and student participants.

JM: Doug's multi-pronged approach to making dance both attractive and accessible to children echoes the best parts of my own career in mid-sized regional dance companies, where we spent much more time teaching and interacting with the communities where we performed than we did on the stage—often using lesser-known children's literature or regionally/culturally relevant mythologies rather than grand (Euro-Western) fairy tales for source material as a way to broaden conversations about the relevance of dance. This approach, when framed within the mission of a university, also incorporates in its rubric measurable accountability to the institution as well as to the participants, both educator and student. When the scales tipped toward production and standardization, however, is hard to say: when did financial concerns, outcomes-based instruction, and "teaching to the test" mandates become more important than the shared experience of learning?

When were curiosity, play, and experimentation pushed aside in favor of providing hard data to the institution, backed up by self-studies and assessment rather than joy and innovation? And when did teachers become expendable, particularly in the arts? Perhaps it had to do with the way that the institution itself did not (and to some extent still does not) understand the difference between preparation and production, and the ways that support systems simply do not exist for people who live and thrive outside the center, where these versatile, sinuous, chameleon-like artists are able to see the spaces that invite change and where they might slip in to create it.

DR: The chapters in Part III were drawn from qualitative-dominant, mixed method research studies I conducted collaboratively over a ten-year period. My co-researchers were also former or current dance teaching artists throughout their careers working in community dance, P-12 schools, professional dance companies, and postsecondary dance and theater degree programs. At the time (circa 2012), the dearth of published literature on dance teaching artists required conducting original research. With my colleague Dr. Mary Elizabeth Anderson, a theater teaching artist at Wayne State University, we conducted a large, international research study on dance and theater teaching artists. The study's findings were published in the edited volume, *Hybrid Lives of Teaching Artists in Dance and Theatre Arts: A Critical Reader* (Anderson and Risner, 2014); they significantly influenced the creation and establishment of the Master of Arts in Theatre and Dance: Teaching Artistry graduate program at Wayne State University in 2016. As the only graduate program of its kind globally, the fully online program allows working teaching artists, P-12 educators, and post-secondary educators to develop their teaching artistry expertise, pedagogy, artistic practice, and research objectives.

My experiences as a dance teaching artist and my interest in dance teaching artistry research continue to stimulate my curiosity and have heightened my advocacy efforts at the same time. Chapter 10, "Preparation, Policy and Workplace Challenges of Dance Teaching Artists in P-12 Schools: Perspectives from the Field" (2021), is my most recent co-authored journal publication, which closely examines the workplace challenges that dance teaching artists confront in P-12 schools today. This chapter draws upon the words, experiences, and wisdom of expert informants in the dance teaching artist field.

JM: As I noted in the introduction to this book, teaching artists occupy a tenuous sliver in an also tenuous field, and while some of them prefer that chameleon-like ability to slip between the world of dance and the world of teaching, others find the negotiation fraught. And yet, no matter the space where a teaching artist practices—community dance centers, pre-professional training programs, public schools, or private studios—their work is often an ongoing series of trial-and-error, different in each iteration because of varying assessments and learning outcomes, equipment and space standards, competency requirements, supports systems, and populations. Preparing an artist to share knowledge with students or preparing an educator to make art with students—these are widely differing journeys, and yet programs that purport to train arts educators and the placements where these teachers find themselves have very little accountability to that very person—or the students they serve.

At the time of this writing, the state of Pennsylvania, where I teach, has voted to provide a direct path to dance teacher certification in PK-12 education; as universities in the state, hopefully including mine, prepare to offer this certification to eager future teachers, I am indebted to Doug for the questions that I learned to hear and the concerns that I learned to notice because of Doug's passionate attentiveness to the journey upon which teachers embark. Listening, really listening to the voices of working teaching artists—what really matters? What are we not paying attention to? These questions should, perhaps, shape nearly all aspects of a teaching program's design and format. In the case of the Wayne State University MA in Teaching Artistry program that Doug designed with his colleague Mary Elizabeth Anderson, it was clear that the first priority was to make it available in a fully online format for current teaching artists who were unable to relocate or uproot their families. It was also clear that continuing their current teaching artist employment while pursuing a master's degree was a high priority, and they wanted options for internships and fieldwork experiences in their area as part of the program. Listening to those who do the work, day in and day out, creates a culture of community, collegiality, and collaboration—often touted as hallmarks of the arts. Why would our teacher preparation and support programs be anything less? And how can we make this the standard that we uphold for all educators? This is the crux of and urgency behind Doug Risner's continued advocacy in the field.

References

Anderson, M. E., & Risner, D. (2014). *Hybrid lives of teaching artists in dance and theatre arts: A critical reader.* Cambria Press.

Risner, D., Horning, S., & Henderson Shea, B. (2021) Preparation, policy, and workplace challenges of dance teaching artists in P-12 schools: Perspectives from the field. *Arts Education Policy Review*, AHEAD-OF-PRINT, 1–14. DOI: 10.1080/10632913.2021.2004959

Hybrid Lives of Teaching Artistry: A Survey of Teaching Artists in Dance

Doug Risner

This paper investigates teaching artists in the USA whose work is rooted in dance and dance-related disciplines. Teaching artists, although the descriptor itself remains both ambiguous and debated in the USA, provide a good deal of arts education delivery in K12 schools and afterschool programs. Based on survey data from a range of dance teaching artists across the nation ($n = 64$), the study presents emergent themes including: (1) insufficient preparation, (2) obstacles and challenges in the workplace and (3) diverse perspectives on teaching artist professionalization and credential programs. The paper concludes with recommendations for post-secondary (tertiary) curriculum development in dance programs.

Introduction

In the USA, the teaching artist field in dance is a diverse assemblage of individuals who see their work from a variety of perspectives: dance artists who teach as part of their professional responsibilities; dance arts educators working in school and community settings; cultural workers who employ dance for constructive social change; activists who use dance arts to improve people's lives and circumstances; professional dance artists and performers who supplement their income with teaching; and those who clearly classify themselves as professional teaching artists in dance. From a broad perspective, today's teaching artist plays a significant role in numerous educational settings and contexts (Rabkin and Hedberg 2011; Remer 2010). The work of the teaching artist during the past decade has garnered increasing professional and research consideration: the Association of Teaching Artists (ATA),[1] founded in 1998, supports and advocates for the teaching artist profession; the *Teaching Artist Journal*, first published in 2003, offers applied and theoretical research, as well as critical networks and community-building opportunities; the National Opinion Research Center (NORC) completed its five-year study, Teaching Artist Research Project in 2011;[2] and the research survey, "Teaching Artists and Their Work", was published in 2010 by the Association of Teaching Artists.[3] With a focus on teaching artists in dance, this study seeks to expand this burgeoning area of inquiry.

In dance, given the diversity of teaching artist practices and identities, unearthing relevant and meaningful research requires a close investigation of the practitioners and contexts under consideration. The field of dance education in particular, largely under-represented in arts education generally US schools (Bonbright 2002, 2011; Rabkin and Hedberg 2011; Remer 2003, 2010), hinges weightily on the work of teaching artists for delivery of educational programs. Thus, this study also explores the lacunae-like position the teaching artist in dance holds – a position that importantly fills a number of empty spaces, missing gaps – both in arts education and community-based outreach programs.

This paper, drawn from a larger, ongoing international study of teaching artists in dance (Anderson and Risner 2012), offers a comprehensive examination of participants' artistic and academic preparation, entry into the teaching artist field, challenges encountered in their work and attitudes about professionalization and potential credential programs. Implications for post-secondary curriculum and degree programs are featured and the paper concludes with recommendations for imaginative and prophetic curriculum development in higher education dance.

Research design and methods

As part of a three-year mixed-method research study, this paper seeks to develop a cogent body of knowledge about arts education and outreach programs as developed and delivered by teaching artists in dance. The absence of research in this area required basic quantitative data and qualitative narrative data to enrich the former. While some research theorists concentrate on the irreconcilability of qualitative and quantitative research designs (Lincoln and Guba 1985), this study's primary research questions necessitated a fruitful blend of designs (Patton 1990), which included an extensive survey instrument conducted online. In order to conduct this research consistent with these research assumptions and problems, a mixed-method design was employed. Procedures included literature review of secondary resources, primary resources from an online survey (n = 64) and in-depth interviews. Surveys were statistically analyzed and interviews were coded for emergent themes. Human subject approval was received from author's institutional review board.

The study's central research questions included: (1) What kinds of skill preparation, academic training and artistic experience characterize teaching artists in dance? (2) What background, experiences and situations motivated individuals to become teaching artists? (3) How prepared were study participants upon entering the teaching artist field? (4) What challenges do participants confront in their current teaching artist practice? (5) What beliefs and attitudes do teaching artists hold about the professionalization of the teaching artist profession?

Dance arts education in the USA

In order to situate the work of teaching artists in the larger sphere of dance arts education in the USA, a brief outline of instruction types in school-based pre-kindergarten through 12 (P12) education today is necessary. The three primary modes of instruction are those delivered by specialist teachers in dance, general classroom teachers and teaching artists in dance. These categories of instruction hold distinctive functions within the school environment and curriculum. Similarly, each kind of instructor's required educational preparation, certification or licensure and artistic expertise differs according to instruction type.

Specialist teachers in dance hold certification or licensure like other specialist teachers in math, English, history or biology. Dance specialists' educational preparation concentrates on dance as an art form as well as teaching dance. All specialists hold undergraduate degrees: some completed the professional Bachelor of Fine Arts (BFA) degree program, others completed a liberal arts degree program, such as the Bachelor of Arts (BA) in dance or Bachelor of Science (BS) in dance. These teachers deliver curriculum-based programs in dance in one or more schools on a regular basis.

In elementary (or primary education), general classroom teachers are certified or licensed as generalist teachers. The majority of these teachers do not possess the educational preparation or credentials to teach dance. However, there is a range of interest and expertise among generalist teachers about learning through the arts and incorporating dance in their classrooms.

Many schools in the USA have few or no prospect of having, specialist dance teachers. Only 7% of US children in P12 education receive instruction from qualified dance educators (Bonbright 2011). Teaching artists, generally not certified, but trained in one or more arts disciplines, play an important visiting or adjunct role in many school settings. For the vast majority of schools, teaching artists provide some dance instruction where otherwise there would be none. In administrative and policy circles, the term "teaching artist" refers to nearly anyone teaching the arts who is not a certified school-based arts specialist teacher. These teaching artists in dance are the focus of this paper, as described below.

Defining teaching artists in dance

Dance artists serve schools and communities in numerous ways. Their educational work takes many approaches from a variety of perspectives. Without reducing this breadth and complexity, I briefly summarize three primary populations of teaching artists as identified and reported by participants in this study.

Individual artists

Individual dance artists often assume teaching responsibilities as part of their larger professional work and goals. Others teach to generate supplemental income – either for themselves or for their respective professional dance companies (Parrish 2009; Sweeney 2003). Some individual dance artists prioritize community-based, educational projects for socially-responsive outcomes. Often this work is built into their professional commitments and schedules. Integrating artistry, teaching and advocacy, these projects primarily marshal the instrumental aims of dance. By engagement with dance as an art form, individuals find a renewed understanding of themselves and their multiple connections to their communities. In the present study, 27% of participants identified as individual dance artists as described above.

Professional dance companies and presenting organizations

Most professional dance companies and presenting organizations in the USA have developed educational and community programs, frequently aligned with strategies that seek to increase audience development, revenue generation and in some instances, recruitment of young talent (Americans for the Arts 2007; Brown and

Novak 2007; McCarthy and Jinnett 2001). In these organizations, educational and community outreach programs are often delivered by drawing upon dance company members and artistic personnel who receive some form of teaching artist training or mentoring. Today, large dance companies commonly employ an education director and administrative staff, many of whom also serve as teaching artists for the organization's educational programming. Of this study's participants, 29% identified as teaching artists working for professional dance companies and organizations.

Professional teaching artists

A third and increasing sector of dance educational programs are delivered by independent professional teaching artists. As defined by the Association of Teaching Artists (2009), three fundamental capacities are necessary for professional teaching artists: understanding one's art form; understanding classroom environment, pedagogy and human development; and understanding the collaborative process of working in a school environment. Most participants in this study work primarily in K12 schools (75%) or community- and school-collaborative settings (58%). The University of Chicago's National Opinion Research Center reports:

> Remarkable advances have taken place over the past decade and a half in arts education, both in and out of schools, due largely to the creativity of teaching artists. Their best efforts are redefining the roles the arts play in public education; and their work is central to arts organizations' strategies for civic engagement and audience diversity. (NORC 2009, n.p.)

In the present study, 44% of participants identified as professional teaching artists in dance as articulated above.

Although these populations and modes of delivery have been presented as distinct categories, it must be acknowledged that, in practice, there are increasing boundary crossings between them. For instance in the USA, the American Ballet Theatre (ABT) delivers its educational programs through a cohort of ABT Teaching Artists hired specifically for project-driven work. Some are current or retired ABT dancers, others may have credentials in education and some are traditional teaching artists in schools.

Survey findings

The extensive online survey in this study was organized into five broad sections: (1) demographic information, (2) education, training and experience, (3) teaching artist work and support, (4) attitudes and perspectives and (5) open-ended questions allowing participants to revisit and comment on issues and concerns raised earlier in the survey. In this section, I report and summarize survey findings as applicable to the current research questions under consideration.

Employment status and educational populations served

The employment status of participants was reported as: employed by a K12 school or post-secondary institution (46%); self-employed as an individual teaching artist (33%); employed or contracted by an agency or organization that provides teaching artist services (29%); employed or contracted by a dance or theatre company that provides teaching artist services (25%); and employed by an arts council: local, regional, national (3%). Participants' average length of time in the teaching artist profession was 12 years. Respondents reported their teaching artist work in terms of their overall workload as: 100% time (27%); 75% time (25%); 50% time (23%); 25% time or less (25%). The vast majority of participants' teaching artist work has been carried out in K12 schools (see Table 1). For age groups served, participants' current work was reported with: young children (38%); young adults (23%); adolescents (22%); all ages (14%); and adults (3%).

Education, preparation and training

To assemble comprehensive data about teaching artists' education, preparation and training, a number of survey questions were posed. In terms of academic credentials, participants completed the following degrees: bachelor's (79%); master's (51%); doctorate (18%). Of participants, 17% attended a professional school or training program in dance; 6% attended university but did not graduate.

Of participants, 97% reported professional experience (see Table 2). When asked to describe their direct training and preparation for their career as a teaching artist, participants reported the following most frequent responses: research on my own (65%); self-taught (48%); and graduate degree program (44%). Beyond arts training, education and professional experience, participants were also asked to describe any additional educational study or coursework that prepared them for becoming teaching artists (see Table 3).

Career motivation, preparedness and significant influences

In order to gather supplemental data regarding participants' early years as a teaching artist, survey questions centered upon entry into the teaching artist profession,

Table 1. Populations served by teaching artists (*n* = 192).

	n	%
K12 schools	48	75
University programs	27	42
Afterschool programs	21	33
Recreation or community center	16	25
Early childhood	15	23
At-risk youth	14	22
Differently abled	13	20
Under-represented populations	11	17
Audience development	11	17
Mentoring programs	9	14
Seniors and elderly	5	8
Hospitals/therapeutic	1	2
Gay, lesbian, bisexual, transgender and queer	1	2
Domestic abuse/violence	0	0
Incarcerated populations	0	0
Drug abuse/rehabilitation	0	0
Detention facilities	0	0

Table 2. Primary professional experience of teaching artist participants ($n = 64$).

	n	%
Professional dance company	17	27
Dancer	17	27
Choreographer	15	23
Director	5	8
Professional dance/theatre company	4	6
Actor	2	3
Musical theatre performer	2	3
No professional experience	2	3
Total	64	100

Table 3. Additional educational study and coursework ($n = 229$).

	n	%
Teaching methods	37	58
Pedagogy	36	56
Learning styles	30	46
Educational philosophy	28	44
Education theory	26	41
Assessment and evaluation	24	38
Multicultural education	24	38
Social foundations	14	22
None of the above	10	15

their preparedness and influential persons and events which contributed significantly to participants becoming effective teaching artists. When asked to describe their motivations for entering the teaching artist profession, participants completed the statement, "I became a teaching artist because ..." with the following most common responses:

- At my core I'm a teacher (73%)
- Learning through the arts is important for all people (71%)
- It was a logical progression in my career (65%)
- I believe the arts transform people's lives (62%)
- I am interested in the power of the arts in community (56%)
- Opportunities came my way (52% dance)

As one of a series of open-ended questions, participants were asked to respond to the question, "What attracted you to the teaching artist profession?" participants, narrative responses focused on their passion for dance, love of teaching, working with children, the influence of their parents who were teachers and the logical progression of their dance careers (enabling them to stay in the field). In terms of participants' perspectives on their own preparedness, the survey asked, "When you first began working as a teaching artist, how prepared did you feel? "Nearly half reported they were not prepared as indicated in the following responses: very prepared (10%); prepared (8%); somewhat prepared (38%); not prepared (44%). Excerpts from two participants' narrative comments offer more detail about their lack of preparation:

> I felt pretty unprepared for my first job as a teaching artist. I just came across an old note I wrote during that time and it read something like, I know how to teach technique class but I am unclear how to connect our course work with the students' lives and experiences outside of our classroom. [A]t a loss as to how to create a positive movement experience that is meaningful and relevant for students with no previous experience with dance.

> [For my] work with high-risk youth I was not prepared at all. This work was part of Americorps and they basically dropped me off at a school and said, "do your thing". This was dangerous for both me and the children involved.

When asked to identify the most influential events and people leading to their becoming an effective teaching artist, participants' most frequent responses were: learning on-the-job (79%); learning from other teaching artists (73%); my own research and study (69%); professional development opportunities (69%); and my mentors and role models (66%). One of the least chosen responses was "specific teaching artist training: certificate or training program" (21%).

Challenges and obstacles

A number of basic challenges confronted by the general teaching artist population in the USA[4] have been identified: low pay; inadequate facilities and physical resources; lack of support; and the inability to find work (Association of Teaching Artists 2010). For the present study, survey questions sought to collect a wide-ranging swath of data about participants' current teaching artist practice including the nature of work, work contexts, how participants perceive themselves (identity) and their work (impact, rewards, challenges and obstacles). The following section briefly presents the challenges participants reported in their teaching practice.

When asked to complete the survey statement, "The biggest challenges I confront as a teaching artist are …", the majority of participants reported administrative bureaucracy and policies, followed by low pay and scheduling and calendar issues (see Table 4). Respondents' open-ended comments centered on lack of time, bureaucratic and administrative problems, disinterested classroom teachers and lack of support from schools. Additional challenges reported were large class size, inadequate facilities and misconceptions of dance as an art form.

Participants' narrative responses allow further insight into the obstacles they confront:

> Getting the regular teachers and administrators on board. Public school teachers are my heroes and I understand that by coming into their schools, I am interrupting their

Table 4. Teaching artist challenges in the workplace ($n = 131$).

	n	%
Administrative bureaucracy and policies	31	49
Low pay	23	36
Scheduling and calendar issues	22	34
Difficult administrators and policy makers	20	31
Lack of continuity in their work	19	29
Insufficient work to support themselves	16	25

day, often taking precious class time away from their lessons, test preps, etc. But in reality, what I do as a teaching artist enhances what teachers are teaching and give [sic] the students a fresh perspective and physical outlet that will make them better students!

A big challenge is creating opportunities for critical and creative work and imparting that these are fundamental aspects of dance learning. Educating administrators and students that learning in dance is much more rigorous and engaging than "teaching routines". Even when those in charge believe that art and dance is useful, they often have no idea what our needs are.

Professional development and professionalization of the field

At the conclusion of the survey, participants were asked questions about their own professional development and activity, as well as their beliefs and attitudes about the professionalization of the teaching artist profession and its needs for the future. When asked to identify their professional development experiences and professional activity, the majority of respondents reported that they: regularly attend conferences and workshops to develop my content, methods and teaching materials (71%); and network with other teaching artists to develop my own content and methods (56%). Additionally, 42% present workshops and professional development seminars for other teaching artists. In open-ended questions about professional development, participants indicated an array of definitions, with accompanying contexts for their professional development as teaching artists. While attending conferences, workshops, trainings and meetings of professional organizations was reported by more than half of participants, a number of other contexts and settings were also cited. For example, participants reported "taking dance technique classes regularly and attending professional dance intensives." A number of others cited their ongoing professional work as a dancer or choreographer as their professional development activity. Some dance participants expressed difficulty in identifying professional development opportunities that were relevant for them. Participants who do not attend cited lack of funding (both the lack of personal funds and employer subsidized funding). Others referenced their use of books, networking, relationships with other teaching artists and attending professional productions. A number of respondents indicated affordability as a profound obstacle, especially for those working less than full time as teaching artists.

Preliminary research for this study indicated the need to know more about participants' attitudes concerning the professionalization of the field over the past decade and its future development. Therefore, the final survey questions asked participants to share their opinions in this respect and to consider the usefulness of a potential credential or certificate program specifically designed for teaching artists in dance.

On this topic participants were first asked, "In terms of the future of the teaching artist field, what would you suggest for further development and professionalization?" The majority of responses strongly favored continued professionalization of the field including: increased training; national standards and training programs; post-secondary dance curriculum development to include vigorous teaching and pedagogy coursework; and certification programs. At the same time, nearly a quarter of participants opposed professionalization of the teaching profession and advocated for: less or no influence or involvement from academia; less standardization and codified programs; encouragement of creativity (rather than 'best practices');

increased integration of teaching artists into the professional world of dance; and greater flexibility and informality. Another 25% of responses addressed professionalization by emphasizing the need for teaching artist cohesiveness, collective organizing and unionization, which would advocate for teaching artists and negotiate reasonable pay scales, working conditions and benefit options.

The last open-ended survey question, "From your own experience, would a specific credential or certificate program for teaching artists in dance be valuable – why or why not?" prompted equally split responses. Narrative comments from participants who found high value in the possibility of a specific credential or certificate program (32%) stressed the significance of pedagogical skills and educational philosophy; improving teaching; in-depth training and specialization; time for reflection on artistic and teaching practice; unification of the profession;, larger pool of highly qualified teaching artists; and elevating the field (legitimacy, respect, prestige, greater public awareness).

Participants who found little or no value in a potential credential program (24%) cited the following rationales: diversity of artists too broad; certification not a guarantee of good teaching; increased bureaucracy, time, burden and expense; currency in one's art form more important than certification; general lack of employment in the field; and constraints of standardization.

Of participants, 44% were conflicted in their comments, often prefacing their responses with "maybe" or "I don't know". Many voiced guarded stipulations that indicated both what a potential credential program should do and should not do. In the participants' own words, a program should: "give credit for previous professional work"; "address the diverse range of the field"; "find a common thread between, and connections to, other teaching artists"; "quantify life experience in relation to the requirements of the program"; "be broad and present a variety of ideas and approaches" and "elevate the profession". Conversely, participants stated that a credential program should not: "reproduce Arts Specialists' programs"; "isolate us further"; "be too expensive or unable to complete while working"; "have a single vision of arts education"; "copy dance education for school-based instruction"; and, finally, "be just another hurdle for dancers to overcome in creating a sustainable career".

Of participants who expressed mixed opinions, a subset group suggested other options to a certificate or credential program. These alternatives focused on post-secondary dance degree programs, as summarized below in the words of five participants:

> Build the idea of becoming a professional teaching artist into a dance major college curriculum. Talk with college students and professional artists about educational outreach/teaching artist work early on.

> I think that it [teaching artist preparation] should be incorporated into undergraduate and graduate programs. My own Master's program included only one dance teaching course. Many dancers want to enter the teaching artist field but lack the training and experience.

> [University] dance programs often are old-fashioned and can only imagine school-based instruction. Many post-secondary institutions have divided their programs into dance performance and dance education. The idea of successful arts education needs to be broader in university programs and to present a variety of approaches and ideas.

I strongly believe that undergraduate dance majors need pedagogy!! My own master's [degree] included only one dance education course. Dancers who have been trained primarily through technique classes do not have the understanding of the nature of movement to apply and adapt to a variety of settings such as schools, community dance, and special needs.

[Teaching artist] training mandates across MFA and BFA programs in dance ... a real hard look at what programs look like today and how our needs are changing in the twenty-first century.

Summary of findings

In summary, the majority of participants' teaching artist work is in K12 schools mostly with young children. While nearly a third of respondents hold full-time teaching artist employment, most teaching artist work is delivered on a part-time basis. The majority of participants hold bachelors and master's degrees and have diverse professional experience in dance. Research on their own, teaching themselves and completing their graduate program served as their direct training and preparation as teaching artists. In terms of additional educational study and coursework, the majority of dance participants completed courses in teaching methods and pedagogy.

Participants' motivations for entering the teaching artist field were: seeing themselves primarily as teachers; believing that the arts are important to, and transform, people's lives and communities; and taking advantage of opportunities that arose as a logical progression in their careers. Participants' attractions to the profession included: a passion for, and commitment to, their art form; working with children and young people; and the ability to stay in their respective art discipline.

Most participants did not feel adequately prepared for their teaching artist work and became effective by primarily learning on-the-job through their own research and learning from other teaching artists. In terms of the challenges participants confront as teaching artists, the majority reported: administrative bureaucracy; low pay; disconnection between teaching artists, teachers and administrators; and lack of support from schools.

Professional development was defined by respondents in a variety of ways and contexts. Most participants regularly attended conferences, workshops and annual meetings of their respective professional organizations. Developing networks with other teaching artists figured prominently. Beliefs and perspectives about professionalization of the teaching artist profession were divided between those who support increased training in teaching and pedagogy in university degree programs, national standards and certificate programs and those who support much the opposite – less involvement from academia, less standardization and more emphasis on artistry. Participants' perspectives on the value of a potential credential or certificate program specifically for dance were equally polarized with similar rationales; however, some alternatives with implications for post-secondary dance curriculum development were strongly advocated.

Discussion: hybrid lives in a 'third space'

The quantitative survey data presented here depict a dance teaching artist population deeply embedded in, and committed to, P12 schools and the young children they reach. The qualitative narratives heard, though brief, enable us to better comprehend the hybrid lives of participants, their perspectives and challenges – often filling empty spaces and missing gaps in dance arts education – not the space of specialist teachers (Huddy and Stevens 2011) or the space of traditional artists, but as a third space. This lacunae-like position is described by one of the study's participants:

> Mapping this consciousness is what I think distinguishes the teaching artist from an artist who takes up a residency in a school or a school teacher. The teaching artist needs to be able to exist in the 'third space' between artistry and teaching – combine and separate the both when needed. It is this capacity that the teaching artist needs to develop and is a part of the course of their own self-knowing and being able to assist others to come to some semblance of self-knowing and explore deep creativity.

The study's findings provide ample lenses for looking more closely at the hybrid nature of teaching artistry in dance. For the purposes of this paper, discussion centers on emergent 'third space' themes of insufficient preparation in teaching and pedagogy and the role of post-secondary degree programs in dance in the USA.

Highly trained, less than prepared

Teaching artist participants in this study are highly trained in their art form and hold advanced degrees on levels approaching that of dance faculty in post-secondary institutions in the USA.[5] While participants acknowledged their graduate study as a primary influence on their training as teaching artists, the vast majority felt inadequately prepared to teach. Becoming an effective teaching artist was achieved mainly by learning on-the-job and being self-taught through their own experiences and research. This contradiction – highly trained yet less than prepared – generates numerous questions about participants' academic training in artistry and pedagogy, particularly for this highly-degreed population. To gain greater insight about the preparation teaching artists with academic degrees receive in the USA, this discussion first turns to undergraduate programs in dance.

Undergraduate degree programs in dance

At least 80% of participants hold bachelor's degrees in dance[6] and identified their primary area of preparation and training as: dance (71%), dance education (15%) and dance and theatre (14%). Academic degrees in dance were reported as baccalaureate degree (79%), master's degree (51%) and doctorate (18%).

Of current accredited bachelor's degree dance programs in the USA (HEADS 2011), 42% are liberal arts degree programs, 46% are professional Bachelor of Fine Arts degree programs – degree programs in dance education comprise only 12% of all undergraduate programs. The total US undergraduate dance student enrollment in 2011 was: liberal arts (48% of dance students), BFA (47% of dance students) and dance education (5% of dance students). While baccalaureate degrees with P12 teacher preparation in dance require extensive pedagogy and teaching coursework (National Association of Schools of Dance [NASD] 2010, 89–92), information on these programs has limited application to this study in which most participants (85%) did not complete undergraduate teacher preparation programs. Rather, for this discussion, we must look more closely at liberal arts and professional degree requirements for teaching and pedagogy.

For liberal arts degree programs in dance[7] (Bachelor of Arts; Bachelor of Science), coursework in teaching is elective, among numerous other choices like dance notation, living dance, anatomy and kinesiology, philosophy of dance, dance ethnology and music for dance (NASD 2010, 85). If not required, it is unlikely that students place value on teaching or see its relevance for their career aspirations as professional dancers and choreographers. Moreover, many young dancers do not see themselves becoming teachers or teaching artists during their post-secondary education and training.

In professional degree programs (BFA), which focus primarily on technique, performance and choreography, standards for teaching coursework are more specific:

> VIII. B. 4. Teaching. Students must develop basic knowledge and skills in dance pedagogy. The program should include the equivalent of at least one course in pedagogy and teaching experience. (NASD 2010, 88)

However, research indicates that a one-course requirement of pedagogy for BFA students is likely insufficient given that the majority of these students will not dance professionally and will instead earn a significant portion of their living by teaching (Bennett 2009; Montgomery and Robinson 2003; Warburton 2004).

It is also difficult to know the ways in which even minimal standard requirements, such as "the equivalent of at least one course", are satisfied by accredited institutions in the USA, as dance departments are given considerable flexibility in adapting guidelines and standards based on their own missions and prerogatives.

Graduate programs in dance

The predominant graduate degree program in dance in the USA is the Master of Fine Arts (see Table 5). From 2004 to 2009, post-secondary dance prioritized its professionalization by introducing a number of new Master of Fine Arts (MFA) programs, a 15% increase during this five-year period (HEADS 2004, 2009; Risner 2010). Focused on artistic practice, the MFA degree is recognized as the credential for teaching artistic subjects in most institutions of higher education; as such, MFA programs emphasize the creation and presentation of dance (NASD 2010, 101).

Table 5. Graduate degree programs and degrees awarded in dance, accredited institutions in the USA.

	($n = 25$) Degree program		($n = 91$) Degrees awarded*	
	n	%	n	%
Initial Master's**	6	24	15	17
[Dance Education]	[2]	[8]	[2]	[2]
Master of Fine Arts	16	64	72	79
Doctorate***	3	12	4	4
Total	25	100	91	100

Notes: *July 1, 2009 through June 30, 2010; **MA, MS, EdM; ***PhD.
Source: HEADS Dance Summary, 2011.

For this discussion a closer investigation of the MFA credential and its requirements is necessary, first, due to its preponderance in the field (both in number of degree programs and degrees awarded), second, because of its emphasis on artistry, creation and performance and, finally, because of the scarcity of initial master's programs in the USA, especially in dance education that comprise only 8% of accredited programs in dance (HEADS 2011). Additionally, and as a reminder, 15% of this study's participants indicated dance education as their primary area of preparation and training. This discussion is targeted toward the other 85% of participants and their teaching and pedagogical preparation (or lack thereof).

MFA: Teaching preparation and curricular structure

National accreditation standards for teaching preparation in MFA programs in the USA address these requirements as part of the fundamental purposes and principles for graduate programs in dance:

> XII. A. 7. b. Teaching. Many of those who are in graduate degrees in dance are or will be engaged in dance teaching of some type during the course of their professional careers. Institutions are therefore strongly encouraged to give attention to the preparation of graduate students as teachers. Whenever possible, experiences should include teaching dance to both dance majors and non-dance majors. Graduate students, particularly at the MFA and doctoral level, should have opportunities for direct teaching experiences appropriate to their major and minor areas under the supervision of master teachers. As appropriate to primary and secondary areas of concentration and to individual career objectives, preparation for teaching should include an introduction to the pedagogy of subject matter considered fundamental to curricula for undergraduate dance majors, including performance, choreography, dance theory and history, dance from a breadth of cultures, technology, and performance. (NASD 2010, 95)

For this discussion it is important to clarify that teaching, as described above, refers to preparation for post-secondary teaching, not for P12 teaching contexts in which 75% of participants in this study teach and make their livelihoods as teaching artists.

Additionally, national accreditation standards for MFA degree programs include pedagogy, among a number of other areas of study as listed below:

> A minimum of 15% of the total credits for the degree should be in academic studies in areas such as aesthetics, critical analysis, dance science, history, theory, pedagogy, and related humanities and social sciences concerned with dance. (NASD 2010, 101)

Between artistry and pedagogy: the 'third space'

This review of the standards for MFA programs suggests that teaching is seen as part of – rather than separate from – the professional life of an artist in dance. While MFA teaching preparation is specifically targeted at post-secondary teaching contexts rather than P12, it would logically follow that MFA programs, if it were their prerogative,[8] would also adopt strategies for including teaching artist preparation in their curricula. Flexible curricular structures in accreditation requirements in the USA afford plentiful space for design and implementation of a teaching artistry track or core curriculum.[9] Developing an MFA track that has an increased focus on teaching, while retaining the artistic core that makes the MFA distinctive, is clearly possible within the framework of national standards and illustrates the real possibility of a 'third space' preparation for teaching artists.

More to the point, the "highly trained yet less than prepared" contradiction found in this study documents the need for envisioning programs that balance focused artistry with pedagogy and teaching. For example, a recent survey of graduate program directors in post-secondary dance (Risner 2009) showed the following areas as most important overall to MFA programs: artistic practice (84%), improvisation/choreography (72%) and performance (56%). The significance of teaching and pedagogy was rated much lower (33%). Consistent with the character of the MFA degree as a practice-oriented degree focused on artistry and production, these data are not surprising. Later in that study, however, narrative comments from graduate directors constantly stressed the significance of teaching preparation for MFA career paths.

In the present study, we know that by a small majority participants completed courses in teaching methods (58%) and pedagogy (46%). However, 44% reported they were unprepared to teach upon entry into the teaching artist profession. Taken in sum, these factors and the study's findings contribute to what might be called the "accidental teaching artist" phenomenon: many young artists do not see themselves becoming teachers during their post-secondary education and training. Therefore, they do not prepare themselves for teaching, but then are subsequently drawn into the teaching artist profession. At the same time, a review of pedagogical preparation in BFA and MFA program requirements indicates significant deficiencies for developing teaching expertise in contexts other than the university setting. This level of inconsistency highlights the need to reconcile goals of artistry and pedagogy in more commensurate and meaningful ways. Programs that integrate practical training in teaching artistry with appropriate curricular support and participation from master teachers with experience in a range of contexts are in a better position to prepare graduates for the demands they will face as teaching artists.

Recommendations: rethinking artist versus educator discourses

Although the findings of this study provide new understanding of dance teaching artists and their work in P12 schools, enduring debates continue to surround questions about artists in US schools. Jane Remer (2010) reminds us that:

> The problem has almost always been one of competition for recognition, respect, status, space, time, and money. Some artists dismiss arts educators on the grounds of what they perceive as a lack of artistry and artistic methods. Professional arts educators with degrees and school experience, on the other hand, resent the implication that they possess lower levels of sensitivity, intelligence, and status. (89)

The growing prominence of the teaching artist during the past decade is a prophetic example of rethinking the limitations of 'artist versus educator' binaries. Therefore, the recommendations I offer below find their grounding in two basic assumptions: (1) teaching artists make important contributions to dance arts education in schools and (2) teaching artists should receive high-quality preparation and support commensurate with their responsibilities in schools and communities. As this paper has described, the challenges are numerous and complex, yet not unsolvable if we are willing to re-cast these obstacles through a holistic lens – "one rooted in enhancing arts education for all children and young people but *centered* on developing relevant post-secondary programs that value teaching, pedagogy and community engagement alongside artistic practice, technique and performance" (Anderson and Risner 2012, 12). In this spirit, this paper concludes with recommendations for integrating teaching artistry in dance curriculum and degree programs. Strategies for implementation include those that emanate from collaborative approaches: finding common values across and among stakeholders and constituencies, as well as informed institutional decision-making.

Teaching artistry competency in undergraduate programs

Based on the present study's findings and the participants' perspectives, it is critical to introduce and develop teaching artistry *competency* at the undergraduate level in dance. Offer curriculum (either existing or newly developed) that introduces undergraduates to teaching in diverse contexts and builds teaching artistry proficiency throughout the four-year degree program. Beyond coursework teaching and pedagogy, provide classes such as dance in community, dance for special populations, interdisciplinary arts teaching and dance in alternative settings.[10]

For students already committed to a teaching artist career, design and implement a degree concentration that draws from some courses in dance specialist teacher curriculum. Substitute general teacher education coursework with classes and practicum experiences in teaching artist career management, professional development and school residency design.

Re-envision senior thesis projects in ways that expand format, content, methods and dissemination venues to encourage and support options for teaching artistry projects. In addition to traditional performance-based thesis projects, develop hybrid approaches that equitably support artistry and pedagogy; highlight the relationships they share.

As a related example, encourage dance faculty to share their perspectives on teaching in transparent and meaningful ways. Integrate faculty teaching values throughout the curriculum within the specific courses they teach. Understanding the "why" and "how" of teaching artistry that faculty can provide will deepen undergraduates understanding and appreciation of teaching. In similar fashion, include invited guest artists and master teachers as critical resources for understanding the significance of teaching artistry in the professional realm. Incorporate regular activities or events that give guests the opportunity to share their perspectives on teaching as professional dance artists, as well as the role teaching artistry plays in their careers. In terms of professional BFA programs, implement these recommendations with greater depth for developing teaching artist *proficiency*; concentrate particularly on relationships between artistry and pedagogy.

Teaching artistry proficiency in graduate programs

The following recommendations for graduate study focus on two distinct areas: first, the MFA degree – the terminal degree recognized by dance professions and higher education in the USA for studio-related areas and, second, post-baccalaureate certificate programs in teaching artistry in dance arts.

MFA teaching artist track

Based on the study's findings, participant data, and a close examination of graduate programs in dance in the USA, the design and implementation of a teaching artistry track of core courses into current or newly-designed MFA degree programs in dance is recommended. National accreditation standards, as discussed earlier, offer ample opportunities for implementing a teaching artistry track while maintaining the artistic focus that characterizes the distinctive MFA credential.

A teaching artistry core curriculum would be comprised of a series of relevant courses (12–15 credits) that expands graduate student knowledge and skill sets for teaching in diverse contexts including schools, community and alternative settings. Constructed on the prerogative of the institution, faculty expertise, institutional resources, local dance artists and the unit's community relationships, assemble course offerings from the following areas: pedagogy and teaching methods; education (philosophy, theory, social foundations, multicultural education, learning styles); schooling and school culture; community arts; professional teaching artist issues (career management, evaluation and assessment, classroom management, administration and funding); human development; and integrated arts education. Mentoring, fieldwork experiences, apprenticeships and residency work for graduate students are strongly encouraged.

Position the teaching artistry track within national accreditation guidelines for additional academic studies in the MFA program (10–20% of credit hours) and elective studies (10% of credit hours).[11] For MFA thesis projects, expand form and content, as well as dissemination venues, to foster and support theses grounded in both artistry and teaching and community when appropriate.[12] Supplement traditional performance-based thesis productions with hybrid, 'third space' approaches that nurture and affirm teaching artist interests, aptitudes and contexts.

Post-baccalaureate teaching artist certificate program

With the exception of specialist teacher certification, post-secondary dance institutions in the USA rarely take advantage of certificate program offerings; most institutions focus on full degree programming. The following recommendation requires thinking about current or potential resources for expanding offerings that would generate local, regional and institutional appeal, while at the same time provide relevant learning opportunities for graduates and dance artists and educators in the community. For those inclined, I recommend the development and implementation of a post-baccalaureate teaching artist certificate program specifically in dance.

In the USA certificate programs typically range from 12–20 credit hours. Many programs combine traditional and online learning delivery with a few intensive periods of study, often during the summer months. Based on this study's findings, accessibility and affordability are key considerations; therefore, consider offering the certificate program through continuing education units (CEU) or other institutionally-based, affordable programs.

In regard to curriculum, develop a program of coursework, practicum and residency projects that builds the post-baccalaureate dance student's capacity for accomplished dance teaching artistry in schools and community settings. Similar to the teaching artist track suggested above, a balance of theoretical and applied experiences would combine the dance student's study of learning theory, human development and educational foundations with immersion experiences in professional management, arts integration and assessment and residency work.[13] As identified in the present study, strong mentoring and effective role models are essential components for developing teaching artistry (Lichtenstein 2009; Saraniero 2011; Seidel

1998). Well-mentored individuals experience increased career satisfaction and professional achievement. Ongoing mentorship (by faculty, master teaching artists, classroom teachers and dance specialist teachers) throughout the certificate program is highly recommended.

Collaboration and common values

In large part, the work necessary to advance the value of dance teaching and teaching artistry in academia often demands that we develop approaches that appeal persuasively and realistically to our faculty colleagues and administrators (department chairs, school and unit directors and deans) who identify firmly, if not staunchly, with performance and production-based curricula and professional degree programs (BFA, MFA). In order to communicate effectively with these individuals and to garner their support, the most compelling rationales will likely be those that articulate how teaching preparation, in its broadest sense, will significantly benefit BFA and MFA students and the realities and demands of students' career options. The literature, study findings and recommendations[14] shared here supply plentiful examples and provide persuasive evidence for identifying common values shared between artistry and pedagogy.

Notes

1. See the Association for Teaching Artists at http://www.teachingartists.com/aboutus.htm
2. Findings of the NORC Teaching Artist Research Project are available at http://www.norc.org/PDFs/TARP%20Findings/Teaching_Artists_Research_Project_Final_Report_%209-14-11.pdf
3. For information on the research survey, Teaching Artists and Their Work, see: http://www.teachingartists.com/Association%20of%20Teaching%20Artists%20Survey%20Results.pdf
4. The Association for Teaching Artists identifies the following teaching artist disciplines: dance, film and electronic media, folk arts, literature, multidisciplinary, music, theatre and visual arts.
5. Higher Education Arts Data Services (2011) reports advanced degrees for post-secondary faculty in dance as master's degree (64%) and doctorate (12%).
6. Because some participants in the survey selected their highest degree rather than all degrees received, it is likely that those who hold baccalaureate degrees exceed 80%.
7. I refer here to National Association of Schools of Dance guidelines and standards for US baccalaureate degrees that do not include specific P12 teacher preparation programs.
8. Beyond basic NASD requirements and frameworks, the nature and requirements for graduate study are largely the prerogative of each institution, especially for terminal degrees such as the MFA.
9. See NASD Handbook (2010), III. M. Flexibility and Innovation (74); NAST (2010) Handbook, III. M. Flexibility and Innovation (73).
10. Alternative teaching settings in dance include the following: differently abled, at-risk youth, under-represented populations, incarcerated populations, detention facilities, hospitals/therapeutic, drug abuse and rehabilitation, domestic abuse and violence, gay, lesbian, bisexual, transgender and queer, seniors and elderly, among others.
11. See NASD 2010 (101).
12. There are numerous connections and partnerships that can be forged between MFA teaching artist tracks and community. See NASD 2010, Dance Education and Local Community (126–7).
13. See, for example, the required curriculum for teaching artist certification (visual arts, performing arts, literary, media and crafts) at the University of the Arts at http://cs.uarts.edu/ce/certificate-programs/teaching-artist

14. This study is made possible through the generous support of the President's Research Enhancement Program for the Arts and Humanities, Wayne State University, Office of the Vice President for Research.

References

Americans for the Arts. 2007. *Arts and economic prosperity III: The economic impact of nonprofit arts and culture organizations and their audiences*. Washington, DC: Americans for the Arts.

Anderson, M., and D. Risner. 2012. A survey of teaching artists in dance and theater: Implications for preparation, curriculum, and professional degree programs. *Arts Education Policy Review* 113: 1–16.

Association for Teaching Artists. 2009. Getting started as a teaching artist. http://teachingartists.com//gettingstartedTA.htm

Association for Teaching Artists. 2010. Teaching artists and their work. http://www.teachingartists.com/Association%20of%20Teaching%20Artists%20Survey%20Results.pdf

Bennett, D. 2009. Careers in dance. Beyond performance to the real world of work. *Journal of Dance Education* 9, no. 1: 27–34.

Bonbright, J. 2002. The status of dance teacher certification in the United States. *Journal of Dance Education* 2, no. 2: 63–7.

Bonbright, J. 2011. Threats to dance education: Our field at risk. *Journal of Dance Education* 11, no. 3: 107–9.

Brown, A., and J. Novak. 2007. *Assessing the intrinsic impacts of a live performance. Commissioned by 14 major university presenters*. San Francisco, CA: Wolf Brown.

Higher Education Arts Data Services [HEADS]. 2004. *Dance data summaries 2003–2004*. Reston, VA: Author.

Higher Education Arts Data Services [HEADS]. 2009. *Dance data summaries 2008–2009*. Reston, VA: Author.

Higher Education Arts Data Services [HEADS]. 2011. *Dance data summaries 2010–2011*. Reston, VA: Author.

Huddy, A., and K. Stevens. 2011. The teaching artist: A model for university dance teacher training. *Research in Dance Education* 12, no. 2: 157–71.

Lichtenstein, A. 2009. Learning to love this more: Mentorship for the new teaching artist. *Teaching Artist Journal* 7, no. 3: 155–64.

Lincoln, Y., and E. Guba. 1985. *Naturalistic inquiry*. Beverly Hills, CA: Sage.

McCarthy, K., and K. Jinnett. 2001. *A new framework for building participation in the arts*. Santa Monica, CA: RAND.

Montgomery, S., and M. Robinson. 2003. What becomes of undergraduate dance majors? *Journal of Cultural Economics* 27: 57–71.

National Association of Schools of Dance (NASD). 2010. *National Association of Schools of Dance Handbook 20010–2011*. Reston, VA: Author.

National Opinion Research Center (NORC). 2009. Teaching artist research project. http://www.norc.org/Research/Projects/Pages/Teaching-Artists-Research-Project-TARP.aspx

Parrish, M. 2009. David Dorfman's "Here": A community-building approach to dance education. *Journal of Dance Education* 9, no. 3: 74–80.

Patton, M. 1990. *Qualitative evaluation and research methods*. (2nd ed). Newbury Park, CA: Sage.

Rabkin, N., and E. Hedberg. 2011. *Arts education in America: What the declines mean for arts participation (based on the 2008 Survey of Public Participation in the Arts).* Washington: National Endowment for the Arts.

Remer, J. 2003. Artist-educators in context: A brief history of artists in K–12 American public schooling. *Teaching Artist Journal* 1, no. 2: 69–79.

Remer, J. 2010. From lessons learned to local action: Building your own policies for effective arts education. *Arts Education Policy Review* 111: 81–96.

Risner, D. 2009. *Survey of dance graduate programs in the US: Research priorities.* Detroit, MI: Wayne State University. http://www.dougrisner.com/html/cordceparesearch.html

Risner, D. 2010. Dance education matters: Rebuilding post-secondary dance education for 21st century relevance and resonance. *Arts Education Policy Review* 111, no. 4: 123–35.

Saraniero, P. 2011. I teach what I do, I do what I teach: Study of the experiences and impacts of teaching artists. Association for Teaching Artists. Research on Teaching Artists. http://www.teachingartists.com/researchonTA.htm

Seidel, S. 1998. Stand and unfold yourself: A monograph on the Shakespeare & Company Research Study. In *Champions of change*, ed. E. Fiske, 79–90. Washington, DC: Arts Education Partnership.

Sweeney, S. 2003. Living in a political world? A symposium hosted by the Dance UK in collaboration with Dance Umbrella, South Bank Centre, London. Criticaldance. http://www.criticaldance.com/magazine/200401/articles/LivinginaPoliticalWorld2003100.html

Warburton, E. 2004. Who cares? Teaching and learning care in dance. *Journal of Dance Education* 4, no. 3: 88–96.

ABSTRACT

How do teaching artists perceive the need and usefulness of a credential program specifically designed for teaching artists in dance and theatre arts?

The Credential Question: Attitudes of Dance and Theatre Teaching Artists

Doug Risner

Mary Elizabeth Anderson

Introduction

Questions about the need and relevance of a teaching artist credential continue to receive considerable debate in the field and research literature (Anderson and Risner, "A Survey"; Reeder; Rabkin et al.; Risner; Saraniero; Stanley). In her 2009 study of teaching artists in theatre, dance, visual art, and music, Saraniero reported that the majority of participants (60%) believed that there should not be a teaching artist credential; however, nearly the same number of participants (55.7%) indicated that they would pursue a credential if there was one available (241). Saraniero concludes, "What is clear from the findings of this study is that any type of certificate must be developed in conjunction with the teaching artist community" (243).

In the same year, Reeder noted, "Political leadership, sources and losses of funding, research evidence, and a spike in demand are conspiring to bring certification of teaching artistry firmly into the national dialogue" (244). In the same publication, Reeder announced,

> Certification Is Here: The University of the Arts ... is offering a Teaching Artist Certificate through the university's Continuing Studies Division. The research-based certificate program is inclusive of visual, performing, literary, media, and crafts and aims to build the knowledge and capacity of artists to work alongside teachers and arts specialists in pre-K–12 classrooms and community settings to create and implement best practices residency programs that support learning in and through the arts. (244)

Many teaching artist practitioners, those who train and mentor them, and arts education directors welcomed this innovative development for the profession. The effectiveness and outcomes of the certificate program remain undocumented in the literature. According to its website, the program was temporarily suspended but is scheduled to be relaunched in an online format for fall 2014.

The extensive three-year study, the Teaching Artist Research Project conducted by Rabkin, Reynolds, Hedberg, and Shelby, collected data about attitudes toward a professional credential or certification from artists, teaching artists, managers, funders, teachers, and principals, as well as district and civic leaders. For the purposes of this article, a summary of the Teaching Artist Research Project study data from teaching artists themselves is most important:

> TAs [teaching artists] expressed broad skepticism about both certification and the role of higher education in training. They feared that it would become overly academic and were not confident certification would warrant quality or expand career opportunities for them. The [teaching artist] focus groups wrestled with the idea of credentials and certification. ... Though they were attracted to the possibility of professionalizing the work, they were concerned about standardizing it ... and skeptical that it would change anything fundamental about the market for their services. (17, 209)

Most recently in this journal, Stanley argued,

> During these difficult budgetary years, we may have an ideal window of time to forge a credentialing system for TAs that would simultaneously acknowledge every type of TA, and provide information about the level of expertise possessed by a TA at a given time. Our affinity for our fringe position, and our recognition of the positive aspects of this position, can inform our choices and efforts. We, as a profession, can take beginning steps toward this goal. (167)

Taken in sum, a number of competing narratives surround the complexity of the credential question. There are fears that something critically important about the profession's artistry might be lost in a credential or certificate program, or that the market doesn't warrant the time and expense of completing a program for willing and interested practitioners. At the same time, the growing momentum for creating a credential or certificate program for teaching artists may move forward with or without input from those whom it would serve (Rabkin et al.)

While some studies have addressed these concerns in the general teaching artist population, this analysis examines the credential question and ongoing debates among dance and theatre teaching artists working in the United States and internationally. Unlike previous research, this analysis asks questions surrounding the possibility of a specific credential in theatre and dance teaching artistry.

Methodology

Drawn from the authors' larger study of teaching artists in dance and theatre arts (Anderson and Risner, *Hybrid Lives*), this analysis investigated participants' ($n = 172$) attitudes and beliefs about the need and relevance of a teaching artist credential or certificate. Data were obtained through an in-depth, online survey, electronic questionnaires, and selected interviews. From those in the survey pool who indicated interest in completing an electronic questionnaire or interview, 10% (17 participants) were randomly selected (eight dance, nine theatre). Each questionnaire and interview protocol was unique to the participant's earlier survey data (quantitative and qualitative), as well as the participant's own interests and perspectives (Kvale & Brinkmann). Analysis of data generated was based on procedures of interpretive inquiry (Lincoln & Guba). Extraneous material was eliminated while emerging themes and patterns were identified and coded (Bernard & Ryan). Human investigation approval was received and maintained from authors' Institutional Review Board for the duration of the study.

Data for the present analysis were collected from participants' perspectives on the professionalization of the teaching artist field and its future growth and development. Within this portion of the study, a subset of open-ended questions (survey and questionnaire) and interview queries asked participants to share their candid opinions about a potential credential or certificate program specifically designed for teaching artists in dance and theatre and to contemplate its possible usefulness and relevance. When appropriate, we asked questionnaire and interview participants to describe important elements and components of an effective, meaningful certificate or credential program.

Overview of Teaching Artist Attitudes

In general, survey participants defined professional development in a variety of ways and contexts. The majority of participants regularly attended conferences, workshops, and annual meetings of their respective professional organizations. Affordability figured prominently in attendance. Networking with other teaching artists was also seen as important. However, when moving from considerations of their own professional development activities to the development and professionalization of the field, we must acknowledge the conflictedness of participant responses. No other portion of open-ended questions in the larger study garnered such strong emotions and divided perspectives.

Within the professional development section of the survey, participants were first asked the open-ended question, "In terms of the future of the teaching artist field, what would you suggest for further development and professionalization?" Responses were split between two divergent perspectives: (1) those who strongly favored increased training, national standards and training programs, postsecondary dance and theatre curriculum changes to include robust teaching and pedagogy coursework, and certification programs and licensure, and (2) those who strongly advocated for less or no influence or involvement from academia, less standardization and codified programs, encouragement of creativity (rather than "best practices"), increased integration of teaching artists into the professional worlds of dance and theatre, and greater flexibility and informality. A third category of responses, though less prominent, emphasized the need for teaching artist cohesiveness, collective organizing, and unionization, which would provide advocacy for teaching artists and the ability to negotiate reasonable pay scales, working conditions, and benefit options.

The second open-ended survey question, "From your own experience, would a specific credential or certificate program for teaching artists in dance and theatre be valuable—why or why not?" elicited similarly strong and divided opinions. Narrative comments from participants who found high value in the possibility of a specific credential or certificate program (40%) stressed the significance of pedagogical skills and educational philosophy, improving teaching, in-depth training and specialization, time for reflection on artistic and teaching practice, unification of the profession, larger pool of highly qualified teaching artists, and elevating the field (legitimacy; respect; prestige; greater public awareness).

Participants who found little or no value in a potential credential program (18%) cited the following rationales: diversity of artists too broad; inevitability of inadequate teachers ("a person who can't teach, can't be taught to teach"); certification not a guarantee of good teaching; increased bureaucracy, time, burden, and expense; currency in one's art form more important than certification; and constraints of standardization.

Forty-two percent of participants were conflicted in their comments, which frequently began with "maybe" or "I'm not sure." Many expressed cautious caveats that indicated both what a potential credential program should do and should not do. In the participants' own words, a program should "give credit for previous professional work," "address the diverse range of the field," "find a common thread between, and connections to, other teaching artists," "be affordable and easily accessible," "quantify life experience in relation to the requirements of the program," "be broad and present a variety of ideas and approaches," and "elevate the profession."

Conversely, the same group of conflicted participants stated that a credential program should not "satisfy administrators' needs only," "be elitist," "reproduce arts specialists' programs," "isolate us further," "be too expensive or unable to complete while working," "have a single vision of arts education," and "copy dance and theatre education for school-based instruction."

Alternative Views: The Role of Postsecondary Dance and Theatre

A subgroup of conflicted participants who reported mixed opinions suggested alternatives to a certificate or credential program that would still address further development and professionalization of the field. These alternatives focused on postsecondary dance and theatre programs and their responsibilities for effectively preparing students for teaching artist careers, as exemplified next in five participants' own words:

> The training of the work of a teaching artist should be a requirement in the graduate field of training (if not before). For example, actors should have a year-long course in their training empowering them as teachers in the field moving beyond the stage and studio. (Anh, theatre)

> I think that it [teaching artist preparation] should be incorporated into undergraduate and graduate programs. My own Master's program included only one dance teaching course. Many dancers want to enter the teaching artist field but lack the training and experience. (Alex, dance and performing arts)

> I think a solid education in your art form is most essential, but I see great potential for incorporating opportunities for developing students into teaching artists in our university theatre programs. (Sasha, theatre)

> Yes, we do need more highly qualified teaching artists in dance, but we also need more teaching artists with the required certification to teach in public schools, which vary from place to place. (Liz, dance and performing arts)

> Is this not why we have MFA programs for the university level? All theatre programs need to incorporate all aspects of the discipline but generally that experience is only obtained through a double major (theatre and then the content area that NCLB allows you to teach in). (Miranda, theatre)

Although many of these responses likely replicate similar concerns voiced in previous research on the general teaching artist population, they do call attention more directly to the ethical obligations and responsibilities of postsecondary degree programs in theatre and dance—which may or may not apply to music and visual arts. At minimum, these attitudes confirm the importance of teaching methods and pedagogical training in postsecondary degree programs in the arts. As Rabkin et al. noted, "New research suggests that more than half of arts graduates—there are some 120,000 a year—teach at some point during their careers" (37). Whether these graduates will pursue full-fledged careers as teaching artists, the message for postsecondary arts programs is clear: Developing knowledge and proficiency in teaching is critical.

Credential Question Discourses

Narrative data from questionnaires and interviews supplemented the participants' survey comments and provided enhanced detail of participants' attitudes and beliefs about a potential credential program and what it might look like. In the spirit of interpretive inquiry, we present responses from 16 participants[1] in a dialogical format—allowing their arguments, rationales, and apprehensions to be heard in conversation with one another. On this topic, we first asked, "From your own experience would a specific credential program for teaching artists in dance and theatre be valuable? Why or why not?"

Affirmative Dialogues

> Anne (Theatre): Absolutely YES. We need programs where teacher artists can be trained! From my study and observations so far, teacher artists need training in their field of artistic interest and as pedagogues. We should

---

[1] At the time of the study, these sixteen teaching artist participants were primarily employed in the United States (ten), United Kingdom (three), Australia (two) and Singapore (one), though some worked in both the United States and United Kingdom.

be given a place in the culture of education that can serve to bridge the worlds between teaching and artistry. This person is the "new" pedagogue, the new educator!

Jarrod (Dance): Yes, it seems important that everyone has a degree these days, so yes. It would need to have a new model of matriculation, a way to quantify life experience in relation to entrance to the program.

Betsy (Theatre): Yes, an online program with projects and practica negotiated in one's local area and portfolio-driven. But probably one more cost to risk against an outlay of money against the probability of sustainable employment.

Rob (Theatre Education): Yes, legitimacy in the eyes of administrators and proper basic training for everyone in the field. A good artist does not always translate into a good TA.

Sybil (Dance and Theatre): Yes—confidence builder initially and to learn some fundamental teaching skills. May as well learn from what others likeminded have done. Programs help establish real enduring networks of the interested thus some back up and support. They allow people to mentally rehearse what's ahead. [A credential program should] support research and engage in the latest debates about the nature and realities of these kinds of endeavors. They are much debated on the ground and by others so why not concentrate the minds of those going on to work in this mode.

Trevor (Theatre): Yes, more systematic training opportunities and international exchange of research and practice; recognition by mainstream creative industries and political institutions. There are many people entering the sector underprepared and delivering uncritical practice.

Adverse Dialogues

Sheila (Dance): No. I think the most important thing about being a teaching artist is staying active and connected in the field locally, nationally and internationally. Many excellent teaching artists are also incredible performers and choreographers who do not have the resources to go back to college.

Evan (Theatre): No, like painting by numbers, enforcing deadening consistency. [There needs to be] greater flexibility and informality, less emphasis on formal qualifications. Not sure I like the idea of professionalization.

Claire (Dance): No, I do not put very much stock in this. [There should be] less standardization. I work with teachers in the UK who have all received this training. It is like syllabus training. The teacher can rely on the tick-boxes and not on their imagination and experience. I am no more impressed with them than I am with American colleagues. Dance is an art form that stems from the artist, not from a guidebook.

Jill (Theatre): No. It would be something else we would have to pay for in order to be considered valuable in our field. What makes a TA is the passion. You can't teach someone how to really teach art. You can teach them how to incorporate facets of into their curriculum, but a true teaching artist has a passion, and that passion creates the method. My methodology has been created through experience and passion. I am wary of a program/credential because it homogenizes the teaching artist.

Apprehensive Dialogues

Sara (Theatre): I'm torn on the [credential] issue. I would like to see formal acknowledgement of the skills and expertise of Master Teaching Artists, but I think that there should be many avenues to achieve this status.

Jayme (Dance Education): There needs to be a better, easier way for artists to see teaching as a viable profession (part or full time). While certificates and degrees seem like an answer, they cannot substitute the value of apprenticeships and internships. This information cannot be taught in a class, workshop, or degree program.

Stephen (Theatre): I'm not sure. I think a solid education in your art form is most essential. I see great potential for incorporating opportunities for developing students into teaching/community artists in university programs, perhaps as a minor. I think the post-graduate level is probably the best place to really prepare students who are serious about working in this field, but that doesn't mean we can't expose them to it at some point in their undergraduate career.

Bebe (Dance): We are low on the totem and often our work isn't even viewed as a profession. Perhaps a way for TAs to get "certification" so that their work is more *respected and perhaps compensated better. But then we become "teachers" which carries that baggage. Teaching as a profession is not highly regarded.*

Eric (Theatre Education): I go back and forth on this issue. Credentialing programs are great, but mostly to those not directly in the profession. A school or agency would love to see some credentials, it speaks to training. However, I have noticed that graduates of programs tend to enter the field thinking the way their program did things is the only way to do things.

Samantha (Dance): It [a credential/program] could be, if we pay attention to the vast, diverse range of what the field has and can be. I believe a Teaching Artist must be an Artist first and they must know and be solid in their artistic voice before they are a Teaching Artist. Secondly, this is a field different from Arts Specialists. This distinction is essential.

Whether adverse, affirmative, or apprehensive about a credential program, these voices illuminate diverse perspectives about the future of the field, and in many ways give a rich and compelling snapshot of teaching artist experiences in dance and theatre arts today. While there is clear commitment to their own professional development, participants' attitudes about professionalization of the field itself remains in question. We conclude by turning to participants' recommendations for a credential or certificate program grounded in their own needs, concerns, and visions.

Credential Visions and Possibilities

When appropriate,[2] questionnaire and interview participants were asked to specifically describe important elements, components, and systems of delivery for what they believed would provide

---

[2] In most instances, participants who indicated some degree of positive support for a teaching artist credential or certificate program were then asked to describe what they believed would constitute an effective and meaningful program.

Taken in sum, a number of competing narratives surround the complexity of the credential question. There are fears that something critically important about the profession's artistry might be lost in a credential or certificate program, or that the market doesn't warrant the time and expense of completing a program for willing and interested practitioners.

---

an effective, meaningful credential or certificate program. Unsurprisingly, their responses reiterated a good deal of what we summarized earlier from the survey findings regarding potential credential program form and content. However, a number of additional aims and elements emerged in the additional narrative data collected. Table 1 summarizes recommendations of participants, organized by program aims, coursework and content, learning experiences, professional development, and accessibility and delivery.

In sum, attitudes and perspectives on professionalization of the teaching artist profession were widely divided between those who support increased training in teaching and pedagogy, national standards, and certificate programs and those who support much the opposite—less involvement from academia, less standardization, greater flexibility and informality, and more emphasis on artistry. Participants' perspectives on the value of a potential credential or certificate program specifically for dance and theatre artists were mixed, with 40% in favor of a potential credential or certificate program, 18% not in favor, and 42% conflicted over the value and impact of such a program. Within the overall narrative comments heard here, a number of possibilities and recommendations with implications for postsecondary dance and theatre programs were advocated. The visions and possibilities heard here contribute to a larger conversation about the professionalization of teaching artistry

TABLE 1. Participant Recommendations: Credential Program in Dance and Theatre Teaching Artistry

Program Elements	Participant Recommendations
Aims and Goals	• Address the diverse range of the field • Present a broad variety of ideas and approaches • Make affordable and easily accessible • Find common threads and connections to other teaching artists • Recognize and elevate the profession
Coursework and Content	• Pedagogy and educational philosophy • Artistic practice and reflection • Human development • Curriculum and lesson plan design • Community and school cultures/environments • Assessment and evaluation • Creative and applied research • Career management and planning
Learning Experiences	• Apprenticeships and internships • Practicum and projects • Collaboration with teachers and other teaching artists • Fieldwork and observations • Portfolio development
Professional Development	• Mentoring and relationship building in the field • Networking and support systems • Continuing artistic development and mastery • Collaborating for shared-discovery and growth • Communicating one's work (conferences, journals, newsletters, blogs)
Accessibility and Delivery	• Affordable tuition and easy access • Flexible program scheduling and timeline to completion • Ability to continue to work while completing the program • Online program with projects/practicum completed in one's local area • Credit or waiver for previous or current professional work as a teaching artist • Student-centered approach to coursework and requirements

and emerging developments in higher education, as Stanley recently described in this journal:

> In the work toward active professionalization of the field, many varied approaches may be seen: Some universities are establishing arts integration degree programs at undergraduate and graduate levels, and conservatories and arts schools are beginning to offer course work specific to teaching artistry. (167)

Concluding Thoughts

As former and current teaching artists now responsible for undergraduate and graduate programs in theatre and dance at a large public university in the United States, we find the participants' recommendations to be insightful, well reasoned, and visionary possibilities for a potential credential program. It's important to note that the attitudes, perspectives, and recommendations documented in this article emerged from a participant sample that was highly experienced in the teaching artist field; the vast majority (75%) had been employed as a teaching artists for at least six years, while 50% had ten to more than twenty years' experience. Although this population provides critically important perspectives from seasoned teaching artists, a study of relatively new teaching artists might produce different results, needs, and recommendations. In the near future, we hope to conduct additional research focused on those just entering or in their early years of teaching artistry.

We also understand our closeness to this intense research project over the past three years and acknowledge that this might affect, though completely unintended, our perspectives to some degree. However, we have endeavored to present this work in ways that readers will come to their own understandings and develop their own conclusions of the findings and our analyses. Additionally, this inquiry has attempted to provide the field with cogent and timely research that addresses Saraniero's 2009 call that "any type of certificate must be developed in conjunction with the teaching artist community" (243). While this research does not speak for the teaching artist field as a whole, we hope these findings move the collective profession forward from a more informed place rooted in teaching artists' perspectives, needs, and commitments to the field's professionalization and its wider recognition and elevation.

Works Cited

- Anderson, Mary, and Doug Risner. "A Survey of Teaching Artists in Dance and Theater: Implications for Preparation, Curriculum, and Professional Degree Programs." *Arts Education Policy Review* 113 (2012): 1–16. Print.

- ———. *Hybrid Lives of Teaching Artists in Dance and Theatre Arts: A Critical Reader.* Amherst, NY: Cambria Press, 2014. Print.

- Bernard, H. Russell, and Gery Ryan. Eds. *Analyzing Qualitative Data: Systematic Approaches.* London: Sage, 2010. Print.

- Kvale, Steinar, and Svend Brinkmann. *Interviews: Learning the Craft of Qualitative Research Interviewing*. Thousand Oaks: Sage, 2008.

- Lincoln, Yvonna, and Egon Guba. "But Is It Rigorous? Trustworthiness and Authenticity in Naturalistic Evaluation." *Naturalistic Evaluation* 30 (2004): 73–84. Print.

- Rabkin, Nick, Michael Reynolds, Eric Hedberg, and Justin Shelby. *Teaching Artists and the Future of Education: A Report on the Teaching Artist Research Project*. Chicago: National Opinion Research Center, 2011.

- Reeder, Laura. "Newsbreak." *Teaching Artist Journal* 7 (2009): 244–53. Print.

- Risner, Doug. "Hybrid Lives of Teaching Artistry: A Study of Teaching Artists in Dance in the USA." *Research in Dance Education* 13 (2012): 175–93. Print.

- Saraniero, Patti. "Training and Preparation of Teaching Artists." *Teaching Artist Journal* 7 (2009): 236–43. Print.

- Stanley, Faye. "Teaching Artistry: Education's Extreme Sport." *Teaching Artist Journal* 113 (2013): 161–7. Print.

Preparation, Policy and Workplace Challenges of Dance Teaching Artists in P-12 Schools: Perspectives from the Field

Doug Risner, Sam Horning and Bryant Henderson Shea

ABSTRACT
The primary aims of this qualitative interpretive inquiry were to gain better understanding of dance teaching artists' preparation and preparedness, workplace challenges, and the role and impact of policy and regulations in P-12 schools. A secondary aim focused upon identifying school environments that support effective and purposeful dance teaching artistry. The collective knowledge and experiences of six expert informants provide important insights and critical questions about dance teaching artist status and marginalization, bureaucratic challenges, and obstacles in developing relevant postsecondary programs that value teaching, pedagogy and community engagement alongside artistic practice, technique, and performance. Findings suggest an adept teaching artist adapts to shifting environmental conditions of the school and its administration. A flexible teaching artist carefully devises and revises lesson plans, objectives, and goals in relation to each particular group of students. A receptive teaching artist skillfully hones their pedagogy and teaching methods in alignment with curriculum and curricular goals. A sensitive teaching artist translates and fulfills the needs of the school and the student communities they serve with a strong desire to collaborate with classroom teachers and dance specialist teachers.

Introduction

For the special issue, *Arts Education Policy and the Preparation of Teaching Artists*, the authors pursued four guiding questions that form the basis of this interpretive inquiry: What preparation, academic training, and artistic experience characterize teaching artists in dance and how prepared are they upon entering the field? What workplace challenges do dance teaching artists confront in their practice? In what ways do policies and regulations foster or deter the successful work of dance teaching artists in P-12 schools? What kind of P-12 environments support effective and meaningful dance teaching artist programs?

Focused on the areas of preparation and preparedness, coupled with policy at the local, state, and organizational levels toward which dance teaching artists are bound, this study examines the ways in which these aspects and conditions may influence dance teaching artists' experiences and labor in P-12 school settings. To ensure a range of vantage points from key stakeholders, expert informants were solicited and identified from a pool of interested respondents who associated themselves with at least one of the following: a full-time or part-time dance teaching artist in a P-12 school; full-time or part-time dance educator in a P-12 school; a manager or administrator of dance teaching artists in P-12 schools; and an employer or researcher of dance teaching artists in P-12 schools.

For this research, we used the term, "expert informant," to distinguish their role from a "participant" in traditional research studies in which participants' anonymity is of critical importance. An expert informant in qualitative inquiry possesses specialized knowledge regarding a specific culture. In this study, that culture is dance teaching artistry; expert informants build relationships with dance teaching artists and share knowledge about the culture and members' thinking, values, practices and beliefs (Field-Springer, 2018). In addition, informants are able "to identify any organizational shifts or patterns of change throughout time, while offering insight into why changes have occurred" (Field-Springer, 2018, p. 702). Taken together, the collective knowledge and experiences of expert informants provide important insights and questions–often lingering ones–about the status, challenges and barriers, and value of dance teaching artistry in P-12 education. As such, this research will be of interest to policy-makers, school administrators, art education directors and researchers, as well as stakeholder-educators at the school level including dance teaching artists, P-12 classroom teachers and dance specialist teachers.

Stakeholders in dance education

Since the majority of dance teaching artists deliver programs in P–12 schools (Anderson & Risner, 2014; Risner, 2012; Snyder & Fisk, 2016a), some distinctions require elaboration. First, three categories of teachers figure prominently in policy considerations: specialist teachers in dance, general classroom teachers, and dance teaching artists. Respectively, each educator possesses a distinctive purpose within the school environment, and therefore, education, training, and certification may differ depending upon the type of instructor (Risner, 2012). In general, "Many hiring institutions advertise teaching artists positions with language that encourages applicants to have both thriving artistic practices while also having significant classroom experience, but degrees in education or other types of alternative certification are for the most part not required" (Kresek, 2018, p. 21). Although requirements for licensure vary by state, dance specialist teacher programs in higher education provide education and training in dance (e.g., technique, history, choreography, performance) alongside dance education study including pedagogy, teaching methods and curriculum design (Anderson & Risner, 2014).

While postsecondary dance programs vary widely among public and private institutions, specialist teachers may pursue a number of paths for dance education at the undergraduate level. Many elect a liberal arts degree (Bachelor of Arts in Dance) combined with a dance education minor or concentration, or specialist degree (Bachelor of Science in Dance) leading to teacher certification. Others may opt for a professional undergraduate degree (Bachelor of Fine Arts in Dance or Bachelor of Performing Arts in Dance) focused on artistic development supplemented by a dance education minor or concentration. Anderson and Risner (2012) note:

> Some dance specialists have completed the Master of Fine Arts (MFA) degree, indicating a high level of artistic training. Dance specialist teachers are normally certified or credentialed and have parity with specialist teachers in other school disciplines; their function is to operate regularly scheduled curriculum-based programs in dance in one or more schools. (p. 2)

Second, general classroom teachers, especially those in elementary education, may have a range of interests in the arts and the desire to incorporate arts-based instruction in their curriculum and pedagogy; however, they may not possess the educational background, training or credentials to teach or integrate the arts successfully (Anderson & Risner, 2014). Similar to specialist dance teachers, general classroom teachers likewise operate within and are integral to a curriculum-based school structure.

Third, teaching artists who are educated and trained in one or more arts disciplines, play a visiting, short-term or an extended, part-time role, which is crucial to many P-12 schools for providing arts education instruction and experiences (Risner & Anderson, 2015). While these artist-educator distinctions produce clear economic implications and outcomes, for dance artist-educators "identifying oneself as a teaching artist remains malleable. For example, some P-12 specialist teachers in dance identify strongly as teaching artists" (Anderson & Risner, 2014, vii). Teaching artists, though normally not certified, often work alongside classroom teachers in creative, esthetic, and integrative collaborations that provide powerful arts learning experiences for students, their families, caregivers and teachers (Snyder & Fisk, 2016a, 2016b).

The primary aims of this interpretive inquiry were to gain better understanding of dance teaching artists' preparation and preparedness, workplace challenges, and the role and impact of policy and regulations in P-12 schools. A secondary aim focused upon identifying school environments that support effective and purposeful dance teaching artistry. A range of stakeholders were identified including current and former dance teaching artists, persons who facilitate, implement, and manage arts education and dance teaching artist programs, as well as those professionals in P-12 schools with whom dance teaching artists engage, collaborate, and partner. From this pool, a group of six expert informants was formed.

Research approach and procedures

As a qualitative conceptual framework, interpretive research design seeks enhanced understanding of what it means to be human and to engender meaning and understanding rather than proving or disproving facts (Denzin & Lincoln, 2011). In an interpretive approach, meaning is revealed in multiple ways and compels researchers to engage conceptual frameworks and research methods that consider and amplify the voices of diverse perspectives and account for contextualization and complexity. The lived experiences of research informants, heard through their words and narratives, are contemplated by the researcher as multiple, socially constructed and contextual (Creswell, 2014).

Simultaneously, the interpretive researcher employs processes and methods of qualitative design in order to construct concepts, devise grounded theories, and identify emergent patterns via interpretation and contextual analyses (Denzin & Lincoln, 2011), or more simply, what each informant's text and language convey. Further clarifying this research orientation, Erickson (2005) asserted, "The interpretive qualitative researcher would say that the question 'what is happening?' is always accompanied by another question: 'and what do those happenings mean to those who are engaged in them?' And a critical qualitative researcher would add a third question, 'and are these happenings just and in the best interests of people generally?'" (p. 7).

Given the study's multiple-stakeholder approach, a national call for expert informants generated 32 responses to an extensive online questionnaire that concluded with an invitation to participate in an individual virtual Zoom interview. Eleven informants accepted our invitation, from which six were selected for in-depth interviews based on range of experiences, length of time in the field, and consideration for wide stakeholder engagement in dance-based arts education and teaching artistry. In identifying their positionality, expert informants self-selected from employment descriptors with instructions to "check all that apply" (See Table 1).

Open-ended interview prompts allowed informants to revisit and elaborate issues raised in their interviews with greater specificity. Interviews were recorded and transcribed and checked for inaccuracies. Thematic analysis of qualitative data was based on procedures of interpretive inquiry (Creswell, 2014). Pre-analysis methods included transcribing, coding, and categorizing qualitative data from questionnaires and interviews for emergent themes and unique or discrepant cases. In-depth, substantive analyses reviewed qualitative data from questionnaires and interviews based upon interpretive inquiry standards (Creswell, 2014). Individual case studies were created for each of the six expert informants selected for this interpretive inquiry.

What we know about dance teaching artists: A review of literature

Teaching artists in dance today serve schools, communities, and organizations in myriad ways; as such, their teaching artistry takes a variety of shapes and pathways for diverse educational environments. Anderson and Risner (2014), in their study of dance and theater teaching artists (n = 172) reported that dance teaching artists are employed in multiple settings, often simultaneously. However, most teach in P-12 schools. With regard to age groups served, dance teaching artists engage: young children and adolescents (60%); young adults (23%); all ages (14%); and adults (3%) (Risner, 2012). These findings are critically important because the majority of dance teaching artists serve P-12 schools, whereas Rabkin and colleagues' (Rabkin et al., 2011) found that only 12 percent of all teaching artists serve P-12 schools. Therefore, generalizing data from teaching artists overall as a homogeneous group is misleading in many

Table 1. Expert informants by employment.

	Gina Buntz	Emily Hoch-Windus	Ashlyn Keller	Hetty King	Anna Mansbridge	Kelly Williams	Totals
Full-Time Dance Teaching Artist (P-12)	X	X	X				3
Part-Time Dance Teaching Artist (P-12)				X	X	X	3
Full-Time Dance Educator (P-12)		X				X	2
Part-Time Dance Educator (P-12)					X		1
Employer of Dance Teaching Artists	X						1
Manager of Dance Teaching Artists	X						1
Administrator of Dance Teaching Artists	X						1
Teacher of Dance Teaching Artists		X					1

instances, especially when considering dance teaching artists. In addition, dance arts education in P-12 schools is already a significantly marginalized art form: "a sobering fact is that dance is included in less than three percent of all schools in the US" (Young-Overby, 2014, p. 20).

Preparation, education, and training

Published research on dance teaching artists' preparation, training, and academic credentials remains limited. However, in regard to degrees earned, Risner (2012) reported that dance teaching artists hold the following: bachelor's (79%); master's (51%); doctorate (18%); some attended a professional school or training program (17%), while others attended university but did not graduate (6%). In the same study, when participants were asked to describe their direct training and preparation for their careers as dance teaching artists, participants cited "research on my own" (65%), "self-taught" (48%), and graduate degree program (44%) (Risner, 2012, p. 179). In addition, participants in that study described additional educational study or coursework that prepared them for becoming teaching artists as teaching methods (58%), pedagogy (56%), and learning styles (46%) (Risner, 2012, p.180). In regard to their overall preparedness, nearly half reported they were not prepared (44%), while others indicated they were somewhat prepared (38%), followed by a small number who felt very prepared (10%) and prepared (8%). (Risner, 2012, p.180). Taken together, these findings indicate that dance teaching artists confront significant challenges in preparation for effective work in P-12 schools.

Workplace challenges

The Association of Teaching Artists (ATA) determined primary challenges confronted by the general teaching artist population included low pay, inadequate facilities and physical resources, lack of support, and the inability to find work (Association for Teaching Artists, 2010). More specifically, challenges reported by dance teaching artists comprised: administrative bureaucracy and policies (47%); low pay (35%); scheduling and calendar issues (29%); difficult administrators and policy-makers (28%); and insufficient work to support themselves (24%) (Anderson & Risner, 2014). Qualitative narratives from participants in the same study spoke to challenges rooted in lack of time, bureaucratic and administrative problems, disinterested classroom teachers, lack of school support, and misconceptions of dance as an art form (Anderson & Risner, 2014; Bernard, 2020).

Arts education policy and teaching artists

For nearly 40 years, the realm of P-12 arts education policy has maintained permanent tensions about the role of the teaching artist, especially in states where certification or specialized credentials are available in the fine and performing arts. According to the National Dance Education Organization (National Dance Education Organization, 2021), 35 states (69%) currently offer certification in dance in P-12 schools. However, once state certification is established, its continuance is not guaranteed. For example, in the state of Michigan (the first author's location), dance specialist certification had been available since the 1990s, but was recently repealed by the state legislature in 2018. As stated by the Michigan Department of Education:

> School districts may assign any teacher to a Recreation or Dance course who provides evidence of content knowledge and skills along with holding an endorsement for the grade level at which the course is offered. Note: Dance is NO LONGER considered a core subject area.[1]

Teacher certification in music and visual arts continues with both art forms considered core subject areas in Michigan. The power and influence of policy-makers at the state-level cannot be underestimated, privileging already dominant art forms while further marginalizing others.

At the same time, tensions surrounding teaching artists emerge and develop differently based on whether or not certification is available. For example, specialist teachers in dance who hold certification and often possess extensive significant artistic achievement and credentials, may sense that advocacy for teaching artists produces negative policy consequences at the school and school district level, and that advocating for teaching artists reaffirms the notion that the arts, particularly dance and theater, are the only subjects that when declared basic, don't require or deserve full-time specialist teachers. (Anderson & Risner, 2014). Taken together, teaching artist advocacy and its policy effects can produce further tensions by pitting visiting teaching artists and classroom teachers against full-time specialist teachers and support for their work.

In addition, teaching artist advocacy may unwittingly marginalize the arts as subject and content worthy of P-12 curriculum and appropriate funding, thereby decreasing and diminishing the position of the arts in policy decisions. A powerful counter assertion is "that schools have little or no prospect of having specialist arts teachers and that teaching artists provide some arts instruction where there would otherwise be none," which is particularly the case for dance (Anderson & Risner, 2014).

Perspectives on preparedness

In telling the stories of six expert informants, we begin by examining dance teaching artists' preparation, academic training, and artistic experiences. Each expert informant has benefited from rigorous education and professional training, and as a collective, share a devotion to the field of dance developed throughout their lives as dancers, choreographers, collaborators, educators, administrators, and producers. In terms of teaching artist preparation, the informants bring unique backgrounds that prepared them to teach dance in P-12 schools. We introduce each expert informant accompanied by relevant information on her preparation, education, and training.

Dance teaching artist preparation

All expert informants in this study hold a bachelor's degree, and a majority hold one or two master's degrees. When asked about the relationship between informants' academic training in their undergraduate work and dance teaching artist preparation, Emily Hoch-Windus, a full-time dance teaching artist, activities director, and arts integration specialist at the Doral Academy of Colorado noted, "I was hired right after graduation to teach dance part-time at the community college in town. I was also teaching at private dance studios part-time as well, and continued to do that for several years." Emily holds a Master's degree in Dance Education, and as an instructional coach, she works closely with classroom teachers to design arts integrated teaching methods and curriculum. She has taught in public schools, private sector dance studios, community colleges, for professional dance teams, and serves on the board of directors for Colorado Dance Educators Organization (CoDEO).

For Kelly Williams, her bachelor's degree program provided opportunities to choreograph, perform, and teach, which included touring with the university's dance company: she noted, "during the day we would go into the public schools to teach. I remember teaching creative dance in elementary schools helped to prepare me as a teaching artist." Kelly is a full-time, credentialed physical educator and part-time dance teaching artist in the San Juan Unified School District of Sacramento, CA where she leads creative movement programs. Kelly works closely with school administrators and teachers to design and teach physical education and dance classes designed for elementary school students. She holds a BA in Modern Dance from Brigham Young University.

Another expert informant, Anna Mansbridge, reported that her Bachelor of Education degree "trained teachers to work in secondary schools, which included preparing us to teach GCSE [secondary education] and A Level Dance [college preparatory for dance]." She is a part-time dance teaching artist, part-time dance educator in P-12 schools, and faculty member at the Creative Dance Center, Seattle, Washington, where she directs Kaleidoscope Dance Company for youth ages 8–17 and teaches Anne Green-Gilbert's Brain-Compatible Dance Education. Anna is a specialist in European and Renaissance Court Dances.

After earning her BFA in dance, Ashlyn Keller worked as free-lance professional dancer and taught in several dance studios: she recalled the importance of her undergraduate degree for securing a dance teaching position in P-12 schools:

> I was approached by a former [school] principal of mine who knew I had a degree in dance. [The state of] North Carolina had recently implemented an initiative called "Arts are Basic," and dance was to be added to the elementary and middle schools in the state. I interviewed and was hired to teach 6–8th grades.

Ashlyn is a full-time dance teaching artist and department chair at the Jesse C. Carson High School Arts Academy. She has held a variety of roles as a professional dancer, choreographer, dance teaching artist, and administrator. Ashlyn earned her MA in dance teaching artistry from Wayne State University and BFA in dance from the University of North Carolina at Greensboro. She performed with Charlotte Ballet and Louisville Ballet companies. Ashlyn's participation in an undergraduate teaching internship at an elementary school uncovered her joy for teaching young students. She stated, "…it was that particular experience that kind of eventually led me to want to become a K-12 teacher."

Kelly and Anna also articulated how their undergraduate degrees supported their work as teaching artists in P-12 education: "The most important preparation was the experience of teaching creative dance in public schools in my undergrad classes" (Kelly).

Similarly, Anna noted the significance of her undergraduate experiences:

> Because the focus of the degree was teaching, my B.Ed honors degree in England gave me a diverse tool box to draw from, and also an excellent foundation for my work as an artist in a variety of schools with different socio-economic backgrounds, from a rural school in Northern England, to an inner-city school in London.

Many expert informants also received master's degrees. Gina Buntz holds an MFA in Dance from the University of Michigan and recalled, "My MFA degree was really a culmination of my background as a professional dancer. The MFA did very little to support my preparation as a teaching artist." Gina holds a BA in Dance from Stephens College, and is a full-time dance teaching artist, as well as an employer, manager, and administrator of dance teaching artists. Currently, she is Director of Dance at The Fine Arts Center (Greenville, SC) for grades 9–12. Gina has served on the faculties of the New World School of Arts, the Dreyfoos School of the Arts, Cranbrook Schools and was Dance Chair of the Los Angeles County High School for the Arts. She is a five-time recipient of a Choreographer's Fellowship from the National Endowment for the Arts.

Anna, who completed her MFA in dance at Mills College, described:

> I had just come from this very cerebral MFA program, and I went back to teaching dance and I landed with a bump. Because I had to kind of let go of all that because it (teaching dance) was on a very different level. It was a little bit of a culture shock, coming back and going into schools, responding to the culture –which was very different– adapting and realizing how much I didn't know.

Both Ashlyn and Emily elected Master of Arts degree programs for their graduate study, which they described as transformative and rigorous preparation. Having completed a master's program in dance teaching artistry, Ashlyn noted, "My work in the MA program at Wayne State University has also been transformative for my personal pedagogy and values as a teaching artist. The work helped me to realize the importance of building relationships with my students and giving them space to forge bonds with each other." Emily connected the theories and methodologies she learned in an exacting MA program in dance education to the practicalities and realities of teaching in public schools. She recalled, "I was diving deeply into studying arts and dance integration in my master's program, and was able to conduct my [master's] thesis research for my MA Degree while in my first year teaching."

Additionally, informants reported participation in continuing education in pedagogy and teaching methods[2] and emphasized the need for professional development in order to maintain and develop their knowledge and currency in educational standards in dance, as well as national and local policies. Ashlyn noted her participation in the National Dance Institute in New York City: "We took what we learned in the two-week, hands-on intensive in NDI pedagogy and applied the techniques immediately in a school in Chinatown where I interned. The experience was invaluable and changed the way I taught dance."

Hetty King, MFA, CMA, is a part-time dance teaching artist in P-12 schools. She recalled the importance of professional development early in her teaching artist career. "When I first came to teaching artist work the institutions that hired me, namely Lincoln Center Institute (LCI), offered training and mentorship." Hetty is an experienced dance educator with a demonstrated history of working in the education industry creating and implementing dance education programs for P-12 schools with a focus on early childhood. Currently, she holds an Arnhold Fellowship as a doctoral candidate at Teachers College, Columbia University, and part-time dance teaching artist positions at Hollingworth Preschool, a university-based early childhood center located on the campus, and at Third Street Music Settlement at the 92nd St. Y in their Dance Education Laboratory (DEL) and Department of Education (DOE).

Becoming a dance teaching artist: Entering the field

Although the path to becoming a dance teaching artist may take a number of different routes, a strong desire to meld the knowledge, expertise, and skills of one's chosen art form with a deep commitment to engage others in arts-based learning typifies teaching artistry preparation (Jaffe, 2012). Questions of preparedness upon entering the field figure prominently.

When expert informants were asked how prepared they were for beginning work as a dance teaching artist, many informants recalled that having a mentor and professional development experiences were integral to their preparation, as Gina explained, "What was most important for me was the mentoring of my teaching that I received from top administrators who were supportive and provided a sounding board for me." Hetty emphasized that learning to teach in a P-12 environment is an ongoing process: "I am still learning – always learning how to work with each group of students, their teachers, and the culture of the school." Informant responses illustrate how professional development and knowledge are continuously gained through in-practice experiences, which supports the notion that teaching artists commonly "piece together their own course of professional development once they begin their practice" (Anderson et al., 2013, p. 18).

Gina asserted that peer and mentor support in the classroom can encourage teaching artist preparedness. "When a teaching artist receives peer support there are opportunities for observation, dialogue, and the possibility for creation of new strategies and methodologies." The impact of being mentored early in teaching artists' preparation can influence their career paths in profound ways, as Hetty explained: "In the Lincoln Center Institute program, we were really well mentored. I had a mentor who followed me into my first residency and who came with me to my first class. That was awesome." Gina and Hetty highlighted the importance of being mentored and developing professional relationships through formal and informal mentor/mentee programs.

In summary, mentorship and peer support enrich dance teaching artists' preparedness for entry into P-12 schools. Cultivating 'on the job' opportunities for collaboration and exchanges buttress ongoing learning with each group of students and school culture. Opportunities rendered by postsecondary institutions and professional development programs build the foundation for teaching artists in P-12 environments, especially when 'on the ground' practices and circumstances are integrated into teaching artist programs.

Professional development and artistic praxis

The benefits of practicing their teaching artistry during their training prior to entering P-12 schools was voiced by the informants. Emily shared "I was really well prepared for teaching in P-12 schools from my education, training, experiences and professional development. The most important professional development was my experience of teaching creative dance in the public schools in my undergrad classes." In preparing to teach at a specific P-12 school, Gina asserted the need for professional development and enrichment prior to beginning a residency or long-term position:

> I think teaching artists should make a visit to the school at least a month or two in advance, and watch and observe classes with the classroom teacher, and to have a little Q&A with the students. I think you have to create an orientation for the teaching artist, classroom teacher, and the students – kind of an early, initial 'common ground and initiation ceremony.

Some described feeling ill-prepared for classroom management. Kelly acknowledged, "The behavior management piece is huge. I was really lucky when I first started teaching dance in a public school without a credential, and the classroom teacher had to stay in the room with about 30 students who may or may not have wanted to be there." Likewise, Emily recalled, "Being able to work with teachers that have more experience in the classroom, and co-teach with them has really helped with classroom management."

The significance of informants' dance studio practice and artistic development emerged as important and supportive in their teaching artist preparation. Hetty noted, "My studio-based degrees meant I spent a lot of time in dance studios learning my craft in those degrees, which offered me a broader perspective on dance that I think has been useful in all of my teaching artistry work." Likewise, Emily also discussed the transferable skills she developed while working in private sector studios. She stated:

> I'm thankful for all the years I've had working in private dance studios putting on main stage productions, and gaining experience in theater production. From choreography to lighting design, costuming and makeup and even film and projection…teaching my students about these processes along the way has helped me dive more deeply into this at the P-12 level.

Speaking directly to her artistic development and learning through collaboration with others, Ashlyn elaborated:

> My undergraduate degree and certification built my foundation as an artist and helped me to understand myself and my own artistic processes better. I was surrounded by and worked with talented and inspirational artists every day. Working with my professors and fellow students, collaborating and witnessing their creative practices molded me into the performer and artist who evolved into the teaching artist I am today.

Artistic preparation and development for Hetty focused on creative processes and their applications to P-12 students:

> My experiences with choreographers Ralph Lemon and David Dorfman were the most meaningful and impactful for informing my approach to generating material and seeing the choreographic process as a collaboration that feeds off the generative nature of

the dancers present. As a P-12 teaching artist, this is a subtle underpinning of my work with young students…who need structure and the opportunity to learn by doing…taking students through the process of creating a dance where they generate material, giving them the chance to see what it looks and feels like, which gives them more agency as they build dance-making skills.

Taken together, informants' teaching artistry benefits from, and is sustained by, ongoing personal artistic praxis alongside meeting the demands and interests of each school and group of students they engage. Classroom management strategies that foster appropriate behavior were also identified as important areas for additional professional development and training. Moreover, informants indicated demonstrable success when intentional engagement and exchange among P-12 teaching artists, school faculty, administrators, and students occurs.

Workplace challenges

Beyond classroom management obstacles, expert informants identified challenges they confront in their day-to-day teaching artistry. Thematic challenges included limitations on collaboration, expectations for using codified curricula or having no curriculum in place, development of interpersonal and synchronous relationships between dance teaching artists, classroom teachers and dance specialists, and under-appreciation of the art form and its educational values.

For Anna, the challenge is lack of time with students. "I would like to teach them more than a few times a year," which she acknowledged is linked to "insufficient funding and an under-appreciation of the value that dance (and the arts in general) brings to students' learning and educational experience." Hetty identified curriculum and teaching methods challenges that vary between each particular school and organization:

Some have codified ways they want you to approach teaching and learning (i.e., centered on a specific work of art). Others want you to take charge of the material and use your own approach and understanding of teaching dance. In some cases, the curriculum is co-created with others and then pre-packaged. In other schools it is totally self-generated by the teaching artist. I strive to develop relationships with the teachers I work with; some teachers want this while others just want to take a break.

Gina discussed the limitations of ongoing professional development requirements created for, and aimed specifically to, classroom teachers. Teaching artists' expectations are often quite different based on the learning objectives of their art form, which she noted, "is oftentimes not part of the reality of classroom teachers and students in the arts classroom."

Stories rooted in socio-economic and cultural differences between teaching artists and the cultures of students they teach were also obstacles faced by informants. Kelly described challenges she confronted in a specific school environment:

I was not able to teach Creative Dance because the behaviors at the school were really intense. Children came to school with knives, guns, and toys they had turned into weapons. They would try to slice each other open… no one felt safe. This was a growing time for me. I taped down spots on the floor for the students to stand. I needed to teach fast-paced curriculum that was relevant to these K-5 graders, and I needed to develop relationships. Building relationships with them saved me during this time.

Hetty described her experience in alternative schools for students who have been expelled and where violence was commonplace, which is particularly challenging for teaching artists who have little to no training in violence prevention and mitigation. She recalled, "Every day we were there, someone had been injured. On the second day, the assistant principal had her hand in a bandage, her fingers had been broken, breaking up a fight." The perspectives shared by Hetty and Kelly speak to systemic challenges that teaching artists face in P-12 education without the necessary training and resources to be effective. In sum, workplace challenges described by expert informants comprise various value systems regarding the role of dance and dance performance, developing arts-based curriculum, addressing divergences in cultural and socio-economic realities, troubling interpersonal relationships among staff and peers, and ongoing under-appreciation of dance as a viable educational method and learning tool.

Policy, regulations and rules

Discussing arts education policy and its implications for teaching artists without acknowledging the ramifications of the current COVID-19 pandemic would be irresponsible, if not short-sighted. As Dik and colleagues (2021) have recently noted:

Some of the challenges which arts education will face in the policy and political arenas over the next several years will continue the lack of equitable access for students, particularly students in poverty who are often students of color. We may need to rethink how we approach areas of educational policy, particularly the accountability structures of public education, if we are going to address this lack of access now and into the future. (pp. 1–2)

On a localized level, the pandemic created "space for educators to embrace a more process-based approach to artmaking, particularly making use of the responding and connecting aspects of dance national standards where students can individually evaluate, critique and make meaning about art, their own or others" (Dik et al., 2021, p. 3). Dik and colleagues ponder whether or not process-informed pedagogy and teaching methods will continue. More specifically, how might arts educators and teaching artists pursue and embody individual approaches to instruction, providing student agency in the respective art form they study, create, perform, and critique? To do so may take several types of school district policy changes, which expert informants took as their primary focus in their responses to the policy implications of their teaching artistry.

Informants described restrictive financial challenges as well as insufficient support from school administration as primary workplace obstacles. From a budgetary perspective, Gina explained, "Dance receives the least amount of funding compared to music, visual arts, and theater... but I work like crazy to shore up the necessary funds for costumes, guest artists, and commission royalties, etc." Similarly, Ashlyn's concerns echoed lack of support: "Unfortunately, all but one of the principals I worked with those first three years did not support the dance and theater in their schools and offered little, if any, resources." Emily shared a strategy for engaging parents in discussions around funding: "Funding is typically the biggest limitation I currently face, but I have done my best to work around this by having fundraisers, or unique ways to get our parents involved."

Like many expert informants, Kelly acknowledged barriers she faced in administrative and financial support from school staff, emphasizing the necessity for dance teaching artists to work alongside the principal and staff in highlighting the benefits of dance and shaping the performances and engagements. She noted, "You might have an idea of what you want to do when you come in, and they might have a different idea, and so you have to work together." In summary, informant's experiences of policy speak to numerous limitations and obstacles that dance teaching artists often confront in terms of funding and administrative support. Compounded by the COVID-19 pandemic, dance teaching artists risk further restrictions and limitations, ultimately impacting equitable access for students, especially students living in poverty who are often students of color.

Dance teaching artist sites of practice: P-12 environments

The final portion of the study explored dance teaching artists' sites of practice by addressing the specific place, space, and context in which teaching artistry occurs and is delivered. Primary questions investigated the following: What are the P-12 environments in which teaching artists work? How do those settings shape the nature of the teaching artist's work? What types of exchanges transpire between teaching artists, students, participants and communities in these sites of practice? The places, spaces, and contexts of teaching artistry frequently emerge from specific ideas, presumptions, expectations, and pedagogies operating within a particular learning environment. Therefore, we sought to better understand the values and assumptions that operate in P-12 school environments, and how a dance teaching artist's practice affirms, reproduces, resists or challenges those values and assumptions.

Hetty provided insights about P-12 environments that support or inhibit the work of dance teaching artists:

> Each school sees dance as a specific function: as a break, as fun, or as enrichment, and some as entertainment for assemblies. Some, as a link to improvement in other subjects, and some, as part of its core education, vision and philosophy. When a school is choosing to work with an arts education organization with teaching artists in their classrooms, they have determined that dance is of value to their community. This does not always apply to each individual classroom.

Part of the problem Hetty identifies is a lack of clear vision about engaging teaching artists In P-12 settings from the outset, as she said "Do you want to see a performance? Is it going to happen in the studio? Is it going to happen in the auditorium? Are parents going to come? How far should we go with this?" Some expert informants provided creative solutions for navigating and negotiating teaching spaces in P-12 environments. Ashlyn offered specific examples:

> In one school I taught in a trailer, the next was a former auditorium converted to a multipurpose room which worked well. The third school gave me the cafetorium in which I had to teach on a small stage with the curtain drawn for two hours of my day. The

4th school did not give me a room. I had to bounce between a parking lot, an old weight room and a hallway. It was tough but I was determined to build a program despite the lack of administrative support.

Ashlyn's account describes common experiences that many teaching artists confront in terms of environmental support in delivering their programs. Her words reflect the nimbleness and flexibility required when teaching P-12 students, in which each school confronts various structural limitations and resources. When asked about the type of environments that support or inhibit the work of dance teaching artists, Anna responded:

I was teaching in a school last year, and I was in this huge echoing gym, and I had 50 children I just met. It was incredibly challenging to get their attention. I have very rarely taught in a purposely built dance studio. Often I am in the gym, which is usually a very large space, and I need a microphone. I have taught in classrooms where the tables have to be cleared, and then put back after class. The floors are often carpeted. I've had to teach in corridors.

Arriving at a school as a guest or visitor, teaching artists whose work is part-time or residency-based, must cope with numerous environmental challenges. In order to navigate difficult workplace issues as a visiting teaching artist, Anna recommended knowing as much as possible about the residency's teaching spaces beforehand, as she explained:

Going in and seeing the space beforehand and anticipating, like, do you need a microphone? What's the music? How are you going to play the music? And being well prepared, and knowing that you might have to adapt in the space, and that comes with experience. And don't panic, keep calm, keep positive. Teach to the core.

Gina shared a similar idea, "you might have to go into a space and pull the desks aside to create a sacred space for movement." Having the ability to strategize options for adapting dance to diverse environments raises important questions about the role of dance in P-12 environments generally, as well as teaching artists' preparedness for navigating teaching spaces that rarely include a dance studio or similar safe and appropriate space. Given these limitations, larger questions about how well dance/dance education–as both a performing art and arts education–are currently integrated in P-12 schools arise. The abundant environment and space dilemmas, as heard from informants, demonstrate an often unsureness of how, where, and why dance is located within a P-12 school. It appears that adaptability to shifting environments is a key component of "guesthood," one that is vital for continued positive outcomes of dance teaching artists and their P-12 students.

Learning from dance teaching artist practitioners

A number of overlapping themes and confluences emerged from expert informants' stories about their labor as dance teaching artists in P-12 schools: adaptability, flexibility, receptivity, and sensitivity. An adept teaching artist adapts to shifting environmental conditions of the school and its administration. A flexible teaching artist carefully devises and revises lesson plans, objectives, and goals in relation to each particular group of students. A receptive teaching artist skillfully hones their pedagogy and teaching methods in alignment with curriculum and curricular goals. A sensitive teaching artist translates and fulfills the needs of the school and the student communities they serve with a strong desire to collaborate with classroom teachers and dance specialist teachers. In sum, a prerequisite for effective and meaningful dance teaching artistry builds relationships with the people, places, policies, resources, curricula, and environments with which they engage (Jaffe, 2012).

As Anderson and Risner (2012) noted: "Teaching artists are guests. Generally, they are not permanently employed in full-time positions by the institutions in which they conduct workshops and residencies" (p. 13). The notion of "guest-hood," articulated by James Thompson (2005), describes the term as "a carefully negotiated position that is acutely sensitive in relation to the histories of colonization and exploitation" (p. 9). Moreover, the guest's or visitor's challenges come from the fact that teaching artists often work in short-term residencies and "need to figure out the lay of the land relatively quickly" (Snyder-Young, 2014, p. 264). Historically, teaching artists' work has been "accordingly itinerant, contingent, and based on the specific project-based needs of individual classroom teachers…[and] although invited guests, teaching artists were nonetheless met with a degree of suspicion and anxiety" (Anderson & Risner, 2012, p.3).

Classroom teachers and dance specialist teachers regularly navigate complicated local power structures and engage "institutional authorities whose rules and values (both explicit and implicit) govern the spaces in which teaching artists function" (Anderson & Risner, 2014, p. 88). Dance teaching artists, as outsiders, "endeavor to 'fit' into complex and often political environments, while simultaneously serving as ambassadors of the arts, frequently without job security" (Anderson & Risner, 2014, p. 88). At the same time, as teaching artists negotiate the complexity of 'guest-hood' upon entry into P-12 educational environments, they do so alongside reconciliation of their creative interests and artistic praxis within regulations, rules, and policies of respective school locales. The expert informants' stories illustrate the ways in which purposeful and committed integration of dance teaching artists into P-12 schools, when unified with care, collaboration, and mentoring, may produce sustainable and enriching dance arts education benefitting all stakeholders.

One key divergence among informants was the value of dance master's degree programs and the extent to which these programs prepared them as entry-level teaching artists in P-12 schools. Informants who completed MFA degrees in dance found little that prepared them for careers as teaching artists, especially their work in P-12 schools. Conversely, informants who completed MA degrees in dance described how these programs provided comprehensive curricula and meaningful learning experiences that prepared them for careers as P-12 dance teaching artists.

In the US, the MFA is the most prevalent degree offered by graduate dance programs: "64% MFA, 27% MA, EdM, and 9% PhD, EdD" (Higher Education Arts Data Services (HEADS), 2021, pp.11–12). With an emphasis on artistry (performance, technique, choreography), the MFA is widely accepted as a credential for teaching dance in postsecondary education and focuses upon the creation, production and performance of dance. Therefore, it is not surprising that dance teaching artists with MFA degrees find themselves ill-prepared for teaching in P-12 schools. Conversely, because initial master's degrees in dance and dance education (MA, EdM, MS) provide study options in teaching, pedagogy, curriculum, education philosophy, and learning theory, prospective dance teaching artists may find these programs more aligned with their interests and aspirations, beyond teaching dance in higher education. It comes as no surprise that 89% of MFA programs focus on choreography and performance. Unfortunately, over the past two decades, initial master's degrees in dance have been in decline (Anderson & Risner, 2014). However, it is worth noting that the majority of initial master's degree graduates (64%) pursue dance education as their primary course of study (NASD 2021, p. 11). Yet, the fact remains that MFA degree programs in dance outnumber initial master's degrees in dance by nearly three to one, often limiting choice and access while adding significant costs for relocation.

Further considerations: call for action

Lingering considerations and their attendant questions emerge from the findings of this qualitative, interpretive inquiry based on two primary assumptions: first, dance teaching artists make profound contributions to arts education in P-12 schools, and second, dance teaching artists should receive high quality preparation and support commensurate with their responsibilities and obligations in P-12 schools (Anderson & Risner, 2014, p. 280). The obstacles for dance teaching artists remain complex; however, these challenges are not insurmountable if the field's stakeholders, as a collective, are "willing to frame these challenges through a holistic lens—one rooted in enhancing arts education for all people— but also centered on the responsibilities for developing relevant postsecondary programs that value teaching, pedagogy and community engagement alongside artistic practice, technique, and performance" (Anderson & Risner, 2014, p. 280), understood broadly. A holistic approach provides engagement and support for dance teaching artists as whole persons, not only their status as guests, visitors, or outsiders. Therefore, we conclude by asking larger emergent questions drawn from informants' expertise and insights as well as published literature as a call for action.

Highly trained, less than prepared

What role and responsibilities might postsecondary dance programs hold for educating and preparing dance teaching artists for work in P-12 schools? Based on previous research (Anderson & Risner, 2014) and this study's findings, teaching artists entering the field are highly trained in dance performance and choreography, but many do not feel adequately prepared to teach. Most rely upon learning on the job and their own trial and error efforts. Addressing the paradox of highly trained yet less than prepared, begs the questions: what is the relationship between artistry and pedagogy? And why is this relationship important to dance teaching artists and stakeholders? To a large extent, the marginalized status of dance education is an outgrowth of long-standing "artist versus educator" binaries (Kerr-Berry, 2007; Risner, 2007) that "privilege dance performance and choreography while marginalizing commitments to teaching pedagogy, and dance in community" (Risner, 2010, p.124). On the other hand, music education and art education often function as non-binary disciplines in which distinctions between artist and teacher are frequently blurred, holding two identities at the same time is commonplace and accepted.

When the majority of postsecondary dance graduates will not dance professionally or pursue professional careers as performers or choreographers (Bennett, 2009; Montgomery & Robinson, 2003;) but will instead earn a significant portion of their living by teaching dance (Risner, 2010; Warburton, 2004), why is postsecondary dance curriculum in pedagogy, teaching methods, dance education theory, human development, and culturally-relevant teaching undervalued and underrepresented in undergraduate and graduate degree programs? From this curricular void, the "accidental teaching artist" phenomenon often emerges, "many young artists do not see themselves becoming teachers during their postsecondary education and training. Therefore, they do not prepare themselves for teaching but then are subsequently drawn into the teaching artist profession" (Anderson & Risner, 2014, p. 283).

Lack of imagination

Why do recurring challenges and obstacles for dance teaching artists in P-12 schools remain unaddressed? Generally, schools and school system bureaucracies are often rigid, stifling, and slow to respond to changing needs of students and teachers, yet at the same time, they are supposed to serve the public interest (Labaree, 2020). Teaching artist stakeholders are well-acquainted with bureaucratic obstacles characterized as inflexible, impersonal, and hierarchical. In short, "bureaucracies make it difficult to accomplish whatever you want to do, forcing you to wade through a relentless proliferation of red tape" (Labaree, 2020, np). Many bureaucratic challenges confound teaching artists' work often due to a lack of imagination and possibility, frequently affecting under-resourced and marginalized populations, including those with developmental or cognitive challenges, those without access generally, or restricted access to the internet and other technology, as well as school systems without financial and human resource support (Elpus, 2020; Iceland & Hernandez, 2017).

In what ways might dance teaching artists, dance specialist teachers, and school administrators actively engage and exchange in collaborative ways to find imaginative and creative solutions for reducing ill-informed bureaucratic and other policy limitations?

Teaching artists can play a vital role by virtue of their guest-hood status; dance teaching artists as guests entering a school and school system can provide new insights and novel strategies for stakeholders who are accustomed to accepting the status quo operating in P-12 cultures. But to do so, they must be invited to the table where their voices are equally heard and valued.

Finding common ground for transformation

Where can support, cooperation, and commitment best be cultivated and established to inform and advocate the significance of P-12 dance in arts education more broadly, including the important collective work of dance teaching artists, dance specialist teachers, and cooperating general classroom teachers?

As the teaching artist expert informants in this study voiced, finding common ground with dance specialists and classroom teachers, school administrators, students, and families/caregivers is a necessary and essential prerogative to develop awareness and excitement about the numerous benefits of dance education. Building a network of committed allies is critical for gaining both horizontal and vertical support for dance education generally. How might a national initiative bring together P-12 dance specialist teachers and dance teaching artists to ameliorate "guest-hood" obstacles and visitor status challenges? For example, what role might the National Dance Education Organization (NDEO) play in fostering new initiatives through collaborative partnerships, finding common goals and values, and developing informed decision-making that benefit P-12 schools, dance teaching artists, dance specialist teachers and classroom teachers at the same time?

Call for action

Dance education comprises varied populations and sectors, including P-12 schools, postsecondary education, private sector, professional schools of dance, dance company education and outreach, community programs, and cultural centers, all of which benefit from the contributions of dance teaching artists. Although diverse in content, environment, and mission, much is shared and reciprocated in achieving common goals for arts education parity, gender equity, inclusion, fair and just access, curricular equality, representation and diversity. We strongly implore dance education stakeholders to actively pursue commonly shared goals, rather than allowing differences and unique aspects to separate and bifurcate the field of dance education, which has often served to divide us and our ability to act collectively.

To these ends, we offer a call for action that asks dance teaching artist stakeholders to consider the following initiatives:

- Seek new partnerships and collectives: Explore mutually beneficial ways to partner with dance populations outside your current perspective or primary dance education framework.
- Blur traditional boundaries: Examine current limitations and obstacles confronted in your own dance education contexts and identify areas where common goals may allow differences to serve as potential sources for development and strength in dance education and teaching artistry.
- Launch new models: Producing new knowledge and information about dance education requires innovative models that bring together practicing teachers, artists, and policy-makers with scholars and researchers.
- Explore and support research collaborations for gaining new and robust information: Initiate and develop cooperative relationships and applied laboratories between dance education practitioners, researchers and dance teaching artists for conducting research studies. The more we know the better we successfully integrate dance education in P-12 schools and their communities.

Much of the tension in arts education in P-12 schools comes from competing narratives about what a specific artform best brings to student learning in conjunction with mandates that require quantifiable, quantitative data on particular areas of improvement and higher test scores in other required curriculum. The lack of imagination that permeates a great deal of P-12 school administration and bureaucracy often comes from ignoring the numerous and inherent possibilities the arts hold for expanding creativity, exploration, imagination, wonderment, and questioning. Albert Einstein (1931) noted that "imagination is more important than knowledge. Knowledge is limited. Imagination encircles the world" (p. 97). His prophetic voice captures the power of imagining the world otherwise and the limits of knowledge. In many ways, knowledge is easy to acquire; however, it is our collective imagination that requires resolve, patience, persistence, and commitment.

Notes

1. Drawn from Michigan Department of Education Retrieved July 1, 2021, from. https://tfa.soe.umich.edu/wp-content/uploads/2015/03/Classes_Taught_396034_7.pdf
2. Informants' continuing education included Laban Movement Analysis, Brain-Compatible Dance Education (Anne Green-Gilbert), Dance Education Laboratory (DEL), and Orff-Schulwerk professional development classes, among other enrichment programs and professional conferences.

ORCID

Bryant Henderson Shea http://orcid.org/0000-0003-0528-0438

References

Anderson, M., & Risner, D. (2012). A survey of teaching artists in dance and theatre: Implications for preparation, curriculum and professional degree programs. *Arts Education Policy Review*, *113*(1), 1–16. https://doi.org/10.1080/10632913.2012.626383

Anderson, M., & Risner, D. (2014). *Hybrid lives of teaching artists in dance and theatre arts: A critical reader*. Cambria Press.

Anderson, M., Risner, D., & Butterworth, M. (2013). The praxis of teaching artists in theatre and dance: International perspectives on preparation, practice and professional identity. *International Journal of Education & the Arts*, *14*(5), 25. Retrieved May 15, 2021, from http://www.ijea.org/v14n5/.

Association for Teaching Artists. (2010). *Teaching artists and their work*. Retrieved July 20, 2010, from http://www.teachingartists.com/Association%20of%20Teaching%20Artists%20Survey%20Results.pdf

Bennett, D. (2009). Careers in dance: Beyond performance to the real world of work. *Journal of Dance Education*, *9*(1), 27–24. https://doi.org/10.1080/15290824.2009.10387381

Bernard, C. F. (2020). Lived experiences: Arts policy at the street level in the New York City Department of Education. *Arts Education Policy Review*, *121*(1), 30–41. https://doi.org/10.1080/10632913.2018.1530713

Creswell, J. (2014). *Research design: Qualitative, quantitative, and mixed methods approaches*. SAGE.

Denzin, N. K., & Lincoln, Y. S. (2011). *The SAGE handbook of qualitative research*. SAGE.

Dik, D., Morrison, R., Sabol, R., & Tuttle, L. (2021). Looking beyond COVID-19: Arts education policy implications and opportunities. *Arts Education Policy Review*, 1–9. https://doi.org/10.1080/10632913.2021.1931603

Einstein, A. (1931). *Einstein on cosmic religion and other opinions and aphorisms*. Covici-Friede, Inc.

Elpus, K. (2020). Access to arts education in America: The availability of visual art, music, dance, and theater courses in U.S. high schools. *Arts Education Policy Review*, *121*, 1–20. https://doi.org/10.1080/10632913.2020.1773365

Erickson, F. (2005). Arts, humanities, and sciences in educational research and social engineering in federal education policy. *Teachers College Record, 107*(1), 4–9. https://doi.org/10.1111/j.1467-9620.2005.00451.x

Field-Springer, K. (2018). Informants. In M. Allen (Ed.), *The SAGE encyclopedia of communication research methods* (pp. 702–705). SAGE Publications, Inc.

Higher Education Arts Data Services (HEADS). (2021). *Dance data summaries 2020-2021*. Higher Education Arts Data Services.

Iceland, J., & Hernandez, E. (2017). Understanding trends in concentrated poverty: 1980-2014. *Social Science Research, 62*, 75–95. https://doi.org/10.1016/j.ssresearch.2016.09.001.

Jaffe, N. (2012). We are allies and we have allies. *Teaching Artist Journal, 10*(3), 143–122. https://doi.org/10.1080/15411796.2012.685694

Kerr-Berry, J. (2007). Dance educator as dancer and artist. *Journal of Dance Education, 7*(1), 5–6. https://doi.org/10.1080/15290824.2007.10387326

Kresek, K. C. (2018). *Invisible terrains: Experiences of nomadic music teaching artists* [Doctoral dissertation]. Teachers College Columbia University. https://academiccommons.columbia.edu/doi/10.7916/D8K661KP

Labaree, D. (2020). Two cheers for school bureaucracy. *Phi Delta Kappan, 101*(6), 53–56. https://kappanonline.org/two-cheers-school-bureaucracy-public-interest-labaree/ https://doi.org/10.1177/0031721720909595

Montgomery, S., & Robinson, M. (2003). What becomes of undergraduate dance majors? *Journal of Cultural Economics, 27*(1), 57–71. https://doi.org/10.1023/A:1021580130420

National Dance Education Organization. (2021). *About PreK-12 dance education in the United States: State certification for PreK-12 education*. Retrieved June 30, 2021, from https://www.ndeo.org/content.aspx?page_id=22&club_id=893257&module_id=194714

Rabkin, N., Reynolds, M., Hedberg, E., & Shelby, J. (2011). *A report on the teaching artist research project* (Rep.). NORC at the University of Chicago. Retrieved September 1, 2013, from http://www.norc.org/PDFs/publications/RabkinN_Teach_Artist_Research_2011.pdf

Risner, D. (2007). Current challenges for K-12 dance education and development: Perspectives from higher education. *Arts Education Policy Review, 108*(4), 17–24. https://doi.org/10.3200/AEPR.108.4.17-24

Risner, D. (2010). Dance education matters: Rebuilding postsecondary dance education for 21st century relevance and resonance. *Arts Education Policy Review, 111*(4), 123–135. https://doi.org/10.1080/10632913.2010.490761

Risner, D. (2012). Hybrid lives of teaching and artistry: A study of teaching artists in dance in the USA. *Research in Dance Education, 13*(2), 175–193. https://doi.org/10.1080/14647893.2012.677426

Risner, D. (2014). A case study of empathetic teaching artistry. *Teaching Artist Journal, 12*(2), 82–88. https://doi.org/10.1080/15411796.2014.878137

Risner, D., & Anderson, M. (2012). The highly satisfied teaching artist in dance: A case study. *Teaching Artist Journal, 10*(2), 94–101. https://doi.org/10.1080/15411796.2012.658311

Risner, D., & Anderson, M. (2015). The credential question: Attitudes of teaching artists in dance and theatre arts. *Teaching Artist Journal, 13*(1), 28–35. https://doi.org/10.1080/15411796.2014.966025

Snyder, S., & Fisk, T. (2016a). A national survey of teaching artists working in schools: Background, preparation, efficacy and school experiences. *Journal of Research in Education, 26*, 1–30.

Snyder, S., & Fisk, T. (2016b). Applying Bandura's model to identifying sources of self-efficacy of teaching artists. *Research in the Schools, 23*, 38–50.

Snyder-Young, D. (2014). Ethical problems for hybrid teaching artist-researchers. In M. Anderson & D. Risner (Eds.), *Hybrid lives of teaching artists in dance and theatre arts: A critical reader* (pp. 253–268). Cambria Press.

Thompson, J. (2005). *Digging up stories: Applied theatre performance and war*. Manchester University Press.

Warburton, E. (2004). Who cares? Teaching and learning care in dance. *Journal of Dance Education, 4*(3), 88–96. https://doi.org/10.1080/15290824.2004.10387264

Young-Overby, L. (2014). Learning programs: A case study of dance teaching artists. In M. Anderson & D. Risner (Eds.), *Hybrid lives of teaching artists in dance and theatre arts: A critical reader* (pp.19–30). Cambria Press.

Part IV
Dance, Gender, and Sexual Identity

Prelude

"When we speak about "what we know about boys and dance" we have to carefully undo any assumptions we have that there is one uniform male dance student. Boys who dance, dance for different reasons and purposes. What's more, boys and males dance diverse dance forms and genres. From hip hop to hula, ballet to tap, clogging to cha-cha, male social status, privilege, and marginalization vary widely across the globe." (Risner et al., 2018, p. 28)

Jennifer McNamara: Gender studies and the perspectives of and on males in dance are the research areas where I first came to know Doug Risner's work, in spite of having taken his pedagogy course through the NDEO's Online Professional Development Institute. Perhaps this is because at the time, I was close to the end of my own performing career and hadn't quite drawn the connection between education and dance; I wasn't looking for research on the social foundations of teaching and their essential, underlying influence on the ideas of who was invited to dance. I subscribed to worn-out notions about recruiting and retaining males in dance, marketing to males and their parents, and ideas about subsidized dance education for males as perfectly legitimate—even when that also included special treatment for them—all of which were dangerous and deleterious for the male and female dancers. Because males in dance were and still are a rare commodity, this kind of attitude both reinforced their divine stature while simultaneously erasing their individual identities—because, of course, we needed them to be the counterpoint to the dancing feminine body/ideal. And this line of thinking, of course, marginalizes the work that the more numerous female dancers had to do to achieve as much as the fewer, rarer male dancers did, while simultaneously reducing dancers of all genders to mere bodies in opposition to one another.

Doug Risner: During my doctoral study (1998–2001), the relationships between dance, gender, and sexual identity in education became the focus of my research and scholarship. At the time, Ramsay Burt in the United Kingdom and Michael Gard in Australia were leading the charge for investigating, bringing forward, and uplifting males and masculinities in dance. Burt's work focused on professional male dancers, while Gard's scholarship tended toward dance education and sport. Their important theorizing often emanated from a dance studies perspective as a hybrid form combining aspects of performance studies, masculinity studies, and queer theory. While their highly influential and much-cited work was rigorous and pioneering, I was not interested in repeating or competing with what Burt and Gard had successfully carved out. In addition, I wasn't prepared to move their work forward.

Therefore, I pursued research inquiry about dance and masculinity from educational perspectives, more specifically social foundations of education, critical pedagogy (Freire), critical feminist pedagogy (hooks), and critical feminist dance pedagogy (Stinson), as these paradigms meshed closely with my own reservations about and problems with traditional, authoritarian dance training and dance education. To these ends, I realized that my interests in scholarship and research were quite different in aims, values, pedagogy, and epistemology. I wanted to learn more about the lived experiences of dancing and a life in dance directly from adolescent boys and young males who danced.

My first publication on this topic, "Sexual Orientation and Male Participation in Dance Education: Revisiting the Open Secret" (2002) in the *Journal of Dance Education*, emerged from a qualitative research study I conducted while completing my PhD. A second article, titled "Rehearsing Heterosexuality: Unspoken Truths in Dance Education" (2002a), quickly followed and was published in *Dance Research Journal*. In it, I outed myself for a second time as a queer, cis-gendered male dance educator—a cathartic endeavor after years of secrecy and struggles learning how to rehearse, perform, merge, and ultimately authentically live both my sexual identity and professional persona.

JM: As a white, able-bodied, cis-female, I have not often been asked to perform as anything other than a persona that matches the identity I present as outwardly facing, character studies in the classical ballet canon notwithstanding—they are all still predicated on an understanding of human relationships that matches my own experience of living in the world. Reading Doug's work on gender, masculinity, and identity, however, challenged my perception of my place in the greater dance milieu, as I acknowledged my complicity in the complexities of male experience, as well as in the ways I have participated in the marginalization of male and female voices, my own included. Upholding dominant paradigms limits the potential for shift in perceived ideals, from aesthetics to accessibility to ideas about what is true or real, which is itself colored by nuanced layers of inequitable experiences that dancers, care-givers, dance-makers, and dance educators have noted for generations.

DR: Chapter 11, "Rehearsing Masculinity: Challenging the 'Boy Code' in Dance Education" (2007), my most cited journal article, was drawn from exploratory research in preparation for writing my first book, *Stigma and Perseverance in the Lives of Boys Who Dance* (2009). My focus was to center the voices of boys who dance as they told their stories of how they experience dancing, as well as inviting and holding space for the parents/caregivers responses to their sons' dancing.

The next chapter I chose to include here, "Bullying, Victimization, and Social Support of Adolescent Male Dance Students" (2014), emerged from a subset of the data gathered from male participants (13- to 18-year-old students) as part of research for my book, *Stigma and Perseverance* (2009), which examined bullying and harassment of young males who dance. As my fourth most cited journal publication, the findings of this article ask readers to contemplate the challenges that males in dance confront from a very early age.

Chapter 13, "Gender Problems in Western Theatrical Dance: Little Girls, Big Sissies and the 'Baryshnikov Complex'" (2014), was written for undergraduate students fulfilling their performing arts requirement in postsecondary general education, such as Introduction to Dance, Dance in Culture, and Gender in the Arts. Having taught general education courses in dance for many years, I thoroughly enjoyed deconstructing gender studies and masculinity studies in straightforward language applicable to dominant notions about people who dance. This novel approach integrates actual student comments and responses from general education courses I taught over more than a decade.

Section IV concludes with Chapter 14, the keynote address I presented at the Men in Dance: Bridging the Gap Symposium organized by the National Dance Education Organization—two years to the day that I was released from the hospital to begin outpatient cancer rehabilitation, starting with learning how to walk again. The thrust of my keynote focused on asking new questions about boys in dance, rather than the field's eternal fixation on how to get more males in dance:

> Based largely on heterocentrism [seeing all the world as heterosexual] and influenced heavily by the professional dance world, the obsession for attracting and retaining male students, often at the expense of highly skilled females, may ultimately contribute to significant gender inequities and biases. Even if we believe more male students would benefit our dance programs, we must at some point ask, "How many males is 'enough'?" And "what and who are we willing to sacrifice to achieve this goal?" (Risner et al., 2018, p. 26)

Preparing this keynote along with the many dialogues and conversations throughout the symposium led me to edit and write the collected volume, *Masculinity, Intersectionality, and Identity: Why Boys (Don't) Dance* (2022) with Beccy Watson.

JM: The research that Doug brought forward in these chapters, centering a marginalized voice that also exists in a double-bind, was one of the seminal ways in which his work has allowed the field to expand without becoming homogeneous. As he urgently advocated in his dissertation, being the center, or even adjacent to the center, runs the risk of being subsumed by dominant theories and beliefs. Maintaining a distinct identity and holding the space of difference while still speaking in ways that can be heard by those in a place of privilege means navigating an orbit that wobbles, corrects, stretches, and tugs on the gravitational forces that seek to contain and equalize it, without accounting for its own predilections and curiosities. Such work can only be undertaken if there is a history of trust, ethical decision-making, and bold tenderness. Rehearsing many iterations of self can obscure these frameworks, but for Doug Risner, the work provided a clarity that both encompassed and flung wide open the space between, allowing him to be both potter and clay, drawing once more from the analogy by potter, poet, and educator Mary Caroline Richards to which he referred in "Exploring Dance Rehearsal—The Neglected Issues Revealed" (Risner, 1992) in part one of this book.

References

Risner, D., Blumenfeld, B., Janetti, A., Kaddar, Y., & Rutt, C., 2018

Risner, D. (1992). Exploring dance rehearsal: The neglected issues revealed. *Journal of Physical Education, Recreation & Dance, 63*(6), 61–65. DOI: 10.1080/07303084.1992.10606621

Risner, D. (2002). Sexual orientation and male participation in dance education: Revisiting the open secret. *Journal of Dance Education, 2*(3), 84–92. DOI: 10.1080/15290824.2002.10387214

Risner, D. (2002a). Rehearsing heterosexuality: Unspoken truths in dance education. *Dance Research Journal, 34*(2), 63–78. DOI: 10.2307/1478460

Risner, D. (2007). Rehearsing masculinity: Challenging the 'boy code' in dance education. *Research in Dance Education, 8*(2), 139–153. DOI: 10.1080/14647890701706107

Risner, D. (2009). *Stigma and perseverance in the lives of boys who dance*. Mellen Press.

Risner, D. (2014). Bullying, victimization, and social support of adolescent male dance students. *Research in Dance Education, 15*(2), 179–201. DOI:10.1080/14647893.2014.891847

Risner, D. (2014a). Gender problems in western theatrical dance: Little girls, big sissies and the "Baryshnikov complex." *International Journal of Education and the Arts, 15*(10), 1–22. Retrieved from http://www.ijea.org/v15n10/

Risner, D., Blumenfeld, B., Janetti, A., Kaddar, Y., & Rutt, C. (2018). Men in dance: Bridging the gap symposium. *Dance Education in Practice, 4*(1), 25–31. DOI: 10.1080/23734833.2018.1417212

Risner, D., & Watson, B. (2022). *Masculinity, intersectionality, and identity: Why boys (don't) dance.* Palgrave McMillan.

Rehearsing Masculinity: Challenging the "Boy Code" in Dance Education

Doug Risner

Dance education experiences of boys and male youth are investigated in terms of dominant constructions of contemporary Western masculinity and the potential limitations these hegemonic discourses may place on male participation. Recent research on boys and male youth in dance, although limited, suggests prevailing social stigma, heteronormative assumptions, narrow definitions of masculinity, and internalized homophobia in the field. For boys and young males, however, choosing to dance may be an important vehicle for investigating dominant notions about masculinity, gender, sexual orientation, and the body. From emerging research, this review essay explores the ways in which male youth in dance confront heterocentric bias, gender norms, and gendered bodies, as well as peer pressure and dominant cultural ideology in dance training and education. Focal points include key social questions of difference, pleasure, marginalization, and the larger effects and limitations of contemporary masculinity.

Introduction

This review essay explores dance education experiences of boys and young males in Western theatrical concert dance[1] through a lens of dominant constructions of contemporary masculinity (Pollack, 1999; Kimmel, 2005) and the effects these hegemonic discourses place on dance more broadly. Although research indicates that 50 per cent of male dancers in the United States are gay or bisexual (Bailey & Oberschneider, 1997; Hamilton, 1998), the dance community has only recently begun to illuminate the silence that surrounds gay and bisexual males' experiences in Western theatrical dance and its training. Recent scholarship on male youth in dance education suggests various kinds of prevailing social stigma, including narrow definitions of masculinity, heterosexist justifications for males in dance, and internalized homophobia in the field. Illuminating the experiences of boys and young males in dance education provides an important vehicle for researchers interested in exposing dominant notions about masculinity, gender, privilege, sexual orientation, and the body.

From emerging research in the US (Risner, 2002a,b, 2003b, 2007; Risner & Thompson, 2005; Williams, 2003), Australia (Gard, 2001b, 2003a, b, 2006), the United Kingdom (Keyworth, 2001), and Finland (Lehikoinen, 2005), the aim of this paper is to identify and synthesize literature that investigates the ways in which male youth in dance experience heterocentric bias, gender norms, and gendered bodies, as well as social pressures through dominant cultural ideology in dance training and education. Presented as a review of literature, this paper examines social questions of gender, difference, pleasure, marginalization, and the larger effects of contemporary masculinity within the realm of dance education.

At the outset, it is important to note the dearth of research and scholarly attention applied to this burgeoning area of dance education study; much of the literature reviewed here emerges from studies with small sample sizes and therefore drawing firm, generalized conclusions is not the aim. Rather, this review seeks to assemble a useful body of knowledge, albeit limited, providing some evidentiary resources in an under-researched field for further inquiry. In tandem, the nascent development of research in this area also requires a wide-ranging review of literature, providing context and point of reference for readers.

Given this range of literature, I employ the term 'dance education' in this paper to broadly reference education, training, and preparation in Western theatrical concert dance settings. The use of 'dance education' implies formalized dance study in K-12 (age group 5–17 years), teacher preparation programs, postsecondary, tertiary, private studio, and other professional conservatories and schools. Within this context and where possible, I briefly identify each study's particular dance education context and sample description.

Gender and dance education

Dance education and training have long been associated with gender and gender roles in world culture (Kraus *et al.*, 1991; Sanderson, 1996; Posey, 2002; Stinson, 2005). While dance in many cultures has been, and continues to be viewed as an appropriate 'male' activity, the Western European cultural paradigm situates dance as primarily a 'female' art form, and has done so since the sixteenth century (Hasbrook, 1993). Moreover, research indicates that the overwhelming majority of the student population engaged in dance education and training is female.[2] Dance education researchers have gleaned considerable energy from the area of social foundations in education, especially in the realm of schooling and its impact on gender identity. With hybrid research agendas and methodologies from feminist thought, critical theory, gender studies, critical pedagogy, and most recently, men's studies, dance education literature has begun to focus on the ways in which socially embedded assumptions about gender and dominant structural power relations produce unjust educational and socio-cultural outcomes.[3]

Gender and its social construction play an important role in students' participation and attitudes regarding dance study.[4] Beginning as early as three years of age, girls, unlike boys, often grow up in dance as a taken-for-granted activity of childhood, adopting values 'which teach that it is good to be obedient and silent, good not to question authority or to have ideas which might conflict with what one is being asked to do' (Van Dyke, 1992, p. 120). Thomas (1996) asserts that understanding 'the "feminization" of theatrical dance in the west is critical for studying gender and dance for dance educators, because viewed primarily as a feminine activity, males who dance are always in danger of being classified as effeminate' (p. 507). Due in large part to dualistic thinking which separates mind from body, intellectual activity from physical labor, and dance's close association with girls and women, dance is often perceived as part of the women's domain, whereby its denigration for its dense female population is possible. Historical notions about the body often link the *feminine* with intuition, nature, the body, and evil; conversely, the intellectual, culture, and the mind historically have been perceived as *masculine* (Risner, 2001). Dance education scholar, Edrie Ferdun summarizes:

> The term 'dance' is usually associated with girls and feminine qualities by a significant portion of the dominant culture. Labelling dance as female prevents dance from functioning fully as an educational medium. It limits participation by anyone, male or female, who does not want to be associated with stereotyped gender images and practices. (Ferdun, 1994, p. 46)

Some approaches for confronting gender stereotypes in dance teaching and curriculum have been identified.[5] Central to most of these strategies is a concerted effort to make gender a conscious variable in all aspects of dance education (Ferdun, 1994) and the affirmation of individual differences in gender and culture (Bond, 1994; Kerr-Berry, 1994).

Males in dance often benefit disproportionately because of their gender (Van Dyke, 1996; Garber *et al.*, 2007). Despite women's majority in the dance population, dance does not necessarily offer more opportunities to women than to men (Adair, 1992; Van Dyke, 1996; Samuels, 2001). Because of the seeming legitimacy men bring to dance, although they comprise a definitive minority, males often receive more attention and cultivation in their classes, training, and scholarship awards. Some research indicates that dance teachers may emphasize the need to make boys and young men in dance 'feel more comfortable' by inviting them to actively contribute ideas for movement, music, costumes and choreographic theme (Risner *et al.*, 2004), by developing lesson plans and movement (sports movement, vigorous actions) that allow boys a feeling of ownership (Baumgarten, 2003), and by emphasizing the challenge and satisfaction of jumping higher, shifting weight faster, moving bigger and balancing longer (Gard, 2001b).

In order to cultivate more male participation in dance and dance education, normalizing strategies over the past two decades have frequently centered on noteworthy heterosexual male dancers (Hanna, 1988), masculinist comparisons between sports and dance (Crawford, 1994), and minimizing the significant gay male dance population (Spurgeon, 1999; Risner, 2002a, b). Even so, research continues to indicate that participation in Western European dance remains a culturally suspect endeavor for male adolescents and young adults (Sanderson, 2001; Stinson, 2001; Risner, 2002a; Gard, 2003b, 2006; Williams, 2003; Leihikoinen, 2005; Fisher, 2007).

Dance is for girls: rehearsing masculinity

Current discourses in contemporary masculinity and gender, as well as the findings of leading researchers on boys and young males indicate a direct correlation between post-modern masculine identity and homophobia (Kimmel & Messner, 2001). Understanding more fully the experiences of boys who dance requires particular attention to the parallel relationship between masculinity and homophobic attitudes.

Dance scholar, Ramsay Burt (1995), gives a highly rigorous explication of the cultural, social, and political history of masculine representation in dance, most notably the twentieth century construction of prejudice toward male dancers and the homophobia that today continues to surround gay or straight men in dance. In his seminal text, *The Male Dancer*, Burt (1995) charts the development of homophobia as a means for males to rationalize their close attraction to one another. In this scheme, men can only bond socially when homophobic attitudes accompany such intimacy. In other words, although men might enjoy watching other men dance, in order to do so, they must profess an absolute repulsion for homosexual desire or attraction. Straddling this important boundary between acceptable homosocial bonding and repressed homosexual attraction is the crux for the heterosexual male spectator watching men dance. This notion is a key element in understanding many men's culturally prescribed anxiety toward gay men. It is instructive for dance educators to realize that similarly uncomfortable boundary crossings might reasonably apply for many fathers, siblings and friends attempting to watch or support male dancers. Without facing these foundational aspects of culturally defined masculinity, there is little hope for any real progress. Research in men's studies reveals much the same conclusion; homophobia is a key defining element in contemporary, post-modern masculinity (Kimmel & Messner, 2001).

Within the current politicized debate about boys' achievement and behavior in schools, sociologist Michael Kimmel (2005) notes the importance of examining contemporary masculinity in order to constructively address boys' needs. Although post-modern feminist theory has greatly expanded our understandings of multiple subject positions, as well as the notion of diverse femininities or ways of being female for girls and women, it appears that contemporary masculinity has become even narrower, or like a 'gender straightjacket' for boys and men (Pollack, 1999, p. 6). In the pioneering *Real Boys*, William Pollack (1999) outlines the significance of a cultural re-evaluation of prevailing ideas about boys, men, and masculinity:

> The boys I see in schools and in private practice often are hiding not only a range of their feelings but also some of their creativity and originality ... The Boy Code is so strong, yet so subtle, in its influence that boys may not even know they are living in accordance with it. When they do (stray from the code), however, society tends to let them know—swiftly and forcefully—in the form of a taunt by a sibling, a rebuke by a parent or a teacher, or ostracism by classmates. (p. 7)

The gender straightjacket and Boy Code have profound effects on more than just the lives of boys and young males (Katz & Earp, 1999; Pollack, 1999; Kimmel & Messner, 2001; Kimmel, 2005). Unchecked traditional values of masculinity—emotional detachment, suppression of feelings, feigned bravado and self-confidence, dominance, aggression, and valorized individual achievement—diminish all human experience. Katz and Earp (1999) describe this phenomenon as 'the crisis in masculinity', in which 'behind the bravado and tough guy posturing, there is human complexity ... the results of a sensitive, nuanced experience of the world that rarely airs in public' (Katz & Earp, 1999, p. 3). Sociologist Timothy Curry (2001) reminds readers of the socialization process in which boys learn to be masculine by avoiding all that is feminine, homosexual, or *unmasculine*.

When we consider seriously this mask of dominant masculinity that society imposes on boys and young males, we see more clearly not only the disruptive cultural resistance, but also the courage necessary for our male students to pursue dance study and consider a career in dance. Dance educators would do well to look more closely at the dominant social structures and cultural assumptions that guide our own practice and research, as well as the ways in which our actions wield the power to deplete or enrich an empowering common humanity. Obviously, there are additional complexities involved in unpacking the social experiences and gendered bodies of males in dance: for example, the marginalization of male dancers in a culturally feminized field, combined with the privilege, benefit and authority of being male in a patriarchal society.

What we know about boys who dance

While research on adolescent male dancers and their experiences is scant, what we do know provides cause for concern, linked as it is to dominant notions of masculinity, pervasive homophobia, and boys' neglect and harassment (Gold, 2001; Patrick, 2001; Williams, 2003). Recent research about psychosocial understanding of male adolescent dancers emerges from a quantitative/qualitative study, *Examining Psychosocial Issues of Adolescent Male Dancers*, by Deborah Williams (2003), whose research was conducted from a human development perspective. Using an ethnographic approach, the qualitative portion of the study of 33 boys (12–18 years of age) enrolled in summer intensive dance training programs (at three sites) revealed three significant themes: the participants feel social isolation; have unmet needs; and, despite lack of social support and negative experiences, they persevere in their dance study (Williams, 2003, p. iii).

Williams notes the following aspects of social isolation among her subjects:

- a lack of same-gender peers/teachers in the dance environment
- a need to talk about issues but not having a supportive person to talk with
- in some cases, having family members who did not support or discouraged their desire to dance
- a need to keep their dance life a secret from academic peers
- fear of or actual teasing and harassment by peers
- perceptions of homosexuality regardless of the dancer's sexual orientation
- teachers, parents, and directors attempting to justify dance activities by relating them to sports. (p. 57)

Williams' accompanying qualitative interview data illuminate the boys' social isolation and their frustration with misguided efforts by teachers, parents and directors to justify dance for males in traditionally masculinist ways. As one participant stated, 'I'm an artist, not a football player! Why does everyone keep insisting on comparing me to a sports star who takes ballet for exercise as though that should make it alright to dance?' (Williams, 2003, p. 59). In previous work, I have been critical of these kinds of hegemonic approaches (Risner, 2002a, b) and have advocated, with others (Crawford, 1994; Gard, 2001b, 2003b), for more rigorous questioning and informed strategies that focus on greater understanding of dominant notions of masculinity, societal stigma about males in dance, and that dance education researchers attempt to unearth cogent, relevant research about the experiences of males who dance. Williams' study, though limited in scope and generalization, provides valuable information for future research.

While male adolescent dancers indicate the necessity of perseverance (in their words: *a love for dance*) for confronting negative stereotypes and social isolation outside the dance studio, it appears that an internalized homophobia within dance education may be powerful as well. Teachers, directors, and peers sometimes use homophobic language in order to emphasize the importance of adhering to strictly masculine behavior, gesture, and movement execution. For example, the male teacher who coaches a young male dancer to execute movement more strongly states, 'You're a beautiful dancer, but you dance like a fag. We'll need to show you how to dance like a man' (Williams, 2003, p. 71). For another participant struggling to affirm his gay identity, the pejorative societal stereotype of the gay male dancer looms largely in his consciousness when he states, 'I recently came out [as gay] to my friends and family. I feel guilty because I let my fellow dancers down. I'm exactly what everyone thinks male dancers are. I'm ashamed of that' (Williams, 2003, p. 60). This kind of shame or low social worth is typical of internalized homophobia (Margolies *et al.*, 1987).

Recent research in dance education and physical education has begun to explore the ways in which hegemonic masculinity, as an institution, can be challenged through the participation and experiences of boys and young males in dance (Gard, 2001b, 2003a, b; Keyworth, 2001; Risner, 2002a, b). Central to this work is the notion that dance education may serve as an important means for disrupting dominant cultural assumptions about acceptable ways of moving for males and to challenge cultural stereotypes about male dancers and non-heterosexual modes of sexuality. This is not to say that all boys and young men in dance consciously enter the dance studio with the intention of challenging dominant paradigms of masculinity, nor can it be denied that some males in dance reaffirm narrow definitions of masculinity and heterosexism through their actions and discourses. Rather, this area of research suggests that the experiences of males in dance education can provide powerful insights into hegemonic assumptions about dance, gender and sexuality, as well as dominant codes that govern the former.

Saul Keyworth, in his critical autobiographical (Jackson, 1990) study of himself and nine male participants, found significant feelings of isolation, both for himself and his physical education study's male dance participants who acknowledge their pejorative status, as the 'dancing queens' on campus (Keyworth, 2001). For this qualitative study, Keyworth employed a 'collective story' methodology (Richardson, 1990; Barone, 1992), comparing his own critical narrative with those of his peers engaged in dance study within a teacher training program for physical educators. Although participants in this narrative inquiry enjoyed their dance experiences, many were reluctant to pursue further dance study away from the 'safety' of a university sport and athletic program. While optimistic that more males in dance will be sensitized to 'question and ultimately subvert their own gendered conditioning', Keyworth concludes that participants will 'continue to carry their gendered legacy' (p. 133). More simply, the power of narrowly defined masculinity and its 'boy code' continues to police the behaviors of young men, regardless of the joy and pleasure they experience while dancing. This contribution to the literature opens an important area for future inquiry investigating male pleasure and satisfaction in dance education.

Michael Gard's (2001b, 2003a, b) recent work focuses on the possibilities that dance education offers for 'disruptive and discomforting experiences', as well as pleasurable ones, for students in schools and universities, more specifically, exhuming the taken-for-grantedness of gendered male bodies and heterosexual embodiment (Gard, 2003a, p. 211). In his unpublished doctoral thesis investigating the discursive construction of male theatrical dancers in Western culture, Gard conducted interviews with 19 male dancers of differing ages and career achievements (Gard, 2001a). Within this research the notion of gendered investments, or committed ways of deploying the body, in dance education are explored. In a life history narrative culled from this study with Ralph (pseudonym), a professional male dancer, Gard (2003b) found an interesting correlation between the absence of 'enjoyment' or pleasure and an acute awareness that 'boys don't dance' (p. 109). This kind of love/hate relationship with dance stems from the idea that males are enculturated to manifest a particular kind of body and a specific way of moving that evidences a strict heterosexual regime (or set of governed practices). A highly proficient professional dancer, Ralph's narrative account of dancing is one of repeated ambivalence, 'bereft of any talk of bodily pleasure' (p. 113). Gard argues that this kind of uncertainty hinges upon a struggle to reconcile enjoyment of dancing with other bodily investments more consistent and characteristic of dominant male heterosexuality, like Ralph's skills in rugby and surfing. The study suggests that challenging dominant gender norms, whether intentional or not, requires an intense internal struggle with external forces and expectations.

Previous qualitative research on male participation in dance that I conducted with six introductory level male undergraduate dance students (average age 19) in the US revealed five themes that may illuminate a better understanding of social stigmatization: homophobic stereotypes, narrow definitions of masculinity, heterosexist justifications for male participation, the absence of positive male role models (straight and gay), and internalized homophobia among male dance students (Risner, 2002a). Within the small convenience sample of this action research study, it should be noted that three of the participants in this study self-identified as heterosexual; two self-identified as gay and one as bisexual. While it is unknown how representative this study is to the whole of male undergraduates in dance education, the findings provide some fairly significant insights.

Resisting cultural norms for these young men began with confronting homophobic stereotypes held by their own families and peers, in which the participants' negative preconceptions of male dancers figured prominently as each contemplated and began dance study. At the same time, participants later spoke eloquently about the personal satisfaction they felt while studying dance. Similar to the work of Gard (2003b), Keyworth (2001), and Lehikoinen (2005), understanding the ways in which young men in dance balance these competing narratives deserves further examination. Although males' dance education appears to be an important source of joy, satisfaction, and affirmation, their masculinity and sexual orientation is repeatedly questioned and surveilled. Complicated meta-narratives may also require equally complicated coping mechanisms for young men in dance (Risner, 2003b). Justifying their participation in dance emerges as an important arbiter of masculinity for young men who dance. Justification, or 'excuses' as Gard refers to them, often result in heteronormative half-truths; that is to say that a 'real male' would never actively choose dance study on his own volition. As AJ (pseudonym), whose degree program requires coursework in dance, acknowledges, 'You don't have to show that you're interested, but of course I am. I did use it [the requirement] as an excuse with my friends back home, my family' (Risner, 2002a, p. 87). Like Williams' study of male adolescents discussed earlier, many of the male students described their frustration with the lack of positive male role models in dance, citing the need for more affirming examples of men as dance teachers, professional dancers, as well as popular media images of men dancing. Without strong role models to challenge narrow views of masculinity, some of the participants suggested, homosexual stereotypes become so embedded in the culture's association with dance that young males in dance accept the homophobic responses their dancing frequently garners (Risner, 2002a, p. 88).

While there is little doubt that the physical nature of dance is commensurate with that of football or soccer, discourses that colonialize dance in traditionally masculinist ways obfuscate critical issues of homophobia and societal stigma directed toward male dancers (Gard, 2001b; Stinson, 2001; Garber et al., 2007; Risner, 2007). With the intention of making dance more accessible for boys and palatable to their peers, family and culture, these discourses regularly position dance for males as acceptable only as sport. Nor is it doubted, for those participants who are straight, the ontological significance of their heterosexual orientation and the ways in which dancing may challenge some of their deepest feelings about what it means to be male. However, masculinist justifications frequently serve to not only buttress homophobic stereotypes, but also to erase the otherwise positive and pleasurable experiences of young men in dance. First, why do these young men engaged in dance study—gay and straight—reaffirm some of the very stereotypes they repeatedly confront themselves? Second, why do these men feel it necessary to deny the presence of gay/bisexual men in dance education in order to legitimate their own participation? While one can certainly acknowledge the kind of courage required of the young men like those discussed in these various studies, it is also important to recognize the myriad ways in which denigrating some people serves to privilege others—in this case, heterosexual males and dominant notions of masculinity.

Dominant masculinity and gay males in dance

For young gay males, the protection offered by the dance studio often carries the cost of isolation for a number of reasons (Risner, 2002b; Williams, 2003). First, young girls significantly outnumber their male counterparts in dance. Second, both gay and straight boys who suffer from negative stigma associated with males in dance often go to great lengths to display traditional heterosexual markers, often isolating themselves further from peers, family and their own sexual orientation or questioning. Leaving the dance studio often means returning to the embarrassment, humiliation, and contempt of being labelled the 'pansy', 'fag', or 'queer'. Although studies are limited, research appears to indicate that young gay and bisexual males in dance receive far less parental/family encouragement and support for dancing than their heterosexual peers (Bailey & Oberschneider, 1997; Risner, 2002a).

Young boys' avoidance of their homosexual orientation is facilitated by social devices perpetrated by a pervasively heterocentric culture, especially when considering the overwhelmingly ridiculed status of 'sissy boys' in American society. Education researcher Eric Rofes (1995) notes that the widely accepted sissy/jock paradigm operates as a key element in male youth culture, whereby traditional masculinity is narrowly described in highly misogynist ways. Boys in dance, unlike their male peers in athletics and team sports, are participating in an activity that already sheds social suspicion on their masculinity and heterosexuality. For gay male youth in dance, coping with this double bind situation (marginal in a marginalized field), is a complicated dilemma. While there is vast individual variation, many young gay males tend to begin homosexual activity during early or mid-adolescence; similar activity for lesbian females begins around age 20 (Anderson, 1995, p. 18). Because adolescents are only beginning to possess the capacity for abstract thought or formal reasoning skills to cognitively integrate their sexual experiences, dance educators must realize that boys and especially young gay males in dance are extremely vulnerable to gendered criticism, homophobic attitudes, anti-gay slurs, and the absence of positive gay male role models.

Young gay males may also develop internalized homophobia, in which self-hate, low self-esteem, destructive behavior, and further confusion characterize their underlying attitudes and conduct. Many gays, incapable of resisting persistent heterocentrism and homophobic prejudice, internalize negative attitudes about homosexuality, themselves, and other gay people (Lehne, 1976; Margolies *et al.*, 1987). As Luke (self-identified as gay) told me, 'I never talk to men in class … we [speaking for himself as a gay man] don't identify with other gay guys. This sounds stupid, but I really don't like gay people that often … who wants to talk to a bitchy male dancer?' (Risner, 2002a, p. 89). When the gay and bisexual participants were asked if they felt dance was a supportive environment for gay men, the group believed that dance provides an open and supportive atmosphere for gays, though each struggled to articulate how they experienced that support. One participant summarized, 'There's some sense of support in that nobody's calling you names. It's not hostile' or 'It's a big escape in the studio ... when I come out of dance class I feel it all back on me' (Risner, 2002a, p. 90). The emerging picture this small sample of young gay/bisexual men paints appears to be a contradictory landscape characterized by a strong sense of gay/bisexual support and affirmation on the one hand, but an internalized homophobia on the other. This landscape, when combined with the homophobic attitudes characteristic of homosocial bonding, tends to isolate gay males from their straight male classmates, as well as from each other. Although speculative at this time, taken in conjunction with other research findings in this review, this small picture may be showing us that young males in dance—gay and straight—tend to distance themselves from gay males and homosexuality at all costs.

This kind of environment is stressful and often threatening for gay and bisexual male students, particularly since they are vulnerable young people who are struggling to claim and affirm their sexual orientation in an often hostile atmosphere of homosexual denigration. For closeted gay youth, the weight of this burden over a long period of time causes many other psychological and emotional hardships, though at the time, recognition of these dilemmas may be unacknowledged (Besner & Spungin, 1995, p. 95).

Summary: challenging the 'boy code'

The aim of this paper has been to identify and synthesize literature on male youth experiences in dance education, with particular attention to social pressures of dominant masculinity, or the 'boy code' including questions of gender, difference, pleasure, marginalization, and the larger effects of contemporary masculinity within the realm of dance education. Much of the literature reviewed emerges from recent studies with small sample sizes; drawing generalized conclusions has not been the aim. Instead, this review has sought to assemble a useful, although limited, body of knowledge, to provide some significant resources in an under-researched field for further inquiry. To conclude, let me briefly summarize the larger salient points and make a few recommendations for future research.

First, it is critical to understand that dehumanizing discourses and their continued implications for boys who dance are part of a much larger cultural re-evaluation, one I believe compellingly requires participation by the dance education community. Much of the prevailing societal stigma associated with boys in dance can be traced to powerful, long-standing meta-narratives that, though sometimes well-intentioned, have reproduced a deleterious mythology about *all* males in dance, regardless of sexual orientation. Until recently, many of these narrowly defined heterocentric paradigms have gone unquestioned. Future research might include larger studies on boys' affective domains and self-concepts in diverse dance education environments.

Second, while the appeal of cultivating a larger male population in dance, one that more closely resembles its particular community, school, and culture, is admirable and worthwhile, denying the presence of gay and bisexual male dancers is likely to be pragmatic and short-sighted. Though well-intentioned, masculinist comparisons have most probably forfeited opportunities for educating the dance profession about homophobic prejudice and heterocentric assumptions. When recruitment strategies ignore important issues of sexual orientation, gender identity, and homophobic attitudes, dance education may unintentionally reproduce narrow derogatory stereotypes of gay dancers, and in so doing, demean the entire male dance population, its diverse contribution, and the field of dance as a whole. The field would benefit significantly from research that investigates its current male population's attraction and retention to dance training and education.

Third, a number of liberatory pedagogical approaches have been identified that overlap critical feminist approaches to teaching dance, including choreographic exploration of the body as a living laboratory (Arkin, 1994); use of African dance to encourage male and female students to express themselves through gender-flexible movements (Kerr-Berry, 1994); openly discussing gender identification and the experiences of dance students (Risner, 2002b); and exploring gender-bias, sexism, homophobia, elitism, and power relations (Horwitz, 1995). Based on these studies, future pedagogical research might investigate approaches for teaching practices that address non-gender-specific movement, gendered bodies, and the social construction of gender, and gender identity.

Finally, dance educators would benefit from taking an inventory of their own unwitting heterosexist beliefs, gender assumptions, and taken-for-granted actions that unintentionally create an environment of shame, humiliation or embarrassment for males in the studio and classroom.[6] Although dance teachers probably understand their authority and power as positive role models for dancers, as well as the respect teachers inherently garner from their students, it is important to identify teaching methods and in-class language and practices that reinforce narrow definitions of femininity and masculinity. Research in the future might investigate teacher and student perceptions of sexist and homophobic practices in dance education and training.

In conclusion, it is important to acknowledge that 'boy code' extremes (individualism, independence, emotional detachment, and bravado), by social osmosis, may also influence our own individual interactions, relationships and teaching practices. By definition, dominant discourses prevail and hold sustained sway because they often remain unquestioned. It is my intention that this review at minimum heightens readers' sensitivity to issues of males in dance education, and more specifically, motivates awareness of the need for continued questioning and future inquiry.

Notes

1. Throughout this paper, the term 'dance' is intended as a synonym for concert dance, theatrical dance, and Western European dance.
2. Though seemingly obvious, see for example Adair, 1992; Van Dyke, 1992, 1996; Sanderson, 2001; Higher Education Arts Data Survey/HEADS, 2003.
3. The last decade's work in dance education scholarship and research in this area includes Arkin, 1994; Clark, 1994; Horwitz, 1995; Marques, 1998; Shapiro, 1998, 2004; Smith, 1998; Green,

2000, 2002–03, 2004; Keyworth, 2001; Schaffman, 2001; Doi, 2002; Risner, 2002a, 2004a, 2005; Blume, 2003; Gard, 2003a, b; Letts & Nobles, 2003.
4. Social construction of gender in dance education receives interrogation in the following important works: Stinson *et al.*, 1990; Flintoff, 1991; Van Dyke, 1992; Cushway, 1996; Sanderson, 1996, 2001; Stinson, 1998a, b, 2001; Gard, 2001b, 2003a, 2006; Green, 2001, 2002–03, 2004; Risner, 2002a, b, 2004 .
5. Readers may be interested in approaches for confronting gender issues and inequity in dance teaching and curriculum as articulated by Arkin, 1994; Bond, 1994; Crawford, 1994; Daly, 1994; Ferdun, 1994; Kerr-Berry, 1994; Risner, 2002b; Clark, 2004; Dils, 2004; Stinson, 2005.
6. See for example Morrow and Gill (2003), documenting heterosexism and homophobia in physical education.

References

Adair, C. (1992) *Women and dance: sylphs and sirens* (New York, New York University Press).
Anderson, D. (1995) Lesbian and gay adolescents: social and developmental considerations, in: G. Unks (Ed.) *The gay teen* (New York, Routledge), 17–30.
Arkin, L. (1994) Dancing the body: women and dance performance, *Journal of Physical Education, Recreation and Dance*, 65(2), 36–38, 43.
Bailey, J. & Oberschneider, M. (1997) Sexual orientation and professional dance, *Archives of Sexual Behavior*, 26, 433–444.
Barone, T. (1992) Beyond theory and method: a case of critical storytelling, *Theory into Practice*, 31(2), 142–146.
Baumgarten, S. (2003) Boys dancing? You bet! *Teaching Elementary Physical Education*, 14(5), 12–13.
Besner, F. & Spungin, C. (1995) *Gay & lesbian students: understanding their needs* (Philadelphia, Taylor & Francis).
Blume, L. B. (2003) Embodied [by] dance: adolescent de/constructions of body, sex and gender in physical educator, *Sex Education*, 3(2), 95–103.
Bond, K. (1994) How 'wild things' tamed gender distinctions, *Journal of Physical Education, Recreation and Dance*, 65(2), 28–33.
Burt, R. (1995) *The male dancer: bodies, spectacle, sexualities* (New York, Routledge).
Clark, D. (1994) Voices of women dance educators: considering issues of hegemony and the education/performer identity, *Impulse*, 2(2), 122–130.
Clark, D. (2004) Considering the issue of sexploitation of young women in dance: K-12 perspectives, *Journal of Dance Education*, 4(1), 17–23.
Crawford, J. (1994) Encouraging male participation in dance, *Journal of Physical Education, Recreation and Dance*, 65(2), 40–43.
Curry, T. (2001) Fraternal bonding in the locker room: a profeminist analysis of talk about competition and women, in: M. Kimmel & M. Messner (Eds) *Men's lives* (Needham Heights, MA, Allyn and Bacon), 188–201.

Cushway, D. (1996) Changing the dance curriculum, *Women's Studies Quarterly*, 24(3–4), 118–122.
Daly, A. (1994) Gender issues in dance history pedagogy, *Journal of Physical Education, Recreation and Dance*, 65(2), 34–35, 39.
Dils, A. (2004) Sexuality and sexual identity: critical possibilities for teaching dance appreciation and dance history, *Journal of Dance Education*, 4(1), 10–16.
Doi, M. M. (2002) *Gesture, gender, nation: dance and social change in Uzbekistan* (Westport, CT, Bergin and Garvey Publishers).
Ferdun, E. (1994) Facing gender issues across the curriculum, *Journal of Physical Education, Recreation and Dance*, 65(2), 46–47.
Fisher, J. (2007) Make it maverick: rethinking the 'make it macho' strategy for men in ballet, *Dance Chronicle*, 30, 45–66.
Flintoff, A. (1991) Dance, masculinity and teacher education, *The British Journal of Physical Education*, Winter, 31–35.
Garber, E., Stankiewicz, M., Sandell, R. & Risner, D. (2007) Gender equity in the visual arts and dance education, in: S. Klein (Ed.) *Handbook for achieving gender equity through education* (Mahwah, NJ, Lawrence Erlbaum).
Gard, M. (2001a) *Athletics, aesthetics, and art: a study of men who dance*. Unpublished PhD thesis, Wollongong, University of Wollongong.
Gard, M. (2001b) Dancing around the 'problem' of boys and dance, *Discourse: Studies in the Cultural Politics of Education*, 22, 213–225.
Gard, M. (2003a) Being someone else: using dance in anti-oppressive teaching, *Educational Review*, 55(2), 211–223.
Gard, M. (2003b) Moving and belonging: dance, sport and sexuality, *Sex Education*, 3(2), 105–118.
Gard, M. (2006) *Men who dance: aesthetics, athletics and the art of masculinity* (New York, Peter Lang Publishing, Inc).
Gold, R. (2001) Confessions of a boy dancer, *Dance Magazine*, 125(11), 52.
Green, J. (2000) Emancipatory pedagogy? Women's bodies and the creative process in dance, *Frontiers*, 21(3), 124–140.
Green, J. (2001) Socially constructed bodies in American dance classrooms, *Research in Dance Education*, 2(2), 155–173.
Green, J. (2002–03) Foucault and the training of docile bodies in dance education, *Arts and Learning*, 19(1), 99–126.
Green, J. (2004) The politics and ethics of health in dance education in the United States, in: E. Anttila, S. Hamalainen & L. Rouhiainen (Eds) *Ethics and politics embodied in dance* (Helsinki, Theatre Academy of Finland), 65–76.
Hamilton, L. (1998) *Advice for dancers: emotional counsel and practical strategies* (New York, Jossey-Bass).
Hanna, J. L. (1988) *Dance, sex, and gender: signs of identity, dominance, defiance, and desire* (Chicago, IL, University of Chicago Press).
Hasbrook, C. (1993) Sociocultural aspects of physical activity, *Research Quarterly for Exercise and Sport*, 64(1), 106–115.
Higher Education Arts Data Services (2003) *Dance Annual Summary 2002–2003* (Reston, VA, National Association of Schools of Dance).
Horwitz, C. (1995) *Challenging dominant gender ideology through dance: contact improvisation*. PhD dissertation, University of Iowa, DAI 56/06, 2023.
Jackson, D. (1990) *Unmasking masculinity: a critical autobiography* (St. Leonards, NSW, Allen & Unwin).
Katz, J. & Earp, J. (1999) *Tough guise: violence, media & the crisis in masculinity* (Sut Jhally, Dir.) (North Hampton, MA, Media Education Foundation).
Kerr-Berry, J. (1994) Using the power of Western African dance to combat gender issues, *Journal of Physical Education, Recreation and Dance*, 65(2), 44–45, 48.

Keyworth, S. (2001) Critical autobiography: 'straightening' out dance education, *Research in Dance Education*, 2(2), 117–137.

Kimmel, M. (2005) What about the boys? in: H. Shapiro & D. Purpel (Eds) *Critical social issues in American education: democracy and meaning in a globalizing world* (Mahwah, NJ, Lawrence Erlbaum Associates).

Kimmel, M. & Messner, M. (Eds) (2001) *Men's lives* (Needham Heights, MA, Allyn and Bacon).

Kraus, R., Hilsendager, S. & Dixon, B. (1991) *History of the dance in art and education* (3rd edn) (Englewood Cliffs, NJ, Prentice-Hall).

Lehikoinen, K. (2005) *Stepping queerly: discourses in dance education for boys in late 20th century Finland* (Oxford, Peter Lang).

Lehne, G. (1976) Homophobia among men, in: D. David & R. Brannon (Eds) *The forty-nine percent majority: the male sex role* (Reading, MA, Addison-Wesley), 66–88.

Letts, W. & Nobles, C. (2003) Embodied [by] curriculum: a critical pedagogy of embodiment, *Sex Education*, 3(2), 91–94.

Margolies, L., Becker, M. & Jackson-Brewer, K. (1987) Internalized homophobia in gay men, in: J. Gonsiorek (Ed.) *Homosexuality and psychotherapy: a practitioner's handbook of affirmative models* (New York, The Haworth Press, Inc.), 59–69.

Marques, I. (1998) Dance education in/and the postmodern, in: S. Shapiro (Ed.) *Dance, power, and difference: critical and feminist perspectives on dance* (Champaign, IL, Human Kinetics), 171–185.

Morrow, R. & Gill, D. (2003) Perceptions of homophobia and heterosexism in physical education, *Research Quarterly for Exercise and Sport*, 74(2), 205–214.

Patrick, K. (2001) Speaking out: more male dancers tell it like it is, *Dance Magazine*, 125(11), 53–55.

Pollack, W. (1999) *Real boys: rescuing our boys from the myths of boyhood* (New York, Random House).

Posey, E. (2002) Dance education in dance schools in the private sector: meeting the demands of the marketplace, *Journal of Dance Education*, 2(2), 43–49.

Richardson, L. (1990) *Writing strategies: reaching diverse audiences* (London, Sage).

Risner, D. (2001) *Blurring the boundaries: hope and possibility in the presence of the necessary stranger in gay liberation*. PhD dissertation, University of North Carolina at Greensboro, DAI 62/03, 1236.

Risner, D. (2002a) Male participation and sexual orientation in dance education: revisiting the open secret, *Journal of Dance Education*, 2(3), 84–92.

Risner, D. (2002b) Re-educating dance education to its homosexuality: an invitation for critical analysis and professional unification, *Research in Dance Education*, 3(2), 181–187.

Risner, D. (2003a) What Matthew Shepard would tell us: gay and lesbian issues in education, in: H. Shapiro, S. Harden & A. Pennell (Eds) *The institution of education* (Boston, MA, Pearson). Reprinted in: H. Shapiro (Ed.) (2005) *Critical social issues in education: democracy and meaning in a globalizing world* (Mahwah, NJ, Lawrence Erlbaum Associates).

Risner, D. (2003b) Rehearsing heterosexuality: unspoken truths in dance education, *Dance Research Journal*, 34(2), 63–81.

Risner, D. (2004a) Dance, sexuality, and education today: observations for dance educators, *Journal of Dance Education*, 4(1), 5–9.

Risner, D. (2004b) The politics of student-centered practices in dance in higher education: challenges to the ethical treatment of undergraduate dance students in the US, paper presented at the *Ethics and Politics Embodied in Dance International Research Symposium: Special Strand, Everyday Life in Dance Institution, Teatterikorkeakoulu Teaterhogskolan*, Helsinki, Theatre Academy of Finland, 9–14 December.

Risner, D. (2005) Dance & sexuality: opportunities for teaching and learning in dance education, *Journal of Dance Education*, 5(2), 41–42.

Risner, D. (2007) Critical social issues in dance education research, in: L. Bresler (Ed.) *International handbook for research in arts education* (New York, Springer).

Risner, D. & Thompson, S. (2005) HIV/AIDS in dance education: a pilot study in higher education, *Journal of Dance Education*, 5(2), 70–76.

Risner, D., Godfrey, H. & Simmons, L. (2004) The impact of sexuality in contemporary culture: an interpretive study of perceptions and choices in private sector dance education, *Journal of Dance Education,* 4(1), 23–32.
Rofes, E. (1995) Making our schools safe for sissies, in: G. Unks (Ed.) *The gay teen* (New York, Routledge), 79–84.
Samuels, S. (2001) Study exposes dance gender gap, *Dance Magazine,*March, 35–37.
Sanderson, P. (1996) Dance within the national curriculum for physical education of England and Wales, *European Physical Education Review,* 2(1), 54–63.
Sanderson, P. (2001) Age and gender issues in adolescent attitudes to dance, *European Physical Education Review,* 7(2), 117–136.
Schaffman, K. (2001) *From the margins to the mainstream: contact improvisation and the commodification of touch.* PhD dissertation, University of California at Riverside, 62/07, 2270.
Shapiro, S. (1998) Toward transformative teachers: critical and feminist perspectives in dance education, in: S. Shapiro (Ed.) *Dance, power, and difference: critical and feminist perspectives on dance education* (Champaign, IL, Human Kinetics), 7–21.
Shapiro, S. (2004) Recovering girlhood: a pedagogy of embodiment, *Journal of Dance Education,* 4(1), 35–36.
Smith, C. (1998) On authoritarianism in the dance classroom, in: S. Shapiro (Ed.) *Dance, power, and difference: critical and feminist perspectives on dance education* (Champaign, IL, Human Kinetics), 123–146.
Spurgeon, D. (1999) The men's movement, paper presented at *Congress on Research in Dance,* Pomona College, Claremont, CA, December.
Stinson, S. (1998a) Places where I've been: reflections on issues of gender in dance education, research, and administration, *Choreography and Dance,* 5(1), 117–127.
Stinson, S. (1998b) Seeking a feminist pedagogy for children's dance, in: S. Shapiro (Ed.) *Dance, power, and difference: critical and feminist perspectives on dance education* (Champaign, IL, Human Kinetics), 23–47.
Stinson, S. (2001) Voices from adolescent males, *DACI in Print,* 2, 4–6.
Stinson, S. (2005) The hidden curriculum of gender in dance education, *Journal of Dance Education,* 5(2), 51–57.
Stinson, S., Blumenfeld-Jones, D. & Van Dyke, J. (1990) Voices of young women dance students: an interpretive study of meaning in dance, *Dance Research Journal,* 22(2), 13–22.
Thomas, H. (1996) Dancing the difference, *Women's Studies International Forum,* 19(5), 505–511.
Van Dyke, J. (1992) *Modern dance in a postmodern world: an analysis of federal arts funding and its impact on the field of modern dance* (Reston, VA, American Alliance for Health, Physical Education, Recreation, and Dance).
Van Dyke, J. (1996) Gender and success in the American dance world, *Women's Studies International Forum,* 19(5), 535–543.
Williams, D. (2003) *Examining psychosocial issues of adolescent male dancers.* PhD dissertation, Marywood University, UMI 2090242.

Bullying Victimization and Social Support of Adolescent Male Dance Students

Doug Risner

This analysis ($n=33$), drawn from the findings of the author's larger mixed method research study, investigated bullying and harassment of adolescent male students (ages 13–18) pursuing dance study at the pre-professional level in the United States. Procedures for this analysis included review of primary and secondary sources from the international literature in psychology, adolescent and public health, paediatrics, sexuality studies, and dance education, an adapted version of the Dancer's Social Support Scale, and data from online surveys and in-depth interviews. Findings indicate significant bullying of adolescent males engaging in western concert dance training. Analyses reveal pervasive heterocentric discourses and continued homophobic attitudes surrounding the adolescent male dancer and his experiences regardless of his sexual orientation. The importance of social support in and outside the dance studio especially support from his dance teacher-director, best friend in dance or school, and his mother figure prominently. Findings from research on bullying in the general and sexual minority populations are discussed. Pragmatic and critical approaches for understanding bullying and supporting bullied adolescent male dancers are presented.

1. Introduction

As a global public health concern, bullying affects significant numbers of adolescents (Craig et al. 2009). Bullying victimisation over the past decade has been recognised as a leading adolescent health problem throughout the world (Craig and Pepler 2003; Nansel et al. 2003; Due, Holstein, and Lynch 2005). In their 40-country analysis, Craig et al. (2009) found that "Bullying involvement transcends cultural and geographic boundaries" (219). Adolescent "children who are unusual in some way" are more likely than others to suffer bullying and harassment (Berger 2007, 105). Boys perceived to be or who identify as non-heterosexual are especially at risk. Bullied frequently and severely, these boys report "distressing and intrusive memories of those events of their school days and being victimized" (Rivers 2004, 171). Additionally, Berlan et al. (2010) report that:

> [S]exual minority youth (gay, lesbian, bisexual, questioning) are more likely than their heterosexual peers to be threatened or injured at school, skip school because of feeling unsafe, be violently attacked requiring medical treatment and witness violence, and experience sexual and physical abuse. (366)

Questions surrounding the male dancer in western concert dance, especially those about his masculinity and sexual orientation, have dominated popular discourses and societal assumptions for more than a century. Regrettably, society's propensity to denigrate qualities associated with femininity makes gender conformity more difficult on non-conforming boys than on non-conforming girls (Meyer 2008). Creativity, expressiveness, caring and empathy – often considered feminine characteristics – signal weakness in boys. Based on these dominant signals, the prevailing stereotype of boys who dance is that they are unmanly, effeminate, and gay (Gard 2003; Risner 2007). These social descriptors clearly position dancing boys, as Berger (2007) asserts, as children who are unusual, and particularly susceptible to bullying and harassment, and research confirms that teasing, verbal and physical harassment, and aggression directed toward adolescent males in dance training and education have been empirically documented in the international literature (Williams 2003; Gard 2006; Lehikoinen 2006; Risner 2009). Based on adolescent development research (Rivers 2004; Berlan et al. 2010) and given the significant sexual minority of male adolescent population in which 47% identify as non-heterosexual (Risner 2009), boys in dance are additionally vulnerable to bullying.

In this investigation the lives of boys who dance provide an important lens for investigating bullying, harassment and aggression in the general adolescent population as well as the ability to develop an informed understanding of and proactive strategies for, confronting bullying behaviour and supporting adolescent male dance students. Therefore, the present investigation sought to extend and develop the findings of Risner (2009) by comparative analyses with bullying and social support literature from the fields of psychology, adolescent and public health, paediatrics, and sexuality studies.

2. Literature review

2.1. Bullying in the general adolescent population

Beginning in the late 1990s, a number of highly publicised school attacks linked student violence with bullying behaviour and victimisation. These incidents drew international attention to the climate of bullying and harassment occurring in schools (Spriggs et al. 2007). Since that time, research conducted on bullying and victimisation has grown significantly throughout the world (Swearer et al. 2010). The professional literature generally defines adolescent bullying "as a specific form of aggression, which is intentional, repeated, and involves a disparity of power between the victim and perpetrators" (Wang, Iannotti, and Nansel 2009, 368); bullying behaviour can be perpetrated in various forms, such as verbal, physical, and relational or social (Olweus 1993; Crick and Grotpeter 1995). Bullying of a verbal nature includes name-calling, taunting, and teasing in a purposely hurtful manner. In physical form, bullying behaviour includes hitting, slapping, pushing, shoving, and kicking. Both verbal and physical bullying are direct forms, "while relational bullying refers to an indirect form of bullying, such as social exclusion and spreading rumors" (Wang, Iannotti, and Nansel 2009, 368). Berger (2007) reports,

> The first wave of research reported that bullying decreased steadily with age, and that more boys were bullies and victims than girls. Later research confirmed that physical bullying declines with age but found that other forms increase, with a sizable bump between ages 11 and 15 when children experience puberty and change schools. (97)

In a cross-national study of adolescents (*n* = 202,056) from 40 countries, 11% indicated bullying others, 12.6% reported being bullied, and 3.6% indicated that they were both a bully and a victim of bullying (Craig et al. 2009). Regular and repeated bullying victimisation or bullying others has been linked to high risks of depression and suicidal ideation and suicidal attempts compared with adolescents not involved in bullying behaviour; adolescents who are both victims and bullies run the highest risk and are the most troubled (Klomek et al. 2007). Over the past decade, a number of anti-bullying campaigns have been launched on local and national levels,[1] and as Berger (2007) notes, "Thousands of popular books and guides for parents, children, and teachers promulgate untested and sometimes destructive suggestions ... often it seems as if the scientific method has been forgotten" (93).

For the purposes of this analysis, understanding the experiences of bullied adolescents and their victimisation is particularly important. The effects of bullying on victims have been closely associated with physical and mental health difficulties (Hymel, Rocke-Henderson, and Bonanno 2005). Dislike of school and avoidance of school are often by-products of being bullied, which in turn can affect academic performance and positive socialisation (Juvonen, Nishina, and Graham 2000). Alcaraz, Kim, and Gendron (2010) summarise the literature:

> Research on victims of bullying behavior has demonstrated that these individuals are more likely to report loneliness and greater difficulty making new friends compared to non-involved peers. Victims have also been found to be lower in social acceptance, in terms of number of friends and amount of time socializing with other peers. Compared to non-victimized counterparts, victims of bullying are more likely to be anxious and insecure, exhibit higher rates of depression, diminished performance in school, and are lower in self-esteem. (3)

Hymel, Rocke-Henderson, and Bonanno (2005) conclude, "Perhaps most alarming is the number of teens who have ended their own lives because of both bullying and victimization" (1).

2.2. *Bullying in the adolescent sexual minority population*

In order to understand young male dancers' heightened vulnerability, I review the literature on bullying victimisation in the adolescent sexual minority population. Studies indicate that nearly half of male dance students self-identify as sexual minority youth (Risner 2002, 2009).[2] The adolescent health profession defines sexual minority youth as "young people with same-sex or both-sex sexual attraction and/or partners or youth who self-identify as gay, lesbian, or bisexual" (Berlan et al. 2010, 366). Research studies demonstrate that sexual minority youth are subject to high levels of bullying, from verbal harassment to physical injury (D'Augelli, Pilkington, and Herschberger 2002).

At the foundation of much sexual minority bullying and harassment are idealised notions of masculinity and femininity – socially constructed and well-rehearsed in schools, mass media, and society (Meyer 2008). Boys who do not adhere to dominant codes of masculinity are in peril, whether they identify as gay or are perceived to be gay. Meyer (2008) notes "The pressure on boys to conform to traditional notions of masculinity is great and the risk of being perceived as gay is an effective threat in policing the boundaries of acceptable behavior" (39). A former male dance student explains:

> When I was in elementary school, I did a lot of ballet. I was at the National Ballet School one summer. And that sort of stigma (laugh) which I never thought was a stigma, or could be a stigma, but which became a stigma, followed me into high school. And that was followed with comments continually – "fag," you know, "fag." I think that was actually ... one of the reasons why I eventually gave up ballet was just because of the constant harassment, and also pursuing other interests. But I think that was at the back of my mind a lot of the time with the harassment, and realizing that they're right. That's what I was. I knew that that's what I was. (Smith 1998, 322)

In a study of 522 middle and high school students in the northeastern US, Gruber and Fineran (2008) reported that sexual minorities experience higher levels of bullying and sexual harassment than their heterosexual peers. Similarly, a Canadian school-based study of high school adolescents ($n = 1598$) reported that lesbian, gay, bisexual, and youth who are questioning their sexual orientation reported more bullying experiences than heterosexual youth (Williams et al. 2005). A statewide survey of public high students ($n = 3522$) found that sexual minority youth were significantly more likely than other students "to have been bullied (44% vs. 23%), to have skipped school because they felt unsafe (13% vs. 3%), have been in a physical fight (42% vs. 28%), and been threatened or injured with a weapon at school (14% vs. 5%)" (Massachusetts Department of Education 2006).

Schooling, as an extension and reproduction of dominant social ideology, often privileges and valorises individual strength, competition, aggressiveness, independence, and toughness, typical of traditional codes of masculinity (Risner 2007). From this masculinist perspective, it is no revelation that "typical victims are described as physically weak ... tended to be timid, anxious, sensitive and shy ... [I]n contrast, bullies were physically strong, aggressive, and impulsive, and had a strong need to dominate others" (Hoover and Juul 1993, cited in Meyer 2008, 35). Readers may be familiar with the "It Gets Better" anti-bullying campaign founded by American writer Dan Savage with his partner Terry Miller after a number of gay youth suicides in 2010. The high-profile project's website "invited adults to submit videos that offer messages of hope and encouragement to youth who may be struggling with their sexualities in difficult environments" (Mason 2012, 83). Later the project received widespread criticism from the LGBTQ community and scholars, especially for its adult-centred evasiveness of homophobia, heterosexism, and realistic strategies for confronting adolescent sexual minority bullying and violence.

The lasting effects of bullying and harassment on victims are well documented and severe (Rivers 2004). Adolescent targets of sexual and homophobic harassment are at increased risk for harmful behaviours and leaving school (Williams et al. 2005). Meyer (2008) indicates that many of these "students perceive school as a dangerous place, and that causes significant damage to their level of engagement in the school community" (35).

3. Research design

This mixed method empirical analysis ($n = 33$), drawn from the data of a larger three-year research project (Risner 2009), investigated the prevalence and severity of bullying and harassment of adolescent male students (ages 13–18) pursuing dance study at the pre-professional level in the United States. It is important to note that the larger study did not focus specifically on bullying perpetration and victimisation. Rather, the theme of bullying emerged from the findings of the larger study. The purpose of the present investigation was to extend and analyse participants' bullying victimisation and harassment, as well as the social support resources available to them.

Procedures for this analysis included: review of secondary sources from the international literature in psychology, adolescent and public health, sexuality studies, and dance education; data from an adapted version of the Dancer's Social Support Scale (Williams 2003; Risner 2009); participant data from an extensive online survey; and participant narratives from in-depth interviews. Beyond traditional strategies, recruitment of participants was also facilitated by the endorsement and support of a well-established national dance company and its educational training programmes in the US. This allowed participants to be identified from across the nation, ensuring a large cross-section of male adolescents and dance genres (ballet, contemporary, modern, jazz, and musical theatre). Participant assent and informed consent from participants' parents were obtained, based upon the requirements of human subject investigation approval from Wayne State University.

3.1. *Mixed methods framework*

At the outset, readers are encouraged to see the author's three-year study for a full description of the research design and mixed methods framework from which the data for this article were drawn (Risner 2009). Interpretive research frameworks allow researchers to render a better understanding of what it is to be human in the world and to bring forth meaning and understanding rather than proving or disproving facts (Denzin and Lincoln 2011). Meaning is revealed in diverse ways and requires that researchers engage conceptual frameworks and methodologies that account for multiple perspectives, contextualisation, and complexity. The realities of participants are considered multiple, socially constructed, and contextual (Creswell 2014).

For the present analysis, I briefly outline the purpose and necessity of employing a mixed methods approach from both a pragmatic researcher's (what works best now) and a critical researcher's (what empowers positive social change and action) perspective. Describing the pragmatic researcher's turn, Creswell (2003) notes:

> Truth is what works at the time; it is not based in a strict dualism between the mind and a reality completely independent of the mind. Thus, in mixed methods research, investigators use both quantitative and qualitative data because they work to provide the best understanding of a research problem. (12)

Prior to 2009, the lack of published, empirical research on bullying victimisation experiences of male adolescents pursuing pre-professional dance training required quantifiable baseline data from which tentative and cautious generalisations could be formulated. Therefore, collecting and analysing quantitative survey data on a relatively large scale about teasing, verbal and physical harassment, threatening behaviour, and physical harm was necessary.

At the same time and from an interpretive researcher perspective, the processes and methods of qualitative research design and generated data allow researchers to assemble concepts, develop grounded theories, and seek emergent patterns through interpretation and contextual analyses (Denzin and Lincoln 2011). When coupled with a critical approach, Johnson, Onwuegbuzie, and Turner (2007) state that:

> Qualitative dominant mixed methods research is the type of mixed research in which one relies on a qualitative, constructivist-poststructuralist-critical view of the research process, while concurrently recognizing that the addition of quantitative data and approaches are likely to benefit most research projects. (124)

Extending this research perspective further, Erickson (2005) elaborates that:

> The interpretive qualitative researcher would say that the question "what is happening?" is always accompanied by another question: "and what do those happenings mean to those who are engaged in them?" And a critical qualitative researcher would add a third question, "and are these happenings just and in the best interests of people generally?" (7)

Therefore, the present analysis and the larger study utilised a mixed methods, qualitative design from a critical interpretive perspective.

3.2. Methods and procedures

The author's larger study ($n = 75$), from which data were utilised in the present investigation ($n = 33$), included the following research methods: review of secondary sources; qualitative and quantitative data from an extensive online survey; narrative data from in-depth participant interviews with 20 participants of geographic diversity across the US. The extensive online survey required 30–45 min to complete. Each of the 20-participant subset selected was interviewed once; interviews were 90–120 minutes in duration.

Comprised of eight sections, the online survey generated the following participant data: (1) demographic information; (2) school data; (3) dance education and training experience; (4) attitudes about dance and dance study; (5) an adapted version of the Dancer's Social Support Scale (Williams 2003; Risner 2009); (6) written responses to questions regarding interest, attraction, enjoyment, support, peers, challenges, and advice to other boys in dance; (7) participant gender and sexual identity; and (8) interest in participating in an interview. From those in the survey pool who indicated interest in completing an interview, randomly selected survey participants ($n = 20$) were invited to participate in semi-structured interviews that took the form of guided conversations based on participants' survey data.

Interview protocols centred on participants' experiences and attitudes as boys and young men in pre-professional dance training. Formatted in a semi-structured, open-ended fashion, interview questions allowed participants to speak candidly about themselves and their experiences (Kvale and Brinkmann 2008). As in previous interview research conducted by the Risner (2000):

> [W]hat we want to know informs how we conduct our research. The questions we ask shape the words and stories we record, analyse, and interpret. The questions pursued by the narrative researcher are therefore broad and heuristic in order to allow and facilitate individual authorship. Interpretive inquiry, then, often illuminates a slice of the proverbial pie previously unseen or unexpected. Narrative research reveals the plurality of our human experience as evidenced by the singularity of our individual existence. (158)

In this spirit, each interview protocol was unique to the participant's earlier survey data (quantitative and qualitative), as well as his own interests and inclinations within the interview itself. Participants were encouraged to share stories and to give examples when possible. Interview data were recorded on audio tape, transcribed, and then destroyed. Analysis of data generated was based on procedures of interpretive inquiry (Lincoln and Guba 2004). Extraneous material was eliminated while emerging themes and patterns in each narrative account were identified and coded (Bernard and Ryan 2009) with an independent researcher verifying edited reductions. Although each interview protocol was unique, sample questions and prompts included:

- Tell me how you came to study dance.
- What were your perceptions about dance before you began pre-professional study?
- What, if any, obstacles (personal or otherwise) did you encounter in deciding to study dance?
- What does it mean to you to as a male to study dance?
- What do you find satisfying about studying dance?
- Who gives you the most support for dancing?
- Do you have male role models as a dancer?
- Tell me about what you find interesting about dancing.
- What role does dancing play in your life?
- What might other males find satisfying about dancing?
- Why do you think so few males pursue dance study?
- What would be necessary to attract more males to dance?
- Have your attitudes about dance changed since you began studying?

3.3. Participant profile

The participant population (ages 13–18) for this analysis was comprised of the following age groups: 13–15 years old (28%); 16–17 years old (36%); and 18 years old (36%). By ethnicity, participants self-reported as white or Caucasian (82%); black or African-American (9%); Hispanic or Latino (6%); and American Indian or Alaskan Native (3%). The majority of participants' familial living arrangements included mother and father, or mother, father, and siblings (73%), with remaining family structures: mother (9%); mother and siblings (6%); and other familial arrangements including grandparents and siblings (6%). In terms of demographics, participants resided in: suburb of large city (39%); medium-sized city (27%); small town (21%); and large city (12%).

School attendance data for participants included the following: public or charter high school (39%); university (27%); home school (12%); performing arts middle or high school (9%); public or charter middle school (6%); liberal arts college (3%); and private high school (3%). Regarding academic achievement, participants reported they received: mostly grades of A and B (45%); usually B grades (27%); all A grades (15%); mostly grades of B and C (9%); and 3% reported that their school does not give grades. Beyond their interests in dance and the arts, school subjects of highest interest to participants included English and literature, history, and sciences. Other co-curricular activities in which participants actively participated were reported as: dance/dance company (75%); drama/plays (50%); and musical theatre (47%). In terms of sport activities, 20% of the overall population reported participation in organised sports, with swimming/diving and soccer as the primary activities.

The vast majority of participants have studied dance for six years or more (70%). Primary dance study environments were described as: dance studio (39%); college or university dance programme (27%); performing arts high school (15%); dance academy (12%); and professional dance school affiliated with a dance company (7%). Additional pre-professional dance training was reported by 8 out of 10 participants who attended summer dance workshops (local and regional), as well as summer dance study at national intensive training programmes. Participants reported that their dance teachers were three times as likely to be female than male, with 63% of all participants reporting zero to one male dance teacher in their studio or programme setting. In terms of sexual orientation, participants self-identified as heterosexual (52%), gay (44%), and bisexual (4%).

4. Presentation of data

The aim of this analysis was to investigate bullying, harassment, and aggression in the lives of adolescent male dance students (ages 13–18) pursuing dance study at the pre-professional level in the US. Data for this analysis were drawn from the Risner (2009) larger research study of male dance students' lived experiences and the meaning they construct from dancing and dance training. In the following, I report the survey data and provide additional narrative data to support the quantitative results organised around the following emergent themes: (1) social environment; (2) bullying, harassment, and aggression; and (3) social support.

4.1. Social environment of adolescent male dancers

The stigma associated with boys in western concert dance is longstanding and generally linked to dominant attitudes about dance and its feminisation (Williams 2003; Risner 2002, 2009). More specifically, the stigma that boys who dance garner marks them as effeminate, homosexual, and not real men (dance is for girls). In order to better understand this stigmatisation and the social isolation that often accompanies it, the larger study's survey posed questions about adolescent males' social environment and relationships. In the following, relevant data are presented.

Inside the dance world (studio, school, conservatory, academy, or programme), boys encounter a gendered social environment in their dance study and training. When asked the question, "How many other male students study in your studio/school or program?" participants reported none (12%); one to three males (18%); four to five males (33%); six to nine males (15%); and 10 or more males (21%). The majority of male adolescents (63%) studied in programmes with five or fewer male peers. However, when asked "How many other male students are enrolled in your class/level?" participants reported considerably lower numbers of male peers: no other males (48%); one to three males (34%); four to five males (10%); and 10 or more males (8%). In terms of male adolescents' daily training, the vast majority (82%) studied with three or fewer male peers.

Survey data indicated that participants' dance teachers were four times as likely to be female than male, with 63% of all participants reporting zero to one male dance teacher in their studio or programme setting. In relation to their peers and the predominance of dance teachers who are women, male adolescents in dance encountered an overwhelmingly female social environment inside the studio, both in terms of peers and authority. Over half of the participants (55%) indicated the importance of male role models in dance; however, only 38% reported that having a male dance instructor had a positive effect on their dance study.

For adolescent males pursuing pre-professional dance study, issues of marginality and privilege play out in complicated and often contradictory ways. Within the dance environment, males hold highly valued status but leaving the dance studio often means enduring social isolation, stigma, and questions about their masculinity. Open-ended survey questions asked participants about their experiences outside the confines of dance:

Survey Question 30: How do people react when you tell them that you are a dancer?[3]

- (Carson, 14 years old) Some people are a little weirded out at first, they sometimes question it because it is thought to be feminine by some people. There are always the people who hate me for some reason and just say "he's gay" and will never give me the time of day.
- (Ben, 17 years old) They are generally very surprised and they sometimes drop gay jokes.
- (Alex, 15 years old) Some people tease you or assume you're gay. The people who would make fun of me or react badly are, frankly, not the people I try to hang out with.
- (Jeffrey, 13 years old) They are in shock and usually start to question me and automatically say that I am gay. It's happened like 30 times.
- (Carlos, 16 years old) People would respond with, "oh do you wear tights," "are you gay" and things of that sort.
- (Ryan, 13 years old) Girls immediately think im gay and just open themselves up to me. Guys think im gay and kick me out of anything that they say, "isn't for girls."
- (Jesse, 18 years old) It's not like there disgusted when i tell them i just don't think its what they were expecting from a boy.
- (Rob, 14 years old) Well, if it is a girl there is this look like hmmm is he gay? Then I tell them I am not gay and they say oh haha. On the other hand, if I tell a guy they get this look on their face like "SHIT! I am talking to a gay person!!!!!"
- (Eric, 15 years old) I don't generally call myself a dancer
- (Josh, 17 years old) It's usually a tone of, "Well, yeah ... you're gay." It generally gets me all up in arms and defensive of the straight guys I dance with. A lot of my uncles and older male cousins think that I'm "girly" or "a pansy" because I dance.

These narrative accounts provide a deeper understanding of the daily stigma and social environment that male adolescent dancers repeatedly confront outside their dance sphere. Additionally, these findings not only corroborate and extend previous research that has identified social isolation as a prominent theme in male dancers' experience (Gard 2001, 2003; Keyworth 2001; Risner 2002, 2009; Williams 2003), they also place adolescent dancing males at higher risk for bullying and victimisation as indicated by the professional literature discussed earlier. Social support findings will be presented later in this section.

4.2. Bullying, harassment, and aggression

The prevalence of bullying and harassment in the lives of participants was addressed directly in one survey question, "As a male who studies dance, I have experienced …" Four possible responses were listed, based on findings from previous research studies on male dancers (Risner 2002; Williams 2003; Lehikoinen 2006). Participants were asked to select "all that apply." Five participants did not respond to this question; however, 85% of participants reported the following experiences:

- Teasing and name calling (93%).
- Verbal or physical harassment (68%).
- Verbal threats or threatening behaviour (39%).
- Physical harm or injury (11%).

Self-identified non-heterosexual participants reported that they experienced verbal threats or threatening behaviour at nearly three times the rate of self-identified heterosexual participants.

In order to learn more about the minority status of adolescent males in dance study, the survey asked participants to complete the sentence, "I think more boys would study dance if …," which participants completed by choosing from a number of different answers based on previous research findings on adolescent male dance students (Williams 2003). Participants were instructed to select all applicable answers. The majority of responses were: "if boys/males weren't teased and harassed so much about dancing" (87%); "if boys/males knew more male friends who dance" (71%); "if parents were more supportive and encouraging" (68%); and "if there were more male role models" (55%). Only 8% selected "if teachers made dance more like sports."

In tandem and based on a similar methodology, participants were then asked to complete the sentence, "I think that some boys stop studying dance because." The most cited responses were: "because they were tired of teasing and harassment as a male dancer" (84%); "because some people thought they were gay because they studied dance" (78%); and "because their parents weren't supportive" (59%). The words of the participants below illuminate the survey data in tangible and meaningful ways. Their accounts reveal more clearly the sometimes stark survey percentages reported earlier:

Survey Question 34: Has anyone ever teased, harassed, threatened, or hurt you because you study dance?

- (Jackson, 18 years old) Yeah, a lot of the people I went to high school with would make fun of me a lot because I was a dancer. They all assumed I was gay, and that I was not "cool" enough for them to be friends with.
- (Matt, 17 years old) ALLLLLLLLLL the time.
- (Luke, 16 years old) Yes, especially in elementary school. I was bullied so much that I hid the fact that I danced from about fourth grade through ninth

from everyone. If it hadn't been for some male teachers, I probably would have quit, but they helped me become more sure of myself and confident.
- (Mason, 13 years old) Everyday.
- (Kyle 14 years old) uhhhh ya. only every day of my life. I always get someone asking me if I like guys. or if I have balls or a penis.
- (Willie, 15 years old) Yes. All throughout Middle school. I rarely told anyone i danced because of it.
- (Bailey, 13 years old) Yes I have been teased forever. My mom once told me that if everyone likes you your doing something wrong.
- (Kevin, 13 years old) By uncles and older male cousins on my mom's side, and the occasional trophy-jock who's generally homophobic anyway.
- (Adrian, 16 years old) Yes. Extremely bad.
- (Grant, 14 years old) The people that it affects me the most to be teased by are my siblings.

When asked a more general, open-ended question about the most significant challenges they confront, nearly half of the participants focused on pejorative stereotypes, teasing, and harassment:

Survey Question 35: What are the biggest challenges you face as a male dancer?

- (Evan, 15 years old) Fighting the negative opinions that people have toward me.
- (Rob 14 years old) The biggest challenge ... well it is the teasing.
- (Mason, 13 years old) The assumption that dance is only for girls and gay men.
- (Sean, 14 years old) Stereo-types and harassment.
- (Jared, 17 years old) Overcoming all the name calling and harassment as a young dancer was a huge challenge for me when i started dancing.
- (Adam, 13 years old) Harassment from other boys.
- (Marc, 15 years old) Teasing, judging and probably being an outcast.
- (Josh, 17 years old) Homophobic attitude of some.

Hearing the experiences of male dance students who are regularly disparaged and repeatedly ridiculed gives a more complete picture. Boys in pre-professional dance training often report feelings of being different or being perceived as different in social contexts (Earl 1988; Williams 2003). Often these perspectives include feeling different in one's own family, especially with fathers, brothers, and other male relatives (Risner 2002). While there is a wide range of male experience in dance study, boys overwhelmingly report lack of social support from important core male family members (Williams 2003; Risner 2010). Research, though limited, appears to indicate that the underlying reason for this lack of support is rooted in heterocentric cultural beliefs and homophobic attitudes (Risner 2009). When being different carries with it scorn, harassment, and "outsider" status, it results in a kind of contagious exclusion that permits unchecked bullying and fosters the social isolation of stigmatised individuals in a far more substantial swath (Dorais 2004; Risner 2009).

4.3. *Social support in dancing boys' lives*

An adapted version of Williams's Dancer's Social Support Scale (2003) was utilised to gather data pertaining to boys' social support. The scale measures participants' beliefs about important people in their lives and the level of support for dancing from these individuals. The Likert-type scale listed 21 individuals with a five-level set of responses ranging from 1 – *not at all helpful or supportive* to 5 – *very helpful or supportive*.

Participants reported individuals who were *very helpful or supportive* as follows: best friend in dance (84%); best friend at school (75%); favourite dance teacher-director (71%); and mother (69%). A comparative group of adolescent female students in pre-professional dance study reported *very helpful or supportive* individuals as mother (92%), father (62%), and favourite dance teacher-director (30%). In terms of *unsupportive or unhelpful* individuals, boys reported gym teacher (47%), step-mother (38%), father (23%), and step-father (22%). Males were more than twice as likely as females to report their favourite dance teacher-director as a primary source for help and support.

Male participants reported their overall social support satisfaction as *highly satisfied* or *satisfied* (63%), *somewhat satisfied* (6%); and nearly one in three males indicated they were *dissatisfied* or *highly dissatisfied* (31%). Comparative data found females' overall support satisfaction (80%) higher than males. Overall dissatisfaction for females (*dissatisfied* or *highly dissatisfied*) was significantly lower than males (3%, females; 31%, males).

Overall data provide for additional analyses. Based on the scale range (1 = *highly dissatisfied* with support, 5 = *highly satisfied* with support), average support satisfaction for the study's male population was 3.56 or at the very low end of *somewhat satisfied* with the support they receive for dancing. The female comparative group average was 4.20, indicating that girls were *satisfied* with the support they receive. As shown earlier, females reported significantly higher levels of support from both parents than males did. The higher level of support for females may indicate the significance of parental support in the overall analysis. That is, while males report strong support from a best friend in dance, best friend in school, mother, and dance teacher, having support from both parents may colour females' overall positive perception of support.

Male participants' responses to open-ended survey questions provide qualitative data for understanding the source and level of boys' social support, which the quantitative data have shown, relies heavily on support from best friend in dance and at school (84% and 75%, respectively), favourite dance teacher-director (71%), and mother (69%). The boys' narrative responses focused primarily on support from their mothers, and then favourite dance teacher, as the examples illustrate below:

Survey Question 29: What important person gives you the most support for your dancing?

- (Bailey, 13 years old) My mother gives me the most support throughout dancing. She always has believed in my talent and told me to follow my heart so that is what I am doing.
- (Sean, 14 years old) My mom. she's always been there and always keeps me going when i feel completely overwhelmed.
- (Alec, 18 years old) My mom has to deserve the credit for mostly anything I do.
- (Josh, 17 years old) My main dance instructor for she sees much potential in me and encourages me to try my hardest and put forth my all. She really wants to see me succeed.

- (Christopher, 16 years old) My high school dance director really encourages me to pursue my passion for drama and dance. She has known me since I was a child and has help bring me up in the arts.

Participant narrative responses also illuminate the perceived support deficit that boys experience from male family members and male school peers. These empirical findings flesh out the challenges dancing boys confront more clearly and add an important dimension for understanding teasing, bullying, and harassment in their lives – some of which may be buttressed, if not affirmed, by the lack of support and approval from male family members:

Survey Question 32: What important person gives you the least support for your dancing?

- (Evan, 15 years old) The person that gives me the least support as a dancer would have to be my father.
- (Grant, 14 years old) The males within my family show little or no support.
- (Brett, 13 years old) The guys at school and football jocks.
- (Will, 14 years old) My father, he's never seen me dance.
- (Stephen, 16 years old) My Dad and brothers.
- (Matt, 17 years old) The sports boys at school who think they are soooooo cool.

In summary, data indicate that most participants: experienced a predominantly female environment in dance with few male peers; encountered a social environment of teasing and harassment outside the studio based on their status as males in dance; reported insufficient support and affirmation for their dancing from family members (especially males); and, face questioning and repeated surveillance as to their sexual orientation.

4.4. Disconfirming evidence

Creswell and Miller (2000) explain the process of searching for disconfirming or negative evidence:

> [I]nvestigators first establish the preliminary themes or categories in a study and then search through the data for evidence that is consistent with or disconfirms these themes. In this process, researchers rely on their own lens, and this represents a constructivist approach in that it is less systematic than other procedures and relies on examining all of the multiple perspectives on a theme or category. Further, the disconfirming evidence should not outweigh the confirming evidence. As evidence for the validity of a narrative account, however, this search for disconfirming evidence provides further support of the account's credibility because reality, according to constructivists, is multiple and complex. (127)

The confirming data evidence presented in this section was reported in terms of majority responses of participants; however, disconfirming evidence was also found for some topics: (1) five participants (15%) reported no experiences of teasing or name-calling, verbal or physical harassment, threatening behaviour, or physical harm of injury; (2) self-identified heterosexual participants reported far fewer verbal threats or threatening behaviours but reported physical harm or injury more frequently; and (3) while fathers were ranked 15th out of 21 individuals who provide support, 40% of the participants reported their father as *very helpful or supportive*. This discrepant data provide opportunities for further research and study.

5. Discussion

The findings of this analysis, when taken together with recent bullying research in the general adolescent and adolescent sexual minority populations, bring up a number of questions and quandaries. Some questions are relatively easy to answer. First, how does the level of bullying experienced by boys in dance compare to that experienced by other adolescents? Based on numerous studies, there is general research consensus that 9–12% of adolescents in the US are the victims of moderate to frequent bullying (Berger 2007; Spriggs et al. 2007). Based on the present investigation's findings, it appears that male adolescent dancers (85%) are at least seven times more likely than the general adolescent population to be bullied (9–12%). Beyond the bullying that results from the feminisation (dance is for girls) of western theatrical dance training (Gard 2006; Risner 2009), another plausible factor in adolescent male dancers' high level of bully victimisation is likely tied to their self-identified or perceived sexual minority status (Berlan et al. 2010). Regardless of his sexual orientation, as we have seen, the adolescent male dancer experiences significant teasing and harassment.

5.1. What keeps male adolescents dancing?

A second series of questions centred on coping strategies and support systems: How do young male dance students navigate bullying and harassment? What sources of support and interpersonal relationships provide meaningful assistance and encouragement? More simply, what keeps male adolescents dancing? Attempting to answer these questions must be prefaced by acknowledging that neither this analysis nor any other studies have been conducted on male adolescents who dropped out of dance training. We might get a much better picture of the impact of teasing, harassment, and bullying, among other influences, from studying that population. However, what we can glean from this investigation in relation to bullying research provides some new knowledge for the field.

Part of navigating the difficulties of repeated bullying is likely tethered to the meaning that dance brings to boys' lives. The majority of participants articulated their attraction to dance for its expressive qualities, movement opportunities, physical and emotional pleasure, and their desires for encountering the world in more creative ways. Although their responses to questions about the meaning dance brings to their lives resulted in mostly positive affirmations of enjoyment, satisfaction, and pleasure, when asked to give advice to younger male dancers, participants' personal struggles surfaced quickly, often agitated in tone:

- (Evan, 15 years old) Don't let what anyone else thinks of you affect your want to dance. There will always be negative opinions towards you.
- (Grant, 14 years old) I'd say don't listen to other people. Don't listen to the jokes or stereotypes.
- (Ben, 17 years old) FUCK everyone and their bias opinions. Do what pleases you, if it be dance or not.

- (Jake, 16 years old) Don't let any rude or obscene comments kill your want to dance.
- (Matt, 17 years old) You will get bullied and harassed, but every male dancer gets it so don't let it knock you down.

Their narratives are also characterised by self-described acquiescence to the marginalised status boys in dance encounter outside the studio and then often internalise in their personal lives. In this internalisation, negativity, stereotypes, bias, and harassment are accepted as commonplace – expected, negotiated, and endured. Still, passion and perseverance remain the central messages telegraphed to their younger peers.

Understanding what participants believe others need to know about male dancers and their experiences provides additional insight into the challenges they confront or the feeling they have not been heard. The following comments summarise the majority of participants' perspectives in response to the question, "What would you like others to know about dance for young males?"

- (Sean, 14 years old) Be more nurturing for males ... parents also need to support the art, just because you are a male and you dance doesn't mean you're gay.
- (Ben, 17 years old) First off, the stigma and the jokes have to stop. We don't make fun of guys on sports teams for being blockheads (which they certainly aren't), so why should male dancers be made fun of?
- (Jake, 16 years old) Dancing for young males will NOT turn them gay. Its perfectly fine for men to express themselves through dance.
- (Ryan, 13 years old) Well, just let all parents know that if that's what your kid really wants, take him to class let him try it for a while and if he is really interested keep taking him and make sure that he knows that he has your support.
- (Evan, 15 years old) Don't make us out to be wimps. What we do is just as difficult as any sport you play.
- (Brett, 13 years old) That it can be hard while growing up to be dancing because of the many changes one goes through especially if you are dealing with your sexual orientation.

Stating and affirming the significance of parental support was critical for participants. Challenging dominant cultural stereotypes of male dancers as gay (effeminate, weak, not athletic, and not real boys) was equally important, as well as repeatedly reminding others that *not all male dancers are homosexual*. Most participants' narratives also rehearsed well-worn "dance as sport" discourses (Crawford 1994; Risner 2002, 2003, 2009), attempting to rehabilitate the stigmatised dancing male. Both recuperative strategies likely emerge from participants' numerous life experiences of defending themselves and their dancing to others. Regardless of their own sexual orientation, participants indicated a keen awareness of the pejorative status male dancers hold in society. Although male dancers (straight, gay, bisexual, or unsure) experience homophobic bias, teasing, and verbal and physical harassment, they feel strongly compelled to voice denial of the non-heterosexual population of male dancers. The level and degree of distancing themselves from gay and bisexual male dancers indicates continued internalised homophobia, which deserves further investigation.

5.2. What social support and interpersonal relationships provide meaningful assistance and encouragement?

For adolescents, social support from parents, peers, and adults of significance is a key element of transition to a healthy adult life (Fenzel 2000). The stress-buffering benefits of positive social support alleviate the impacts of frustration experienced by adolescents (Dumont and Provost 1999). From the findings, we know that the majority of participants perceived high levels of support from their best friend in dance (84%), best friend at school (75%), their favourite dance teacher-director (71%), and mother (69%). However, nearly a combined third of participants were *dissatisfied* or *highly dissatisfied* with the support their dancing receives. Taken together, qualitative and quantitative data indicated insufficient familial support and affirmation, especially from male family members.

Social psychology researchers find that perceived social support is of more significance than actual support received (Ross, Lutz, and Lakey 1999) and positive perception of support decreases depression and anxiety, leads to higher self-esteem and fewer physical ailments/injuries, and mitigates distress and the effects of life stressors (Antunes and Fontaine 2002). Therefore, rather than focusing on participants' perceived support deficits (Risner 2009, 2010), the following discussion looks more closely at supportive interpersonal relationships identified by the participants and the ways in which these relationships contribute to their well-being and emotional health.

5.2.1. Support from best friend in dance, or at school

Adolescent victims of bullying have been shown to have "fewer friends and are rejected by classmates more than non-involved peers, leaving them vulnerable to aggressive peers" (Spriggs et al. 2007, 2). Research confirms the benefit and value of peer friendship (Bollmer et al. 2005). Having more friends reduces the likelihood of victimisation, "suggesting a 'friendship protection' hypothesis" (Wang, Iannotti, and Nansel 2009, 2). Berger (2007) notes, "Friends not only protect victims, they also help bullies change their ways by decreasing their reliance on dominance, power, and defiance" (98). The high level of perceived support from participants' best friend in dance and best friend in school appears to confirm the value of strong friendships and may also explain participants' ability to cope and persevere. However, the question of number of friends versus one best friend remains. For example, only 34% of the participants indicated "friends in dance" as an important reason for their dancing. Initiating research on adolescent peer interaction and relationships in dance is needed, as Warburton (2009) suggests, "[a] focus on peer-to-peer influences and interactions between adolescent boys and girls may be a profitable way to combat harmful stereotypes, strengthen relations between male and female dancers, and build healthy dance communities" (145).

5.2.2. Support from favourite dance teacher-director

Participants perceived high levels of support from their favourite dance teacher-director, confirming research from previous studies (Williams 2003, Risner 2009). It appears that dance teachers are uniquely positioned to provide support for the young male dancer. In fact, boys may depend on their favourite teachers for advice, mentoring, and counsel well beyond teachers' current understanding – both in terms of need and kind of support. Bullying research from adolescent development and education psychology provides important insights for teachers,

> Teachers play a key role in preventing and intervening with bullying at school, yet they receive little if any help or training in how to effectively deal with such problems. Although teachers have the benefit of understanding the social context of bullying, they do not necessarily know how to best use this knowledge to intervene. In school settings, bullying and victimization are often considered as personal problems of individual youth rather than problems requiring a collective response. (Juvonen, Graham, and Schuster 2003, 1236)

Research has shown that teachers are "more likely to stop direct physical bullying than indirect relational attacks, even though the latter probably is more harmful in the long run" (Bauman and Del Rio 2006 cited in Berger 2007, 95). Additionally, victims demonstrate "quiet signs" of distress, which teachers may not readily detect (Juvonen, Graham, and Schuster 2003, 1236). From the adolescent's perspective, Berger (2007) notes:

> Children themselves do not put much faith in adult intervention. A study of 9–11-year olds in the Netherlands found that only 53% of bullied children told their teachers. When they were told, teachers usually tried to intervene, with half of them helping, a third making no difference, and a third making things worse (Fekkes, Pijper, and Verloove-Vanhorick 2005). A US study of elementary school children found that, particularly for boys, telling a teacher sometimes backfired (Kochenderfer-Ladd and Skinner 2002), and a British study of adolescents (Smith and Shu 2000) found that telling peers was much more helpful than telling adults. (112)

As primary sources, dance teachers and directors should realise the significance of their support (or lack thereof), to "intervene effectively with incidents of bullying" (Juvonen, Graham, and Schuster 2003, 1236), as well as the ways they can encourage peer and familial support.

5.2.3. Support from mother

High levels of perceived maternal support have been reported by male dancers in previous studies (Williams 2003; Risner 2009; Polasek and Roper 2011) and are confirmed by the present findings. Male adolescent dancers in Deborah Williams's (2003) study reported mothers as the most supportive individual of their dancing. Research indicates that "During adolescence, emotional closeness and trust within the mother-adolescent relationship also may buffer problems occurring within the peer or school context" (Williams et al. 2005, 473).

The family origins of bullying victims have received considerable investigation. According to Berger (2007), "Boy victims often are unusually close to their mothers, although their fathers may be more distant" (110). This line of research also studies bullying in terms of family genes:

> Genetic influences are now recognized as pervasive, affecting every behavior. Some children are genetically predisposed to be unusually aggressive, impulsive, or submissive. Could becoming a bully or victim be the result? ... A genetic tendency to be weak and submissive by nature and being bullied by older brothers but protected by one's mother is likely to produce a victim. (Berger 2007, 109)

Obviously, we have no inkling of participants' genetic composition in the present study; however, the bullying victim profile described above closely resembles the majority of participants' experiences. When analysing this study's data by participants' self-identified sexual orientation (52% heterosexual; 44% gay; and 4% bisexual), we see that maternal support becomes more complex, as does social support from best friends discussed earlier. Participants who self-identified as non-heterosexual were more than twice as likely as heterosexual participants to report their mother as unsupportive or not supportive at all. These findings confirm Williams et al. (2005) study of peer victimisation and social support of sexual minority adolescents, which found that:

> Sexual minority youths indicated that they felt significantly less closeness with their mothers and less companionship with their best friends than did heterosexual youths. Although it is unknown whether these adolescents are "out" to their mothers or best friends, this particular finding may reflect the tension arising from keeping their sexual orientation from their mothers and/or best friend. Out of fear, adolescents may withdraw from family and other close relationships to avoid discussing concerns about their sexual orientation. This may be a reaction to fear of parental rejection, or a desire to avoid hurting or disappointing parents. Fear may also extend to losing one's best friend. Compared to their heterosexual peers, sexual minority youth reported more sexual harassment, more bullying, less closeness with their mothers and less companionship with their best friends. (471)

To be clear, the point here is to better understand bullying victimisation based on extensive research and the implications for male adolescent dancers, not to judge or evaluate a mother's (or father's lack of) support of her son's dancing. Understanding the complexity of bullying is tantamount for taking informed action. The work of Spriggs et al. (2007) reminds us that most bullying prevention programmes neglect the importance of familial contexts and "failure to address these contexts ignores important sources of adolescents' learning and norms which perpetuate maladaptive behavior" (8).

5.3. Long-term effects of bullying victimisation

Little is known about the long-term effects of bullying and harassment experienced by male dancers. Adult male dancers tend to minimise their adolescent experiences of verbal abuse and harassment, as well as the lack of support they experienced in their teen years (Risner 2009). These post-harassment narratives often take a "rite of passage" tone, not dissimilar from other dance training discourses in which dealing with inhumane practices and behaviours is tolerated, but then valorised (Abra 1987; Smith 1998; Risner 2009). In the area of bullying research in the general population, studies have found that "Retrospective accounts are biased, although it is not known precisely how much, in what direction, and when" (Brainard and Reyna 2005). However, Berger (2007) found that "victims experience anxiety, fear, and depression, not only when they are victimized but for years afterwards" (105). Longitudinal studies in dance, especially in regard to quality of life, are needed.

6. Further thoughts
6.1. The need for research

This analysis has attempted to trace in detail the level and scope of bullying that adolescent male dancers experience – what researchers in the field of adolescent health and child development, if they were aware of it – would likely consider a public health crisis in the arts. At the same time, there is still much we do not know. Although the previous decade of dance education research could be considered an explication of male experience in dance education and the challenges of homophobia and harassment,[4] subsequent research for understanding and confronting bullying has been limited. Most studies have replicated previous findings with little to no empirical research specifically addressing bullying from teacher, student, or school perspectives. The need for additional research is dire.

6.2. *The problem with and for bystanders*

> Bullies do not act alone; they seek victims and an audience. (Berger 2007, 97)

Based on the complexity of bullying perpetration and victimisation, it is unsurprising that most organised anti-bullying initiatives in the US result in mixed outcomes and that "meta-analysis of intervention research finds that bullying outcomes showed no significant change" (Alcaraz, Kim, and Gendron 2010, 3). Part of the problem may be attributed to intense concentration on identified bullies and victims themselves, which ignores the social context of bullying and the significant role that bystanders play, as Berger (2007) articulates:

> Research on intervention has discovered some aspects that seem pivotal. One is the recognition that bullying is a social interaction, part of peer culture, a fact stressed by most European experts (Smith 2003). This leads to a strategy of turning bystanders into defenders, an effort that seems successful before puberty (Salmivalli, Kaukiainen, and Voeten 2005). This social perspective may be one reason European interventions seem more successful than those in North America, where "bullying and victimization are often considered as personal problems of individual youth rather than problems requiring a collective response" (Juvonen, Graham, and Schuster 2003, 1236). (113)

In their research, Hymel, Rocke-Henderson, and Bonanno (2005) reported that "although peers are present in most bullying situations (85–88%), they seldom intervene on behalf of victims (11–25% of the time)" (1). While these observers are not directly participating in the situation, bystanders provide an audience, and without intervening, give silent but powerful endorsement of the bully's behaviour and the victim's harassment (Alcaraz, Kim, and Gendron 2010). Research also indicates that it is detrimental to one's mental health to be a silent bystander in which feelings of culpability, helplessness, and remorse develop. Rivers et al. (2009) found that,

> Witnesses may worry about or assume that they too will be victimized at some point and this may account for the higher levels of interpersonal sensitivity we observed. Some students who witness others being bullied, but who are nevertheless not directly involved, may experience a degree of cognitive dissonance resulting from the discrepancy between their desire to intervene and their lack of action. (220)

Participants' descriptions of bullying and harassment in this study did not directly address bystanders or observers; however, overall social support dissatisfaction (31%) of participants may have been influenced by perceptions that their peers and teachers did not intervene or take supportive action. Based on the findings of this study, dance educators are encouraged to reflect upon their own bystander experiences (whether silent or active) and to revisit notions about intervention in their teaching practices.

6.3. Deep listening

Although much of the literature investigated here emerges from a social-cognitive perspective, I finish in my voice as a critical interpretive researcher and by turning to the moral aspects of bullying and harassment, "insofar as it involves intending to hurt another person or behaving in a way that causes harm to others" (Bosacki, Marini, and Dane 2006, 231). A moral education approach to bullying extends beyond formulating, articulating, posting, and policing rules, as Jacobson (2010) describes:

> Moral education moves from a program or a set of tools, to a conversation, a relationship between student and teacher; a relationship that involves listening, knowing and learning. [D]eep listening requires a reciprocity ... not only students listening to teachers, but teachers listening to students. Moral education means taking seriously those we educate, living in reciprocal relationships with them. And, again, relationship always requires deep listening. (446)

Every time a courageous nine-year-old boy in one of our dance classes is teased and humiliated in front of his peers, we have failed to listen deeply to our programme and school. Every time a 12-year-old boy who has mustered the self-confidence to study dance is denigrated by his father and brothers, we have failed to listen deeply to our programme and our relationships with parents. Every time a devoted ninth-grader in our dance company drops out because he can no longer tolerate getting slammed into his locker and being threatened physically, we have failed to listen deeply to him, our school, and our personal responsibility. Every time we accept that "this is just how it is," we have failed to listen deeply to ourselves and the aims of dance education. Careful empathetic listening allows dance educators to call upon our strongest commitments to human dignity and our beliefs about dance education.

Notes

1. For example, see the US Department of Health and Human Services "Stop Bullying" programme at http://www.stopbullying.gov/.
2. Research indicates that approximately 50% of professional male dancers and male dance students in the US are gay or bisexual as compared to 4–10% in the general population (see Bailey and Oberschneider 1997; Hamilton 1998; Risner 2009).
3. Qualitative survey data are presented by bringing the participants' words into conversation with one another (pseudonyms used). Their responses are verbatim, without grammar editing or spelling and punctuation correction. Selection of participants' open-ended responses was based on a triangulation of quantitative survey data, open-ended qualitative responses, and dominant themes.
4. Extensive research on male dancers' experiences has been published since 2001. See Gard (2001–2006), Keyworth (2001), Lehikoinen (2006), Polesek and Roper (2011), Risner (2002–2010), and Williams (2003), among others.

References

Abra, J. 1987. "The Dancer as Masochist." *Dance Research Journal* 19 (2): 33–39.
Alcaraz, R., T. Kim, and B. Gendron. 2010. *Bullying in Schools*. Riverside: Southern California Academic Center of Excellence on Youth Violence Prevention, University of California.
Antunes, C., and A. Fontaine. 2002. "Relations between Self-concept and Social Support Appraisals during Adolescence: A Longitudinal Study." *Psychology: The Journal of Hellenic Psychological Society* 7 (3): 339–353.
Bailey, J., and M. Oberschneider. 1997. "Sexual Orientation and Professional Dance." *Archives of Sexual Behavior* 26: 33–444.
Bauman, S., and A. Del Rio. 2006. "Preservice Teachers' Responses to Bullying Scenarios: Comparing Physical, Verbal, and Relational Bullying." *Journal of Educational Psychology* 98: 219–231.
Berger, K. 2007. "Update on Bullying at School: Science Forgotten?" *Developmental Review* 27: 90–126.
Berlan, E., H. Corliss, A. Field, E. Goodman, and S. Bryn Austin. 2010. "Sexual Orientation and Bullying among Adolescents in the Growing up Today Study." *Journal of Adolescent Health* 46 (4): 366–371.
Bernard, R., and G. Ryan. 2009. *Analyzing Qualitative Data, Systematic Approaches*. London: Sage.
Bollmer, J., R. Milich, J. Harris, and M. Maras. 2005. "A Friend in Need: The Role of Friendship Quality as a Protective Factor in Peer Victimization and Bullying." *Journal of Interpersonal Violence* 20: 701–712.
Bosacki, S., Z. Marini, and A. Dane. 2006. "Voices from the Classroom: Pictorial and Narrative Representations of Children's Bullying Experiences." *Journal of Moral Education* 35 (2): 231–245.
Brainard, C., and V. Reyna. 2005. *The Science of False Memory*. Oxford: Oxford University Press.
Craig, W., Y. Harel-Fisch, H. Fogel-Grinvald, S. Dostaler, J. Hetland, B. Simons-Morton, M. Molcho, et al. 2009. "A Cross-national Profile of Bullying and Victimization among Adolescents in 40 Countries." *International Journal of Public Health* 54 (S2): 216–224.
Craig, W., and D. Pepler. 2003. "Identifying and Targeting Risk for Involvement in Bullying and Victimization." *Canadian Journal of Psychiatry* 48: 577–582.
Crawford, J. 1994. "Encouraging Male Participation in Dance." *Journal of Physical Education, Recreation and Dance* 65 (2): 40–43.
Creswell, J. 2003. *Research Design: Qualitative, Quantitative, Mixed Methods Approaches*. Thousand Oaks, CA: Sage.
Creswell, J. 2014. *Research Design: Qualitative, Quantitative, and Mixed Methods Approaches*. Thousand Oaks, CA: Sage.
Creswell, J., and D. Miller. 2000. "Determining Validity in Qualitative Inquiry." *Theory into Practice* 39 (3): 124–130.
Crick, N., and J. Grotpeter. 1995. "Relational Aggression, Gender, and Social-psychological Adjustment." *Child Development* 66 (3): 710–722.
D'Augelli, A., N. Pilkington, and S. Hershberger. 2002. "Incidence and Mental Health Impact of Sexual Orientation Victimization of Lesbian, Gay, and Bisexual Youths in High School." *School Psychology Quarterly* 17 (2): 148–167.
Denzin, N., and Y. Lincoln. 2011. "Discipline and Practice of Qualitative Research." In *The Sage Handbook of Qualitative Research*, edited by N. Denzin and Y. Lincoln, 1–19. Thousand Oaks, CA: Sage.
Dorais, M. 2004. *Dead Boys can't Dance: Sexual Orientation, Masculinity, and Suicide*. Montreal: McGill-Queen's University Press.
Due, P., P. Holstein, and J. Lynch. 2005. "Bullying and Symptoms among School-aged Children: International Comparative Cross Sectional Study in 28 Countries." *European Journal of Public Health* 15: 128–132.
Dumont, M., and A. Provost. 1999. "Resilience in Adolescence: Protective Role of Social Support, Coping Strategies, Self-esteem and Social Activities on Experiences of Stress and Depression." *Journal of Youth and Adolescence* 28 (3): 343–363.

Earl, W. 1988. *A Dancer Takes Flight: Psychological Concerns in the Development of the American Male Dancer*. New York: University Press of America.

Erickson, F. 2005. "Arts, Humanities, and Sciences in Educational Research and Social Engineering in Federal Education Policy." *Teachers College Record* 107 (1): 4–9.

Fekkes, M., F. Pijper, and S. Verloove-Vanhorick. 2005. "Bullying: Who Does What, When and Where? Involvement of Children, Teachers and Parents in Bullying Behavior." *Health Education Research* 20: 81–91.

Fenzel, L. 2000. "Prospective Study of Changes in Global Self-worth and Strain during the Transition to Middle School." *The Journal of Early Adolescence* 20 (1): 93–116.

Gard, M. 2001. "Dancing around the 'Problem' of Boys and Dance." *Discourse: Studies in the Cultural Politics of Education* 22: 213–225.

Gard, M. 2003. "Being Someone Else: Using Dance in Anti-oppressive Teaching." *Educational Review* 55 (2): 211–223.

Gard, M. 2006. *Men Who Dance: Aesthetics, Athletics and the Art of Masculinity*. New York: Peter Lang.

Gruber, J., and S. Fineran. 2008. "Comparing the Impact of Bullying and Sexual Harassment Victimization on the Mental and Physical Health of Adolescents." *Sex Roles* 59: 1–13.

Hamilton, L. 1998. *Advice for Dancers: Emotional Counsel and Practical Strategies*. New York: Jossey-Bass.

Hoover, J., and K. Juul. 1993. "Bullying in Europe and the United States." *Journal of Emotional and Behavioral Problems* 2 (1): 25–29.

Hymel, S., N. Rocke-Henderson, and R. Bonanno. 2005. "Moral Disengagement: A Framework for Understanding Bullying among Adolescents." *Journal of Social Sciences* 8: 1–11.

Jacobson, R. 2010. "On Bullshit and Bullying: Taking Seriously Those We Educate." *Journal of Moral Education* 39 (4): 437–448.

Johnson, R., A. Onwuegbuzie, and L. Turner. 2007. "Toward a Definition of Mixed Methods Research." *Journal of Mixed Methods Research* 1 (2): 112–133.

Juvonen, J., S. Graham, and M. Schuster. 2003. "Bullying among Young Adolescents: The Strong, the Weak, and the Troubled." *Pediatrics* 112: 1231–1237.

Juvonen, J., A. Nishina, and S. Graham. 2000. "Peer Harassment, Psychological Adjustment, and School Functioning in Early Adolescence." *Journal of Educational Psychology* 92: 349–359.

Keyworth, S. 2001. "Critical Autobiography: 'Straightening' out Dance Education." *Research in Dance Education* 2 (2): 117–137.

Klomek, A., F. Marrocco, M. Kleinman, I. Schonfeld, and M. Gould. 2007. "Bullying, Depression, and Suicidality in Adolescents." *Journal of the American Academy of Child Adolescent Psychiatry* 46 (1): 40–49.

Kochenderfer-Ladd, B., and K. Skinner. 2002. "Children's Coping Strategies: Moderators of the Effects of Peer Victimization?" *Developmental Psychology* 38: 267–278.

Kvale, S., and S. Brinkmann. 2008. *Interviews: Learning the Craft of Qualitative Research Interviewing*. Thousand Oaks, CA: Sage.

Lehikoinen, K. 2006. *Stepping Queerly: Discourses in Dance Education for Boys in Late 20th Century Finland*. Oxford: Peter Lang.

Lincoln, S., and E. Guba. 2004. "But is It Rigorous? Trustworthiness and Authenticity in Naturalistic Evaluation." *Naturalistic Evaluation* 30: 73–84.

Mason, D. 2012. "On Children's Literature and the (Im)possibility of It Gets Better." *English Studies in Canada* 38 (3–4): 83–91.

Massachusetts Department of Education. 2006. *The 2005 Massachusetts Youth Risk Behavior Survey Results*. Malden, MA: Author.

Meyer, E. 2008. "A Feminist Reframing of Bullying and Harassment: Transforming Schools through Critical Pedagogy." *McGill Journal of Education* 43 (1): 33–48.

Nansel, T., M. Overpeck, D. Haynie, W. Ruan, and P. Scheidt. 2003. "Relationships between Bullying and Violence among US Youth." *Archives of Pediatrics and Adolescent Medicine* 157: 348–353.

Olweus, D. 1993. *Bullying at School What We Know and What We can Do*. Cambridge, MA: Blackwell.

Polasek, K., and E. Roper. 2011. "Negotiating the Gay Male Stereotype in Ballet and Modern Dance." *Research in Dance Education* 12 (2): 173–193.

Risner, D. 2000. "Making Dance, Making Sense: Epistemology and Choreography." *Research in Dance Education* 1 (2): 156–172.

Risner, D. 2002. "Male Participation and Sexual Orientation in Dance Education: Revisiting the Open Secret." *Journal of Dance Education* 2 (3): 84–92.

Risner, D. 2003. "Rehearsing Heterosexuality: Unspoken Truths in Dance Education." *Dance Research Journal* 34 (2): 63–81.

Risner, D. 2007. "Rehearsing Masculinity: Challenging the 'Boy code' in Dance Education." *Research in Dance Education* 8 (2): 139–153.

Risner, D. 2009. *Stigma and Perseverance in the Lives of Boys Who Dance: An Empirical Study of Male Identities in Western Theatrical Dance Training*. Lewiston, NY: Mellen.

Risner, D. 2010. "Dancing Boys' Lives: A Study of Male Participation in Pre-Professional Dance Training and Education in the U.S." In *Dance: Current Selected Research*, edited by L. Overby and B. Lepczyk, Vol. 7, 179–204. Brooklyn, NY: AMS.

Rivers, I. 2004. "Recollections of Bullying at School and their Long-term Implications for Lesbians, Gay Men, and Bisexuals." *Crisis* 25 (4): 1–7.

Rivers, I., V. Poteat, N. Noret, and N. Ashurst. 2009. "Observing Bullying at School: The Mental Health Implications of Witness Status." *School Psychology Quarterly* 24 (4): 211–223.

Ross, L., C. Lutz, and B. Lakey. 1999. "Perceived Social Support and Attributions for Failed Support." *Personality and Social Psychology Bulletin* 25 (7): 896–908.

Salmivalli, C., A. Kaukiainen, and M. Voeten. 2005. "Anti-Bullying Intervention: Implementation and Outcome." *British Journal of Educational Psychology* 75: 465–487.

Smith, C. 1998. "On Authoritarianism in the Dance Classroom." In *Dance, Power and Difference: Critical and Feminist Perspectives on Dance Education*, edited by S. Shapiro, 123–146. Champaign, IL: Human Kinetics.

Smith, P. 2003. "Violence in Schools: An Overview." In *Violence in Schools: The Response in Europe*, edited by P. K. Smith, 1–14. London: RoutledgeFalmer.

Smith, P., and S. Shu. 2000. "What Good Schools Can Do about Bullying: Findings from a Survey in English Schools after a Decade of Research and Action." *Childhood* 7: 193–212.

Spriggs, A., R. Iannotti, T. Nansel, and D. Haynie. 2007. "Adolescent Bullying Involvement and Perceived Family, Peer and School Relations: Commonalities and Differences across Race/Ethnicity." *Journal of Adolescent Health* 41 (3): 283–293.

Swearer, S., D. Espelage, T. Vaillancourt, and S. Hymel. 2010. "What can be Done about School Bullying? Linking Research to Educational Practice." *Educational Researcher* 39 (1): 38–47.

Wang, J., R. Iannotti, and T. Nansel. 2009. "School Bullying among Adolescents in the United States: Physical, Verbal, Relational, and Cyber." *Journal of Adolescent Health* 45 (4): 368–375.

Warburton, E. 2009. "Of Boys and Girls." *Research in Dance Education* 10 (2): 145–148.

Williams, D. 2003. "Examining Psychosocial Issues of Adolescent Male Dancers." Doctoral diss., Marywood University, DAI-A 64/05, p. 1444, 2003.

Williams, T., J. Connolly, D. Pepler, and W. Craig. 2005. "Peer Victimization, Social Support, and Psychosocial Adjustment of Sexual Minority Adolescents." *Journal of Youth and Adolescence* 34 (5): 471–482.

🔓 OPEN ACCESS

Gender Problems in Western Theatrical Dance: Little Girls, Big Sissies and the "Baryshnikov Complex"

Doug Risner

Abstract

General education programs, in postsecondary institutions, provide a broad base of learning in the liberal arts and sciences with common goals that prepare undergraduate students for living informed and satisfying lives. In the United States, dance units in public institutions, offering general education coursework for non-majors (dance appreciation and history, dance studies, world dance), generate 50 percent of their total credit hours per year from these courses (HEADS 2012). Rooted in the body, culture, society, and performance, dance provides ample opportunities for investigating gender. The purpose of this study was to develop an accessible, research-based essay written specifically for and directed toward students enrolled in general education courses in postsecondary dance by drawing upon qualitative data gathered from five years of discussion board postings on the topic of gender compiled from the author's courses. Student (n=312) narratives illuminate the complex relationships between dance and gender, socioeconomic status, race and ethnicity, and sexual orientation. The essay, intended for student readers, concludes with additional discussion questions and prompts.

© 2014 The Author(s).
This is an Open Access article distributed under the terms of the Creative Commons Attribution Non-Commercial License (CC BY-NC). This license ensures that original authorship is properly and fully attributed. This article was originally published in the *International Journal of Education & the Arts*.

Audio Clip 1: For teachers ~ Research problem and methodology

Preface

If you're like most undergraduate students across the United States taking a general education course in dance, chances are: you're female, have an interest in dance or took dances classes as a child or teenager and are completing this class to satisfy your general education requirement in the visual and performing arts. If, on the other hand, you're a male in this course, it's likely that you are in the definitive minority, struggled about even registering for this "dance" class, and have given some serious thought to dropping it and taking a popular music history survey course next semester. Let me ask you to stay through this essay before deciding.

Dance and its training teach us many things about the cultures and societies in which we live. One of the most powerful lessons that dance offers is about gender, specifically: Who should dance or not dance, and why? Does dance simply reinforce what is taught elsewhere in society about what girls do and what boys do? Let's face it, dancing bodies on stage bring up questions about traditional gender roles and sexuality. If we look more deeply into these questions, we can see that they rest on gender stereotypes: Dance (at least western theatrical dance such as ballet, and modern, jazz, and musical theatre dance) is for girls, and "only sissy boys dance."

These stereotypes probably have less to do with dance than with how we think about gender in our society. In particular, we assume that only a narrow range of behaviors are "normal." When we speak about sexuality, normal is almost always defined as heterosexual; people who study gender often use the term heteronormative to refer to this assumption, and use the word heterocentric when discussing practices that emphasize heterosexuality as a central value and dominant standard.

The dance profession in many ways reinforces the value system found throughout the rest of society: this is evident in choreography, performance and training, where heterosexual themes, content, and sensibilities, as well as heterosexual male dancers, are privileged. These heteronormative values maintain and glorify heralded straight male dancers (called *danseurs* in ballet) through, what this essay describes as, the Baryshnikov Complex. In contrast, Mark Morris's *The Hard Nut* (1990) and Matthew Bourne's *Swan Lake* (1995), among other choreographies, provide substantial challenges to heterocentric discourses and offer new ways of thinking about dance, gender and society.

My teaching of university general education courses in dance history and appreciation[1] provides the grounding for this essay's focus on perennial gender issues that remain troubled in western theatrical dance and its training. The voices that you will hear in much of this essay emerge from actual class discussion boards.[2] Therefore, you may sometimes recognize yourself or your classmates in the words and conversations that follow, or you may hear new perspectives and insights.

Dance and Gender: What's the Problem?

Dance training and performance have long been associated with gender and gender roles in world culture (Hagood, 2000; Kraus, Hilsendager, and Dixon, 1991; Posey, 2002; Stinson, 2005). Although dancing in many cultures has been and continues to be viewed as an appropriate "male" activity, the western European cultural paradigm has situated dance as primarily a "female" art form since the 18th century (Hasbrook, 1993). Today, the overwhelming majority of the student population engaged in dance education and training is female (Adair, 1993; HEADS, 2012; Van Dyke, 1996). The social construction of gender, or what society dictates as socially-appropriate behavior for girls and boys, plays an important role in students' attitudes regarding dance study and whether or not they participate in dance (Green, 2000, 2002-03; Smith, 1998; Stinson, 1998a).

So, what's the problem? Let's look at the experience of the majority population in dance first. For many young girls, dance classes are an assumed part of their childhood. Girls often grow up in dance, beginning as early as two or three years of age, adopting values "which teach that it is good to be obedient and silent, good not to question authority or to have ideas which might conflict with what one is being asked to do" (Van Dyke, 1992, p. 120). Susan Stinson

---

[1] Little is known about general education students' attitudes and beliefs about dance and dance history. Most educational literature on dance in higher education focuses upon the intrinsic values of professional western concert dance training and education for students actively pursuing competitive careers in performance and choreography. The findings of this descriptive study add to the educational literature on the instrumental values of studying dance and its history from a liberal arts perspective of general education students at the undergraduate level. Teachers will benefit from understanding undergraduate student perspectives and attitudes about contemporary issues in dance and dance history.

[2] Methodology: Existing data from Blackboard discussion board posts on topics of contemporary issues in dance from the author's undergraduate, general education course (Dance History 1800 to Present) over the past five years were obtained from eight sections of the course (312 students) taught from 2008-2012. Data presented here are from a wide range of students that is characteristic of this large, urban university including: traditional aged undergraduates, returning students and non-traditional students completing degrees later in life. All posts were de-identified. Narrative data were coded for emerging themes. Students are identified here by pseudonyms only. Human subject approval was granted from the author's institutional review board (IRB).

(1998b) cautions that traditional dance pedagogy and training emphasize silent conformity in which dancers reproduce what they receive rather than critique, question, or create it, and that "there is a kind of freedom in obedience, the freedom from responsibility" (p. 118). This hidden curriculum in dance reinforces traditional gender expectations for girls, including passivity, obedience, and escapism (Smith, 1998; Stinson, 2005; Van Dyke, 1992). While dance provides girls with important outlets for self-expression, creativity, and performance, this environment can also produce passive followers rather than active leaders.

A second and related gender problem presented by girls and women in dance is the idealized female body, known in western concert dance for its iconic beauty, heightened expressiveness, graceful docility, eternal youthfulness and svelte frame, as well as its extreme flexibility—all of which are presented as completely natural and thoroughly effortless. Of course, we know that this is not every woman's body; or even close to most. Nor is it produced and maintained naturally or without effort. Puberty, maternity, aging, and all natural processes produce significant challenges for the idealized female dancing body (Arkin, 1994). The traditional, gendered dance body (always female) is frozen in time, a statue of idealized perfection. Ideals of any kind are rarely met by flesh-and-blood people. What's important (and sometimes harmful) about them, however, is the way they function—to provide constant reminders of what is most valued, most important, and usually unattainable. At the same time, we see that idealized values vary greatly depending upon gender.

Students in my introduction to dance history course begin to discuss gender issues during the first week of the class. I open the conversation by asking, "What comes to mind when you think about ballet?" Immediate responses include "ballerina," "pointe shoes," "princess," and "little girls dancing on their toes." I follow by asking them why they associate ballet so strongly with the female gender:

> *Jacqui*: Because of the romantic notion of it. Little girls dream of being a ballerina, it's a fairy tale for girls to be dressed in pink tutus and ballerina shoes twirling on the stage gracefully.

> *Macayla*: Ballet is thought of as sensual and beautiful and basically describes everything that a woman is supposed to be. With specific "gender roles" set in our minds, men should not be doing something beautiful and delicate; they should be doing "manly" things, which would never include dancing.

> *Anee*: That's because society pushes certain views on each gender. From the day that we are born, certain rules are given to us based solely on the fact of whether we are male or female: pink for girls, blue for boys. The little boy should play sports and the

little girl should dance or do gymnastics. Ballet is such a beautiful dance and it certainly would not be the same without men who are brave enough to defy the view that "real men don't dance."

Marin: But what if a girl isn't delicate, tender and sensitive? If she behaves as a strong person, she's seen as a "tom-boy."

Robbie: Dance isn't like competitive sports. There is no physical contact between opposing sides trying to dominate over each other. Rather, dance is more about creativity and self-expression. Men who dance are often stigmatized and even have their sexuality questioned. "Real men" are seen as having physical strength, dominating others, and taking big risks. I'm new to all of this but I can tell you, it is very hard for us to imagine a "real man" ever being a dancer.

Maurice: I have never seen any ballet until this class but my first impression honestly is that these guys are sissies. I guess it's because they do not exhibit masculine behavior. But to see them jump around waiving their hands and arms like women takes some getting used to. I guess some of us have a lot to learn.

Siedah: Men will always play an important role in dance, but I don't think we'll ever get past the soft, delicate waif-like image of the ballerina. Any man thought to embody those qualities will have a hard time proving his "manhood" in today's society.

Rebekah: People tend to think women's bodies are more fit, beautiful and pleasant to watch—look at advertising and magazines—the focus is always the woman's beautiful body. Even though ballet takes an incredible amount of strength, the whole point is to make it look easy and effortless, which takes away from the idea of male strength.

We summarize our lively discussions by noting that most romantic and classical ballets preserve and maintain traditional gender roles, gendered bodies, and societal expectations for women and men that may, in many instances, no longer reflect society's current views.

Dancing in the Margin

Let's now look at the experience of the minority population in western concert dance. Some significant problems emerge from the stereotype of dance as an activity for girls. These problems center on the ways in which dance is marginalized in society and then, more specifically, on the minority male population in dance. Because western theatrical dance is a feminized profession (think: nursing, hairdressing, and public school teaching), male participation remains a culturally suspect endeavor (Gard, 2003; Risner, 2002; Sanderson,

2001; Stinson, 2001). Helen Thomas (1996), a sociologist who has looked at concert dance, asserts that understanding "the 'feminization' of theatrical dance in the west is critical for studying gender and dance" (p. 507). Because it is viewed primarily as a feminine activity, dance, when performed by males, is always in danger of being classified as effeminate.

Due in large part to dualistic thinking which separates mind from body, intellectual activity from physical labor, and the close association of dance to girls and women, it is often perceived and denigrated as part of women's domain (Adair, 1992). Historical notions about the body often link the *feminine* with intuition, nature, the body, and evil; conversely, the intellectual, cultural, and mind historically have been perceived as *masculine* (Risner, 2001). Dance education scholar Edrie Ferdun (1994) summarizes:

> The term "dance" is usually associated with girls and feminine qualities by a significant portion of the dominant culture. Labeling dance as female prevents dance from functioning fully as an educational medium. It limits participation by anyone, male or female, who does not want to be associated with stereotyped gender images and practices. (p. 46)

While the feminization of dance begins early in children's lives, its pervasiveness extends well into adulthood. For example, in the United States, although men are just as likely as women to attend music concerts (jazz, classical, opera) and theatre productions (plays and musicals), women are twice as likely as men to attend ballet performances (NEA, 2004). According to the *National Endowment for the Arts* (*NEA*), Americans are three times more likely to attend a ballet performance than all other forms, defined as other than ballet, including modern, folk, and tap (NEA, 2004).

As our class discussions on gender continue throughout the semester, we focus on developing a more comprehensive understanding of the feminization of western concert dance and, from such, the marginalized place it holds in American society. I begin this conversation by asking, "Why do you think most people automatically think 'ballet' when they think of dance?" Their responses reveal that issues of social class, economic status, and education level come into play when we attempt to understand the links between traditional gender stereotypes and dance's place in the margins of society.

> *Devona*: It's about what ballet represents. Looking back, people who attended ballet were the educated people, the royalty and the rich. You had to be able to mingle with the higher echelons of society. Attending a ballet today gives the sense of accomplishment and being a part of a world that many can't experience. In short, it's still a fairy tale for dreaming about love and romanticism.

Meghan: I'm really shocked by the NEA survey. Personally, I would rather go to a modern dance performance than a ballet. Maybe more people prefer ballet because it tends to tell a story. But I must say that modern dances that don't tell a story have literally brought me to tears because they were so powerful and physical.

Jenna: With ballet performances, I know what I am going to see. Even though the stories differ, ballet is always ballet, and it's always entertaining. Like most people, when I am spending money on a performance, I want to make sure I will enjoy the show no matter what.

Ali: Ballet has a long history and is viewed by society as upscale and high class. The performances are also very traditional with the ballerina always front and center.

Starkesha: I think more people think of dance as ballet and are likely to attend a ballet more than any other style because America is Eurocentric. Were the people in the (NEA) survey mostly white?

Therese: Personally, I'd rather go to a ballet. For me, it's because the gracefulness and beauty of the dancers absolutely captivates me. It's amazing how much poise and balance they have, especially while dancing on their toes, doing difficult lifts and the synchronicity of all dancers on stage.

Marcus: Where does National Endowment for the Arts get its statistics from? Do they gather data from all cultures or just a few? How many low income families did they ask this question to? I just know that ballet would not be my first choice. I believe that they got their information from upper society.

Geoff: With contemporary or modern dance, people are afraid—they don't know exactly how the performance will play out. It's a comfort level thing. I don't think people have yet opened up their minds to other forms of dance—like we've watched in this class—especially dances where females are strong and athletic.

Sudha: Ballet still provides a night of escape from the drudgery of daily life with fantastic stories and ethereal ballerinas, ballerinas that many little girls have dreamed of being.

Jason: Perhaps a man knows his wife likes dance, so for her birthday he decides to buy her tickets to a dance performance. While he's at the box office or ticket website, he plain and simple does not know what he is looking for. When he finds a ballet on the list he will be inclined to choose it because he's probably heard the title before, like *Swan Lake*. I could be way off, but I truly believe people are not aware of concert dance styles—I know I didn't before this semester.

Maurice: When this class started with ballet, I didn't know what to think. But now, I seem to scratch my head more times watching modern dance than ballet. To me modern just does not seem very spectacular, at least not enough to spend my money on.

Jacqui: I feel that a lot of this—people's lack of information and knowledge of other dance types—has something to do with demographics and SES (Social Economic Status).

Throughout these discussions, students begin to identify other factors that emerge from and surround gender problems in dance. Most notably, their conversations illuminate the socioeconomic and educational issues that contribute to dance's marginal status. In fact, income level and formal education figure prominently in predicting dance performance attendance; most people who attend dance performances have high incomes (over $75,000) and attended graduate school (NEA, 2004).

Between the lines of the students' discussion, we also hear the beginnings of racial asymmetries operating in western concert dance and its audiences. Audiences of ballet in the United States have the smallest representation of racial and ethnic minorities of all performing arts [88% of ballet audiences are non-Hispanic whites] (NEA, 2004). Today's major ballet companies in the U.S., like *American Ballet Theatre, New York City Ballet, San Francisco Ballet, Atlanta Ballet,* and *Houston Ballet,* are comprised primarily of white American, Europeans, and South American dancers. African-American and African dancers are significantly under-represented in the professional ballet world. Of these ballet companies, Nyama McCarthy-Brown (2010) reports only one African-American principal ballerina since 1990. This problem, a big one, requires that we look carefully at race whenever we attempt to consider gender. Because when we do, we see that many times the feminization of dance also inherently values a particular, white femininity.

However, a few smaller contemporary ballet companies are comprised of African-American and other ethnic group dancers, like *Alonzo King LINES BALLET* and *Complexions Contemporary Ballet.* Still, the vast majority of working professional ballet dancers in the United States is white. Therefore, recognizing the complexity of studying gender and dance also means looking carefully at social and economic status, race/ethnicity, and education.

More simply, it is impossible to examine dance from gender perspectives without considering the whole of social issues.

Dance and Masculinity ("Dance is for Sissies")

To a certain degree, all stereotypes begin with a particular aspect of a certain population that is then applied to the entire group uniformly (e.g. "all male dancers are gay"). Assumptions about men and boys in dance are part of what D. A. Miller (1988) describes as the "open secret," a knowledge that is present and understood, yet unspoken and unarticulated. More simply, an open secret is one that everyone hides because everyone holds (p. 207). For males in western concert dance, we needn't say more—you already know it—the assumption is that they're all sissies (queers, fags, homos).

To open this discussion with students, I ask them to respond to the following Blackboard prompt based upon estimates from my own research: *For ages 12-17 in professional dance training in the U.S., girls (93%) significantly outnumber boys (7%). Why do you think this is?*

> *Annette*: There are fewer males involved in dance because they are afraid of being stereotyped as gay. I think that if we look at hip hop, you'll find that there are more males because it is viewed as masculine dancing. But when it comes to standing on your toes, this is looked at as feminine, dancing that should only be performed by women.

> *Dani*: There are so few boys because of the sociological issues with society. I don't think it's because they don't have talent. I think it's because of the way that parents influence their children. Girls are born to play with babies. Boys are born to play with trucks. It's always been like that and it probably always will be.

> *Sanit*: Parents' attitudes, for the most, steer their children where THEY want them to go, not necessarily where or what the child is most interested in.

> *Patti*: But I don't want my son to become gay and most men do not want their son becoming a dancer because they believe he's going to become gay. A lot of male dancers and teachers are openly gay and that just does not sit well with parents. I myself am having that same problem—I want my son to dance but I don't want him to be gay nor do I want him to think it's ok to be gay.

> *Joshua*: A young male growing up just wants to fit in with their peer group, period. He wants to play soccer with his classmates and be considered cool. Anything that would make him un-cool he will not want to do. Gay stereotypes are a big part of it, but it

goes much deeper than that. If the majority of males at a certain school were involved in dance, then certainly more boys would join. However, that is not the case in our society today, nor do I expect it to change in our lifetimes.

Valerie: People don't know how much physical strength and stamina it takes for dancing. Male dancers are just like athletes. I mean dance is a kind of sport. I don't understand why a heterosexual male wouldn't want to spend most of his day with cute chicks in spandex, when he's outnumbered 20 to 1.

Alicia: Many male dancers are gay, so most people assume that all of them are gay. For a straight male, it can be very embarrassing when people are questioning his sexual orientation. Also, many parents think that boys belong in sports where there is aggression involved. Dads don't let their sons dance because they are afraid they will turn out gay. But I can't understand how any parent could ignore or discourage their son's dance talents.

Natalie: Dads don't want to brag about their son's dance performance. They want to brag about their son scoring a touchdown.

Eileen: Well, I have three daughters and one son and I already know that when my son is old enough he's going to be entered in football because his father wants him there. That's just the way it is, but my daughters have already started dancing.

Micki: Homosexual stereotypes are a large reason why boys are not a part of the dancing world, plus all the bullying that goes with it. Considering how much strength it takes to be a male dancer, this is really sad.

Beth: I'd be very hesitant to put my son in a dance class. I'd fear that he would get picked on from other kids and maybe even some of the nastier parents. It's hard enough for young boys. As he would grow older I would be afraid that he would get called gay and get bullied in school for being a male ballerina. It would make my son way too easy of a target for the other kids and I wouldn't want to be the source of his teasing and bullying.

Justin: There are many mothers and fathers that label dance as a feminine occupation or art, so they keep their sons from pursuing dance.

Erin: The male-to-female ratio in dance plays in the male's favor... I mean they have their choice from all the females that they dance with. I personally loved all the guys that I danced with. All of them are far from being gay and are very masculine.

Rochelle: I just feel parents, especially the male figure, is going to be totally against their son participating in dance.

Students quickly identify the gay stereotype attached to boys and men who dance. Like all dominant stereotypes, there is some partial truth to the gay stereotype in dance. While gay males make up approximately 9 percent of the US population[3], research indicates that gay and bisexual men comprise approximately half the male population in professional dance and training in the US (Bailey and Oberschneider, 1997; Hamilton, 1998; Risner, 2009). While much of the dance field accepts that there is a higher percentage of gay men in dance than in the general population, meaningful discussion within the dance profession has begun to emerge only recently (think: "open secret").

In their class discussions, students assert that the gay stereotype, and all the social assumptions that come with it, may bring harm to all males in dance—whether they are gay, straight, or questioning their sexual orientation. Stereotypes aside, what I notice is missing from their responses is: If a person actually is gay, what's the problem? And if it is, whose problem is it?

Parents, as you heard many students suggest, hold significant influence on boys' participation in dance (Risner, 2009). Whether they support their son's desire to dance or discourage it, parents' attitudes and behavior carry a lot of weight in boys' decision making and significantly impact their feelings about being supported in dance. Consider this: in a recent study of students (age 13 – 22) in pre-professional dance training in the U. S., male dancers were eight times more likely than female dancers to report dissatisfaction with the support they receive for their dancing (Risner, 2009). Understanding the experiences of boys and men who dance requires that we pay attention to the lockstep relationship between dominant masculinity and homophobic attitudes. In his book *The Male Dancer*, dance historian Ramsay

---

[3] Estimates in the US have varied since Alfred Kinsey's 1948 book, *Sexual Behavior in the Human Male*, which suggested that 10 percent of the male population is gay (Kinsey, Pomeroy, and Martin, 1948). The 1993 Janus Report estimated that nine percent of men had more than "occasional" homosexual relationships (Janus and Janus, 1993). The National Survey of Sexual Health and Behavior (2010) reported that 8 percent of men identify as gay or bisexual.

Burt (1995) explains how prejudice toward males in western theatrical dance developed and the ways that homophobia continues to surround boys and men in dance today.

Burt argues that homophobia arises from the need for males to rationalize their close attraction to other men. In this scheme men can only bond socially when homophobic attitudes and language accompany closeness, intimacy, and attraction in their social relationships with other men (think: Monday Night Football). In other words, cultural norms require that males profess an absolute repulsion for same-sex desire or attraction and to vocalize this disgust openly and repeatedly.

Therefore in dance, men watching and enjoying other men dancing presents a particularly difficult impasse. While men might certainly enjoy viewing and affirming other men in dance, this kind of attraction to males in the feminized environment of western concert dance sets in motion the required repulsive responses men have learned as socially necessary from a very young age (think: bullying in elementary and middle school).

Burt's explanation helps us better understand the problems that boys in dance confront with male family members and male peers. For example, boys in pre-professional dance training often report feelings of being different or being perceived as different in social and family contexts (Earl, 1988; Risner, 2002; Williams, 2003). Often these perspectives include feeling different in the boy's own family, especially with fathers, brothers, and other male relatives (Risner, 2002, 2009; Williams, 2003). Therefore, parents and family members need to look carefully at their own personal prejudices and biases about gay, lesbian, and bisexual people and then evaluate how they condone or reaffirm anti-gay prejudice in their children.

For students like Patti and Beth (quoted earlier), it's important to understand that a dance teacher's sexual orientation does not determine his or her ability to be an effective and respected professional. All parents and family members will benefit from exploring the ways in which they support or discourage their son's or brother's choices, including the possibility of dancing. Research indicates that the underlying reason for this lack of support is rooted in heterocentric cultural beliefs and homophobic attitudes (Risner, 2002, 2009; Williams, 2003). For the young male dancer, this stigma and marginalization is often experienced both at home and in his wider social world.

Rehearsing Heterosexuality in Dance ("The Baryshnikov Complex")

For an individual or a group of people on the societal margin—like dancers or dance in general—one approach for making your way to the society's center is to show how similar you are to those who hold power and rights in the culture's dominant center (think: Equal Rights Amendment for women, which, by the way, is still not part of the US Constitution; or the Americans with Disabilities Act). While there is no legislative mechanism to elevate the social value of dance to that of music or visual art, dance has frequently sought its rightful place in society by emphasizing traditional heterosexual values and highlighting heterosexual male dancers and choreographers. To do so, however, the dance profession has often harbored and affirmed heterosexist and homophobic attitudes.

You may be asking how this would be possible given the significant gay male population in dance. The answer is—like what most marginalized groups do—erase your difference as much as possible. To be a part of the dominant center requires re-positioning yourself or group to be as similar to the people in the center as you can. For western concert dance over the past century, this has meant developing strategies that negate or hide non-heterosexual males in dance and attracting more boys to the profession by making dance more "masculine."

Encouraging increased male participation has historically involved well-intentioned but frequently heteronormative approaches: these focus on "manly" sport comparisons between male athletes (presumably heterosexual), and male dancers (Crawford, 1994), encourage greater male participation by minimizing or ignoring the significant population of gay males in dance (Risner, 2009), and idealize noteworthy heterosexual male dancers (Hanna, 1988).

As noted in the student comments earlier, some of these heteronormative strategies circulate in the general public. Valerie argued that "male dancers are just like athletes." Speaking from her personal experience with male dancers, Erin stated that they were "far from gay" and "very masculine." Both students emphasized the heterosexual benefits that would attract and retain straight males to dance (outnumbered 20 to 1 by "cute chicks in spandex").

Taken together, these heteronormative approaches project and glorify heralded straight male dancers through what I call the Baryshnikov Complex—a phenomenon based loosely on heterosexual ballet superstar Mikhail Baryshnikov's (b. 1948) penchant for womanizing in the 1970s and 1980s, and the larger public mythology that developed from his bad-boy brilliance and tyrannical reputation. Three decades later the heteronormative message of the Baryshnikov Complex continues, as Joseph Carman (2006) of *Dance Magazine* recently noted:

> Lest anyone think that men in tights are always gay, let's not forget that ballet's biggest box-office attraction was Mikhail Baryshnikov, a ladies' man who made a number of straight men think ballet class might be a good way to meet chicks. (np)

Because the dance profession confronts the desire and need to attract more males to dance when at the same time many male dancers are gay, the "macho man" heterosexual messages of the Baryshnikov Complex seek to refute the open secret about gay male dancers. It's used by teachers, directors, schools, programs, and dance companies, some parents and family members of male dancers, and male dancers themselves confronting the gay stereotype. But, do these approaches effectively recruit all males (gay, bisexual, questioning, straight), or just heterosexual males?

As a researcher who has interviewed many male youth pursuing serious dance training (Risner, 2009), I am sympathetic to efforts for increasing male involvement. However, I believe that most of the field's approaches have likely made matters worse, exacerbating the homophobic stereotyping that most males in dance repeatedly encounter. It is one thing to promote dance, for example, as an activity of self-expression and physical challenge for all children, both girls and boys. It is quite another to encourage male involvement by denigrating boys who do not conform to dominant notions of masculinity and heterosexuality. What's more, over the past ten years of my research I have found no evidence that would suggest any differences between what attracts straight males to dance and what attracts gay or bisexual males to the art form.

A real commitment to cultivating increased male participation, one that would enrich the art form and its audiences, would center on questioning the ways in which western society discourages all young boys and men from participation. Without such questions about dance, we ignore important social issues of sexual orientation, gender identity, homophobic attitudes, and bullying and harassment (Risner, 2014). Rather than trying to increase male numbers with strategies that attempt to re-engender dance in traditionally masculine ways (i.e., dance as sports, competition, jumping and turning), or to recast dance in misogynist ways for "real" boys, a more responsive inquiry into male students' social context and what, in fact, attracts and affirms them in pre-professional dance study is needed. The findings of a recent research study of young males (age 13 – 22) in pre-professional dance training in the US give us a good starting point:

> Male participants articulate their attraction to dance for its expressive qualities, movement opportunities, physical and emotional pleasure, and for their own desires for encountering the world in more creative ways. In terms of enjoyment and satisfaction, participants' narratives illuminate the significance of dance as fun; as achievement through performance, physical challenge, and expression; and as a creative outlet opportunity otherwise not part of their daily worlds. (Risner, 2009, p. 141)

By not only acknowledging, but also acting upon the educative potential the profession holds for reducing homophobia and antigay stigmatization, dance education has the ability to play a profoundly important leadership role in re-shaping our culture's negative messages about difference and prejudice.

Troubling Traditional Gender Assumptions

The complicated gender problems you have thought about in this essay are sociological ones: how people see themselves and others in society. We have looked at how these play out in dance performance and training, especially from dance's place in the margins of society. Much of the profession's response focuses on showing its similarity to societal norms and gender assumptions (think: fitting in), rather than questioning them.

However, some pockets of western concert dance challenge assumptions about gender and society, seeking to "trouble" traditional ideas and the status quo. Because males in western concert dance present great challenges to dominant western masculinity, let's conclude our discussion of "troubling gender" with two evening-length works that reinterpret revered classical ballets. I hope you might view these dances in your class or on your own.

Using the holiday ballet *The Nutcracker* (1892) as his starting point, modern dance choreographer Mark Morris (b. 1956) turns gender and social class upside down in *The Hard Nut* (1991). In his caricature version of the beloved ballet, coveted roles reverse to the opposite sex, sometimes in parody (think: RuPaul's Drag Race), other times in strikingly poignant critiques of traditional female beauty and masculine brawn in which both genders don tutus and pointe shoes.

Carefully crafting humor with satire, Morris troubles the very notions of what we think is feminine and masculine—really, what gender is equated with love, tenderness, or sensuality? In many ways, Morris's questions heighten our understanding of gender philosopher Judith Butler's idea that all of gender is a learned performance (Butler, 1990), in which socially appropriate performance of gender, when matched exactly with dominant social and cultural norms, is both affirmed and rewarded. As Butler (1988) notes, "those who fail to do their gender right are regularly punished" (p. 522). *The Hard Nut* gets through to us because we laugh at how we judge people daily, and then because we reflect more seriously about how another person's difference consumes us as a society (think: Defense of Marriage Act).

Many of my male students get a big kick out of Morris's gender parody, noting that it helps them begin to understand their own performance of masculine behavior as something they *do*, rather than who they *are*. *The Hard Nut*'s gender-bending snow scene (always a rousing piece in the original *Nutcracker* anyway) is a highlight for female students because of the athleticism and power of both female and male snowflakes.

Matthew Bourne's (b. 1960) re-telling of the classic *Swan Lake* (1895), originally choreographed by Marius Petipa and Lev Ivanov, moves beyond gender parody by directly challenging preconceptions about masculinity and opposite sex attraction. Bourne's *Swan Lake* (1996), unlike the traditional story of Odette with the princess transformed into the Swan Queen by an evil sorcerer, turns its focus to the prince and his struggle from boyhood to manhood in modern day London. The Swan Queen, as well as the entire flock of swans, has changed from female to male: "bare-chested, barefoot and hairy, they [dance] sharply and aggressively around the stage under the reign of The Swan [male]" (Drummond, 2003, p. 236).

Although the sex of the swans changed, the new *Swan Lake* did not eliminate the attraction and desire between the Prince and The Swan, now both males (Drummond, 2003). However, unlike the traditional ballerina swan—elusive, shy, ephemeral, in downy headdress—this male Swan is "a hunk with a buzz haircut, a gleaming bare chest and lush, feathery thighs" (Hohenadel, 1997, np). Dancer Adam Cooper, who created the role, believes that the Swan, through the Prince's eyes, represents masculinity, power, and freedom (Fisher, 1997). Bourne himself has described the role as a combination of "father figure, lost love, alter ego, unattainable ideal" and an "omnisexual, whip-wielding gate-crasher in black leather pants" (Hohenadel, 1997, np).

This *Swan Lake* repeatedly shows us unresolved longings for intimacy between two men; well, a man and a male swan, that is. Still, the notion of homoeroticism (think: same-sex fantasizing without acting upon it) comes through clearly. But to call this a gay ballet is too simple-minded, because Bourne's choreography depicts "a spectrum of ways of being masculine" (Drummond, 2003, p. 244) through "parts that were lyrical without being emasculating and sexually charged without being hyper-macho" (Bourne cited in Lancioni, 2006, p. 710). These nuanced depictions are rarely seen in western theatrical dance. At the same time, the critical and commercial success of the new *Swan Lake* tells us that mainstream audiences may be more open to shifting gender norms and accepting of wider notions of sexual attraction. While you might think that student discussion of Bourne's *Swan Lake* would focus primarily on gay issues, my previous students have centered on how the ballet brings up contemporary questions about what is considered "beautiful," "emotional," and "expressive," and how societal views on gender norms and traditionally female ways of being are changing.

Reflections

Throughout this essay you have learned how western concert dance encounters a number of gender problems when it's seen traditionally as only something for little girls and big sissy boys. Gender norms and homophobic stereotypes are challenged by the relatively large population of gay boys and males who dance, but at the same time the profession (and some of the public) continues to rehearse the "hyper-straight dude" image of the Baryshnikov Complex. Choreographers like Mark Morris and Matthew Bourne trouble these gender assumptions on a deeper level, creating new ways of seeing femininity, masculinity, attraction, intimacy, and even freedom.

You have also seen, maybe unexpectedly, that looking critically at western concert dance brings up a number of larger social questions in current public debates—many of which are political (think: who's got the power?). The heated politics of gender, sexual orientation, race, and social class have not been as hotly debated since the 1960s (think: your grandparents). Dance serves as a cultural TiVo, if you will, recording and replaying both highly traditional social values as well as alternatives that challenge and resist "the way things are."

Knowing what you know now, I leave you with a few questions to think about on your own or to discuss with classmates:

- From your own experience, can you identify situations in which your own gender identity or sexual orientation was questioned? If so, what was this like for you? If not, why do you think it wasn't?

- In your own life, has your gender-race-social class ever determined what you could or could not pursue? How so? And how did you know?

- After reading this essay, has your notion about male dancers and masculinity changed? If so, in what ways?

- What connections do you see between sexual orientation in dance and larger public debates about gays serving in the military and marriage equality? How are these discussions similar and different?

- If/when you become a parent, how will you address gender norms and social pressures as you raise your own child?

- For dance students, how does this knowledge about gender and dance impact your own work as a dancer and choreographer?

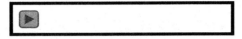

Audio Clip 2: For teachers ~ General education in dance today[4]

References

Adair, C. (1992). *Women and dance: Sylphs and sirens.* New York: New York University Press.

Aleman, D., Frichtel, M., Gerdes, E., & Warchal-King, J. (2010). "Embodying pluralism:" A 21st century design for dance in higher education. In K. Bond and M. Frichtel (Eds.), *Focus on dance education: Creativity, innovation and 21st century skills*, Proceedings of the National Dance Education Organization, (pp. 111-117). Bethesda, MD: National Dance Education Organization.

Arkin, L. (1994). Dancing the body: Women and dance performance. *Journal of Physical Education, Recreation and Dance,* 65(2), 36-38, 43. Bailey, J., & Oberschneider, M. (1997). Sexual orientation and professional dance. *Archives of Sexual Behavior,* 26, 433-444.

Bond, K., & Etwaroo, I. (2005). If I really see you...:" Experiences of identity and difference in a higher-education setting. In M. Powell and V. Marcow-Speiser (Eds.), *The arts, education, and social change: Little signs of hope,* (pp. 87-99). New York: Peter Lang.

Bond, K., & Gerdes, E. (2013). Student performance in a dance-based humanities course at "Diversity U." In S. Stinson and C. Nielsen (Eds.), *Proceedings of the World Dance Alliance/Dance and the Child International.* http://ausdance.org.au/publications/details/dance-young-people-and-change

Bourne, M., & Mumford, P. (1995, 1998). *Matthew Bourne's Swan Lake.* Derby, England: NVC Arts.

Burns, C., Diamond, M., & Morris, M. (1990, 2007). The *Hard Nut: Mark Morris Dance Group.* New York: Nonesuch.

Burt, R. (1995). *The male dancer: Bodies, spectacles, sexualities.* London: Routledge.

Butler, J. (1988). Performative acts and gender constitution: An essay in phenomenology and feminist theory. *Theatre Journal,* 40(4), 519-531.

---

[4] As referenced in this audio, see Aleman, Frichtel, Gerdes and Warchal-King (2010), Bond and Etwaroo (2005), Bond and Gerdes (2013), Dils (2004, 2007), Frichtel (2012), Morgan (2011), Narva (2004) and Stark (2009).

Butler, J. (1990). *Gender trouble: Feminism and the subversion of identity.* London: Routledge.

Carman, J. (2006). Gay men and dance: What's the connection? *Dance Magazine.* Retrieved from: http://www.thefreelibrary.com/_/print/PrintEssay.aspx?id=154003601

Crawford, J. (1994). Encouraging male participation in dance. *Journal of Physical Education, Recreation and Dance,* 65(2), 40-43.

Dils, A. (2004). Sexuality and sexual identity: Critical possibilities for teaching dance appreciation and dance history. *Journal of Dance Education,* 4(1), 10-16.

Dils, A. (2007). Moving into dance: Dance appreciation as dance literacy. In L. Bresler (Ed.), *International handbook of research in arts education* (pp. 569-580). Dordrecht, Netherlands: Springer.

Drummond, K. (2003). The queering of Swan Lake: A new male gaze for the performance of sexual desire. *Journal of Homosexuality,* 45(2), 235-255.

Earl, W. (1988). *A dancer takes flight: Psychological concerns in the development of the American male dancer.* New York: University Press of America.

Ferdun, E. (1994). Facing gender issues across the curriculum. *Journal of Physical Education, Recreation and Dance,* 65(2), 46-47.

Fisher, J. (1997). "His wings of desire." Interview with Adam Cooper, 2 May 1997. *Los Angeles Times.* Retrieved from: http://www.dance90210.com/swanintercoop.html

Frichtel, M. (2012). Freedom, transformation, and community: Student meanings of engagement in a dance-based general education course. (Doctoral dissertation). Retrieved from ProQuest Dissertations and Thesis database (ATT 3509061).

Gard, M. (2003). Moving and belonging: Dance, sport and sexuality. *Sex Education,* 3(2), 105–118.

Green, J. (2000). Emancipatory pedagogy? Women's bodies and the creative process in dance. *Frontiers,* 21(3), 124-140.

Green, J. (2002-03). Foucault and the training of docile bodies in dance education. *Arts and Learning,* 19(1), 99-126.

Hagood, T. (2000). *A history of dance in American higher education: Dance and the American university.* Lewiston, ME: Mellen Press.

Hamilton, L. (1998). *Advice for dancers: Emotional counsel and practical strategies.* New York: Jossey-Bass.

Hanna, J. (1988). *Dance, sex, and gender: Signs of identity, dominance, defiance, and desire.* Chicago: University of Chicago Press.

Hasbrook, C. (1993). Sociocultural aspects of physical activity. *Research Quarterly for Exercise and Sport,* 64(1), 106-115. Higher Education Arts Data Services (HEADS). (2012). *Dance Data Summaries: 2011-2012.* Reston, VA: National Association of Schools of Dance.

Hohenadel, K. (1997). Guys and swans: Interview with Matthew Bourne, 20 Apr. 1997. *Los Angeles Times.* Retrieved from http://articles.latimes.com/1997-04-20/entertainment/ca-50430_1_swan-lake

Janus, S., & Janus, C. (1993). *The Janus report on sexual behavior.* New York: John Wiley & Sons.

Kinsey, A., Pomeroy, W., & Martin, C. (1948). *Sexual behavior in the human male.* Philadelphia: W.B. Saunders.

Kraus, R., Hilsendager, S., & Dixon, B. (1991). *History of dance in art and education.* Englewood Cliffs, NJ: Prentice-Hall.

Lancioni, J. (2006). Cinderella dances Swan Lake: Reading Billy Elliot as fairytale. *Journal of Popular Culture,* 39(5), 709-728.

McCarthy-Brown, N. (2010). Dancing in the margins: Experiences of African American ballerinas. *Journal of African American Studies,* 15(3), 385-408.

Miller, D. (1988). *The novel and the police.* Berkeley, CA: University of California Press.

Morgan, I. (2011) "Empowerment in this dance? You love this Dance?" Instructor and student together online. *Journal of Dance Education,* 11(4), 119-123.

Narva, S. (2004). Body knowing: Embodied education in theory and practice. Unpublished master's thesis, Temple University, Philadelphia, USA.

National Endowment for the Arts. (2004). *2002 Survey of public participation in the arts.* Research Division Report 45. Retrieved from http://www.nea.gov/research/NEASurvey2004.pdf

National Survey of Sexual Health and Behavior (NSSHB). (2010). Findings from the National Survey of Sexual Health and Behavior, Centre for Sexual Health Promotion, Indiana University. *Journal of Sexual Medicine,* Vol. 7, Supplement 5.

Posey, E. (2002). Dance education in dance schools: Meeting the demands of the marketplace. *Journal of Dance Education,* 2(2), 43-49.

Risner, D. (2001). *Blurring the boundaries: Hope and possibility in the presence of the necessary stranger in gay liberation.* Dissertation Abstracts International, 62/03, 1236.

Risner, D. (2002). Sexual orientation and male participation in dance education: Revisiting the open secret. *Journal of Dance Education,* 2(3): 84-92.

Risner, D. (2009). *Stigma and perseverance in the lives of boys who dance: An empirical study of masculine identities in western theatrical dance training.* Lewiston, NY: Mellen Press.

Risner, D. (2014). Bullying victimisation and social support of adolescent male dance students: An analysis of findings. *Research in Dance Education,* 15(2), 179-201.

Sanderson, P. (2001). Age and gender Issues in adolescent attitudes to dance. *European Physical Education Review,* 7(2), 117-136.

Smith, C. (1998). On authoritarianism in the dance classroom. In S. Shapiro (Ed.) *Dance, Power and Difference* (pp. 7-21). Champaign, IL: Human Kinetics.

Stark, K. (2009). Connecting to dance: Merging theory with practice. *Journal of Dance Education,* 9(2), 61-68.

Stinson, S. (1998a). Seeking a feminist pedagogy for children's dance. In S. Shapiro (Ed.) *Dance, Power and Difference* (pp. 23-47). Champaign, IL: Human Kinetics.

Stinson, S. (1998b). Places where I've been: Reflections on Issues of gender in dance education, research, and administration, *Choreography and Dance,* 5(1), 117-127.

Stinson, S. (2001). Voices from adolescent males. *daCi in Print,* 2, 4–6.

Stinson, S. (2005). The hidden curriculum of gender in dance education. *Journal of Dance Education,* 5(2), 51-57. Thomas, H. (1996). Dancing the difference. *Women's Studies International Forum,* 19(5), 505-511.

Van Dyke, J. (1992). *Modern dance in a postmodern world: An analysis of federal arts funding and its impact on the field of modern dance.* Reston, VA: American Alliance for Health, Physical Education, Recreation, and Dance.

Van Dyke, J. (1996). Gender and success in the American dance world. *Women's Studies International Forum,* 19(5), 535-543.

Williams, D. (2003). *Examining psychosocial issues of adolescent male dancers.* Dissertation abstract in *UMI,* 2090242.

Men in Dance, Bridging the Gap Symposium: Gender Inequities in Dance Education: Asking New Questions

Conference organizers: Christopher Rutt, Barry Blumenfeld, Andrew Janetti, and Yoav Kaddar.

INTRODUCTION

Doug Risner

One of the many ways that the National Dance Education Organization (NDEO) addresses member needs is through its special interest groups (SIGs) that provide and encourage online and annual meeting discussion forums among members with shared educational interests and common professional bonds. The Men in Dance SIG was established in 2010 to address issues and concerns related to teaching boys and supporting men in the field of dance education. Males in dance education in the United States comprise relatively small percentages: 34 percent of dance faculty in higher education, 14 percent of undergraduate dance majors in postsecondary institutions, and 4 percent of NDEO's membership. The Men in Dance SIG examines myriad topics and challenges of gender imbalance and seeks ways to improve the educational and professional lives of boys and men in dance education.

The vision to present the first symposium of its kind came directly from leaders in the Men in Dance SIG, who believed that the time had come to move beyond meeting to talk about the topic of dancing boys and men once per year at the NDEO annual meeting. These leaders— Barry Blumenfeld, Andrew Jannetti, Yoav Kaddar, and Christopher Rutt— became the organizers of the Men in Dance: Bridging the Gap symposium held at West Virginia University, June 29 through July 1, 2017, hosted by NDEO as part of its Special Topics Conference Program.

This symposium, the first event of its kind to focus on issues affecting boys and men in dance and dance education, comprised the keynote, presentations, panels, workshops, and technique classes in the following areas: Masculinities; What Teachers Need to Know; Professional Dancers; Media, Culture, Socialization; and Developing Resources. The symposium's opening event, "What Young Male Dancers Tell Us," included Dr. Doug Risner's keynote presentation along with film director and producer Scott Gormley's screening of his new documentary film, *DANSEUR*, which focuses on young, male ballet dancers. The final day of the symposium included full-group sessions for identifying and summarizing themes, as well as brainstorming and planning for the future. Symposium organizers committed to the long-term sustainability of the conversation beyond this event. The Men in Dance SIG and its Online Forum will continue as integral parts of ongoing efforts, resource sharing, and gender equity advancements.

KEYNOTE ADDRESS

GENDER INEQUITIES IN DANCE EDUCATION: ASKING NEW QUESTIONS

Doug Risner

We gather this weekend at the first symposium focusing on males in dance as a lifelong vocation. The organizers invited dance educators of all genders who want to share their teaching experiences of boys and men. While contemplating the overall status of males in dance, this symposium, as the call for papers stated, "seeks pragmatic solutions to address the dearth of male dancers in our studios, schools, and companies as students, professionals, and educators." As part of NDEO's campaign, Decade of Dance Education 2015–2025, addressing gender equity is a primary goal. The Men in Dance symposium plays an important role for addressing gender equality in the dance classroom, rehearsal studio, concert stage, school, and community. Presenters and panelists over the next two days will take us on journeys through their scholarly and applied investigations on male presence, participation, transcendence, and the expectations of those who educate and train boys and young males. The vision and significance of this symposium is certainly not wasted on the impressive audience gathered here.

Like many of you, I can only begin to imagine the discussions and conversations that will happen here, the new colleagues and friendships we'll develop, and the important networks and partnerships that will emerge out of this meeting. Thank you to the Men in Dance Special Interest Group, especially the organizers, Yoav Kaddar, Barry Blumenfeld, Andrew Jannetti, and Christopher Rutt. Thank you very much for this invitation.

Let me begin with one of the many gender assumptions held by both female and male dance educators: Dance needs more male students. As I wrote in my recent book, *Dance and Gender: An Evidence-Based Approach* (Risner and Musil 2017):

This hegemonic assumption— broadly accepted and rarely questioned—has fueled popular and scholarly discourses since the academic "dance boom" of the 1970s. Based largely on heterocentrism [seeing all the world as heterosexual] and influenced heavily by the professional dance world, the obsession for attracting and retaining male students, often at the expense of highly skilled females, may ultimately contribute to significant gender inequities and biases. Even if we believe more male students would benefit our dance programs, we must at some point ask, "How many males is 'enough'?" And "what and who are we willing to sacrifice to achieve this goal?" (182)

You're probably thinking to yourself, "Wait, what? What did he just say?"

"Wait, what?" is actually a very effective way of asking for clarification, which is crucial to understanding. It's a question you should ask before drawing a conclusion and before making a decision. It's another way of saying that it's important that you understand an idea before you advocate for it, or against it. I start with it here to make sure everyone's listening, and to emphasize that we need to begin asking new questions about gender inequity in dance education.

As a dance sociologist, I study people, places, and their relationships to one another in dance education and training. When I began researching dance in 1988, little was known about how dancers experienced their education and training, and how they made sense of it. This puzzled me. Why wouldn't this knowledge be important for a field so heavily reliant on human beings, bodies, and expressions? Therefore, my earliest research explored dancers in the rehearsal process looking at the meaning student dancers made of dancing with other dancers (Risner 1992), their relationships with choreographers (Risner 1995), and then later how they learn choreography and often contribute to the choreographic process (Risner 2000). What I found was that learning choreography was far more than simply learning steps, movement, and remembering their organization.

No, dancers were more than finely tuned machines. They brought not only their bodies, but equally agile and flexible minds. Their relationships to one another in rehearsal were just as important to them as learning the dance or understanding the choreographer's process. My findings also showed that the rehearsal process itself was built largely on a faith commitment in which dancers enter the studio on the first day of rehearsal with the firm commitment that a new work will be created, and set of promises to the choreographer and other dancers with whom they dance that a work will be created. This research made me want to learn more about how students pursuing professional careers understand their experiences as dancers and how they make meaning of their lives. By the late 1990s, I began studying gender in Western theatrical dance because its form and content bring up so many social issues and challenging questions about gender, masculinity, and sexual identity (Risner 2002a, 2002b, 2003).

For example, what is it about Western theatrical dance, that when performed by a male, causes such anxiety and discomfort for some men? Especially for the dancing boy's father, brother, and other male extended family? How do young boys and male adolescents pursuing professional careers in theatrical dance experience their lives in an arts discipline populated primarily by girls and women? Where do they look for role models and mentors in a feminized profession? What is it about dancing that gives boys the most satisfaction and meaning? Who supports boys' dancing and dance study most?

From my three books, seven book chapters, twelve articles, and twenty years later, I come together with all of you knowing more about boys and young male dancers than ever before. Studies about dance and masculinity, sexual identity,

Scott Gormley, Producer and Director, *Danseur* (Left). Dr. Doug Risner, Distinguished Professor, Wayne State University, Keynote Presenter (Right).

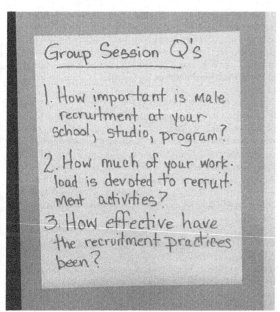

Example of questions explored in one session.

homophobia, and bullying and harassment over the past two decades have significantly changed how we understand males in dance (Risner 2014). In fact, the 2000s could be called the Decade of Males in dance research. Groundbreaking books were published by leading gender and dance scholars: Michael Gard's (2006) *Men Who Dance: Aesthetics, Athletics and the Art of Masculinity* in Australia, Kai Lehikoinen's (2006) *Stepping Queerly? Discourses in Dance Education for Boys in Late 20th-Century* in Finland, and Doug Risner's (2009) *Stigma and Perseverance in the Lives of Boys Who Dance* in the United States, paving the way for male adolescents and young adults to read stories about themselves they had never heard before, paving the way for parents and guardians to read about their dancing boy's challenges and needs like never before, and paving the way for graduate students to focus their master's and doctoral studies on dancing boys and men. New research on males in dance became far more commonplace as journal articles and book chapters. For example, Jennifer Fisher and Anthony Shay's (2009) edited volume, *When Men Dance: Masculinities Across Borders*, gave us a richly diverse anthology that challenged homogeneous notions of boys and men who dance: Taken together, this research clearly shows us that there is no one fixed, uniform male dancer or male student of dance. This, my colleagues, is the first takeaway for us tonight.

Case in point: A good deal of research findings on young males in Western concert dance training differ significantly from young males who participate in dance in general and physical education, as well as in elective dance courses. Zihao Li (2016) reported, in his monograph (adapted doctoral dissertation) of high school boys, that the most prevalent reason for boys taking dance was to "avoid gym class" (80). In contrast, the majority of males age twelve to twenty-four in my 2009 study of preprofessional and university programs, found that males' primary reason for dancing was they "like to perform" (Risner 2009, 114). At the other end of the spectrum, some dance forms are highly masculinized. For example, street dance attracts far more males than females. Of course, in non-Western dance, males perform in numerous traditional dance forms, many reserved solely for boys and men. So when we speak about "what we know about boys and dance" we have to carefully undo any assumptions we have that there is one uniform male dance student. Boys who dance, dance for different reasons and purposes. What's more, boys and males dance diverse dance forms and genres. From hip hop to hula, ballet to tap, clogging to cha-cha, male social status, privilege, and marginalization vary widely across the globe.

For example, another dominant assumption that many in our discipline have held for a long time is that if we just make dance more like sports, more boys will be open to taking dance—or some version of the "dance is like sports" recruitment strategy. Although this approach might work for some boys in general education or elective courses—like some of the twelve boys in Li's study—unfortunately, these attempts to masculinize dance do not work for the overwhelming majority of boys studying Western theatrical dance like ballet, jazz, and modern. Many of these adolescent boys become frustrated with these efforts (Holdsworth 2013), believing that "Dance is nothing like sports, and male dancers know it" (Risner 2009, 148).

In fact, in the same study (Risner 2009), when asked to complete the sentence, "I think more boys would study dance if ...," only 8 percent of participants in my survey of male adolescents and young adults selected the statement, "if teachers made dance more like sports" (108). The top two selected completions were "if boys weren't teased and harassed so much about dancing" (85 percent) and "if parents were more supportive and encouraging" (72 percent) (108). Interestingly, less than half answered "if there were more male dance teachers (40 percent) (108). But again, we are—to some degree here—comparing apples and oranges. Recruiting boys in middle and high schools needs different strategies than recruiting boys into preprofessional schools, studios, and university programs. Or for some boys, maybe we're comparing oranges and tangerines (e.g., there might be some overlap in boys' attraction to dance).

As we begin this symposium and address its call to "seek pragmatic solutions to address the dearth of male dancers in our schools, studios, schools, and companies," we know clearly that boys dance for different reasons and they do so across diverse dance genres and dance education sectors. The second takeaway for your thinking this weekend is to learn more about males in dance by making a commitment to learning from the males in our own programs, schools, and studios. The experiences of these boys and young men are likely your most effective way to informally research why boys dance in your particular setting and location. By doing some informal research each year, everyone can learn a tremendous amount from their male students—why they dance, what dance means in their lives, and why they continue dancing. I'll speak more about this a little later when I discuss opportunities for the future.

Since the 1970s, another dominant assumption about increasing male participation in theatrical concert dance has been that we need to increase the number of male dance teachers and dance faculty to attract male students. However, my recently published research with Pam Musil from Brigham Young University indicates that is no longer the case (Risner and Musil 2017). Although the percentage of male faculty in postsecondary dance has remained relatively unchanged over the past two decades—37 percent in 1994, 34 percent in 2014—the number of male dance majors has steadily increased from 8 percent in 1994 to 14 percent in 2014; this is a 75 percent gain (Risner and Musil 2017, 158, 182).

Although research indicates that young males (age twelve to twenty-four) believe having more male faculty role models in dance is essential (Risner 2009), it appears that the current 34 percent might be sufficient; that is, the male dance major population has increased significantly as male faculty numbers have declined slightly over the last twenty years (37 percent to 34 percent). At least in higher education, the number of male dance faculty doesn't appear to have an impact on increasing male dance students, as long as male dance faculty remain around 35 percent of the total dance faculty. It seems that if we keep doing what we have been doing, based on historical data, we will likely get to 30 percent male participation in another seventeen years, or by 2035.

What's more, the majority of males age twelve to twenty-four say that it doesn't matter if they study dance with a male or female teacher. Although nearly half of them reported the importance of male role models, over two thirds of the participants reported that having a male dance instructor had no positive effect or a slightly negative effect on their dance study. The seeming conflict between these two statements appears to indicate that these adolescent boys and young males do not necessarily view their male teachers as role models.

One of the most ignored findings of my research has been that what attracts boys and young males to pursue dance professional training is very similar to what attracts girls and females to dance. These common elements are (1) they like to perform, (2) dance is the place they can creatively express themselves, and (3) the physicality of dance. The third piece, physicality, is somewhat more prominent for male attraction to dance. My researcher self wants to know why

A movement session. Photo: Barry Blumenfeld.

Group photograph of attendees.

this finding would be ignored. Why would those who are interested in boys dancing hold on to gender differences in dance even when research shows they don't exist? For our purposes here, how can we use this information—that males and females are more similar in terms of their attraction to dance, than they are different? How can this research-based knowledge help us shape more effective recruitment and retention practices for males and females?

The third takeaway I offer is that I am convinced that it's time for dance educators to start asking new questions about gender equity. We have been asking the same "how do we attract more boys" questions for more than forty years. I hope this symposium will to allow us to collectively turn the page in this respect. I look forward to hearing new questions and discussing fresh lines of inquiry about all genders and dance.

It is in asking new, more inclusive questions that we have the opportunity to couple renewed interest with recent momentum for greater gender equity in dance education and training. Some questions to get everyone started might be the following:

- How does my own teaching promote gender equity for both boys and girls?
- What can I learn about gender inequities from both boys and girls in my school, studio, or program?
- How does my program, studio, or school address gender equity in curriculum and policy?
- How do "millennial" moms, dads, and guardians encourage or discourage their child's dancing? What can parents, guardians, and caregivers do to support gender equity initiatives? How can they become involved?
- Knowing that adolescent boys and young males report the most significant person supporting their dancing is their favorite dance teacher, followed by their dance school director, and then their mother, how can you develop or supplement your role?

I also encourage everyone to spend some time during this symposium weekend on creating a culture of gender equity in dance education. For example:

- How is a culture of gender equity cultivated and nurtured in my classroom, school, or program?
- Who are important stakeholders in a gender equitable culture?
- How does my own informal research contribute to building a culture of gender equity? With whom might I partner within my school, program, and community?
- What professional contacts and relationships can I make during this symposium?

In closing let me say thank you to the organizers again: Barry Blumenfeld, Andrew Jannetti, Yoav Kaddar, and Christopher Rutt. To attendees, I hope to meet each one of you here at this symposium. Finally, when you return home, please take time to reflect on your experiences here and then take every opportunity you can for advancing gender equity in dance education.

SUMMARY OF THE MEN IN DANCE SYMPOSIUM

Barry Blumenfeld, Andrew Jannetti, Yoav Kaddar, and Christopher Rutt

Overall the symposium was a success, with a total of thirteen presentations that comprised movement-based sessions, panel discussions, and papers. The majority of the presentations focused on theory, personal reflections, and anecdotes. A few addressed best practices and useful information of what works in the field. Many presenters were presenting for the first time.

Feedback indicated that the participants found the symposium to be empowering and inspiring in terms of dealing with the challenges this overall topic presents. Participants voiced that having the symposium was a start of something new, a "tipping point" in solving these longtime issues. For many, the networking alone was a great benefit, knowing that they are not alone in contending with these matters. The longtime issues and challenges on the topic surfaced throughout the various sessions.

One of the main intentions behind this gathering was to come away from the symposium with some type of action plan. To that end, the final session brought all the participants together for a wrap-up discussion to do just that. The big takeaways were the need for a web-based resource clearinghouse and a larger conference on the topic in the future. The web resource page would hopefully cover a range of topics and offer both tools and networking opportunities. Some suggestions were that it include a registry to help find other educators who are succeeding in similar teaching environments, links to research in the field, information on college programs and resources for parents, as well as advice on how to talk to parents about dance training and careers.

As for future conferences, the hope is that an international conference in the next two to three years could be produced to share information with other cultures. It was also suggested that such a conference involve both students and teachers, and, perhaps, offer sessions for parents as well.

As we look ahead to such future events and gatherings, here are some questions to continue the conversation:

- How do we take this to the next level?
- What might that look like in terms of empowering educators, parents, administrators, and students?
- How might an international event be structured and what value might it bring to the discussion?

One key benefit of an event like this is that there were many issues and subtopics related to the title of the symposium that came up that probably would not have surfaced at a more general dance conference. The topic needs to continue to "live" and be promoted through social media, online forums, NDEO membership, and during the annual NDEO conferences. The challenges of Men in Dance and Dance Education bring up many issues that range from social ideas of masculinity, gender identity, misogyny, social status, and marketability to viable means of income. As we move forward toward an international conference, these inequities and identifications in the field of dance need to continue to be explored to create viable actionable outcomes.

REFERENCES

Fisher, J., and A. Shay. 2009. *When men dance: Masculinities across borders.* New York, NY: Oxford University Press.

Gard, M. 2006. *Men who dance: Aesthetics, athletics and the art of masculinity.* New York, NY: Peter Lang.

Holdsworth, N. 2013. "Boys don't do dance, do they?" *Research in Drama Education* 18(2):168–78.

Lehikoinen, K. 2006. *Stepping queerly? Discourses in dance education for boys in late 20th-century.* Oxford, UK: Peter Lang.

Li, Z. 2016. *Dancing boys: High school males in dance.* Toronto, Canada: University of Toronto Press.

Risner, D. 1992. Exploring dance rehearsal: The neglected issues revealed. *Journal of Physical Education, Recreation & Dance* 63(6):61–66.

———. 1995. Voices seldom heard: The dancer's experience of the choreographic process. *Impulse: The International Journal of Dance Science, Medicine, and Education* 3(2):76–85.

———. 2000. Making dance, making sense: Epistemology and choreography. *Research in Dance Education* 1(2):156–72.

———. 2002a. Male participation and sexual orientation in dance education: Revisiting the open secret. *Journal of Dance Education* 2(3):84–92.

———. 2002b. Re-educating dance education to its homosexuality: An invitation for critical analysis and professional unification. *Research in Dance Education* 3(2):181–87.

———. 2003. Rehearsing heterosexuality: Unspoken truths in dance education. *Dance Research Journal* 34(2):63–81.

———. 2009. *Stigma and perseverance in the lives of boys who dance: An empirical study of male identities in western theatrical dance training.* Lewiston, NY: Mellen.

———. 2014. Bullying victimization and social support of adolescent male dance students: An analysis of findings. *Research in Dance Education* 15(2):179–201.

Risner, D., and P. Musil. 2017. Leadership and gender in postsecondary dance: An exploratory survey of dance administrators in the United States. In *Dance and gender: An evidence-based approach*, ed. W. Oliver and D. Risner, pp. 159–183. Gainesville, FL: University Press of Florida.

Part V
Reflective Practice, Social Justice, and Humanizing Dance Pedagogy

Prelude

"A critical aim of humanizing pedagogy (Jennifer, 2020)—a theory and practice of teaching focused on becoming—is the individual and collective generation of visions of themselves (teachers) and others (students). Becoming more human requires actively examining the tensions inherent in asymmetrical power differentials between dance teachers and students. The aim here is not to disguise, ignore, or mask teacher–student or student–teacher power differences, but instead to critically deconstruct these power structures in order to transform relations of power, and then, to transform the selves that teachers become with their students in the dance studio and classroom. A dance classroom 'that is constantly becoming in the Freirean sense, models humanizing pedagogy, balances relations of power, openly examines tensions, and welcomes complex problems to solve communally.'" (Risner and Schupp, 2020, p. 172)

Doug Risner: I elected to conclude this collected volume with articles whose content and aims typify some of my most fervent commitments to research and scholarship, my obligations as a dance educator and scholar over the past four decades, and the vision I have proposed for a more humanizing dance pedagogy. Its implementation in all sectors of dance education and training along with the multiple and attendant implications and required re-thinking and reconsideration would be the culmination of my life in motion.

Each of these chapters illustrate the arc and growth in my thinking and the inevitable transitions that accompany a career over time. I offer these considerations for future dance educators and researchers who may be contemplating or experiencing the same. As an example, I vividly remember my interview for a well-regarded doctoral program in dance in 1997. After I shared my published research on the rehearsal process and how I, as choreographer and pedagogue, had become invested in researching dancers' experiences of the rehearsal process and collaborative dance making (see chapters in section one for this initial research). Without any hesitation, the PhD program director said that would not be possible. Rather, I would need to focus on choreographies of accomplished, esteemed choreographers of repute, not my own choreographies and the student dancers' experiences of rehearsing and dance making. With all due respect for the work the program has and continues to produce, I remember gently closing my portfolio while nodding accordingly and then exited the interview with a polite "thank you, I am no longer interested in the doctoral program here."

What stands out to me most about this interview experience for a doctoral program is that many graduate programs in dance, especially those culminating in a doctorate, aren't necessarily or even interested in what a prospective doctoral student actually wants to learn or learn much more about. However, and regardless, I have stayed the course I charted, and

I believe I am better for it, as are the readers and scholars who have frequently cited my publications.

I ended up taking my PhD in Curriculum and Teaching at UNC Greensboro (UNCG), whose doctoral faculty in education and dance fully embraced my academic desires and aspirations. At UNCG I was strongly encouraged to dig deeply into what I found most compelling and in need of revision and rethinking for myself and the field of dance education. Therefore, I am grateful to the leadership, guidance, and mentorship of Dr. David Purpel, Dr. Susan W. Stinson, Dr. Svi Shapiro, Dr. Kathleen Casey, and Dr. Jan Van Dyke, all of whom supported the questions I was asking, searching, and researching about education generally and dance education specifically. Their fervent interest in and dedicated commitment to the research I was compelled and determined to pursue gave me not only strength and perseverance to do so but also to instill this commitment to the undergraduate and graduate students I advise and mentor.

JM: Early in his career, Doug was drawn to teaching and studying how to teach because he had struggled under teachers who repeated traditional, authoritarian, banking-method, teacher-centered dance pedagogies that focused on deficits—everything that was wrong with a student's dancing. I had also lived and labored in that reality as a student and professional dancer, and even later, as I began teaching, I found myself falling into those rhythms. Doug's constant push to find and develop ways of engaging in education practices that significantly counteracted the deficiency model was the radical idea I encountered in the pedagogy course I took with him through the National Dance Education Organization.

What kind of teacher do you want to become? And what does it mean to be responsible for someone else's learning? Contemplating these two questions becomes so much more than an inquiry into the steps and the catalogue of knowledge that is shared in a learning exchange; it becomes an ongoing investigation of morality, ethical decision-making, and priorities—both for the person who is in the role of teacher and for those in the role of students. And this, then, is what begins to shift, incrementally, the field, inviting dialogue about what really matters.

Based on those two questions, Doug has spent the last two decades or so, considering and articulating what it might mean to humanize dance pedagogy. Unfortunately, there are still those who cling to, espouse, and reassert the same kinds of deficit models they suffered under and lived through in their own dance training, including pre-professional training programs, commercial dance study, and conservatory training; they dismiss holistic and humanizing approaches to dance teaching and education as too soft, not rigorous enough, or inefficient (and efficiency itself is tied to the practice of slavery); a way of "producing" dancers—which, then, circles back to Doug's earlier inquiry into the tendency to value production over co-learning, particularly in dance education practices. If there are positive lessons that can be gleaned from the COVID pandemic, however, they may include the dual focus on the importance of the mental health and well-being of both students *and teachers:* and perhaps this is where the conversation shifts to see possibility for both/and to exist. Humanizing the way that we teach does not erase or minimize our own experiences as students, professionals, or teachers in other, less compassionate, less functional settings, but nor does it continue to glamorize the flamboyant stories of abuse that permeate the dance field and that are seen as badges of honor amongst those who survived them.

But change is happening. Many dance programs, schools, and conservatories are moving away from de-humanizing pedagogies and teaching methods, and as they do so in the interest of the students' mental and physical health, the conversations around teachers' health are also bubbling to the surface, thankfully.

Doug's commitment to being outdoors and away from screens is the site of his converging interests in the well-being of those inside the studio/educational institution and his own determination to live a good death. When I found out that he walks three to five miles a day, weather permitting, and maintains the outdoor courtyards at his home, I was inspired to start my own journey to meet the fullness of all facets of this thing I know as my life. And being outdoors, walking, breathing, has had a marked impact on my work in the studio: I notice what I pay attention to. I notice what I don't attend to. I notice the cadence, the rhythm, the ebb and flow, the sunrises, and the sunsets—and these gentle fluctuations inform my teaching, the right relationships I cultivate, the shifts I lean into. As Doug notes, this kind of reflexivity requires curiosity, introspection, and honest dialogue with yourself and others, and when you embark on this journey, you also start to identify what is it you want to know, to learn more about, that others in your field need or deserve to know. Your work and your research become inexorably intertwined, both socially relevant and personally resonant: the space between potter and clay, once more.

DR: Published 20 years ago, Chapter 15, "Motion and Marking in Reflective Practice: Artifacts, Autobiographical Narrative, and Sexuality" (2002), was the first time I outed myself as queer in a research publication. Completed during my third year of doctoral study, it was a period when I realized how much I missed being in the dance studio privately—from warming up my body for teaching a dance technique course to creating movement and movement scores, and how to mesh, combine, situate my doctoral study (narratives of the self, sexual identity, and reflective practice) alongside such. From the abstract, I wrote:

> "The paper extends and develops the notion of reassembling 'artifacts' from Watson and Wilcox (2000), in order to expand the possibilities for enlarging methods of reflection. Two forms of artifact are presented: visual illustration and movement vignette. Re-collecting and reading these artifacts, allows the personal history stored in the body, as well as the body's contemporaneous knowledge to become more accessible for examination, dialogue, and reflection. In a dialectic relationship with narrative writing, an example is presented of this reflective model that mines one's impulses for motion and stillness, movement and marking. Drawing upon the researcher's larger concerns, the paper concludes with a critical discussion of autobiographical inquiry and sexuality, heterocentric value systems, and reflective practitioners' ability to exhume the 'taken for granted' oppressions suffered in the world." (Risner, 2002)

A decade later I co-authored Chapter 16, "Moving Social Justice in Dance Pedagogy: Possibilities, Fears and Challenges" (2010), with esteemed dance education researcher and my mentor, Dr. Sue Stinson; the article was published well before recent calls from the Black Lives Matter movement brought forward issues of diversity, equity, and inclusion (DEI) in dance and dance education. Developed from a series of our recorded conversations as dance educators and former administrators in higher education, we carefully examined the history of multiculturalism, multicultural practices in postsecondary dance, their influences on dance teacher education, and the limitations of the multiculturalism movement that emerged from misperceptions about or disregard for differences in culture, gender, ability, ethnicity, and socioeconomic background. We took our charge as prophetic voices for social justice teaching and learning and provided examples of pedagogical approaches and project assignments that aimed to bring social justice learning to the dance education classroom and studio in concrete ways.

Chapter 17, "Activities for Humanizing Dance Pedagogy: Immersive Learning in Practice" (2021), was developed from the edited volume, *Ethical Dilemmas in Dance Education: Case Studies on Dance Education* (Risner and Schupp, 2020), which received both the 2021 NDEO | Ruth Lovell Murray Book Award and 2021 Susan W. Stinson Book Award for Dance Education. This chapter was originally published in *Journal of Dance Education*—a decade after Chapter 16—thereby giving this concluding section of *Dancing Mind, Minding Dance* a three-decade retrospective of my teaching and research emphasizing reflective praxis, social justice, and humanizing dance pedagogies. This chapter seeks to counterbalance the field's current "best practice" dominant paradigm—its "teacher-proof" curriculum, standardization, and methods-centric teacher preparation. I have long been critical of widely accepted "best practice" methods (Barr and Risner 2014; Risner and Barr 2015; Risner and Schupp 2020), which until recently have remained largely unquestioned and under examined—best practices for whom and in what cultural contexts? The best practices movement far too often occurs without examining teachers' own assumptions, values, and beliefs and how this ideological posture informs, often unconsciously, their perceptions and actions when working with politically, socially, and economically subordinated students.

JM: To return to Doug's original questions—What really matters? What am I paying attention to? And what does it mean to be responsible for someone else's learning? Training ourselves to notice what is, what occurs, and what bubbles up in the spaces in between, we begin to understand the focus of distance that allows us to be a part of, and perhaps even locates us in, the ongoingness[1] of a life in dance. This location, however integral to our own being, must necessarily touch and include the margins, the spaces that encourage us to see possibility. Like dance can be understood in terms of negative space (what is between bodies) and intimations (what is not explicit), possibility and potential are found in negative capability—the grace to not have the answers. And when we allow for that weight to be lifted, we find that our minds become ever more nimble, curious, and full of wonder. Doug's journey in dance and life has been marked by patient quicksilver and the shapeshifting, mercurial quality of rehearsing iterations of himself, of sensing both the restfulness and restlessness of otherness, of vacillating between center and margin, between potter and clay, of being porous, of living into a good death (Risner, 2022) while learning how to love and be loved. As he recently noted in *Dancing Across the Lifespan: Negotiating Age, Place and Purpose* (Musil, Risner, and Schupp, 2022):

> As I reflect upon living while dying over the past 61 months, I am increasingly convinced that a life in dance uniquely prepares me, not only for living with a terminal disease, but also for, in Marcy Westerling's (2014) words, dying a "good death." The preparedness I describe comes from experiencing a number of "deaths" or expiration dates over my career span as a performer, choreographer, and technique teacher— each demi-death different in what is lost and what is left. Telling the ensuing expiration stories, I suggest how dancing, living, and dying intertwine throughout the dancer's career and lifespan, which taken together can make for a fulfilling life leading to a "good death." (Risner, 2022, p. 243)

In a field that often has not prioritized the human, relying instead on spectacle, he has urged generations of dancers, dance makers, and dance educators to consider the consequences of their words and actions as only a starting point. He has asked rooms full of strangers what really mattered, continuing the threads of the conversation. He has contemplated what was unseen, unheard, or unexamined. He has considered what it might mean to be responsible for someone else's learning and has shared those moments of uneasy unknowing with us. Without challenging his own assumptions and experiences, he never could have taken the steps to bring the center and the margin into proximity with one another (Risner, 2001), such that they felt that orbiting space between them and entered into "right relationship" (Heyward, 1989) with each other. Dancing and knowing from the inside out means also knowing and dancing from outside to inside—it means marking, rehearsing, noticing, and attending to motion, to thought, to reflexivity in the ongoing practice.

> When we take seriously the enormous responsibility for someone else's learning, which I believe we do, and if we accept the charge for developing cultural understanding, which I believe we should, then our students deserve a far wider comprehension of the politics of dance and its cultural and social meanings. Dance pedagogy that addresses marginalization, privilege, prejudice, equity, and social justice is, then, both our greatest challenge and what I believe is worth knowing. But I wonder if we have the collective energies and commitment to see and teach dance pedagogy coursework through a larger social lens. (Risner, 2010a, p. 206)

The manifestation of this work is the dance that Doug Risner created between mind and body, between life and art, between center and margin, and between potter and clay, always weaving in and through the possibilities. A dancing mind minding the dance, indeed.

Note

1 With thanks to Sarah Manguso for this lovely term, the title of one of her richly evocative memoirs (Manguso, 2015).

References

Barr, S., & Risner, D. (2014). Weaving social foundations through dance pedagogy: A pedagogy of uncovering. *Journal of Dance Education, 14*(4), 136–145. DOI: 10.1080/15290824.2014.934985

Heyward, C. (1989) *Touching our strength: The erotic as power and the love of god.* Harper & Row.

Manguso, S. (2015). *Ongoingness.* Graywolf Press.

Musil, P., Risner, D., & Schupp, K. (2022). *Dancing across the lifespan: Negotiating age, place and purpose.* Palgrave MacMillan.

Risner, D. (2001). *Blurring the boundaries: Hope and possibility in the presence of the necessary stranger in gay liberation.* (UMI No. 3008895) [Doctoral dissertation, University of North Carolina at Greensboro]. ProQuest.

Risner, D. (2002). Motion and marking in reflective practice: Artifacts, autobiographical narrative, and sexuality. *Reflective Practice, 3*(1): 5–19. DOI: 10.1080/14623940220129843

Risner, D. (2010a). *Challenges and opportunities for dance pedagogy: Critical social issues and "unlearning" how to teach.* In T. Randall (Ed.), Global Perspectives on Dance: Research and Pedagogy, Conference Proceedings of the Congress on Research in Dance, pp. 204–209. Leicester, U.K. June 2009. DOI: 10.1017/S2049125500001114

Risner, D. (2022). Narratives on dancing and expiring: An "end of life" autoethnographic essay. In P. Musil, D. Risner, & K. Schupp (Eds.), *Dancing across the lifespan: Negotiating age, place and purpose* (pp. 243–264). Palgrave MacMillan.

Risner, D. & Barr, S. (2015). Troubling methods-centric "teacher production": Social foundations in dance education teacher preparation. *Arts Education Policy Review, 116*(2), 78–91. DOI:10.1080/10632913.2014.944965

Risner, D. & Schupp, K. (2020). *Ethical dilemmas in dance education: Case studies on humanizing dance pedagogy.* McFarland & Company, Inc.

Watson, J. S., & Wilcox, S. (2000). Reading for understanding: Methods of reflecting on practice. *Reflective Practice, 1*(1), 57–67. DOI: 10.1080/713693127

Westerling, M. (2014, October 24). *What I learned about living from dying of cancer.* Yes! Magazine: Solutions Journalism. https://www.yesmagazine.org/issue/poverty/2014/10/24/livingly-dying

Motion and Marking in Reflective Practice: Artifacts, Autobiographical Narrative, and Sexuality

Doug Risner

ABSTRACT This paper introduces a reflective methodology of the body as a resource for reflective practice based on an analysis of my personal response and experience of autobiographical narrative. It offers an approach in which the movements and markings of the body serve as important sites for collecting additional evidence of the daily practices that shape our lives. The paper extends and develops the notion of reassembling 'artifacts' from Watson and Wilcox (2000), in order to expand the possibilities for enlarging methods of reflection. Two forms of artifact are presented: visual illustration and movement vignette. Re-collecting and reading these artifacts, allows the personal history stored in the body, as well as the body's contemporaneous knowledge to become more accessible for examination, dialogue and reflection. In a dialectic relationship with narrative writing, an example is presented of this reflective model that mines one's impulses for motion and stillness, movement and marking. Drawing upon the researcher's larger concerns, the paper concludes with a critical discussion of autobiographical inquiry and sexuality, heterocentric value systems, and reflective practitioners' ability to exhume the 'taken for granted' oppressions suffered in the world.

INTRODUCTION

Reflective practice at its root is about understanding and meaning, both collectively and individually. Learning to reflect involves asking challenging questions about ordinary moments in our lives, both past and present. Beyond re-telling of a story or recollection of a particular experience, reflective practice consciously and in a learning way allows us to "catch ourselves in the act" of living in the world (Watson & Wilcox, 2000, p. 58). By understanding our actions and the meanings that result from these actions, we gain greater insight, grapple with our intentions, wrestle with our own practice and raise further questions.

This paper, rooted in my reflective experiences as a dancer, choreographer and educator, presents a model that integrates autobiographical narrative, reflective practice, and critical theory. This model emerges from a larger attempt to illuminate the reconciliatory powers of understanding diversity, (in this case sexual orientation) and unification as inescapably connected. Although my experience in dance illustrates these tensions and ambiguities from a particular perspective, dance, in this context, is merely emblematic for understanding larger human concerns.

The background of this research seeks to unpack questions of identity and sexuality. To do so, often brings about fragile and complicated circumstances of working with human problems and conditions. Which is to say, there is an inherent difficulty in exploring other realms of sexual possibility within a dominant US culture that views heterosexuality and homosexuality as polarized, fixed and diametrically opposed identities. Reflective practice can enflesh these often muddled conditions because its aim is not absolute certainty, statistical predictability, or law-like, fixed solutions, but rather reflective practice focuses on understanding the complexity and richness of human experience and action.

Confronting issues of sexuality, identity, and homophobia in the mainstream is often confounded by the blindness with which the American public frequently turns its head away from unstable ambivalent issues. The "slimyness" of ambivalence[1] in this instance, both the ways in which homosexuality blurs culturally normative boundaries and more specifically, an understanding of fluctuating sexuality on an often shifting continuum, challenges dominant heterosexuality to be re-thought and reconsidered, as painful and profound as it may be. In order to confront these issues through reflective practice, this paper offers an approach in which the body serves as an important site for collecting additional evidence of our daily motions and markings that shape our lives. These visual and movement artifacts flesh out more of our biographies, our personal histories stored in the body, and the body's contemporaneous concerns as well.

Before discussing in greater detail these guiding research orientations, it is helpful at this juncture to elaborate briefly upon the methodological assumptions at work in this type of critical narrative and the ways in which these methods similarly overlap the ways in which I search for meaning and understanding.

For my purposes, methodology and meaning are intricately linked to making sense of the world and my political practice within it. Having said that, I am also compelled to confess that an attempt to fully articulate my research methodology may inevitably trivialise, or at best may minimize what I consider to be the complex, mysterious connection between my daily encounters, relationships, and experiences in the world with my research, writing, and teaching. This methodology is not one particular, discrete methodology, but rather a composite, or spiralling combination of inquiry traditions which attempts to synthesize both the experiential and theoretical worlds, intentionally capturing stories and intentionally reading them (Watson & Wilcox, 2000, p. 60). Readers should understand that the intimately interwoven nature of this personal inquiry makes telling it from the 'outside' especially prohibitive.

Additionally, as a word of caution, it is important for readers to understand that systematically mining one's own "taken-for-granted" story, although intensely profound, is often deeply painful, sometimes producing anger, hostility, embarrassment and shame. I reassure readers that re-reading these intimate life accounts is necessary, beneficial and cathartic, both personally and professionally.

DOING AUTOBIOGRAPHY

I want to make clear that I understand the nature of autobiographical research broadly, in diverse manifestations and in multiple modes of inquiry. The autobiographical material in this paper arises from first looking, then looking again at familiar experiences, daily encounters which accumulate and constitute the days of my life. *Looking*, in this particular instance, means a spiralling assemblage of word, picture, movement, text, illustration and image. In the hermeneutic tradition, these biographical experiences are repositioned as significant narratives for illuminating theory and informing action. I understand the hermeneutic circle as multi-dimensional, a spiral rather than a circle. This helical structure allows one's personal biography to stand as a central pole, a cylinder around which one's reflections and questions wind—gradually, yet simultaneously receding from and drawing near. Advancing and retreating in a methodological coil enables an intimate exploration of the nature of the individual experience of the public realm, much like Pinar's (1978) notion of *currere* (from the Latin root of the word, 'curriculum'), going underneath our exterior critically.

Mining our interiority importantly guards against the inclination to allow the theoretical to overwhelm or extinguish the personal. At the same time, probing one's own historical and daily data, helps one understand the ways in which what one sees "out there" is lived "in here" in our bodies, minds and practices (Kincheloe, 1998, p. 130). Although Pinar developed his work focused on *currere* during the 1970s in the US, it is well worth reconsideration at this time.

Kincheloe (1998) reminds us that *currere* is a verb and literally translated means running the race course (p. 129). Historically, the word has been reduced to its noun form, the track. Slattery (1995) reiterates the significance of the active process in *currere*, rather than an emphasis on product. This notion of action is particularly important when considering autobiographical narrative, as well as the larger work at hand. Slattery summarizes the importantly contemporaneous nature of a reconstituted post-modern[2] *currere* and the necessity of first, probing one's autobiographical narrative, and second, critically going beneath one's exteriority, in order to facilitate "the journey of becoming a self-aware subject capable of shaping his or her life path" (Kincheloe, 1998, p. 130).

Turning to Pinar's (1988) later work concerning autobiographical method is particularly applicable. According to Pinar, the obstacles imposed by performing roles inauthentic to one's homosexual lived experience in public heterosexist spheres, reveal the significance and purpose of the autobiographical voice:

> Our life histories are not liabilities to be exorcised but are the very precondition for knowing. It is our individual and collective stories in which present projects are situated, and it is awareness of these stories which is the lamp illuminating the dark spots, the rough edges. (p. 148)

I have already indicated the necessity of the intimate nature of telling one's story, its profundity, its pain. Reflecting upon one's "dark spots," as difficult as it may be, allows one to shape one's own practice and life journey. Without deeply inspecting one's "rough edges," one's life appears all too smooth—seemingly unchangeable, fixed and paralyzed.

Much of the exteriority, or what is "out there" in this paper is the realm of professional dance and dance education, but only and importantly, as the pictorial background. The foreground depicts larger social issues, issues that emerge from, and in some cases, are illustrated by oppressive mechanisms operating within the field of dance. The 'in here' of this work re-examines, in the present, memories and recollections from my earliest experiences of dance, family, sexuality and fatherhood. It is offered not as a self-indulgent, personal memoir, but as a means for illuminating a greater collective understanding of what it means to be a part of a diverse and loving humanity.

DOING REFLECTIVE PRACTICE

The questions for the reflective practitioner at their most radical are: What do/did I do? Why do/did I do that?[3] Attempts to answer these questions lead to more insightful understanding of what these moments mean to me and to others. Within this process, the singularity of particular personal experience, in all its complexity and uniqueness, illuminates important pieces of our collective plurality. The reflective practitioner believes that not only do actions frequently speak louder than words, but that by attending to our actions in the ordinary, mundane events of our seemingly routine biographies we: (1) come to understand ourselves and others to a greater degree; (2) recognize our own complicity in oppressive structures we seek to eliminate; and (3) inform our potential for individual and collective action for making a better world.

Let me be more specific regarding the method of reflective practice within this model. Intentionally telling and reading stories from one's life story involves three procedural steps: (1) retrieving the story in words, illustration, and movement, looking again at one's life journey, re-searching biographical particulars; (2) "zooming in" (Watson, 1998) for particularity by looking underneath and in between the lines of the narrative, the drawing or the dance, reading closely one's words, shapes, qualities, preferences, energy and imagery; and (3) "zooming out" (Watson, 1998) or reading the larger concerns revealed from the uniqueness of the personal narrative, reconstituting a perspective by intimately distancing one's self for the purposes of social critique and informed collectivity. "Zooming out" for the reflective practitioner, allows each narrative reflection to speak again, not merely on a purely personal level, but more broadly in dialogue with critical theories for emancipatory change and postpositivist concerns for humanizing social practice.

DOING CRITIQUE

Although the dance profession importantly animates the background of this work, the larger social critique that emerges in the foreground is not confined to all dancers, dance teachers or even all educators. These issues are critically important for all people concerned with liberation and social change. My concerns for removing limits to human freedom, improving social conditions, working for greater emancipation, and reducing needless human suffering emanate from a cultural critique of heterosexual privilege and homosexual oppression. Without diminishing the implications for the dance profession, these social concerns extend to all of humanity, and are importantly embedded in our own and other's daily practices.

The underpinnings of this work are tethered to cultural exploration and critique, and at the same time, are suspended by guide wires of social action, possibility and re-education. Social critique without affirmation renders hollow oversimplification, abundant despair and uninspired hope. Romanticized notions of social change without criticality, on the other hand, create naively optimistic vision, disconnected sentimentality, and unimaginative response. Even with the noblest of intentions, when pursued as separate courses of action, criticality or affirmation alone breed social inaction, meagre expectation, and inadvertent maintenance of the status quo. Notwithstanding the difficulty of managing such a task, this work recognizes the delicate balance characterised by hopeful pessimism and critical affirmation.

Reading our particular stories regarding how we have lived, attempted to make sense, or better yet, how we have explained the world around us illuminates our intimate "inside" and with critical reflection, our deepest hopes for the public "outside." Or more simply, we start with our own story in order to understand more fully the larger stories our culture tells. These cultural narratives tell us what it "means" to be male, to be white, to be an American, to be a father, to be gay, to be a dancer. I tell my story inside these larger social narratives, not to convince readers mine is the story of all gay people, or all white gay men or even white gay dancers. Quite the contrary, I tell and re-read my own story as only one of among many in a collective pursuing greater understanding for what is necessary to affirm a diverse and loving humanity.

I present an example of this model in action from my own experience. I begin with a brief excerpt from one of many narrative reflections recollected during the two-year period of this research. This reflection is accompanied by visual and movement "artifacts" (Watson & Wilcox, 2000, p. 65) which were created either: (1) in response to the narrative account; (2) prior to the writing of the narrative reflection; or (3) simultaneously with the narrative account and illustration. Because this process often integrates word, illustration, and movement at the same time and in conversation with one another, I also present descriptions of my own movement passages (as viewed on videotape recording). It is important to note that a great deal of this process occurs within a "free writing" context, one free of inordinate preparation, judgement or scrutiny. Which is to say, mental and physical filters are minimized in order to facilitate not only more of the story, but also to free the multiple manifestations that constitute such.

MODEL IN ACTION
Never Me

In the first reflection excerpt, I recollect initial memories of rehearsing heterosexuality as a young and confused teenager:

> I stopped taking dance lessons while I was in high school. The harassment and chiding from others was too much to bear. It was however, possible to sing. Singing was serious and competitive; gifted students could win blue ribbons at statewide competitions. Straight guys with popular girlfriends sang with big booming voices. Pretty girls swooned over the boys in music. This I thought I could do. I could continue to dance by virtue of singing with these straight, popular jock-types. At fifteen I thought I might be gay. I knew I had feelings for other guys, and had even acted upon them. There wasn't much talk of bisexuality in the early 70s, and now girls were interested in me. How could I be gay if girls thought I was desirable? I associated being gay and having sexual impulses for men with being fat, undesirable to girls, nerdy and unpopular. Since I was now thin and somewhat attractive, I concluded that I was also straight.
>
> I was quickly thrust into the limelight of music and theatre productions, playing romantic leads opposite pretty young ingenues. I was given dance solos and heartthrob ballads for our touring group performances. My feelings and attraction to my male counterparts however did not subside. And I think being under the pressure of performing love songs to and about women intensified my sexual confusion and frustration. There's something poignantly wrong with crooning a love song like "On the Street Where You Live" to fair lady Eliza Doolittle when you're actually fantasizing about the gorgeous football quarterback playing Henry Higgins. In making my transformation from ugly duckling, I became distant with two close friends who were also same sex curious. My new intimate circle of friends were the professed straightest of the straight; there was no room for my old, now suspect friends in this new elite crowd.
>
> I continued to rehearse my heterosexuality all through high school, especially when it came to dance. Although I was pleased to be dancing and assured of my spot in the show, being pegged as a male dancer (when you already think you might be gay) is all about damage control, constantly reasserting your heterosexual image, weaving an intricate straight story web. I felt guilty and ashamed. I loved dancing, but not the secrecy and shame that came with it.

Initial Retrieval

The 'quick reading' (Watson & Wilcox, 2000, p. 61) of this excerpt reveals a common thread of isolation and shame characteristic of what many of us have felt at different times in our lives. Although heard as a unique pain, it is also one in which all of us can relate ("The harassment and chiding from others was too much to bear"). So too, we recognize the powerful notion of hiding who it is we actually are and the requisite secrecy that ensues.

Intimate Reading

Reading this excerpt more closely, we uncover a more intimate understanding of both the researcher and his culture. Viewing the excerpt's accompanying visual artifacts not only deepens our understanding of alienation and his enduring feelings of loneliness, but also indicates the dialectic, or conversation at work in this process. Although space does not permit a "line by line" reading of this narrative, a few readings are crucial for understanding the profundity of this practice.

"Singing, unlike dancing, was serious and competitive." At the outset, the researcher communicates his cultural understanding of dance's marginalized place within in the larger society. Although the narrative suggests that he has studied and enjoyed dance for a number of years, dance is now seen as frivolous and unimportant. Singing, on the other hand, represents that which has merit, respectability or is seen as something worthwhile and acceptable. Given the researcher's great desire to continue dancing, these words poignantly illustrate his daily dilemma. Singing not only functions as a substitute, or replacement for his most profound desire, but also continues and perpetuates the marginalization of dance and more importantly, the stigmatization of those who dance.

"At fifteen I thought I might be gay." These reflective words indicate an internal exploration, one constituted by a wary cultural awareness of what this proclamation would actually mean, to him and to others. And at the same time, there is a reluctance to admit one's own inner most feelings to one's self. The word choice "might" pledges an uncertainty, an ambivalence toward such an orientation. Moreover, it leaves open the possibility that the researcher "*might*" (hopefully) not be gay. To the contrary, he *might* actually be straight. These words indicate uneasiness with gay self-identification at such a young age. Culturally, we are highly familiar with the notion that, "this is just a phase he's going through." Reading this line more closely, we hear the researcher re-instate the dominant cultural normalization. Which is to say at best, he will grow out of *it*, and at worst, there is always an enduring, socially optimistic hope for heterosexuality.

"How could I be gay if girls thought I was desirable?" Here the researcher's recollection poignantly illustrates his incredulity, as he posits the single question in this autobiographical excerpt. On the one hand, his personal evidence would strongly indicate a gay, if not bisexual, sexual orientation. But on the other hand, the notion that *girls* find him attractive serves to buttress his disbelief and doubt that he is anything other than heterosexual. The confusion surrounding sexual identity is linked much more closely to external forces, rather than to internal compulsions. Being gay, it seems in this narrative, is predicated on one's unattractiveness to other's (fat, nerdy, unpopular), especially to those of the opposite sex.

"I concluded that I was also straight." This statement is not at all an uncommon resolution for teenage boys (straight, bisexual or gay) in the US who experiment sexually, given the immense social pressures of masculinity and homophobia. Nor is it uncommon for boy's self-identification to mirror the polemic sexual binary characterized by American culture, either purely heterosexual or solely homosexual. The ambivalence of bisexuality still arouses a great deal of bewilderment and misunderstanding in the US. The words of his conclusion also indicate a thought process based more on his physical and social transformation, rather than on a discernible change in his attraction toward the same sex. For example, going from *fat* to *thin, undesirable* to *attractive*, and now by extension, from gay to straight indicates the researcher's sense that sexual orientation is malleable, controllable, or more simply put, something one can decide.

"My feelings and attraction to my male counterparts however did not subside." Although the researcher actively attempts to maintain his heterosexual image, the internal contradiction he experiences still struggles to the surface. His reflective words indicate an almost fatalistic optimism, as if these feelings would surely dissipate or that his same sex attractions would dissolve over time. Quite the contrary, by using the word "subside," the researcher shows that his feelings toward other boys most likely continued, without sign of yielding or retreat. Readers also sense that we may be receiving fair warning that this internal contradiction is ongoing and will persist throughout the researcher's struggle.

"I became distant with two close friends who were also same sex curious." An intimate reading of this line poignantly illustrates the great lengths at which concealing one's secret regrettably distances and further isolates those who already feel inadequate, abnormal and marginalized. Rather than advancing the supportive and empathetic relationship with his *two close friends*, the researcher (in order to reaffirm his heterosexual image) retreats from this significant, and most likely (*same sex curious*) beneficial connection. The culturally pejorative nature of remaining socially close to those who are perceived as gay, makes maintaining those relationships especially prohibitive. Put more bluntly, when one is entrenched in constructing a heterosexual image, eliminating guilt by association is the most efficient remedy.

Because the excerpt contains no other rationale for such distancing from these otherwise profoundly intimate friendships, readers are left to ponder the unfortunate and deleterious nature of secrecy and denial in homophobic American culture. At the same time, because these *two close friends who were also same sex curious* indicate a small yet vital community for the researcher, we realize more profoundly the power and domination of heterosexual normalization and a heterocentric value system. Which is to merely say, that seeking social affirmation by the dominant culture carries with it a blindness, one that obfuscates one's innermost feelings, desires, and beliefs in exchange for hollow cultural acceptance.

"I loved dancing, but not the secrecy and shame that came with it." In these words we hear again the researcher's perceived dilemma: how to dance without acknowledging and confessing his gayness. In order to distance himself from the culturally acceptable disdain for male dancers, he harbours his sexual orientation by re-asserting a heterosexual facade. To dance then from this narrative, means to keep a secret, all the while attempting to reconcile the shame and disgust he experiences by not truly accepting his own sexual orientation. For the researcher as a male who dances, he must vehemently assert a heterosexual persona; otherwise dancing is unfathomable. He assumes that dancing, without heterosexual proclamation, means societal disapproval. Regrettably, he is unable to reconcile his love for dance with his sexual orientation. To be a gay male dancer, reaffirms his deepest fears, fears characterized by social alienation, cultural disapproval and reification of the normalizing stereotype of male dancers.

Before a final reading of this narrative account, one that retreats somewhat in order to see the larger issues that emerge, I want to elaborate on two additional resources I use as sites for intimate readings in reflective practice from my own research experience. These methods were initially developed to enlarge my own understanding of autobiographical work through the use of alternative media. As these methods continue to evolve, their usefulness within a variety of contexts has become apparent.

Visual Artifacts

The term "artifact" is used as an affirmation of the Watson and Wilcox methodology (2000, p. 64) but also as a means for development of the term in order to expand the possibilities for enlarging methods of reflective practice. Their work suggests that practitioners collect artifacts that "represent the daily conventions of their practice and then, in the hermeneutic tradition, do a close reading (or annotation) of them" (p. 64). Suggestions include daily written evidence from the workplace, such as letters, proposals, memos and handouts. In addition, one might create an artifact by drawing or simply representing one's self in daily practice.

I have developed this notion in a non-verbal approach in which the body, in its singular parts and combined totality, serves as a site for collecting additional evidence of our daily movements and motions that shape our lives. The visual artifacts, or artworks (I use the term loosely) in this instance, flesh out more of the autobiographical material through the body's movement, motion, and markings. Let me make clear that I am not a visual artist, nor does this practice require such of reflective practitioners. This approach requires no particular confidence, skill, training or facility in movement or drawing; rather it requires a curious, honest authenticism not always facilitated by artistic acumen and technique. The approach seeks rather, an ability to "free associate" with crayon, marker or pastel in hand, one's innermost thoughts, feelings, and responses, not in isolation, but in dialogue with the words and movement at hand.

Movement Artifacts

Each of the visual illustrations is accompanied by a series of improvisational movement vignettes created by the researcher and captured on videotape for later viewing/reading. In much the same manner in which the visual illustrations are created, these improvised "dance" sequences have very little, if anything, to do with technical dance skill or artistic virtuosity. Which is not to say there is not a "technique" to such a process. Or that there are not skills, *per se*, to be developed within this reflective way of moving. Rather, these movement artifacts come about by cultivating a sensitivity directed toward the ordinary motions, shapes and energies of our bodies in our daily lives. The personal history stored in the body, as well as the body's contemporaneous concerns become accessible for examination, dialogue and reflection. Following one's impulses for movement and stillness, in a dialectic relationship with narrative writing and visual illustration, the reflective practitioner embodies the personal and archetypal, inner and outer, spiritual and material, certainty and ambiguity. The body as a resource for reflective practice often calls forth what is most essential about our work, practice and human experience.

Reading these movement artifacts is preceded by first reflecting upon the actual experience of creating them. Because these visual and movement artifacts are created simultaneously there is a unique connection between the two, an inherent dialectic between motion and marking. It is often the case that actual body movements literally translate to lines, shapes and energy in the visual artifact. Within this process, one constantly informs the other, and vice versa. Readers might think of this process as similar to a kind of "stream of consciousness" writing, but for movement and illustration.

READING THE ARTIFACTS

The first of two visual artifacts (Figure 1) that accompany the reflection is a visual depiction that was created in response to both the autobiographical narrative and a series of movement vignettes composed from and with the researcher's interaction with the narrative account and the visual artifact itself. For clarity of discussion, I have titled this visual depiction, *Never Me/Dark House*. Both phrases appear prominently in the illustration.

An initial reading of the large illustration shows a series of black hatch-like marks in rows covering the upper right quadrant. An abstract shape of black and grey shadings occupies the opposite center and lower left portion of the artwork. The illustration is balanced with two word phrases in the remaining two quadrants; "never me" is written in grey and yellow pastels respectively, while the words, "dark house" occupy the lower right quadrant in heavy black letters.

When we read the illustration more closely and in conversation with the researcher's biography, three more concrete forms emerge. First, the hatch-like markings noted earlier seem to appear as rows of empty theatre seats. In a second instance, (Figure 2) upon closer inspection the abstract shape in the centre of the artifact reveals portions of a human face. Finally, in conjunction with both of the former, the lower left quadrant appears to be a stage platform with a curved front apron.

The words "dark house" take on greater significance when readers consider the researcher's professional career in dance. "Dark" in theatre jargon translates to no scheduled

FIGURE 1 Never Me/Dark House.

FIGURE 2 Never Me/Dark House.

performance. For example, "We're dark on Monday" means no performance on Monday. "House" refers to the space in the theatre where an audience views the production. Taken together with the visual aspects of a sole performer on stage playing to an empty audience, we understand more profoundly the researcher's sense of loneliness and feelings of alienation. In addition, the words "never me" articulate more completely the internal contradiction we read earlier in the narrative account, but now the researcher's words are more strikingly definitive. Maintaining his homosexual secrecy renders the understanding that he has never embraced his real identity, his truthful *me*. As such, he has metaphorically played his life out in emptiness, without benefit of others in community.

Within the movement artifact (documented on videotape), two types of movement accompany the *Never Me/Dark House* illustration. The first movement style is repetitive in nature and could be described as angular in shape,

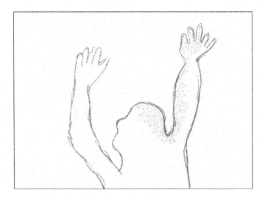

FIGURE 3 Male/Female.

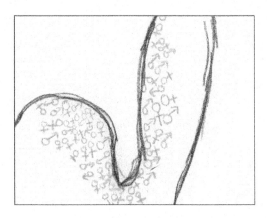

FIGURE 4 Male/Female.

percussive in quality. A second type of movement, performed by the researcher's torso and arms, flows in a more fluid manner with softly curved elbows and wrists. Both movement styles are evidenced in the visual illustration. The angular, percussive motions correspond to the heavy black, hatch-like markings, previously identified as an empty theatre; the more amorphous shapes of the theatrical stage and human figure correspond to the fluidly curved movement.

"Zooming in" (Watson, 1998) for a closer reading of this movement artifact reveals a kind of angered tenacity in the repetitious angular motions of the researcher. An attitude of defiance emerges, one in which he continuously struggles to "be seen" by an audience that is consistently never present, the *dark house*. At the same time, an intimate reading of the researcher's fluid movement sequences also exposes a different side of the researcher, one characterized by a sense of organic wholeness and a somewhat softened resolve. By comparison, this gentler portion of the movement vignette speaks to a more authentic identity hiding behind the percussive outward manifestation seen earlier in the movement sequence. Readers might assume that it's not so much that the researcher has been "playing to an empty house," but rather he has been metaphorically performing the "wrong" dance, the heterosexual dance, in this instance.

A cursory reading of the second illustration, *Male/Female* (Figure 3), shows a simple outline of a human figure sketched in black charcoal. Along the right side of the head and neck, and from the right arm extending to the fingers is a small expanse of careful, bright blue patterning. The "quick" reading of this straightforward depiction communicates an easily recognizable human torso in a supine, relaxed position.

Reading this visual artifact more closely, reflective practitioners see that in actuality the intricate patterning on the body is a series of slightly blurred, alternating male/female icons (Figure 4). Because this random pattern commences in an area of the figure's head, one can assume these thoughts in some way characterize the researcher's internal emotional state. In addition, we see the pattern continues to mark the body, extending the emotional, contemplative state not

unlike a birthmark, tattoo or stigmata. The positioning of the body, when read more closely, provokes further questions. Is the subject sleeping? Is this a moment of rest or repose? Or, is the subject in a state of fallen despair? Is this a moment of retreat or abandonment?

When placed beside the narrative reflection and in conjunction with the first visual artifact, readers comprehend more thoroughly the ways in which the researcher's internal confusion permeates his ability to reckon his sexual orientation not only in the realm of dance, but also within the larger social context of his life. Moreover, Figure 3 clearly reaffirms the narrative's earlier warning of this persistent internal contradiction: attracted to males, but still found desirable by females. Although his struggle is ongoing and pervasive, readers remain uncertain about the researcher's current state of being. Which is to suggest, the ambivalence of this illustration keeps open the possibility for enlightened repose, but at the same time, does not rule out a denial-entrenched defeat. Put more simply, this visual depiction asks, is this a moment of further obfuscation, or an instance of calm lucidity? Without benefit of closely reading the *Male/Female* illustration, the complexity of the researcher's situation is understood less well.

The videotape documentation of the accompanying movement artifact for Figure 3 shows the researcher moving in highly minimal ways, movement barely discernible. This movement vignette occurs entirely with the researcher's body on the floor, reclining and subtly shifting as if preparing for an afternoon nap. His arms extend above his head, with the right arm reaching slightly higher. When reading this movement sequence more closely alongside the narrative reflection and visual illustration, practitioners witness a poignant sense of temporary calm and serenity. Although a respite of sorts, the reprieve from his dilemma is short-lived. There is a nagging uneasiness in his motion as he restlessly repositions himself. It appears that although he can escape momentarily, his confusion remains nearly always "on his mind".

When intimately read, these powerful artifacts convey the researcher's deeper sense of pervasive isolation and persistent confusion in ways that the narrative account alone cannot easily communicate. That which is readily available in narrative reflection is significantly enhanced when the body's motions and markings are cultivated as significant cites for reflective practice.

READING FOR INTIMATE DISTANCE

In order to gain further insight and greater understanding from the close reading process in reflective practice, it is necessary to conclude by returning to the overall picture conveyed. From the singularity of particular personal experience, this procedural stage seeks to illuminate important pieces of our collective plurality. Here, we read a perspective from the larger concerns by intimately distancing ourselves for the purposes of greater self-awareness, social critique, and informed action.

Although at first glance it appears this work is a simple, yet moving story about a young male dancer attempting to reconcile his sexual orientation; stepping back a bit allows practitioners to see the larger issues at hand. "Zooming out," (Watson, 1998) reveals the broad and sweeping social nature of discriminatory attitudes like homophobia and anti-gay bias. Viewing the bigger picture, we are moved to understand more clearly the common plight of oppressed and marginalized groups. At the same time, the profound internal struggle communicated by the researcher, illustrates the powerful and pervasive ways in which dominant cultural norms deleteriously harm individuals already alienated and confused.[4]

For me as the researcher, this model reveals other profound concerns and questions about my own practice as both an educator and a gay male. For example, in what ways does secrecy and silence reassert the dominant status quo and marginalization of gay people? Given the nature of a highly heterocentric and homophobic US culture, is it not quite possible that by remaining politely quiet about these attitudes, I in fact, make conditions even worse? The academic dance profession, of which I am a part, is proliferated with gay males. But at the same time is almost always silent on the subject. Considering this enormous opportunity for exploring issues of sexual orientation, one must ask, what systems remain so entrenched that the dance community lags embarrassingly behind in this particular realm?

Reflecting on the larger perspective, it is also important to question to what degree one becomes complicit with anti-gay attitudes when one internalizes (consciously or not) the dominant heterocentric value system in one's teaching, workplace, and practices. Moreover, as an educator, how do I reproduce, make again that which I diligently seek to revise as a more humane and just world? By intimately distancing one's self for the purposes of social critique and informed action, this reflective process means exhuming the "taken for granted" oppressions one regularly endures, but seldom questions. From this renewed questioning and response to such, reflective practitioners are compelled to commit themselves to action against these and other oppressive practices. The inner contradictions we harbour, when attended to and pestered further, may be in actuality our utmost source of energy and hope.

NOTES

1. Bauman (1991) borrows the term 'slimy' from Mary Douglas's (1966) description of "an entity ineradicably ambivalent, blurring a boundary line vital to the construction of a particular social order of a particular life-world" (p. 61). See Douglas, p. 39.
2. Kincheloe (1998), in tandem with Slattery (1995), retitles *currere* in a postmodern context.
3. Watson and Wilcox (2000) ask a similar question. See their article, p. 58.
4. The author develops this notion more completely in the realm of educational foundations. See Risner (2003).

FUNDING

This research was conducted at the University of North Carolina at Greensboro during the author's doctoral study from 1998 to 2001 and supported in part by generous funding from the Luther Winborne Self Doctoral Fellowship.

REFERENCES

Bauman, Z. 1991. *Modernity and Ambivalence* (Ithaca, NY, Cornell University Press).
Douglas, M. 1966. *Purity and Danger* (London, Routledge).
Kincheloe, J. 1998. Pinar's *currere* and identity in hyperreality: grounding the post-formal notion of intrapersonal intelligence, in: W. Pinar (Ed.) *Curriculum: Toward New Identities* (New York, Garland).
Pinar, W. 1978. Currere: toward reconceptualization, in: J. Gress & D. Purpel (Eds) *Curriculum: An Introduction to the Field* (Berkeley, CA, McCutchan).
Pinar, W. 1988. Whole, bright, deep with understanding: issues in qualitative research and autobiographical method, in: W. Pinar (Ed.) *Contemporary Curriculum Discourses* (Scotts-dale, AZ, Gorsuch, Searsbrick).
Risner, D. 2003. What Matthew Shepard Would Tell Us: gay and lesbian issues in education, in: S. Shapiro, S. Harden & A. Pennell (Eds) *The Institution of Education* (4th edn) (Needham Heights, MA, Simon & Schuster).
Slattery, P. 1995. *Curriculum Development in the Postmodern Era* (New York, Garland).
Watson, J. 1998. *Transforming 'Got a minute' Stories into Reflective Narrative*. Proceedings of the Second International Conference on Self-Study of Teacher Education Practices, Conversations in Community, 16–20 August, Herstmonceux, UK.
Watson, J. & Wilcox S. 2000. Reading for understanding: methods of reflecting on practice, *Reflective Practice*, 1 (1), pp. 57–67.

Moving Social Justice in Dance Pedagogy: Possibilities, Fears and Challenges

Doug Risner

Susan W. Stinson

Abstract

This essay explores social justice commitments in dance pedagogy and dance education teacher preparation in the USA as developed through a series of conversations between two dance educators and former administrators in higher education. The authors examine the history of multiculturalism, multicultural practices in postsecondary dance, their influences on dance teacher education, and the limitations of the multiculturalism movement that emerge from misperceptions about, or disregard for differences in culture, gender, ability, ethnicity, and socioeconomic background. Dominant arguments for maintaining status quo perspectives such as scarcity of resources, accreditation standards, and tenured faculty compositions are examined in conversation with a number of prophetic voices for social justice teaching and learning. Examples of pedagogical approaches and project assignments that aim to bring social justice learning to the dance education classroom in concrete ways are presented.

© 2010 The Author(s).
This is an Open Access article distributed under the terms of the Creative Commons Attribution Non-Commercial License (CC BY-NC). This license ensures that original authorship is properly and fully attributed. This article was originally published in *International Journal of Education & the Arts*.

Introduction

Imagine an undergraduate dance education course at the conclusion of a lively discussion on teaching in today's public schools. The conversation has included some dramatic stories illustrating difficult challenges faced by many young people, the corresponding strengths that they also possess, and the responsibility of dance teachers in such a context. One student is looking particularly overwhelmed. When the instructor gently asks her what she is experiencing, she replies honestly, "Why can't I just teach pliés?"

As dance educators, we can sympathize with this prospective teacher. We could easily ask a similar question related to preparing teachers of dance: Why can't we just teach them how to teach pliés and other dance content? Isn't that enough? After all, they are becoming *dance* educators. Why do they need to deal with the individual differences, personal problems, and cultural issues that their students will bring with them?

The pragmatic response is that they will not be successful in teaching dance to many of today's students if they do not deal with all of the issues that can get in the way between the student and learning. How can they help their future students build on their strengths to manage such obstacles? Based on our own experience and the stories we hear from teachers in the field, we have to know more than dance content because *this* one is developmentally delayed, *this* one doesn't understand English, *that* one is in a wheelchair. Much multicultural teacher education has tried to prepare pre-service educators for teaching students with these differences: Good teachers are expected to learn about instruction for young people from every different demographic group, to customize methodology so that all children can learn. As described below, this orientation has led to some positive developments in the field, including appreciation for the diversity that students bring and what dance can offer. Yet it often ends up leaving teachers, including ourselves, feeling overwhelmed by what sometimes seems more like a collection of different needs than a community of learners.

Not all the obstacles to learning are about disabilities and cultural differences; many are a result of students' social and economic circumstances: *This* one's brother is in prison, *this* one doesn't have money for dance clothes, *that* one is homeless, *that* one's parents are fighting, *that* one was raped. Teachers who care are often called to become therapists and social workers for their students. Anyone who doesn't care doesn't belong in the teaching profession. But those who *do* care often become burned out after a few years, because more students with more challenges keep coming. This situation reminds us of a fable (retold in *The Blue Haze*, 2007) about a man standing on shore watching bodies float down a river. Being a compassionate person, he tried to rescue those he could and bury the rest, staying so busy he never had time to ask what was going on upriver that sent so many bodies floating down.

Busy teachers, trying to do the best they can with too many students facing too many challenges, may recognize Sue Books' analogy of education as triage (1994): We don't give much attention to students who will be fine, or those that will never make it, and instead focus on the few that might survive with our help. We triage those kids, but never think about the system that creates these circumstances. To think about the system creating the challenges so many young people face in schools, takes us beyond thinking about individual and cultural differences to thinking about broader issues of social justice. It means we try not just to help future teachers fit into the world as it is, but to create a world that is more just, more fair, as well as one that is more compassionate.

And yet this seems such a daunting task, especially for dance educators. After all, we and our students chose this particular career because it seemed a good match between our skills and our passions. We did not choose to become politicians or community organizers. At the same time, we believe that dance educators have a role to play in creating a better world for their students to enter, and further, that failure to think about the larger social world is problematic for our students, ourselves, and our art.

This essay has developed through a conversation between two American dance educators willing to be honest with themselves, looking at their own histories as white middle class dance educators and former administrators, at or past middle age, self-defined as liberals committed to inclusivity and social justice. At different institutions with different educational contexts, we have struggled to figure out how to live our values within a larger social world that includes some quite different ideas of what that kind of world might *become*. Parts of our ongoing dialogue throughout this process, often incomplete, half-baked, and generally messy, are included in audio excerpts for a number of reasons. First, we seek to draw attention to collaborative thinking, learning and writing. Second, we hope to illuminate the ways in which the written word, though seemingly effortless from sentence to paragraph, from problem to possible solution, actually makes its frequently awkward and sometimes doubtful path to the printed page. Last, we believe that exposing and confessing our imperfections, inadequacies, and incomplete understandings of the world reveal more of our humanity in our struggle as educators and citizens. At the same time, readers may elect to skip these audio dialogues entirely and focus on the written essay in its more traditional scholarly form.

We will first look at the history of multiculturalism and dance education in the USA: how we have gotten to where we are today. We will emphasize practices in higher education in our country, especially those that have most influenced teacher education. Following that analysis, we will discuss some of the most-cited reasons for maintaining the status quo. We will conclude with some promising possibilities, including two from international locations, and some potential sources of energy for realizing the role of dance education in moving toward social justice. We hope that this piece will become part of an expanding international dialogue on issues of social justice in dance education.

http://www.ijea.org/v11n6/audio/audio1.mp3
Audio Clip #1: Reflections on trying to create a better world.

Multiculturalism and Dance Education

Defining multiculturalism is often contingent upon the varied contexts in which it is discussed and deployed. In 1993, Milton Bennett proposed a Developmental Model of Intercultural Sensitivity which has been used by many subsequent researchers to understand how students experience cultural difference. Although there has been some substantive critique of this model (see Hodges and Belcher, 2005), we find it useful here.

Bennett proposes six stages in experiencing cultural difference. He describes the first three as *ethnocentric*; they involve 1) *denial* of cultural difference, 2) raising a *defense* against it, or 3) *minimizing* its importance. The next three stages are termed *ethnorelative*; they involve seeking cultural difference by 4) *accepting* its importance, 5) *adapting* a perspective to take it into account, or 6) *integrating* the whole concept into a definition of identity. In terms of multiculturalism in the United States, Carson's (1999) definition mirrors the integration suggested in stage six of Bennett's model:

> [M]ulticulturalism is a social and political movement and position that holds differences between individuals and groups to be a potential source of strength and renewal rather than of strife. It values the diverse perspectives people develop and maintain through varieties of experience and background stemming from racial, ethnic, gender, sexual orientation and/or class differences in our society. It strives to uphold the ideals of equality, equity and freedom on which the United States is based, and includes respect for individuals and groups as a principle fundamental to the success and growth of our country. (np)

Unfortunately, we have very little research on the actual practice of teaching and learning about diversity and social issues in teacher preparation (Lowenstein, 2009). However, what we do know brings up questions about effectiveness, methods, and pedagogy. Studies have shown that teachers' beliefs and perspectives change only after lengthy and laborious professional development over time (Gomez and Tabachnick, 1992; Noordhoff and Kleinfeld, 1993 cited in Lowenstein, 2009). Multiculturalism in post secondary education during the 1990s stimulated highly-charged debates surrounding the western canon, producing conservative challenges against "political correctness" that continue today in the United States. Regardless, multicultural education and curricula received renewed attention.

http://www.ijea.org/v11n6/audio/audio2.mp3
Audio Clip #2: Frustration, fears, and possibilities with multiculturalism in dance.

Status of the Field

We begin with dance in higher education because this is where prospective teachers of dance typically first encounter discussion about social and cultural issues in dance. During the past decade under-representation has continued to be a major theme in dance literature related to social and cultural issues (DeFrantz, 1996a, 1996b; Gottschild, 1996; Bennefield, 1999; Jackson & Shapiro-Phim, 2008; Risner, 2009). DeFrantz (1996b) notes the grave injustice of under-represented populations in major international ballet companies, while also acknowledging the powerful contributions of contemporary choreographers, such as Dwight Rhoden, David Rousseve, Ronald K. Brown, and Jawole Willa Jo Zollar, to the current wave of dance that challenges social norms. Unfortunately, efforts to make post-secondary dance more multicultural have focused nearly exclusively on exposing students to non-western forms and cultivating an appreciation of someone else's cultural dance form. Though exposure and appreciation initiatives are important first steps, rarely do our programs adapt a multicultural perspective or integrate wider multicultural identities.

For example, we add courses to the curriculum in "global dance" rather than rethinking our assumptions about how we think of *all* dance. Despite the years that have passed since Joanne Kealiinohomoku's famous essay on ballet as ethnic dance (1970), we continue to think of western dance forms as "normal," require these courses, and then conservatively sprinkle non-western dance forms and content like exotic condiments on the traditional western meal of meat and potatoes. At best, our students who are required to take one semester of African dance will emerge with appreciation for this dance form and enough knowledge to teach a unit during Black History Month (in USA schools, the month of February), but will only rarely use their appreciation to challenge taken-for-granted assumptions about what dance is. This is primarily because we in dance education haven't moved beyond superficial treatment of multiple cultures outside our own.

While significant dance scholarship has identified racism as a central component of ethnocentric bias in dance, it is clear that the persistence of such bias in spite of changing values and more inclusive attitudes is a more complex problem (Asante, 1993; Nicholls, 1995; Mills, 1997, Asante, 1999). Using dance of the African Diaspora[1] as an example, Mills suggests,

> In dance, as in other fields, most people are inclined to maintain or reinforce existing images because people tend to perceive information in a way that is consistent with their values. The end result, as Becker posits, is that we either

> misperceive information that is not consistent with existing images in order to avoid any inconsistencies, thereby making us uncomfortable, or disregard the information altogether. Many times we simply cue ourselves to perceive information that is consistent with what we expect, believe, or know. (Mills, 1997, p. 141)

Mills' argument characterizes the outcomes of most current multicultural efforts in dance: misperception of, or disregard for non-western forms because these images are not consistent with what dance faculty and students understand as "dance." This western ethnocentric perspective, dominant in postsecondary dance, situates the amalgam of African dance as "primarily a somatic, "ethnic" [sic] experience compared to an aesthetic experience... outside the realm of an artistic aesthetic experience" (Mills, 1997, p. 143). As such, the art form, as well as other non-western dance styles (such as Native American, see Lutz & Kuhlman, 2000; Barry & Conlon, 2003), remains on the periphery of most dance education.

Kerr-Berry (2004), in her exploration of black content appropriation in teaching, moves this argument further in a pedagogical critique of multiculturalism in dance education:

> [T]he white dance educator must immerse herself in the historical content in order to understand it before she disseminates it. She must be able to acknowledge the painful history that surrounds the content. Accordingly, as the instructor prepares, she must be able to enter African American historical content, not only as a researcher in search of information, but also as a human being capable of empathy. (p. 46)

A recent publication on dance in South African schools (Friedman, 2009) reports similar issues in teacher preparation in that country, which defines itself as "polycultural" but has also had a history of domination of white Western dance forms in educational settings. Sharon Friedman points out that African dance is not just a traditional form; rather, those traditional forms have evolved with urbanization and had impact on contemporary African choreographers and dancers. We would all be wise, we propose, to problematize our notions about what any particular dance form looks like.

With the recognition that *all* dance should be considered "ethnic" or cultural dance, we affirm the need for broadening student horizons to understand and appreciate the breadth of cultural dance, and for cultivating empathy. At the same time, if we stop there, such necessary steps often become ways to keep the world as it is: to put boundaries around "other" forms of dance and then congratulate ourselves for our compassionate appreciation of those who struggle. Even dance departments that attempt to substantially revise their programs with ambitious multicultural approaches and content encounter significant obstacles entrenched in the discipline's traditional ballet and modern dance paradigm (Hagood, 2000).

Multicultural efforts that provide exposure and cultivate appreciation, though necessary and likely well intentioned, are insufficient. So much is left out: access, representation, historical and cultural context, and the systemic biases that lie beneath continued social inequity and injustice. Simultaneously, those faculty who do this kind of challenging may, in fact, be regarded as "difficult," "political," or "activist."

Current Limitations

At this point in our discussion, we begin to see the limitations of the multiculturalism movement and its often meager curricular impact in dance over the past thirty years in the United States, especially when we look closely at the field and the boundaries we continue to impose on "others" and their dancing. These limitations emanate from misperceptions about, or disregard for differences in culture, gender, ability, ethnicity, and socioeconomic background.

In terms of gender and ethnicity, multicultural efforts in dance have not been accompanied by a prioritization of underrepresented faculty hires or underrepresented student recruitment in dance. Statistics from institutions in the USA, collected by the Higher Education Arts Data Services (HEADS), reveal our limited progress. Undergraduate dance students remain overwhelmingly female (89%) and over seven in ten dance students are white (HEADS, 2009). As the United States has become increasingly diverse, a pattern that will accelerate as this century progresses (Gay and Howard, 2000), we wonder if or how the field will respond. How comfortable are we when dance in academe looks less and less like our neighborhoods and communities?

Trends in longitudinal data over the past four years show that post-secondary dance faculty are becoming increasingly white (80% in 2007, a steady increase from 76% in 2003). While the total Hispanic/non-white undergraduate population has fluctuated, it remained stagnant over the same period at 27-30% (HEADS, 2004, 2009). Although multicultural education in dance has grown significantly over the past decade, accompanied by an explosion of non-western scholarship, we have not seen the "trickle down effect" to our student or faculty populations.

Beyond the asymmetries of ethnicity and gender, the limitations of current multicultural efforts in postsecondary dance often ignore socioeconomic diversity and minimize differently abled populations. The ability to enter dance programs usually privileges previous training, normally extensive study in ballet and modern dance. In this respect, auditions serve as a socioeconomic barrier, filtering out students whose backgrounds have not allowed access to formal dance training. From the outset, these sorting mechanisms build homogenous programs as they simultaneously reduce diversity.

The overarching tenet of inclusiveness embedded in multiculturalism also extends to include persons with different abilities. In the professional realm, a number of dance companies comprised of dancers with and without disabilities, have emerged in the past two decades. Much dance education scholarship addressing the concerns of special needs populations in dance (Hill, 1976; Sherrill, 1976; Walberg, 1979; Fitt and Riordan, 1980; Boswell, 1982; Dunn and Craft, 1985; DePauw, 1986; Jay, 1987; Levete, 1993, Dunphy and Scott, 2003) has its roots in the adapted physical education movement.

More recent research focuses on the social construction of disability and the ways in which differently abled bodies challenge and disrupt conventional expectations of bodies in dance. Albright (1997) exposes the implications of the body in performance and its representation of cultural identity through gendered, racial, and social markings, including disability. Following notions of equitable contribution, Albright is critical of dances by disabled performers that reproduce dominant assumptions about dance, particularly aesthetics of grace, speed, agility, strength, and beauty. Her argument deftly illustrates the hegemonic tendency to value and privilege the abled body, even when the focus is on diversity and dancers with different abilities. Kuppers (2000) argues that the disabled dancing body challenges the audience to see past disability, and in so doing, to locate the social construction of disability in the spectator rather than in the differently abled body. For the most part, however, such research and performance remain on the periphery of academic dance and teacher preparation.[2]

Clearly, multicultural curricular initiatives in dance have not been met with the same candor or commitment in terms of diverse student and faculty populations. Given the expansion of non-western content and forms in dance over the past thirty years, the continued homogeneity of our programs brings up a number of additional and troublesome questions: What doesn't happen in dance theory and practice when the conversation excludes the voices of non-whites? Conversely, what *does* happen when so many voices and bodies are left out of the conversation, and what are the implications? What then has been accomplished in multicultural dance? What remains unaddressed? More importantly, how will we address the shortcomings of our less-than-ambitious commitment to "uphold the ideals of equality, equity and freedom" (Carson, 1999)?

We believe that if answers are to be found, dance must first look at its grounding conceptions and guiding assumptions about what counts as "dance" and how these determinations are rooted in the long-standing exoticism of non-western dance. Second, we must also confront our inability to look at ourselves and those who, on the surface, look like us. The whiteness of academic dance generally and dance education more specifically, creates a number of challenges for understanding the socioeconomic complexity of white experience and the multiple realities of white identity in the USA. Without underestimating the advantages of unearned power in white privilege (McIntosh, 1990), many problems surface when we ignore the ways in which whiteness is often disregarded, blurring the complexity of disadvantage and struggle regardless of skin color.

Sharon Welch (1999) cautions educators of the inherent contradictions in unquestioned, debilitating, dualistic ways of thinking that divide communities and classrooms into *us-them*. In her book *Sweet Dreams in America*, a critical re-envisioning of difference, multicultural education, and social change, Welch asserts, "we need a sense of self and community fluid enough to learn *from and with difference and mistakes*" [our emphasis] (p. 61).

The message conveyed here summarizes the limitations of current multicultural dance approaches that focus only on learning "about" the exotic other, rather than learning "from and with" those unlike us, or those whose dancing is different from ours. At the same time, Welch also clarifies the contradictions we unwittingly harbor when we fail to recognize and learn from the social injustices in our own culture in dance. More simply, a multicultural "tourist" conception, based on superficial exposure and less-than-ambitious appreciation (such as Black History Month), leaves out real learning from and with non-western cultural forms as well as all the complex identities and experiences in our own dominant white population. As Charbeneau (2009) reminds us,

> There is not a monolithic Black, Asian American, Latino, or Native American experience nor is there a monolithic White experience. Most of us hold a combination of agent and target group memberships, thus experiencing advantage in some ways and disadvantage in others (i.e., someone who is upper-class and Latina, lower-class and white, gay and white). Doing so also helps us question the normative assumptions of Whiteness. (p. 16)

Variation and complexity in homogenous groups, especially when these groups hold dominance in a particular population like dance, are frequently masked. However, Gollnick (1992) notes that "there is often as much variation within cultural groups as there is between groups" (p. 162). When dance is normalized as white, which we believe has been the case, and whites comprise over 70 percent of our students and 80 percent of our faculty, we ignore our whiteness and continue to impose boundaries on "others." This limits multicultural learning for all of us.

Returning briefly to Bennett's continuum model will provide us with better ways to see our current limitations and move toward a more comprehensive and meaningful approach for multiculturalism rooted in social justice aims. If we think of how postsecondary dance approaches cultural difference, then Bennett's model helps us map our decreasing levels of ethnocentrism in three stages, from *denial* to *defense* to *minimization*. The limitations we have discussed to this point indicate that multicultural efforts in dance have moved through denial: we have a knowledge of difference and understand there are other world views. Similarly, we have worked through portions of the defense stage, opening our cultural views to include other perspectives different from our own in curricula and teaching. However, our collective journey on this map appears to stall here as we consistently uplift our own cultural values as superior (McAllister and Irvine, 2000). At best, we may be on the outskirts of the least ethnocentric territory, which Bennett describes as minimization: that is, we profess our colorblindness, minimize differences, and "continue to interact within our own cultural paradigm, living under the assumption that our actions and values are shared by others" (McAllister and Irvine, 2000, p. 16).

Although as a field we're not there yet, the other side of the continuum importantly charts increasing levels of ethnorelativism (the belief that all groups and subcultures are inherently equal), from *acceptance* to *adaptation* to *integration*. It is this part of the map that provides critical process guideposts for social justice in multicultural education: moving from reaction to interaction with difference, and thinking, learning, and acting from empathetic perspectives within all cultural contexts and social differences.

http://www.ijea.org/v11n6/audio/audio3.mp3

Audio Clip #3: Contemplating social justice teaching

Challenges to Multicultural Dance Education

It is often easy for progressives like ourselves to call for social change. Yet we know that change occurs slowly, and can be demoralizing for those who start with high ambitions. As dance students, we learned that many skills develop slowly, over time, and injuries and other set-backs are commonplace. We think that recognizing some of the powerful arguments against change can help us continue our efforts for progress in spite of them. Two of the most prevalent are scarce resources and the pressures of accreditation standards.

Scarcity of Resources

A frequent objection to changing the status quo is scarcity of resources: How can we have an inclusive dance program without the means to add multiple tenure track positions in non-western dance forms? Even if we had the financial resources, how would we find sufficient faculty who meet the credentialing requirements of our institutions and accrediting organization and have the potential to earn tenure? So we are left with a "core" faculty teaching traditional courses and low-status, part-time adjunct faculty (when available) to provide the variety and spice. At least, that is true if we think about the dance curriculum in the ways we always have.

At our institutions, what we typically have done is make minor changes to the curriculum, not re-imagine it. This is especially true when departments have many tenured faculty whose strengths support the existing program. Most often we end up simply reproducing stronger versions of what we already have, with slightly more of this and a little less of that. What would a dance program look like if it started out from the beginning to be inclusive not just of different dance forms, but of different ways of thinking about dance? Do we even know what those different ways of thinking are?

There are many voices from progressive political (Rosenthal, 2009) and spiritual (Brueggemann, 2009) discourses questioning the "myth of scarcity." Irwin (1996) writes,

> The myth of scarcity says that we have limited resources and there is not enough to go around. Thus, we must fight over what is available...This mentality pervades our society whether we are talking about food and housing, love, or self-esteem. (p. 64)

Fears about scarcity keep us from the kind of thinking that might even generate additional resources. If we have the courage to do so, faculty in higher education might re-imagine possibilities for dance curriculum for the future, i.e., beyond their own retirements and beyond simply reproducing themselves and their own interests.

Accreditation Standards

While acknowledging the significant contributions of our accrediting agencies (national, regional and discipline-specific) in improving dance in higher education, the existence of standards often has the side effect of helping us get better at doing the same things we have always been doing (and measure how well we are doing it), rather than completely rethinking what we are doing; the accreditation process rarely nurtures reconceptualization. As a result, we mostly get better and better at turning out students who will do more of the same (only better, of course).

Similarly, accreditation standards for K-12 teacher education programs have done much to improve teacher education in dance, but also have created obstacles to more significant social change. In states which license dance educators for public school teaching, we are appreciative of the opportunity to provide dance education for so many young people who would otherwise not have it. At the same time, responding to the constant bureaucratic requirements and mandates of teacher education, while well-meaning, can be a major distraction to committed dance education faculty. For example, preparing dance educators for public school teaching in the USA means spending significant time in teaching them about school policies and initiatives (national and state level) and making sure they know enough about other areas of the curriculum to not just integrate learning, but also to tutor students in case their low-performing school faces sanctions as a result of national legislation (No Child Left Behind, 2004). If dance educators are to become valued members of a school faculty, they need to be able to join their colleagues in developing overall school improvement plans, so they need to understand types of assessment that do not apply directly to dance. Further, expectations that teachers be able to help *all* students learn, a cause in which we believe, can often lead us to an overwhelming list of differences and how to accommodate for them; sometimes, due to lack of time, we end up with student teacher candidates simply feeling sorry for those who are facing challenges but not knowing how to make a difference. We as teacher educators do not have all the answers they seek. No wonder we and our students often feel overwhelmed, and lose focus on what matters most.

A 2008 study by Peter Rennert-Ariev sheds light on why even the best accreditation standards do not generate the kinds of changes intended. He studied faculty and students in a teacher education program at a university similar to our own. Although the accrediting organization mandated such important performance-based standards as inquiry and critical reflection on teaching, students' value for more practical and technical knowledge (specific lesson ideas that "work") won out over intellectual engagement. Students professed to have completed tasks on which they wrote reflections, even expressing the value of such assignments, but eventually confessed to the researcher that they had not actually done all the tasks and saw them as unimportant. Rennert-Ariev found that faculty, too, became adept at what he called "bureaucratic ventriloquism," defined as

> a defensive response to external mandates that are issued within a deeply hierarchical structure of authority in teacher education. All program participants—students, faculty, field-based supervisors—were required to demonstrate compliance with external regulations. Many of them found ways to resist external compliance without jeopardizing themselves by making insincere gestures that masked their true responses. The program sent [implicit] messages not only to students but also to faculty and field-based supervisors, that superficial demonstrations of compliance with external mandates were more important that authentic intellectual engagement. (p. 125)

In other words, faculty were resisting authority from the state that made them feel disempowered and minimized their control over their professional decisions. Students also engaged in resistance to practices that did not fit their values. Yet all parties appeared compliant when they were being judged by the external standards.

The Rennert-Ariev study presents interesting issues with reference to teaching for social justice. Courage to practice resistance, whether subversive or otherwise, is requisite for social justice work. Yet active and passive resistance can be applied to anything, including social justice. We hear too many people dismissing respect for others as mere "political correctness" and know that students may simply say what they think we want to hear, even if they don't believe it.

Rennert-Ariev further emphasizes a point we made previously: "A significant body of research has attested to teacher education as a weak intervention—sandwiched in a sense between two powerful forces: previous life history and real life experience in the classroom" (p. 122). How can we make a difference in the relatively small amount of time we have available to us in courses to prepare dance educators for school and community settings?

http://www.ijea.org/v11n6/audio/audio4.mp3
Audio Clip #4: Compassion, social action and angry people.

The [Im]Possibility for Social Justice Teaching

In the face of these kinds of arguments and distractions, it is easy to give up on any expectations for change—it seems too hard, too impossible. A statement by one of our mentors, David Purpel (2004), reminds us of this danger:

> Perhaps the most serious threat of all to our hopes for a better world has been the increase of cynicism and despair about the possibilities of fundamental positive change and with it a significant loss of the energy and vitality that has fueled the impulse to create a more just and loving community. Because of this, I have become convinced that, as educators and citizens, our most important and pressing task is to confront and overcome the paralyzing and debilitating effects of cynicism and despair. (p. 10)

To move beyond cynicism and despair, we need to find sources of inspiration both within and outside dance education. We need first of all to recognize that some things are worth doing even if they do not accomplish the desired results within our lifetimes. We need to remind ourselves how far we have come—not just to congratulate ourselves and stop there, but to recognize that change is possible. Some of us may heed this advice from Purpel: "It may be wiser for educators to see themselves as cultural and moral leaders and critics who choose to focus their efforts on educational institutions…" (2004, p. 4). Others may, for a variety of personal and professional reasons, look for quieter ways to use their power to try to change the attitudes of students within their own daily classrooms. Pierre Bourdieu (1986) reminds us that every child enters the classroom with plentiful cultural capital including languages, symbols, knowledges, aesthetic preferences, and other cultural assets (Fowler, 1997). However, "classrooms often do not value, acknowledge, or use the cultural capital of some groups of students" (Brooks & Thompson, 2005, p. 49). We may find quieter inspiration for opening our classrooms and studios to social justice when we grapple with the fact that some of our students have few or no acceptable ways to communicate and express their own cultural capital (Brooks & Thompson, 2006).

If we choose to see ourselves as cultural leaders and critics in our own classrooms, then we might also gain significant energy by seeing our roles as collaborators with our students, teaching and learning from them and the diverse cultural capital they bring to school. Repositioning the teacher and student as co-editors in the learning process, allows mutual engagement in dismantling and re-assembling multiple cultural ideas and products (McWilliam, 2008) and may move us away from despair and cynicism and instead, closer to social justice learning in the classroom.

Finding One's Social Justice Teaching

In this section, we present a number of pedagogical approaches and project assignments that aim to bring social justice learning to the dance education classroom in concrete ways, trying to enhance student consciousness of social issues and inequities. We preface these perspectives by acknowledging the many challenges that preclude or greatly inhibit teacher educators' ability to present social justice content in their teaching. In a climate of endless outcomes assessment, we also concede that results are uncertain, rarely quantifiable, and therefore frequently marginalized. Knowing this, we offer the examples below, some ours, others from colleagues, to stimulate and inspire readers' own creativity for meaningful and relevant social justice projects in their own post-secondary locales and communities, as restrictive or conducive as these may be.

Social Justice and Context-based Dance Education
Isabel Marques

Isabel Marques has developed an approach to dance education that has been heavily influenced by her work with Paulo Freire in her native Brazil. She has struggled with many of the same issues we have struggled with in this essay, writing the following in 1998:

> Working directly with the urban social realities of Sao Paulo city...I often felt impotent as a teacher and university consultant to...fight against the unfair...urban reality which went beyond my pedagogical work. Likewise, I understood why students who lived every day in poverty and distress were not so often willing or wishing to revisit the same problems in their school work. On the other hand, working with Freirian concepts helped me to learn that to ignore our social, cultural and political reality could lead me to an endless route of escape, of fearing the future, and feeling absolutely powerless to do something about our social situation. (p. 179)

While committed to social justice, Marques was equally committed to the art of dance, seeking a way for students to learn "about dance as they learn about themselves—and *at the same time* they can critically dialogue and engage with the fast technological, social and political changes the world is going through" (Marques, 2007, p. 147). Beginning with her doctoral dissertation in 1996 and continuing since that time, she has developed and practiced a process which she calls "context-based dance education," based on a "tripod" of Dance, Education, and Society. Drawing from a Laban-based understanding of the structure of movement, as well as choreographic principles, improvisation, and dance history, she finds authentic relationships between dance content and the particular social issue to develop in the dance class. Examples of contexts she developed in her teaching are *violence, bodily dialogue, communication, relationships, family, being a woman,* and *religion* (Marques, 1998, p. 181). She has suggested that

> teaching specific dance contents (body, dynamics, space, improvisation, composition, dance history, etc.) should be based on the assumption that students and teachers are co-creators of dance and of the world... So, by dancing and in dancing we should be able to make a difference in the society we live in. By sharing and experiencing bodily possibilities of construction and transformation in dance classes we can also feel empowered to interact with people in different ways. (2007, p. 146)[3]

Social Justice and Embodied Pedagogy
Sherry Shapiro

Sherry Shapiro (1998, 1999, 2008) has also pioneered ways of teaching dance as social justice, growing out of her work with dance students at a southern liberal arts college for women. A graduate of the same doctoral program that we attended, Shapiro's work is an artful blend of theory and practice. As a critical theorist, she has written extensively about "how the body becomes a vehicle for oppression, as well as resistance and liberation" (1999, p. 79). What differentiates her work from that of many other critical theorists who write about the body is that she brings this theory into her practice/praxis as a dance educator and choreographer.

Shapiro describes her approach as a form of "liberatory pedagogy" (1998, p. 13) integrated into a collaborative choreographic process with her students. She has illuminated this process of dance making in different publications, describing dances based on body image (1998), finding voice in a society that so often silences women (1999), and a biblical story that raises "issues of power, jealousy, domination of the stranger, compassion, and the value of women in society" (2008, p. 267).

Her recent work in South Africa (Shapiro, personal communication, 10-21-09) as part of a Fulbright Fellowship focused on female identity in post-apartheid South Africa; she used *hair* as a theme to discuss issues of race, gender, social class and democracy through a process of reflection on the students' own life stories.[4] The students included white upper middle class university dance students, black students from a local township, and mixed race students known in South Africa as "colored." Through dialogue, students learned about differences in each other's lives and how their culture coded women the same and differently as reflected by "hair stories."

What distinguishes Shapiro's work from that of many other choreographers who make artistic use of social themes is that art is not her only goal. As the dancers/students tell the stories of their lives, centered on their embodied experiences, she hopes they will also develop the consciousness and the courage to engage in transformative acts beyond dance. The centrality of the embodied experience in this process is not accidental. Shapiro writes,

> The body experiencing deeply is recognized as that which makes possible the reconnection to our own lives, and others; that which makes possible the recovery of our humanity from its apathetic condition....It is the material foundation upon which the desire for human liberation and social transformation rests. (1999, p. 100)

Social Justice in Pre-service Teaching
Susan Stinson

My approaches to teaching social justice issues have been more conventional in higher education classrooms, including engagement with readings from a variety of perspectives that challenge student ideas about teaching dance. I try to encourage them beyond thinking about dance education as steps and exercises and fun creative activities with a few dance history and anatomy facts added in. One area of growth for me in recent years has been figuring out how critical and reflective watching of dance can be a part of teaching for social justice.

I have long been inspired by Maxine Greene's writings, which have helped me see that arts education and social justice work can support each other, depending on specific content and methodology. Particularly appealing to me has been Greene's belief that arts education should not be "linked entirely to the life of the senses or the emotions, or...subsumed under rubrics like 'literacy'" (1988, p. 13), but should emphasize moving people "to critical awareness, to a sense of moral agency, and to a conscious engagement with the world" (1978, p. 162). Greene advocated doing this by teaching students how to be more thoughtful and reflective in perceiving art, but she recognized that one has to select art works carefully to make them most relevant to social justice.

As someone whose attraction to dance had originated from the power of the movement experience in dancing, it has taken me years, and partnership with dance historian Ann Dils, to figure out how watching dance can be just as powerful. Through use of Dils' collaborative work on curricular materials *Accelerated Motion* (Wesleyan University Press, 2007-2009)[5], a new approach to thinking about dance literacy that I think Greene would laud, I have been able to mentor prospective and current dance educators in using dance works to help them and their students come closer to the critical awareness, sense of moral agency, and conscious engagement with the world that Greene valued. The modules in *Accelerated Motion*, designed for advanced high school and university students but adaptable for younger ones, are designed to help problematize the taken for granted, and not just in dance. For example, a module on "Bodies and Machines" looks at the issue of physical ability in dancing bodies, "from the greatly challenged body to the extraordinarily skilled body." The module titled "Ecologies of Beauty" has been a starting point for my students to develop middle school dance units challenging ideas of what is "beautiful." "Creating American Identities" has been used by my students as a basis for high school lessons that extend understanding of what it means to be "American." All of these lessons include experiences in dancing and dance-making as well as watching, talking, and writing about powerful dance works.

Another assignment I have developed in recent years has been a mentoring project between university dance education students and students at a local high school with a diverse student population. It is a multifaceted project involving electronic correspondence and face-to-face encounters between the two groups, along with autobiographical reflections and readings for the university students. Some of the stories that emerge from both groups are raw and painful, challenging assumptions about what is a "normal" adolescent life. My students come to appreciate what they can learn from high school students and their own peers about realities other than their own, and that there is no single "normal" when it comes to life experiences.

Social Immersion Project
Doug Risner

The purpose of this three-part project is to facilitate dance pedagogy students' better understanding of the social issues generated in class readings, films, and discussions through students' actual involvement and experience with life situations different from their own. By design, I hope to create stimulating, socially-rich learning opportunities that momentarily reduce the abstractions of poverty, homelessness, hunger, mental illness, racism, gender bias, ability, and homophobia, among others. Central to this assignment is that students, although briefly and in a limited way, experience the range of other people's existence. Students select one of the immersion projects below as described in the syllabus:

1. 74 cent meals: For one week live on $.74 per meal. You may multiply the allowable amount to create a budget for the week.[6]
2. Same clothes: Wear exactly the same clothes for one week. You may wash them once.
3. Volunteerism: Volunteer for five hours at a food bank, soup kitchen, homeless shelter, helpline, hospice, or other social service agency.
4. Public transportation: Use *only* public transportation for one week.[7]

The first part of the assignment gives students two weeks to determine their project choice and to plan accordingly. I encourage students to reflect upon this initial process and to contemplate the ways in which their privilege, access and socioeconomic capital influence their project selection. For example, many students immediately dismiss the public transportation project because no public transportation is available near their residence, they couldn't give up their car for a week, or their rehearsal schedule would dictate late night use of public transportation (unsafe in the urban setting of the university). In each of these instances, I encourage students to think more deeply about the privilege that allows them options; many people don't have these kinds of choices in their lives. Students often carry these early realizations with them throughout the entire project.

The second stage of the assignment is completion of the project itself. The vast majority complete the project without incident. Some, however, fail on first attempt and quickly choose a different project. Others willingly confess their missteps and failures at the end of the project. For example, Felicia recounted her dismay that, out of pure habit, she accidentally bought a vending machine bottled water ($1.00 USD) and thereby had to skip her planned 74 cent lunch, as well as 26 cents worth of her evening dinner meal.

The third part of the project results in a reflective paper and its presentation to the class. Using what they have experienced and learned in the immersion project, students are asked to tie together important aspects from the class readings, in-class assignments, films and discussions that correlate to their experience of doing the project and the development of their own personal pedagogy. As a midterm paper, the third part of the social immersion project allows students to go more in-depth about issues, concerns, and questions about teaching and education in relationship to race/ethnicity, social class, gender, and privilege, among other topics they self identify.

I realize that these learning moments at best reduce these abstractions only momentarily. Without rationalizing the relatively minimal impact of these projects, students do overwhelmingly relate the immediacy and visceral nature of learning in these experiences and the ways in which only reading about social inequity leaves out far too much and doesn't help them "learn."

Making the Strange Familiar and the Familiar Strange

In this essay we have attempted to look at the dance educator's role in teaching for social change, while acknowledging the challenges, fears and possibilities. We have examined the shortcomings and limitations of multicultural education, as well as some of the arguments and distractions that teachers committed to social justice teaching confront. The approaches described in the previous section, though diverse, provide a *segue* to summarize this work and compel us to teach not only as dance educators but also as cultural workers and as members of the human race.

Each of the pedagogical perspectives heard earlier is rooted in student learning that seeks to make the strange familiar and the familiar strange in student's lived experience of social (in)equity. In this respect, we try to reduce the abstraction and distance inherent in learning from (even the most innovative) texts, readings, films, and discussions. Though relatively modest, these projects are meant to help students reflect upon the "strangeness" of their own lives as they become more familiar with the lives and experiences of others. If our pedagogies and programs produce students who can move well but not think in empathetic, reflective, and visceral ways, we risk producing dance educators who are skilled technicians, ones able to teach pliés but incapable of moving fluidly between and within diverse populations in a rapidly changing world. We think the skills students develop as dancers—to bend and to stretch, becoming stronger and more flexible in mind and body—can be an important part of this process, as long as teachers help them make connections between the dance studio and classroom and the world beyond these special environments.

This essay began with the recognition that preparing dance educators means preparing them to enter a troubled world, a reality described by Maxine Greene over twenty years ago as one filled with "homelessness, hunger, pollution, crime, censorship, arms build-ups, and threats of war, even as it includes the amassing of fortunes, consumer goods of unprecedented appeal, world travel opportunities, and the flickering faces of the 'rich and famous' on all sides" (Greene, 1988, p. 12). Today's reality is no less troubling, making it tempting for anyone to retreat to the safe, the comfortable, the trivial, and the oversimplified.

Still, knowledge alone will not solve these challenges or the troubled world educators confront. There are those who believe that if people understand the gravity of a particular injustice, they will take action by "doing the right thing." The pedagogical approaches relayed earlier provide committed, if modest examples of human will to do "good." At the same time, many obstacles—from mundane personal perceptions to a person's core values—impede informed action and the will to resist dominant structures, including school/institutional constraints as well as local restrictions, whether perceived or real. In recovering voices from our past and discovering new ones, we are inspired to consider new possibilities for reconceptualizing teacher preparation. Through sharing these voices in this essay, we hope to extend this energy to others and expand the community of dance educators seeking similar goals. Our dialogues in the process of writing have convinced us of the importance of community and colleagueship in any arduous effort. Alone, we can lose heart. Even together, we may not be able to change the world in our lifetimes, but we can contribute to the process of recreating the world. We close with an important reminder from a mentor we have shared:

> I have concluded that there is an inverse relationship between the significance of a problem and its openness to solution. Put more baldly, I do not believe that our most significant problems can be solved. Problems surely can and should be ameliorated, suffering and pain reduced, justice and equity increased, peace furthered, violence lessened, meaning strengthened. To accomplish even such limited gains is exalting and exhilarating for as the Talmud teaches, "It is not for us to finish the task—but neither are we free to take no part in it." (Purpel, 2004, p. 107)

Notes

1. While a good deal of research in non-western dance has focused primarily on African and African American-based dance forms, it should be noted that curricular diversity initiatives comprise additional cultural dance forms (see the following multicultural teaching texts in dance: Dils, Gee, & Brookoff, 2007; Vissicaro, 2004; Dils & Albright, 2001; Highwater, 1992; and Jonas, 1992).

2. Since we think discourse about the differently abled is critical in expanding our ideas of who can dance, what dance is, and what it might be, we are mindful that our language in the remainder of this essay does not explicitly include this marginalized group.

3. Marques' work with her educational dance company since 1996 extends and transforms these "contextualized lessons" into dance performances. Readers who wish to view examples may find them at http://www.youtube.com/watch?v=P4Ia8PnWwiU and http://www.youtube.com/watch?v=eypEavGykNY

4. Initially Shapiro planned to use skin color as a thematic tool for her research in South Africa. Wary that analyses based on socially-constructed ideas about skin color might be too sensitive, she later chose to focus on hair. For reader's familiar with Jawole Willa Jo Zollar's *Hairstories* project (2001-04), Shapiro indicates that the similarities between her research and Zollar's *Urban Bush Women* project are purely coincidental.

5. Accelerated Motion is co-directed by Ann Cooper Albright and Ann Dils. Albright, Dils, and project administrator Emily Quinn made editorial contributions to the mentioned units.

6. Figures are based on Michigan Temporary Assistance to Needy Families (TANF) food assistance for a family of three at/or below the poverty line. 74 cents per meal in the USA is equivalent to .57 EUR; .51 GBP; .82 AUD; 5.12 CNY; 5.61 ZAR.

7. Public transportation in the United States is not widely available; however, many low-wage earners, especially in metropolitan areas, depend solely on public transit systems.

References

Albright, A. C. (1997). *Choreographing difference: The body and identity in contemporary dance*. Hanover, NH: Wesleyan University Press.

Asante, K.W. (1993). African-American dance in curricula: Modes of inclusion. *Journal of Physical Education, Recreation & Dance, 64*(2), 48-51.

Asante, K.W. (Ed.). (1999). *African dance: An artistic, historical and philosophical inquiry*. Trenton, NJ: African World Press.

Barry, N., & Conlon, P. (2003). Powwow in the classroom. *Music Educators Journal, 90*(2), 21-26.

Bennefield, R. (1999). Refocusing the arts aesthetic. *Black Issues in Higher Education*, *16*(3), 32-35.

Bennett, M. J. (1993). Towards ethnorelativism: A developmental model of intercultural sensitivity. In M. Paige (Ed.), *Education for the intercultural experience* (pp. 21-71). Yarmouth, ME: Intercultural Press.

Blue Haze. (2007). Dead bodies and the peaceful city. Retrieved 25th March, 2010 from http://reprotrends.blogspot.com/2007/05/dead-bodies-and-peaceful-city.html

Books, S. (1994). Social foundations in an age of triage. *Education Foundations*, *8*(4), 24-42.

Boswell, B. (1982). Adapted dance for mentally retarded children: An experimental study. (Doctoral dissertation, Texas Woman's University, 1982). Dissertation *Abstracts International*, *43*(09), 2925.

Bourdieu, P. (1986). The forms of capital. In J. Richardson (Ed.), *Handbook of theory and research for the sociology of education* (pp. 241-258). New York: Greenwood.

Brooks, J., & Thompson, E. (2005). Social justice in the classroom. *Educational Leadership*, *63*(1), 48-52.

Brooks, J., & Thompson, E. (2006). Social justice in the classroom. In H. Shapiro, K. Latham, and S. Ross (Eds.), *The Institution of Education* (pp. 449-454). Boston: Pearson Custom Publishing.

Brueggemann, W. (2009). The liturgy of abundance, The myth of scarcity. Retrieved 25th March, 2010 from http://www.religion-online.org/showarticle.asp?title=533

Carson, R. (1999). *Didja ever wonder what this multicultural thing's all about?* Retrieved 25th March, 2010 from http://wso.williams.edu/~rcarson/multiculturalism.html

Charbeneau, J. (2009). *Enactments of whiteness in pedagogical practice: Reproducing and transforming white hegemony in the university classroom*. (Doctoral dissertation, University of Michigan, 2009). Dissertation Abstracts International, *70*(04).

DeFrantz, T. (1996a). Simmering passivity: The black male body in concert dance. In G. Morris (Ed.), *Moving words: Re-writing dance* (pp. 107-120). New York: Routledge.

DeFrantz, T. (1996b). The black body in question. *Village Voice*, *41*(17), 29-32.

DePauw, K. (1986). Toward progressive inclusion and acceptance: Implications for physical education. *Adapted Physical Activity Quarterly*, *6*(3), 95-99.

Dils, A., & Albright, A. (Eds.). (2001). *Moving history/dancing cultures*. Middletown, CT: Wesleyan University Press.

Dils, A., Gee, R. & Brookoff, M. (Eds.). (2007). *Intersections: Dance, place and identity.* Dubuque, IA: Kendall/Hunt.

Dunn, J., & Craft, D. (1985). Mainstreaming theory and practice. *Adapted Physical Activity Quarterly, 2,* 273-276.

Dunphy, K. & Scott, J. (2003). *Freedom to move: Movement and dance for people with intellectual disabilities.* Sydney: Maclennan & Petty.

Fitt, S., & Riordan, A. (Eds.) (1980). Focus on *dance IV: Dance for the handicapped.* Reston, VA: The American Alliance for Health, Physical Education, Recreation and Dance.

Fowler, B. (1997). *Pierre Bourdieu and cultural theory: Critical investigations.* London: Sage.

Friedman, S. (2009). Navigating the byways of polyculturalism—Whose dance are we teaching in South African schools? *Research in Dance Education, 10* (2), 131-144.

Gay, G., & Howard, T. (2000). Multicultural education for the 21st century. *Teacher Education, 36*(1), 1-16.

Gollnick, D. (1992). Multicultural education: Policies and practices in teacher education. In C. A. Grant (Ed.), *Research and multicultural education: From the margins to the mainstream* (pp. 218-239). London: Falmer.

Gomez, M., & Tabachnick, B. (1992). Telling teaching stories. *Teaching Education, 4*(2), 129-138.

Gottschild, B. D. (1996). *Digging the Africanist presence in American performance: Dance and other contexts.* Westport, CT: Greenwood.

Greene, M. (1978). *Landscapes of learning.* New York: Teachers College Press.

Greene, M. (1988). *The dialectic of freedom.* New York: Teachers College Press.

Hagood, T. (2000). *A history of dance in American higher education: Dance and the American university.* Lewiston, NY: Edwin Mellen.

Higher Education Arts Data Services (HEADS), Dance Annual Summary 2003-2004. (2004). Reston, VA: National Association of Schools of Dance.

Higher Education Arts Data Services (HEADS), Dance Annual Summary 2008-2009. (2009). Reston, VA: National Association of Schools of Dance.

Highwater, J. 1992. *Dance: Ritual of experiences,* 3rd edition. New York: Oxford University Press.

Hill, K. (1976). *Dance for physically disabled persons: A manual for teaching ballroom, square and folk dance to users of wheelchairs and crutches*. Reston, VA: American Alliance for Health, Physical Education and Recreation.

Hodges, B.A., & Belcher, D. (2005). *A critique of Milton J. Bennett's developmental model of intercultural sensitivity*. Retrieved 25th March 2010, from http://bama.ua.edu/~bhodges/portfolio/forms/icc_bennett.pdf

Irwin, J. (1996), *Empowering ourselves and transforming schools: Educators making a difference*. Albany, NY: State University of New York Press

Jackson, N., & Shapiro-Phim, T. (Eds.). (2008). *Dance, human rights, and social justice: Dignity in motion*. Lanham, MD: Scarecrow Press.

Jay, D. (1987). *Effects of a dance program in the creativity and movement behavior of preschool handicapped children*. (Doctoral dissertation, Texas Woman's University, 1987). *Dissertation Abstracts International, 48*(04), 826.

Jonas, G. (1992). *Dancing: The pleasure, power, and art of movement*. New York: Harry N. Abrams.

Kealiinohomoku, J. (1970). An anthropologist looks at ballet as a form of ethnic dance. In M. Van Tuyl (Ed.), *Impulse* (pp. 24-33). San Francisco: Impulse Publications.

Kerr-Berry, J. (2004). The skin we dance, the skin we teach: Appropriation of black content in dance education. *Journal of Dance Education, 4*(2), 45-47.

Kuppers, P. (2000). Accessible education: Aesthetics, bodies and disability. *Research in Dance Education, 1*(2), 119-131.

Levete, G. (1993). *No handicap to dance: Creative improvisation for people with and without disabilities*. London: Human Horizons.

Lowenstein, K. (2009). The work of multicultural teacher education: Reconceptualizing white teacher candidates as learners. *Review of Educational Research, 79*(1), 163-196.

Lutz, T., & Kuhlman, W. (2000). Learning about culture through dance in kindergarten classrooms. *Early Childhood Education Journal, 28*(1), 35-40.

Marques, I. (1998). Dance education in/and the postmodern. In S.B. Shapiro (Ed.), *Dance, power, and difference: Critical and feminist perspectives on dance education*. Champaign, IL: Human Kinetics.

Marques, I. (2007). I see a kaleidoscope dancing: Understanding, criticizing and recreating the world around us. In L. Rouhiainen (Ed.), *Ways of knowing in dance and art* (pp. 144-158). Helsinki: Theatre Academy of Finland.

McAllister, G., & Irvine, J. (2000). Cross cultural competency and multicultural teacher education. *Review of Educational Research, 70*, 3-24.

McIntosh, P. (1990). White privilege: Unpacking the invisible knapsack. *Independent School, Winter*, 31-36.

McWilliam, E. (2008). Unlearning how to teach. *Innovations in Education and Teaching International, 45*(3), 263-269.

Mills, G. R. (1997). Is it is or is it ain't: The impact of selective perception on the image making of traditional African dance. *Journal of Black Studies, 28*(2), 139-156.

Nicholls, R. (1995). Dance pedagogy in a traditional African society. *International Journal of African Dance, 2*(1), 51–60.

No Child Left Behind. (2004). Retrieved 25th March, 2010 from http://www.edweek.org/rc/issues/no-child-left-behind

Noordhoff, K., & Kleinfeld, J. (1993). Preparing teachers for multicultural classrooms. *Teaching and Teacher Education, 9*(1), 27-39.

Purpel, D. (2004). *Moral outrage in education.* New York: Peter Lang.

Rennert-Ariev, P. (2008). The hidden curriculum of performance-based teacher education. *Teachers College Record, 110* (1), 105-138.

Risner, D. (2009, June). *Challenges and opportunities for dance pedagogy: Critical social issues and "unlearning" how to teach.* Paper presented at the meeting of the Congress on Research in Dance, Leicester, UK.

Rosenthal, S. (2009). *The myth of scarcity, managed care, and modern Malthusians.* Retrieved 25th March, 2010 from http://susanrosenthal.com/articles/the-myth-of-scarcity

Shapiro, S. B. (1998). Toward transformative teachers: Critical and feminist perspectives in dance education. In S.B. Shapiro (Ed.), *Dance, power, and difference: Critical and feminist perspectives on dance education* (pp. 7-21). Champaign, IL: Human Kinetics.

Shapiro, S. B. (1999). *Pedagogy and the politics of the body: A critical praxis.* New York: Garland.

Shapiro, S. B. (2008). Dance in a world of change: A vision for global aesthetics and universal ethics. In S. B. Shapiro (Ed.), *Dance in a world of change: Reflections on globalization and cultural difference* (pp. 253-274). Champaign, IL: Human Kinetics.

Sherrill, C. (1976). *Adapted physical education and recreation: A multidisciplinary approach.* Dubuque, IA: Wm. C. Brown.

Vissicaro, P. (2004). *Studying dance cultures around the world: An introduction to multicultural dance education*. Dubuque, IA: Kendal/Hunt.

Walberg, F. (1979). *Dancing to learn: A contemporary dance curriculum for learning and physically handicapped adolescents*. Novato, CA: Academic Therapy Publications.

Welch, S. (1999). *Sweet dreams in America: Making ethics and spirituality work*. New York: Routledge.

Wesleyan University Press (2007-2009). *Accelerated motion: Towards a new dance literacy*. Wesleyan University Press and the Academic Media Studio. Retrieved 25th March, 2010 from http://acceleratedmotion.wesleyan.edu

Activities for Humanizing Dance Pedagogy: Immersive Learning in Practice

Doug Risner

ABSTRACT
Based upon Paulo Freire's theory of humanizing pedagogy and informed more recently by Freirean scholars Lilia Bartolomé and Maria del Carmen Salazar, this practice-based article provides two immersive learning experiences in which learners engage and question their educational histories, beliefs, and values, reflecting upon and unpacking their assumptions, connecting emergent ideas to their own and others, and considering how their teaching can evolve throughout the career span. Theoretical and practical applications for dance educators and those who prepare them are offered.

Social constructivists argue that learners[1] are complex and multidimensional (Vygotsky 1978) and "must be actively involved in the learning process and believe that knowledge must first be constructed in a social context and before being appropriated by individuals" (Beckem and Watkins 2012, 62). Situated cognition theory requires embedding learning in context, a perspective applied in immersive learning design to ensure that students experience learning problems focused on real-life contexts (Brown, Collins, and Duguid 1989). When participating in immersive learning, students forget they are even in a lesson.

Activities for Humanizing Dance Pedagogy, the focus of this practice-based article, provide immersive learning experiences, in which I engage learners to question their beliefs, reflect upon and unpack their assumptions, connect emergent ideas to their own and others', and consider how their teaching can evolve throughout the career span (Risner and Schupp 2020). As their commonly accepted beliefs and taken-for-granted assumptions come into question (as they often do when participating in Activities for Humanizing Dance Pedagogy), learners discover myriad social, economic, and cultural incongruities – sometimes vast – within their own educational histories, narratives, and biographies. Discoveries like these can produce strong responses and emotional reactions, sometimes ranging from frustration, anger, and outrage to shame, guilt, and helplessness. Therefore, readers presenting immersive experiences like those that follow should be prepared to support learners' range of responses and realizations.

Education philosopher Paulo Freire's earliest notion of a "humanizing pedagogy" emerged from connections to his praxis theory of liberatory pedagogy in teacher education (Price and Osborne 2000). In *Pedagogy of the Oppressed*, Freire (1970) describes humanizing pedagogy as a revolutionary approach to instruction that "ceases to be an instrument by which teachers can manipulate students, but rather expresses the consciousness of the students themselves" (51). At the same time, Freire asserts that "Teachers who enact humanizing pedagogy engage in a quest for 'mutual humanization' (56) with their students, a process fostered through problem-posing education where students are coinvestigators in dialogue with their teachers" (Salazar 2013, 127). To be clear at the outset, the immersive learning activities I advocate and offer here fall well within the bounds of pedagogical activism, which I define as working for social change in dance education.

Course Description and Aims

Freirean scholar Lilia Bartolomé (1994) asserts that humanizing pedagogy assumes and builds upon sociocultural realities of students' lives, interrogates the sociohistorical and political dimensions of education, and views students as critically engaged, active participants in the co-construction of knowledge alongside teacher and peers. Over time, increasing numbers of humanizing pedagogues continue to answer Freire's initial call for reinventing humanizing pedagogy in their own context (Rodriguez 2008). In this respect, humanizing pedagogy serves as an instrument for *becoming* and draws "from experiences and simultaneously provokes experiences, through contradictory and complex processes as we individually and collectively generate our visions for ourselves and each other" (Salazar 2013).

To these ends, I integrate Humanizing Dance Pedagogy Activities into an upper-level, three-credit undergraduate course, Foundations of Dance Pedagogy. The online hybrid course contains eight sequential modules delivered over a fifteen-week semester via the learning management system, Canvas. Modules vary in length from one to three weeks. Small groups (normally four learners) meet regularly. Course materials include theoretical and practice-based readings, films, and task-based materials. Assignments comprise summary papers and position papers (Risner 2010), reflective writings, evaluative tasks, peer feedback, field observations, and a social immersion project (described in Risner and Stinson 2010).

As defined in the course syllabus, the purpose of the class is, "To develop learners' theoretical and applied understandings of critical pedagogical concerns in dance education including teaching and learning theory, social and cultural issues in education, cultural diversity, social justice, from a social foundations of education and reflective practice." The course aligns closely with the dance program's mission statement, "To prepare learners to be imaginative and innovative leaders for improving people's lives and social circumstances through dance and related professions" (Risner 2013, 58). Although many learners have studied dance for as long as they can remember, many have not had the opportunity, encouragement, or pathway to look critically at their own education and training in historical, philosophical, critical or reflective ways.

From a social foundations of education perspective (Risner and Barr 2015), the course focuses upon social, cultural, political, and economic influences on education and teaching in order to develop learners' humanizing and value-centered pedagogical choices and decision-making. Discussing sociocultural issues related to power and authority, ability, economic considerations, sexuality, gender and gender identity, race and ethnicity, privilege, and marginalization can often be challenging for educators and learners, whether or not they are prepared to do so. However, developing greater awareness of how these factors play out in the dance classroom and studio is critical for honing a humanizing pedagogical praxis that is personally resonant and professionally relevant to twenty-first century dance education. My own commitment to social justice issues and concerns also figures prominently throughout the class with an emphasis on access, diversity, inclusion, privilege, and marginalization in dance education and training (Risner and Stinson 2010).

Context of "Foundations of Dance Pedagogy" Course

At the large, urban state university where I teach in the United States, the department of theater and dance offers two dance major programs (BFA; BS), two dance minor programs (dance; commercial and studio dance), as well as a master's degree in dance teaching artistry (MA). The undergraduate dance pedagogy course I teach is required for BS dance majors and satisfies the teaching course requirement for BFA dance majors.[2] The majority of learners in the class seek teaching preparation for dance careers as teaching artists and dance educators. Many already teach at various local dance schools and studios and continue to do so while pursuing their dance degree. Approximately 20 percent of pedagogy students are nonwhite and 90 percent identify as cisgender female.

I call upon theoretical content to teach humanizing dance pedagogy, such as constructivism, critical feminist pedagogy, culturally relevant pedagogy, connected teaching, democratic pedagogies, and engaged teaching, among others. This is consistent with the ideas that a) learning is a social process, b) knowledge is a social construction, and c) social justice education is centered in the freedom to exercise one's full humanity. Students bring diverse perspectives and understandings to their dance classroom learning. I provide readings, films, topical discussions, assignments and immersive experiences that seek to bring relevancy to learners' life situations and prior knowledge in order for their learning to be valuable and resonant. I make no effort to mask the passion I hold for humanizing dance pedagogy, especially *why* one is an educator and *what* education should look like, feel like, and sound like.

Activities for Humanizing Dance Pedagogy

Over the past two decades, I have developed a series of Activities for Humanizing Dance Pedagogy based upon immersive learning opportunities directed toward issues and challenges often removed from dance pedagogy learners' consideration and awareness. Some activities take a topical approach for generating greater awareness of identity, privilege, and access, such as the "Personal Capital Inventory." Others aim to facilitate learners' deeper sensitivity and comprehension of societal challenges and injustices, for instance "7 days @ 78 cents a meal," and "Screens Out: No Technology This Week." Another portion of Humanizing Dance Pedagogy Activity consists of probing questions such as "Tracking: Who Benefits?" and through movement and written reflection, "Performing Your Values,

What?" provides a space for learners to critically assess how they view performance within dance education, which may include inconsistencies between their educational values and the beliefs they hold about performing and performance. For instance, probing dominant assumptions and beliefs about a "good dancer's" body type conflicts with the premise that a) all children can dance and b) everyone can engage in the art form's intrinsic merits regardless of their body's size, shape, or color.

As a course of study and critical lens, social foundations of education provide learners with a powerful and effective framework for better understanding how dominant assumptions form and remain part of embedded inequities, values, and complexities of educational institutions and the schooling they provide. Expanding students' pedagogical awareness and understanding of social, economic, and cultural issues, offers space to probe their own attitudes in relation to socioeconomic structures and inequities in dance education and the development of their values as engaged teachers and citizens of civil society. Combining Freire's initial call for humanizing pedagogy with social foundations education, a number of educational scholars, researchers, and practitioners over the past five decades have developed and synthesized ten primary principles and practices "to illuminate the perceptible dispositions, knowledge, and skills that educators need to humanize pedagogy" (Salazar 2013, 138); these principles and practices of humanizing pedagogy include:

(1) The reality of the learner is crucial.
(2) Critical consciousness is imperative for students and educators.
(3) Students' sociocultural resources are valued and extended.
(4) Content is meaningful and relevant to students' lives.
(5) Students' prior knowledge is linked to new learning.
(6) Trusting and caring relationships advance the pursuit of humanization.
(7) Mainstream knowledge and discourse styles matter.
(8) Students will achieve through their academic, intellectual, and social abilities.
(9) Student empowerment requires the use of learning strategies.
(10) Challenging inequity in the educational system can promote transformation.

(Salazar 2013, 138)

In this article, I present two Activities for Humanizing Dance Pedagogy, which I treat as bookends to the dance pedagogy course. During the first week of class, "My Education Map," is an immersive, creative activity using a combined critical autobiographical and partnered movement approach for recollecting and then deconstructing the path of the learner's education journey, both in school and in dance. The second activity, "What Should Dance Education Look Like?" is an immersive praxis activity presented during the final week of course, which provides reflective and creative opportunities for learners to appraise how individual values and experiences shape expectations about dance education. Both activities create spaces for learners to locate themselves and their beliefs in relation to dance, dance education, and the larger world, which can generate meaningful teaching and learning moments, leading to pertinent questions about the learner's past, present, and future.

I invite readers to use the activities and resources presented here in their own teaching contexts or as guides for creating their own Activities for Humanizing Dance Pedagogy. Consider giving a pilot of the activity to a group of interested colleagues; discuss potential responses in your undergraduate setting and ways to provide empathy and support to students who may need extra help making sense of their experiences and personal histories as dance students.

My Education Map

Abstract: In this activity, learners have the opportunity to discover how their experiences of school and dance study have shaped their assumptions about dance education and teaching. Mapping one's own education, from its earliest beginnings, can provide an important step in avoiding the dangers of normalizing one's own education and essentializing communities and groups of people.

Schedule & Duration: Presented during the second week of the semester; 75 minutes.

Materials: Large drawing paper or all-purpose newsprint (available at any art supply store or online vendor); crayons, markers, and colored pencils.

Space: Dance studio preferred or a large classroom with movable desks and chairs.

Introduction

Each person's educational experience is unique and valuable, yet, in terms of generalization, highly limited. No two people have the same educational paths, content, challenges, privileges, or successes. Assuming that one's students have had similar experiences in school and dance study and that students learn in the same ways, can have significant consequences.

Activity Description

The format of My Education Map is a "pair and share" activity that concludes with group discussion. Start by asking students to draw their educational journey in school and dance from early childhood or kindergarten through the present, using the materials provided as follows:

- Create the map like an actual roadmap with a clearly defined route, noting significant landmarks to make visible the social geography and terrain of the school and dance study experience.
- Indicate "forks-in-the-road" required by life situations and circumstances, as well as one's choices or decisions, including unexpected "turns or detours," as well as "pit stops and rest areas" on the journey. Note any "closed roads" or places in education or dance training that were not accessible.
- Highlight key persons on the education map who shaped the journey, including teachers, parents, family, caregivers, friends, peers, dance teachers, dance studio directors, guidance counselors, coaches, choreographers, among other important persons.
- Point out important events, powerful experiences, and life changes that shaped the educational journey including "rough roads," "smooth sailing," "steep hills," and "dangerous potholes" encountered and navigated along the way.

Encourage and support students in unpacking significant elements of their experiences that influenced their journeys. Finished maps should provide a strong sense of the history, social aspects, and meaning making of their experiences of schooling and dance education.

Sharing Education Maps

Step 1: When maps are completed, ask learners to pair up and determine "Partner A" and "Partner B." Partners then exchange maps and carefully review each other's education journey. For this first step of sharing, learners carefully review and familiarize themselves with their partner's map, gleaning as much as possible without the partner's assistance or help.

Step 2: Each partner will carefully retrace their education journey, using the map to give details and recollect their school journey in words and movement. To begin sharing: Stand up, with Partner B directly behind Partner A with hands on Partner A's waist.[3] Partner A will then "dance" her education map journey, with Partner B as a connected couple. Holding the map in front of herself, Partner A (as the "driver") explains the journey aloud to Partner B (the backseat passenger) as if in a car – together witnessing the trip physically, reflecting back to each other what each sees in the map.[4] Each partner should present their map in entirety before asking questions about each other's maps. Then repeat the process with Partner B as the driver and Partner A as the backseat passenger.

Step 3: In the third step, partners ask questions, request clarifications and give constructive comments to help flesh out more of their partner's journey. Because life journeys can be quite personal, sharing means sharing what is "shareable," holding onto what is not readily available nor easily shared (or example, something that is overly embarrassing, too painful or personal). However, what remains unshared with the partner can still inform and enlighten the learner in private reflection or later in a reflective paper at the conclusion of the semester.

DISCUSSION: When a learner's individual Education Map receives validation in a personal way like this immersive, creative activity, the process and outcomes remind us that each learner's story matters. Storytelling helps us understand the world differently because it is the act of listening that enables us to connect with, and honor the humanity in one another. In this spirit, discuss the following questions with your partner or in a full-class group discussion.

(1) How does the uniqueness of your map affect the way you lead your life today as a person? As a (future) dance educator or teaching artist?
(2) Think about the Education Maps of your parents, guardians, or caregivers. How similar is your map to theirs? What role did your parents, guardians or caregivers play in your map?
(3) Imagine waking up in the morning living with another dance educator's map instead of your own, maybe your partner's map. What would that be like for you? What did you learn about yourself and your educational journey? Why is your Education Map important for you in this course?

***

What Should Dance Education Look Like?

Abstract: In this creative, open-ended immersive activity, learners encounter reflective and summative opportunities for examining how individual values, beliefs, and experiences shape expectations about dance education. Contemplating what dance education should look like requires taking an informed stance based on learners' overarching development and thinking over the duration of the dance pedagogy course.

Schedule & Duration: Presented during the concluding week of the semester; 75–90 minutes. May be an activity as part of the course final exam or presentations.

Materials: Construction paper, modeling clay/compound, air-dry clay, cardboard, foam, craft sticks, bamboo skewers, crayons and markers, stapler, scissors, glue sticks, tape, among other various craft supplies.

Space: Classroom with desks or tables for providing each student a suitable workspace.

Introduction

Because dance education occurs in a variety of settings and reaches a wide range of students, this activity recognizes the breadth, or full span of pedagogical knowledge experienced throughout the course. At the same time, this activity also acknowledges and may amplify the depth or extensive exploration of specific topics within pedagogy and teaching (aims, purposes, populations, and theory and practice) crucial for dance educators. From this breadth and depth, reflective dance educators can also identify and consider how their individual values and commitments shape their unique perspectives, goals, and aims of dance education.

Narrative Preface

Throughout this course, we have grappled with challenging questions and issues, many that have been perplexing to wrap our heads around because they are vast and profoundly important questions not easily fixed nor solved with simplistic answers or quick-fix solutions. However, large questions, especially the "why" questions, when we attempt to answer them honestly and truthfully, ground us in our own higher purposes as dance educators and teaching artists: What do I do? Why do I do it? At the same time, struggling with questions of vision (although difficult) gives our lives as educators meaning and clarifies our intentions and deepest commitments to dance education and students.

Now at the conclusion of the course, what is your current vision of dance education? What beliefs, ideas, and assumptions form the basis of your vision? What is crucial and non-negotiable in your vision? What cannot be left out? Do you need your own vision of dance education? Or can you use someone else's? Are you using someone else's vision now? In the schools, studios, community centers, among other teaching spaces you are in, what vision of education is going on? In order to have a meaningful vision of dance education, one in which you can ground your daily practices and actions, what realities of race, ethnicity, social class, economics, gender, gender identity, age, ability, and related politics must be taken into consideration as part of the whole picture of your vision?

TASK: Using the materials provided, create a three-dimensional response by asking yourself the following questions: What is the current state of my vision for dance education? What beliefs, ideas, and assumptions inform my vision? What is crucial and non-negotiable in my vision? What cannot be left out? Of course, one's vision is always incomplete; more questions remain, but at this point in your learning, what is your vision now? Use the provided materials to create a visual model of what dance education should look like in three dimensions.

Sharing "What Should Dance Education Look Like?" Models

Step 1: When models are completed, ask learners to move about the space reviewing their peers' models with particular attention to each model's design, content, presentation and overall vision of dance education.

Step 2: Once the review is finished, ask a volunteer to speak about a model they found particularly meaningful or compelling. Give the model's creator an opportunity to respond and/or describe his or her process and vision. Repeat Step 2 as time permits.

DISCUSSION: Learners' visions of dance education near the conclusion of the course benefit from multiple resources and numerous theoretical and practice-based approaches to dance pedagogy that their earlier "My Education Maps" did not. Similarly, the scope and extent of peer relationships and collegiality shared between learners have developed significantly since the beginning of the term. Taken together, learners frequently respond to one another more freely and intensely and use language, reasoning, and examples in far more informed and humanizing ways. With this in mind, conclude this activity by guiding a full-class discussion based on the following recommended prompts.

(1) How did you approach creating your vision model for dance education? Where did your ideas and process come from?
(2) What was it like to work in a non-verbal, three-dimensional format? If you found this format challenging, how did you proceed? What additional issues or concerns came up for you?
(3) Did you have a clear vision for what dance education should look like before this activity? If you did, what impact, if any, did this activity have on your vision? If you did not have a clear vision, do you have one now? Describe.
(4) What do you take away from this group Activity for Humanizing Dance Pedagogy? Explain.

Further Thoughts

The examples of humanizing dance pedagogy presented in this article seek to counterbalance the current "best practices" dominant paradigm – its teacher-proof curriculum[4], standardization, and methods-centric teacher preparation. I, along with colleagues have been critical of widely accepted "best practice" methods (Barr and Risner 2014; Risner and Barr 2015; Risner and Schupp 2020), which until recently have remained largely unquestioned and under examined – best practices for whom, and in what contexts? As Lilia Bartolome (2004) argues, the best practice "focus far too often occurs without examining [preservice] teachers' own assumptions, values, and beliefs and how this ideological posture informs, often unconsciously, their perceptions and actions when working with other politically, socially, and economically subordinated students" (97).

Immersive learning, employed in the activities shared here, is not based upon or concerned with right and wrong answers or solutions; rather, the goal of immersive learning is to provide holistic and life-like experiences, taking into consideration the massive gray areas educators deal with each day. The ways in which one student addresses and solves a problem will be different from another student's approach and solution. What one student gleans from an experience or encounter will be different from that of another. The learner's experience resides at the center of immersive learning and may comprise earlier events or experiences in the life of the learner, current life events, and experiences surfacing from the learner's participation in immersive activities implemented by dance educators and teaching artists. A key distinguishing component of immersive learning occurs when learners – individually, collectively or both – analyze and critique their experience by using reflection, reconstruction, and evaluation to draw meaning from the learner's prior experiences. Reviewing their experiences in this manner often leads to further informed action and understanding. Moreover, students engaged in immersive learning activities also play a significant role in assessing their own learning and growth.

As Maria del Carmen Salazar (2013) reminds us, a humanizing pedagogy "incorporates content that is meaningful to students' lives in that it draws on students' lived experiences [which is] essential for a humanizing pedagogy" (139) in that it "allows for inclusion of students' linguistic, cultural, and social resources" (Salazar 2010, 120). By affirming learners' abilities to empathize deeply with others and others' life circumstances, dance educators and teaching artists can help learners channel their concerns and educational commitments through pedagogical interventions in their own teaching contexts, both now and in the future.

Notes

1. I use the terms "learner" and "student" interchangeably throughout this article, drawing attention to the dichotomy between one who "studies" and one who "learns."
2. In compliance with National Association of Schools of Dance (NASD) standards, BFA dance majors may satisfy their teaching requirement by completing one of the following courses: Foundations of Dance Pedagogy, Secondary Teaching Methods, or Teaching Creative Dance for Children.
3. Alternatively, touch options may include hands on shoulders or holding hands. Non-tactile (no touch) options include standing side by side.
4. Teacher-proof curriculum describes the notion of an ideal curriculum that works for any group of students in any school, largely independent of the teacher.

Funding

This work was supported by the Distinguished Faculty Fellowship, Board of Governors, Wayne State University.

ORCID

Doug Risner http://orcid.org/0000-0003-1038-2025

References

Barr, Sherrie, and Doug Risner. 2014. "Weaving Social Foundations in Dance Pedagogy: A Pedagogy of Uncovering." *Journal of Dance Education* 14 (4):136–45. doi:10.1080/15290824.2014.934985.

Bartolome, Lilia. 1994. "Beyond The Methods Fetish: toward a Humanizing Pedagogy." *Harvard Educational Review* 64 (2):173–194.

Bartolome, Lilia. 2004. "Critical Pedagogy and Teacher Education: Radicalizing Prospective Teachers." *Teacher Education Quarterly* 31 (1):97–122.

Beckem, John M., and Michael Watkins. 2012. "Bringing Life to Learning: Immersive Experiential Learning Simulations for Online and Blended Courses." *Journal of Asynchronous Learning Networks* 16 (5):61–71.

Brown, John Seely, Allan Collins, and Paul Duguid. 1989. "Situated Cognition and the Culture of Learning." *Educational Researcher* 18 (1):32–42. doi:10.3102/0013189X018001032.

Freire, Paulo. 1970. *The Pedagogy of the Oppressed*. New York, NY: Continuum.

Price, Jeremy, and Margery Osborne. 2000. "Challenges of Forging a Humanizing Pedagogy in Teacher Education." *Curriculum and Teaching* 15 (1):27–51. doi:10.7459/ct/15.1.03.

Risner, Doug. 2010. "Summary Paper." In Writing about Dance, by Wendy Oliver, 62–64. Champaign, IL: Human Kinetics.

Risner, Doug. 2013. "Curriculum Revision in Practice: Designing a Liberal Arts Degree in Dance Professions." *Journal of Dance Education* 13 (2):56–60. doi:10.1080/15290824.2012.698340.

Risner, Doug, and Karen Schupp, eds. 2020. *Ethical Dilemmas in Dance Education: Case Studies on Humanizing Dance Pedagogy*. Jefferson, NC: McFarland & Company.

Risner, Doug, and Sherrie Barr. 2015. "Troubling Methods-Centered 'Teacher Production': Social Foundations in Dance Education Teacher Preparation." *Arts Education Policy Review* 116 (2):78–91. doi:10.1080/10632913.2014.944965.

Risner, Doug, and Sue Stinson. 2010. "Moving Social Justice in Dance Pedagogy: Possibilities, Fears and Challenges." *International Journal of Education & the Arts* 11 (6). Accessed April 15, 2010. http://www.ijea.org/v11n6/.

Rodriguez, Arturo. 2008. "Toward a Transformative Teaching Practice: Criticity, Pedagogy and Praxis." *International Journal of Learning* 15 (3):345–52.

Salazar, Maria del Carmen. 2010. "Pedagogical Stances of High School ESL Teachers: "huelgas" in High School ESL Classrooms." *Bilingual Research Journal* 33 (1):111–24. doi:10.1080/15235881003733415.

Salazar, Maria del Carmen. 2013. "A Humanizing Pedagogy: Reinventing the Principles and Practice of Education as A Journey Toward Liberation." *Review of Research in Education* 37 (1):121–48. doi:10.3102/0091732X12464032.

Vygotsky, Lev. 1978. *Mind in Society*. Cambridge, MA: Harvard University Press.

Afterword

Nyama McCarthy-Brown

Doug Risner is a trailblazing dance educator who, as one can read from his body of research collected and shared herein, did not just begin to think about whiteness in dance pedagogy, or decolonizing dance. Issues of social justice are inseparable from dance education and have been at the heart of his research and teaching for decades. As one the most active and cited dance education researchers and prolific writers in the field, Doug's work speaks to our students, teachers, dancers, and society. He has been contributing to the field since his first publication in 1992. As a lifelong learner, he has shared his processes of inquiry, research, and advocacy for a more equitable society for three decades. Through his work he also lifts up the voices of people who are often marginalized in academia and in dance.

I know Doug Risner as one of the most respected scholars in dance education, but I also know him as a great mentor. He is also the only White man to seek me out as an unknown African American woman, for the purpose of centering my voice in his research class. I remember quite vividly, I was living in Brunswick, Maine, as a postdoctoral student in 2012, working on my then-unpublished book but feeling disconnected and invisible in the all-engulfing world of White academia, when I got an email from Doug Risner. He wanted me to do a podcast for his undergraduate students that he could share in his dance education research course to accompany my journal article on Black Ballerinas, which he assigned them to read. At the time I did not think my article had been out long enough for anyone to know about it. I also did not know what a podcast was. I felt honored, seen, and affirmed by his invitation. I thought, "wow!" What a great way to bring authors and their research to life for students. I noted, even in this invitation, that Doug was modeling great teaching practices for serving students (and bringing me into the technology of podcasts as a teaching resource). It was not lost on me that Doug was likely seeking a person with a different background than his to provide his students with perspectives beyond his own. Conversely, I often sought and leaned into his research on boys and gender for similar reasons. Additionally, I admired how attentive Doug was (and continues to be) to new research publications and what's happening in the field. After this personal connection with Doug in 2012, I began to pay even closer attention to his work.

Doug's expertise as a journal editor for *Journal of Dance Education* and *Research in Dance Education* positioned him to be a great mentor for emerging scholars seeking publication. It was not long after that first connection that I reached out to him for advice on this matter or that, pertaining to the process of publishing articles. I needed someone to help me along this road that seemed to have so few guide posts. He was always willing, thoughtful, and generous with his time. Additionally, he modeled collaborative writing and research throughout his career, a research approach I have taken as well, and also thoroughly enjoyed—particularly with some of his esteemed collaborators, including Julie Kerr-Berry, Karen Schupp, and

Sherrie Barr, among others. One of my most favorite—and most used—co-authored articles of his, "Weaving Social Foundations through Dance Pedagogy: A Pedagogy of Uncovering" (Barr and Risner, 2014) in *Journal of Dance Education*, includes an exemplary social immersion project aimed at walking in someone's shoes. To this day, I continue to use the article and update Risner's social immersion model each time I teach a dance education course.

One of my most memorable moments teaching dance pedagogy relates to another of Doug's collaborative articles, "Moving Social Justice: Challenges, Fears and Possibilities in Dance Education" (2010), co-authored with Sue Stinson. It was the first time I taught a dance pedagogy course, and I focused considerably on race, class, gender, and social inequity, which made no sense to many of my dance students. It was just past the midpoint of the course when we read "Moving Social Justice." The class started to discuss the text and one of my students said, "We really should have started with this first, I mean, none of that other stuff [about race, class, gender, and inequity] seemed of any use to me until I read this." Now, when I teach dance pedagogy or other dance education courses, this piece is one of the first I use.

Doug's work, along with that of his co-authors like Sue Stinson, is revolutionary for many dance educators like myself. His work provides momentum and support to those seeking more socially inclusive dance education. As a cis-gendered female dance teacher, looking for research to support my male identifying students, I have looked to Doug's research on gender in dance for over two decades. Part IV of this book, "Dance, Gender and Sexual Identity," reminds us of Doug's wide-reaching research on gender in dance education, with featured articles such as "Rehearsing Masculinity: Challenging the 'Boy Code' in Dance Education" (2007), and "Men in Dance, Bridging the Gap Symposium: Gender Inequities in Dance Education: Asking New Questions" (2018) as prime examples.

Together, as we move the field of dance education forward, let us hold tight to all we have learned from Doug Risner's impressive work. I lift up the following words he shares with students at the beginning of each course he teaches, consistently redirecting us to each other, our humanity, and our community: "We will learn what we learn from, and with, one another. There is no other real learning that will take place in this course" (Risner, 2008, p. 96). Most importantly, and beyond all of the words I have written here—gratitude. Thank you, Professor Doug Risner, for your innumerable contributions and vast body of research to the field of dance education.

References

Barr, S., & Risner, D. (2014). Weaving social foundations in dance pedagogy: A pedagogy of uncovering. *Journal of Dance Education*, 14(4), 136–145. DOI: 10.1080/15290824.2014.934985

Risner, D. (2007). Rehearsing masculinity: Challenging the 'boy code' in dance education. *Research in Dance Education*, 8(2), 139-153. DOI: 10.1080/14647890701706107

Risner, D. (2008). The politics of gender in dance pedagogy. *Journal of Dance Education*, 8(3), 94–97. DOI: 10.1080/15290824.2008.10387364

Risner, D., Blumenfeld, B., Janetti, A., Kaddar, Y., & Rutt, C. (2018). Men in dance: Bridging the gap symposium. *Dance Education in Practice*, 4(1), 25–31. DOI: 10.1080/23734833.2018.1417212

Risner, D., & Stinson. S. (2010). Moving social justice in dance pedagogy: Possibilities, fears, and challenges. *International Journal of Education & the Arts*, 11(6), 1–26.

Index

Note: Page numbers followed by "n" denote endnotes.

accreditation standards 241, 242–244
Acker, S. 93
adolescent male dancers 173–175
adolescent male dance students 149, 166–185
adverse dialogues 129
affirmative dialogues 128
aggression 155, 167, 173, 175, 198
Albright, A. C. 239
Alcaraz, R. 168
Anderson, M. 125, 134–135, 142
Anijar, K. 29
apprehensive dialogues 129
artifacts 220, 224, 226, 228, 229
artistic development 134, 139
artistic praxis 102, 139, 143
artistry 108, 115, 116, 118–122, 129, 130, 143
arts education 58, 82, 107, 109, 114, 128, 134, 140, 142–145, 248; policy 133, 136–137, 140
Asher, T. 84
Association of Teaching Artists (ATA) 60, 106, 136
attitudes 66–68, 70–72, 107, 113, 126, 128, 130, 131, 171, 191, 230; teaching artist 127
autobiographical narrative 220, 224
autobiographical research 225

Baltodano, M. 67
Barr, Sherrie 266
Bartolome, L. 75, 258, 263
Baryshnikov Complex 149, 189, 190, 200–202, 205
Bauman, Z. 231n1
Belenky, M. 28, 84
Bennett, M. J. 69, 235
Berger, K. 167, 168, 181–184
Berlan, E. 166
Best, David 40
Beveridge, T. 76
BFA professionalization 51
bisexuality 227, 228
Blackmore, J. 93
Blumenfeld-Jones, D. 30
body memory 36, 38, 39

Bonanno, R. 168, 184
Bonbright, J. 82
Bourdieu, P. 245
Bourne, M. 190, 204
boy code 84, 149, 151, 154, 157, 160, 266
Breault, D. 79
budget deficits 52
bullying victimization 166–185; long-term effects of 183
bureaucratic ventriloquism 243
Burris, C. 84
Burt, R. 154, 200
Butler, J. 203

career motivation 110
Carman, J. 201
Carson, R. 235
certificate program 55, 113–115, 121, 122, 125–127, 130
Charbeneau, J. 240
choreographic process 9, 11, 19, 28, 29, 34, 35, 38–40, 42
choreography 12, 13, 24–28, 33, 34, 41, 51, 53, 60, 143, 212
Chow, E. 78
Christman, D. 93, 96
Clark, D. 72
classroom management 85, 121, 139
collaboration 76, 93, 94, 105, 122, 139, 140, 143
common values 120, 122
competition 51, 53, 72, 80, 83, 119, 169, 202
competitive resources 51
consciousness 2, 3, 30, 78, 79, 102, 116, 156, 247, 258
constructive action 78
context-based dance education 245, 246
Cooper, Adam 204
corporate university model 56
Craig, W. 166
credential program 114, 127–130
credential visions 130

Creswell, J. 90, 170, 178
critical feminist pedagogies 66–68, 70, 72, 78–80, 82, 148, 259
critical field observations 85, 86
critical pedagogy 27, 39, 67, 77, 78, 148, 152; critical pedagogical approaches 79, 80
critical social frontiers 27
critique 67, 68, 77–79, 85, 86, 141, 192, 226, 263
cultural/culture 67–70, 72, 80, 83, 84, 133, 138–140, 152, 153, 190; diversity 66, 79, 82, 259; exploration 226; studies 27
curriculum 45–47, 54, 57–59, 120, 121, 134, 140, 142, 143, 242, 243; curricular equity 50, 59; theory 59
Curry, T. 155

dance arts education 82, 107, 116, 119, 136
dance education 50–52, 54–56, 58, 59, 61, 62, 79, 80, 82, 145, 149, 151, 152, 156, 262, 266; curricular equity 59–60; curricular inequity 51; doctorates 57, 58; graduate study in 55; matters 46, 49–63; programs 50–52, 54, 55, 59, 62, 63, 80; teacher preparation programs 50, 76
dance educators 3, 4, 36, 39, 40, 50, 62, 68, 79, 218, 233, 234, 243, 262, 263
dance leadership 91, 93, 97, 98
dance pedagogy 47, 53, 65, 66, 68, 75, 76, 79, 80, 218–220, 259, 262, 266; foundations of 82, 259; humanizing 4, 8, 47, 218, 221, 258–260, 263
dancer-choreographer relationship 21–22
dance rehearsal 11, 12, 14, 15, 19, 20, 25, 32, 40; *see also* rehearsal
dancers' stories 21–23
dance teacher-director 166, 177, 181
dance teaching artists 103, 104, 133–145; in P-12 schools 104, 133, 142; practitioners 142–143; preparation 137
Darder, A. 67
data presentation 173
decision making 5, 52, 62–63, 94, 144
deep listening 185
DeFrantz, T. 236
democratic pedagogies 67, 259
Dik, D. 140
Dils, A. 71, 82
disconfirming evidence 178
discourses 78, 128, 156, 158, 242
dissertations 56–58
doctoral degrees 56
Donmoyer, R. 19, 30
Douglas, M. 231n1
Dunn, D. 17

Earp, J. 155
education 4, 46, 47, 58, 67, 68, 70, 76–80, 82–84, 110, 134, 148, 219, 259
educational policy 141

educational populations 109
education maps 260, 261; sharing 261
effective articulation 52
Einstein, A. 145
Eisner, E. 30
embodied pedagogy 246
emotions 68, 71, 84, 248
empathy 76, 84, 167, 237, 260
employment status 109
empowerment 23, 67, 68, 71, 72
encouragement 113, 127, 169, 179, 181, 259
epistemology 27–29, 35–41, 149
Erickson, F. 90, 135, 171
ethnicity 65, 67–69, 72, 78, 80, 84, 85, 238, 259, 262
ethnocentrism 241
ethnorelativism 241
expansive dance education 50, 52
expert informants 104, 133–135, 137, 138, 140–143

feminine qualities 153, 194
femininity 78, 84, 85, 94, 161, 167, 168, 205
feminist pedagogies 67, 68, 70, 71, 76, 79, 80
feminist theory 27
Ferdun, E. 194
field-based supervisors 243
Fineran, S. 169
four-part methodology 91
Freire, Paulo 67, 258

Gamble, John 28
Gard, M. 157, 158, 213
Gardner, H. 28
gender 5, 70, 78, 80, 84, 90–95, 97, 98, 152, 153, 190, 191, 203, 238, 266; bias 79, 85, 95, 249; inequities 210–216; issues 84, 96, 192; problems 149, 189, 192, 203, 204; stereotypes 70, 92, 98, 153, 190; variations 89
Gendron, B. 168
general adolescent population 167, 179
general education students 191
Glaser, B. 42n1
global dance 236
Gollnick, D. 240
Gray, E. 83
Green, J. 40, 42n1
Gruber, J. 169

Hagood, T. 93
harassment 155, 166–170, 173, 175, 176, 178–180, 183, 184, 227
Harding, S. 35
hegemonic masculinity 156
heterosexuality 159, 190, 202, 225, 227; rehearsing 149, 200, 227
higher education: dance in 49, 93, 143, 191, 236, 242
Higher Education Arts Data Services (HEADS) 51, 90, 91

INDEX

historical foundations 80, 82, 83
historical learning 82
homophobic attitudes 154, 159–161, 166, 176, 199–202
homophobic stereotypes 157, 158, 204
hybrid critical pedagogies 78
Hymel, S. 168, 184

imagination, lack of 144, 145
immersive learning 221, 258, 259, 263
individual dance artists 108
individualism 80, 83, 161
initial retrieval 227
internalized homophobia 151, 156, 157, 159, 160
interpersonal construction 33, 41
interpersonal relationships 140, 179, 181
interpretive inquiry 28, 30, 32, 126, 128, 133–135, 143, 171, 172
interpretive research frameworks 90, 170
intimate distance 231
intimate reading 227, 228
Irwin, J. 242

Jacobson, R. 185
Johnson, R. 90, 171
Jones, P. 57

Katz, J. 155
Kealiinohomoku, Joanne 236
Kerr-Berry, J. 237
Keyworth, S. 156, 158
Kim, T. 168
Kimmel, M. 154
Kincheloe, J. 225, 231n2
Knight-Diop, M. 71
knowing, concept 2, 3, 8, 17, 22, 28, 29, 32–41, 222; as certainty 39–40
knowledge 28, 29, 32–37, 39–41, 77, 138, 145, 258; construction 28, 38–41
Kuppers, P. 239
Kvale, S. 42n1

Langer, S. 34
Lather, P. 28
leadership: approach 91, 93, 94, 97; narratives 89; skills 68
Lehikoinen, K. 158, 213
Lewis, J. 78, 80
Li, Z. 213
Loewen, J. 84

MacDonald, J. 8, 14
Madden, M. E. 92, 98
male adolescents 153, 158, 170, 173, 174, 179, 212, 213; dancers 155, 156, 174, 179, 182, 183
male dance students 157, 167–169, 173, 175, 176
male participation 149, 151, 153, 157, 193, 201, 214

masculinity 84, 148, 149, 151, 152, 154–160, 168, 204, 205, 212; rehearsing 84, 149, 151, 154, 266
master's-level dance education 55
McCarthy-Brown, N. 196
McClellan, R. 93, 96
McIntosh, P. 69, 72n2
McNamara, Jennifer 8, 46, 102, 148
McWilliam, E. 72
Mead, D. 54
Medina, Y. 86n1
memorization 37, 38
memory 33, 36, 37, 39, 41, 50, 226
Meyer, E. 168, 169
MFA teaching artist tracks 120–121
Miller, D. A. 178, 197
mixed-method research study 107
mixed methods framework 170
Montgomery, S. 52n2
Morris, M. 190, 203
Moustakas, C. 42n1
movement artifacts 228–230
movement possibilities 12, 17
multicultural dance education 241
multiculturalism 79, 220, 234, 235, 237–239, 241
multiple-stakeholder approach 135
musical memory 37

narratives 35, 36, 39, 41, 68, 70, 71, 90, 91, 93, 94, 180, 258
national accreditation standards 118, 121
National Association of Schools of Dance (NASD) 50, 80
National Dance Education Organization (NDEO) 50, 93
Neumann, R. 80
No Child Left Behind Act (NCLB) 75–78, 128

obstacles 50, 59, 112, 119, 140, 141, 143–145, 225, 233
Oesterreich, H. 71
online survey 91, 93, 96, 107, 109, 126, 170, 171
Onwuegbuzie, A. 90, 171
open-ended survey questions 114, 174, 177

P-12 environments 138, 139, 141, 142
participants 20, 90, 91, 109–116, 126–128, 170, 172, 173, 175, 180, 181; profile 172; work 96–97
pedagogical/pedagogy 46, 50, 52, 60, 61, 66, 68, 70, 72, 79, 82, 84, 86, 115–120, 143; approaches 80, 83, 84, 102, 161, 220, 245, 251; preparation 53; theory 66, 85, 86
peer friendship 181
personal gain 80, 83
personal meaning 16–18, 26, 30, 42, 65; making 18, 26, 29
pervasiveness 194
physical education 51, 56, 58, 137, 156, 213
Pinar, W. 225

policy ramifications 76
Pollack, W. 154
post-baccalaureate teaching artist certificate program 121–122
postsecondary dance education 54, 61; community dance in 54–55
postsecondary dance leadership 89
postsecondary education 47, 51, 76, 97, 143, 144
potential credential program 107, 114, 127, 128, 131
praxis-incorporative approach 75, 76, 80, 83, 86
preliminary research 113
preparedness 110, 111, 133, 134, 136–139, 142, 221
primary workplace obstacles 141
professional dance companies 103, 104, 108, 109
professional dance training 197
professional development 112, 120, 130
professionalization 50, 89, 107, 113, 115, 117, 126–130
professional teaching artists 106, 109, 114
programme memory 38
public education 47, 109, 141
Purpel, D. 244

qualitative interpretive research 29

race 65, 67, 69, 70, 72, 78, 80, 84, 85, 91, 93, 259, 262, 266
ramifications 51, 75, 86, 140
recognition 69, 76, 78, 86, 119, 126, 129, 132, 160, 184, 237
Redfern, H. 33, 34, 40
re-envision 59
reflective practice 66, 82, 220, 224–226, 228, 229, 231, 259
regulations 102, 133, 134, 140, 143
rehearsal 8, 9, 12, 14, 17, 18, 20–22, 24, 25, 31, 32, 34, 41, 42, 212; model 12, 18; process 9, 12, 14, 17, 18, 20, 23–26, 28, 31–33, 35, 39, 212, 218
Reid, L. 28, 29, 36, 37, 40
relationships, dancers 21, 22
Remer, J. 119
Rennert-Ariev, Peter 243
research approach 134, 265
research design 169, 170
research procedures 31
research study design 90
resonant dance education programs 60–61
resources, scarcity of 241–242
responsibilities 13, 17, 21, 22, 24, 67, 68, 72, 84, 86, 90, 128, 143
restrictive financial challenges 141
Rich, A. 78
Risner, D. 4, 9, 46, 47, 73n4, 84, 85, 86n1, 102, 105, 134–136, 142, 148, 150, 167, 171, 173, 211, 213, 265, 266
Rivers, I. 184
Robinson, M. 52n2

Rocke-Henderson, N. 168, 184
Rofes, E. 159
Ross, J. 93

Sabol, F. R. 75
Salazar, Maria del Carmen 263
Sansom, Adrienne 86n1
self-identified heterosexual participants 175, 178
sexuality 65, 72, 80, 84, 156, 190, 193, 220, 224–226
sexual minority populations 166, 168, 179
sexual minority youth 168, 169, 183
sexual orientation 84, 151, 152, 158–161, 166, 167, 178, 180, 183, 205, 228, 231
Shapiro, S. B. 39, 68, 79, 246
Shor, Ira 78
significant issues 18, 23, 24
Slattery, P. 225, 231n2
social change 78, 226, 240, 241, 250, 258
social class 68, 84, 194, 205, 247, 250, 262
social-cognitive perspective 185
social construction 39, 78, 85, 152, 259
social devices 159
social environment 173, 174, 178
social foundations 65–72, 76–80, 85, 86; in dance education 75–86; inclusion 72, 85, 86; issues 66, 71, 84
social immersion project 66, 82, 85, 249, 250, 259, 266
social inequity 85, 238, 250, 266
social interaction 23, 25, 184
social isolation 155, 156, 173, 174, 176
social justice 221, 222, 234, 241, 244–248, 259, 265; and context-based dance education 245–246; learning 220, 245; in pre-service teaching 247–248; teaching 220, 244, 245, 250
social practice 41, 226
social psychology researchers 181
social support 166–185
social transformation 78, 228, 247
Spriggs, A. 183
Spring, J. 83
stakeholders, dance education 134
statistical predictability 30, 225
stereotypes 92, 98, 158, 167, 179–181, 190, 193, 197, 199
stigmatization 227
Stinson, S. W. 29, 30, 40, 42n1, 70, 79, 84
Strauss, A. 42n1
Swain, A. 76

teacher preparation 60, 63, 67, 68, 72, 75–77, 80, 82, 83, 86, 235, 237, 239
teacher production 47, 75
teaching artist advocacy 136
teaching artistry 103, 104, 106, 116, 119, 120, 122, 125, 130–132, 135, 139–141; competency 120; proficiency 120

INDEX

teaching artists 60, 106–110, 112, 113, 115, 116, 119, 126–128, 134, 136, 139–142
theatre teaching artists 125–132
third space 115, 116, 118
Thomas, H. 153, 194
Thompson, J. 142
Torres, R. 67
traditional dance pedagogy 192
traditional gender assumptions 203
training 109, 110, 113, 114, 116, 119, 128, 134, 136, 139, 140, 152, 191, 212, 259
transformation 144, 227, 246, 260
transformative learning 67
Turner, L. 90, 171

undergraduate programs 55, 116, 120

value-charged traditions 30
values 41, 67, 68, 70, 71, 75–77, 83, 94, 130, 141, 181, 243, 260
Van Dyke, J. 30, 89, 93

variation 17, 94, 97, 240
visual artifacts 227–230
voices 8, 9, 66, 69, 71, 89, 93–95, 98, 239, 242, 265

Warburton, E. 181
Watson, J. S. 220, 228, 231n3
Welch, S. 67, 240
Welner, K. 84
Westerling, M. 221
Western theatrical dance 149, 151, 179, 189, 191, 193, 200, 204, 212, 213
white privilege 69, 70, 84, 240
whole body physicality 17–18
Wilcox, S. 220, 228, 231n3
Williams, D. 155, 182
Williams, T. 183
Wood, G. 83
work–life balance 91, 93, 97
workplace challenges 104, 133, 134, 136, 140
world culture 152, 191

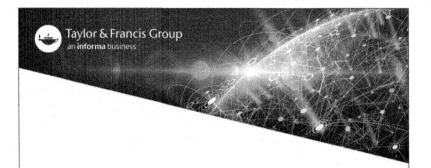